the Ocean of His Words

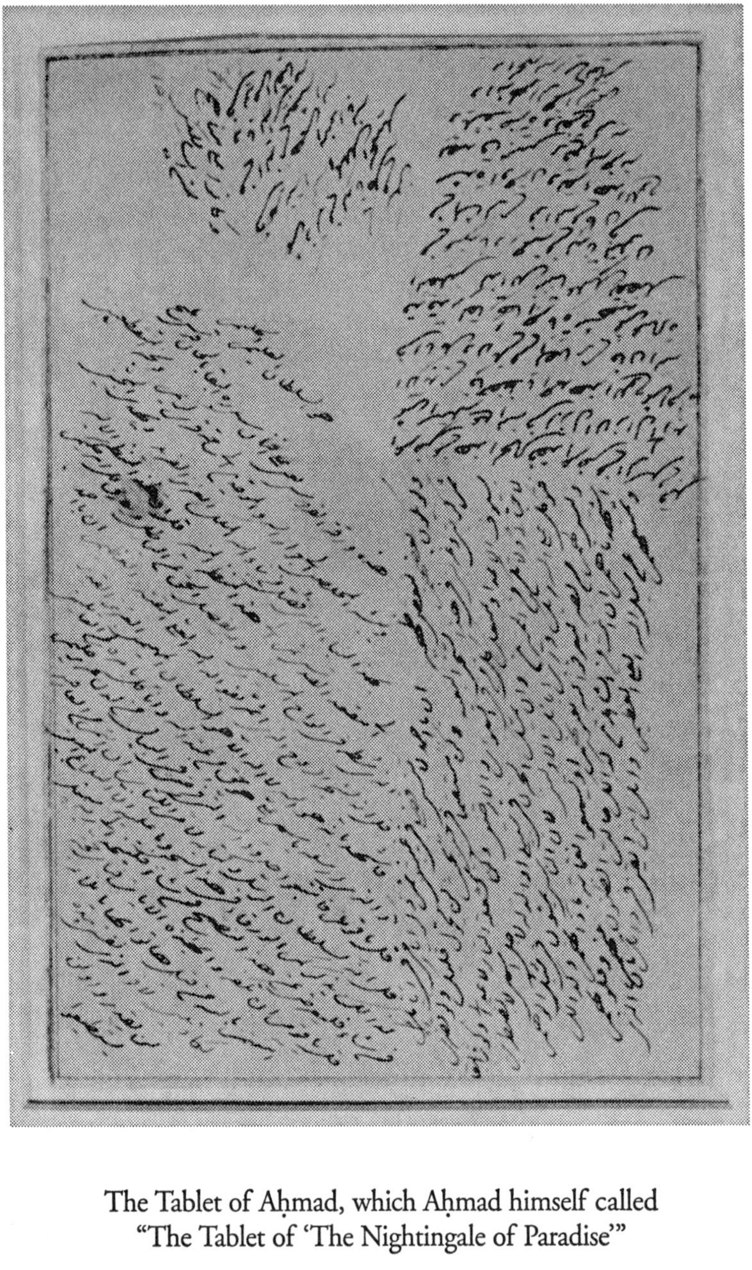

The Tablet of Aḥmad, which Aḥmad himself called
"The Tablet of 'The Nightingale of Paradise'"

the Ocean of His Words

A Reader's Guide to the Art of Bahá'u'lláh

by

John S. Hatcher

Bahá'í Publishing Trust
Wilmette, Illinois 60091

Other Works by John S. Hatcher:

Ali's Dream: The Story of Bahá'u'lláh (1980)
From the Auroral Darkness: The Life and Poetry of Robert E. Hayden (1984)
The Purpose of Physical Reality: The Kingdom of Names (1987)
Conversations (1988)
A Sense of History: A Collection of Poems by John S. Hatcher (1990)
The Arc of Ascent: The Purpose of Physical Reality II (1994)
The Law of Love Enshrined: Selected Essays by John Hatcher and William Hatcher (1996)
The Divine Art of Revelation (1998)
Ali's Dream (1998)
The Journey of the Soul (1999)

Bahá'í Publishing Trust, Wilmette, IL 60091-2886

 Second edition published 2002
Printed in the United States of America

05 04 03 02 4 3 2 1

Library of Congress Cataloging-in-Publication Data

Hatcher, John, Dr.
The ocean of his words : a reader's guide to the art of Bahá'u'lláh / by John S. Hatcher.—2nd ed.
p. cm.
Includes bibliographical references (p.) and index.
ISBN 0-87743-290-2 (alk. paper)
1. Bahá'u'lláh, 1817–1892. I. Title.

BP392.H38 2002
297.9'382—dc21

2001043312

Dedicated to "the learned in Bahá":
the Hands of the Cause of God
Counselors
Auxiliary Board Members
Assistants
and all who diffuse the fragrances
and serve the servants

The reading of the scriptures and holy books is for no other purpose except to enable the reader to apprehend their meaning and unravel their innermost mysteries. Otherwise reading, without understanding, is of no abiding profit unto man.

—Bahá'u'lláh, *The Kitáb-i-Íqán*

O My servants! My holy, My divinely ordained Revelation may be likened unto an ocean in whose depths are concealed innumerable pearls of great price, of surpassing luster. It is the duty of every seeker to bestir himself and strive to attain the shores of this ocean, so that he may, in proportion to the eagerness of his search and the efforts he hath exerted, partake of such benefits as have been pre-ordained in God's irrevocable and hidden Tablets.

—Bahá'u'lláh, *The Tablet of Aḥmad (Persian)*

Contents

Foreword to Second Edition

Since the publication of the first edition of this work, the discussion about what is or is not Bahá'í scholarship and who should be considered a "Bahá'í scholar" has become more animated, thereby eliciting from the Universal House of Justice a number of important observations about the need to foster a more expansive and integrative concept of what constitutes "Bahá'í studies." Among the more important statements is that the terms "Bahá'í scholarship" and "Bahá'í scholar" should not be used "in an exclusive sense, which would effectively establish a demarcation between those admitted into this category and those denied entrance to it."[1]

My sense of this and other similar observations by the Universal House of Justice is that there is an urgent need for everyone to accept his or her individual responsibility for personal spiritual and intellectual development. Conversely, I infer from these comments a mandate for Bahá'í academics to assist the entire community in all fields of study:

> The House of Justice seeks the creation of a Bahá'í community in which the members encourage each other, where there is respect for accomplishment, and common realization that every

1. Universal House of Justice, in *Scholarship* 7.

> one is, in his or her own way, seeking to acquire a deeper understanding of the Revelation of Bahá'u'lláh and to contribute to the advancement of the Faith."[2]

In this regard, the House of Justice has expressed confidence that learned Bahá'ís will begin to engender "more integrative" concepts about what constitutes "Bahá'í study":

> The House of Justice feels confident that, with patience, self-discipline, and unity of faith, Bahá'í academics will be able to contribute to a gradual forging of the more integrative paradigms of scholarship for which thoughtful minds in the international community are increasingly calling.[3]

Thus, while all of us are commanded to become learned to whatever degree we are able, the Bahá'í academic is particularly exhorted to examine the reciprocal relationship between the various fields of study and the Revelation of Bahá'u'lláh. For example, the notion of an associative relationship between body and soul might serve to enlighten the fields of medicine, psychology, and gerontology. The concept of human history as a spiritual dynamic should affect the fields of history, anthropology, and sociology. The image of the universe as an eternal and infinite expression of the unseen divine reality is already finding expression in the fields of theology, physics, and astronomy.

In short, the Bahá'í vision of the essential unity of and the reciprocity between the seen and unseen aspects of reality and of the integration of all human activity in the process of fostering an "ever-advancing civilization" is not confined solely to the realization that true science and true religion are describing one organic creation. Bahá'u'lláh's vision of a "divine economy" implies that all human en-

---

2. Universal House of Justice, in *Scholarship* 7.

3. Universal House of Justice, *Issues Related to the Study of the Bahá'í Faith* 36.

deavors and all areas of scholarship are capable of becoming expressions of this global enterprise.

Stated simply, we cannot relegate our effort to become spiritual to someone else, because no body of scholars within the Bahá'í community has the authority either to guide the community as a whole or to guide Bahá'ís individually:

> . . . Bahá'ís who are trained in various academic disciplines do not constitute a discrete body within the community. While the Bahá'í institutions benefit on an ongoing basis from the advice of believers in many fields of specialization, there is obviously no group of academics who can claim to speak on behalf of Bahá'í scholars generally. Scholarly qualifications enable individuals to make greatly valued contributions to the work of the Cause, but do not set those possessing them apart from the general body of the believers.[4]

However, the role of the academic, of the scholar, of scholarship itself, is no less crucial or valuable in this revised relationship between learned individuals and the community they serve. Indeed, the role of the scholar in the Bahá'í community should assume a far more important status than in previous societies because it has a far more universal application: Scholarly assistance is now relevant and valuable to *everyone* because understanding Bahá'u'lláh's vision of a spiritually based commonwealth has become the job of every single individual.

The Bahá'í scholar in the context of a "Bahá'í society" thus has the duty of striving to be, like 'Abdu'l-Bahá, a servant of the servants of God. But to accomplish this integration of the Bahá'í scholar into the community, a significant change in attitude on the part of the community and the scholar needs to occur. The Bahá'í community needs to

4. Universal House of Justice, *Issues Related to the Study of the Bahá'í Faith* 36.

nourish, to cherish, and to embrace the scholars in its midst. Likewise, the scholars are challenged to discover innovative ways to make even the most specialized areas of study relevant to the new vision of reality that Bahá'u'lláh has bequeathed us.

With this objective in mind I have, in this work, attempted to apply the tools of the somewhat esoteric field of literary critical analysis to the average reader's attempt to learn imaginative approaches to understanding the weighty and complex body of writings that constitutes the authoritative texts of the Bahá'í Faith.

John S. Hatcher, Ph.D.
Professor of English
University of South Florida

Foreword to First Edition

This book is not a final or complete analysis of Bahá'u'lláh's works, nor does it attempt to assess all that has been done in the increasingly rich field of Bahá'í studies. It is my hope that this study will serve to demonstrate how applying the tools of literary criticism can help readers become more creative and confident in studying the art of Bahá'u'lláh.

This study does assume that the reader has some familiarity with Bahá'í concepts, history, and terminology. Consequently, some readers may occasionally find it useful or necessary to consult Bahá'í glossaries or histories for explanations of unfamiliar terms or historical allusions.

Preface

Having taught literature at various universities for more than thirty-five years, I have become confident that all of us are capable of learning how to appreciate literature as art. Whether or not we choose to develop and exercise this capacity is a question of individual determination. In general, the most significant problem with studying the literary arts derives from the fact that the appreciation of belles lettres (literature as art) has become almost totally alien in our society.

It was not always so. Early in all of our cultures art was integral to daily existence, no more separable from life than gathering wood, preparing food, making clothes, or fashioning a shelter. We decorated our bowls, our cups, our bodies, our dwellings with sophisticated artistic symbols of who we were, of what we aspired to be, and of what mysteries we longed to understand. We danced and mimed our joy, our pain, our sorrow. We chanted our shared histories, celebrated our heroes and heroines.

In short, it was through art that we gave concrete expression to our innermost passions, made sensually perceptible through our arts—and thus more understandable to our minds—the passing season, the lost love, the new life. That is what art is capable of doing for us: it can freeze in time the fleeting thought, dress abstraction in the garment of permanence and palpability that we might, in moments of reflection, consider what exactly we have glimpsed through those momentary portals of inspiration that allow us to peek into the etherial world of ideas and forms.

At its best, then, art helps us understand ourselves. And the loss of art from our cultures—or the relegation of art to some obscure and largely ignored segment of our lives—is one major sign that our lives have become *dis-integrated,* that we have gradually become sublimely ignorant about ourselves.

Of course, this relationship between art and successful living is not causal in the reverse direction—we cannot make ourselves whole again by becoming aficionados of art. No, the dissociation of art from our lives is but a symptom of a larger malady—the general decline of self-knowledge, the gradual loss of any sense of exactly who we are as a people and what we aspire to become.

W. B. Yeats excoriates this condition in his poem "The Second Coming," a cynical prophecy about Yeats' millennial expectations for this modern age:

> Turning and turning in the widening gyre
> The falcon cannot hear the falconer;
> Things fall apart; the center cannot hold;
> Mere anarchy is loosed upon the world,
> The blood-dimmed tide is loosed, and everywhere
> The ceremony of innocence is drowned;
> The best lack all conviction, while the worst
> Are full of passionate intensity.
>
> (*The Norton Anthology of Poetry* 883)

The Bahá'í scriptures also depict the perils of this age. In shocking images of our impending decline Bahá'u'lláh presages and portrays a process of turmoil and tribulation in exacting detail. But coupled with Bahá'u'lláh's vision of impending decadence and degeneration is an equally powerful portrait of a Phoenix-like birth of our global identity. The death pangs of our old identity thus merge into the birth pangs of our renovated self, a process Shoghi Effendi alludes to in the opening passages of *The Promised Day Is Come:*

> A tempest, unprecedented in its violence, unpredictable in its course, catastrophic in its immediate effects, unimaginably glorious in its ultimate consequences, is at present sweeping the face of the earth. (¶2)

Because the art of Bahá'u'lláh focuses on the "unimaginably glorious" emergence of this global self, the art of Bahá'u'lláh evokes not doubt, but certitude; not dread, but joyous anticipation of our imminent birth.

From a Bahá'í perspective, Bahá'u'lláh is thus the poet/artist and midwife/architect of an age we have yet to experience. Therefore, we approach His art with immense awe. We are further hindered in understanding His art because we have been bereft for too long of our artistic sensibilities, the skills of interpretation that need constant exercise to become deft and accurate.

We are assured that we can always benefit from His divine art—that mere exposure to Divine utterance is medicinal for us. But there is more that we can do. Even in the throes of what Bahá'í poet Robert Hayden called this "deathbed/childbed age," we can learn how to acquire those skills that will enable us to approach Bahá'u'lláh's art.

This study attempts to show how we can apply certain useful literary tools to help break through the understandable reticence and resistance we feel when we approach the astoundingly vast and complex art that is the Revelation of Bahá'u'lláh. It is a simple process—a series of some six questions derived from literary criticism and applied in the successive chapters of this text. In general, we will employ the questions posed by these several areas of critical concern to uncover and illuminate what we do not understand by assembling all that we can more easily discover.

I have found this process particularly useful in helping students overcome the commonly held misconception that the ability to understand the literary arts is an inborn thing—i.e., one is a "poetry-person" or one is not. It is this same mostly erroneous thinking that finds expression in the groans I sometimes hear when new acquaintances discover I am a professor of literature. They think their groan is saying, "I just don't get poetry, plays, and stuff." I choose to hear that groan as a plea for help, because over the years I have come to believe that, given enough time and the right tools, we can all become "poetry people."

Even though this process is based to some extent on the tools of academic study, this is hardly an impersonal or unspiritual approach to the art of Bahá'u'lláh. After all, Bahá'u'lláh commands each of us to become students of His art, to immerse ourselves in the ocean of His words, that we might "unravel its secrets, and discover all the pearls of wisdom that lie hid in its depths" (Kitáb-i-Aqdas ¶182), not so that we should flail about and drown.

Acknowledgments

I wish to express my appreciation to a number of individuals who assisted me in editing this work: Sonia Zamir, Duane Troxel, Ross Woodman, and my wife, Lucia Hatcher. I am also indebted to Suni Hannan, Operations Manager at the Bahá'í Publishing Trust, for co-ordinating this project, and to my colleagues at the University of South Florida for awarding me a sabbatical during which time I was able to conclude this work. Finally, I am grateful to my grandfather, William Benjamin Hardman (1865–1918), without whose foresight this project would not have been possible.

the Ocean of His Words

Chapter 1
Revelation as Art

. . . [I]n the writings of Bahá'u'lláh there is an influence not dwelling elsewhere in literature or philosophy. That influence permeates and proceeds from a literary and philosophic form, but the power of the influence well-nigh shatters the cup of speech. . . . Our categories and our systems fail to contain this writing, as engineers would fail to dam the sea. Our critical faculties even prevent us from approaching its outpouring effect, for its very purpose is to create new faculties as standards in the mind.

—Horace Holley

A. The Rejection of the Prophet-Artist

Worthwhile art requires something of us. It insists that we become participants, what J. R. R. Tolkien has called "sub-creators," in the process of understanding the ideas and insights to which the artist has given sensually perceptible form. Art which does not require this creative effort on our part usually has little of importance to say to us. Art which has no subtlety, which does not stretch us beyond our present awareness, simply reminds us of what we already know.

The art of the Manifestations of God is carefully fashioned to challenge us, to perplex us, to tease us out of complacency, to coax us into thought. Bahá'u'lláh in the Kitáb-i-Íqán discusses this feature of divine utterance and cites one tradition which states, "'Verily Our Word is abstruse, bewilderingly abstruse'" and another tradition which observes the same quality about the process of revelation as a whole: "'Our Cause is sorely trying, highly perplexing; none can bear it except a favorite of heaven, or an inspired Prophet, or he whose faith God hath tested'" (*Kitáb-i-Íqán* 82).

It is common throughout the history of literature that those artists who have been content to remind us of what we already understand, who do not require that we strive beyond our reach, are usually the most celebrated during their lifetimes. In the short run, these artists are also usually the most successful, at least in terms of public acclaim. It is an equally common occurrence that those artists whom the ages in time adjudge as being the true masters achieve little notoriety during their own lifetimes. How many biographies of great painters, composers, or poets conclude with the plaintive observation that the artist died in misery, penniless, alone, never having received any critical acclaim or public regard? Conversely, if we examine the lists of those artists who were most celebrated during their own lives, we often discover names that we now scarcely recognize.

Of course, it is only in retrospect that we discover this irony. With twenty-twenty hindsight, we scoff at the ignorance of those audiences of the past, believing that surely we would have known the true artist from the imitator, the struggling genius from the celebrated hack. We would have befriended Mozart, rescued Van Gogh. We might well pause to wonder, however, whether we now recognize the enduring talents presently among us.

In a fictionalized dialogue between "the poet" and "the citizen," John Ciardi studies this irony. In particular he notes that over the course of time true art will endure, will take its proper place in our collective regard, as will the repute and acclaim of the true artist. The influence of the true artist will be far more lasting over the long haul, more substantial than the public acclaim that is garnered by the artist who caters to public whim.

To support his contention, Ciardi distinguishes between the accolades of the "horizontal audience" (those who might praise the poet during his lifetime), and the accumulated appreciation of the "vertical audience," those who will in succeeding ages come to discern the merit of the poet's work. "You are going to be dead the next time anyone looks," Ciardi's poet says to the citizen. "We all are for that matter. But not the poem. Not if it's made right" ("Dialogue with the Audience," *Saturday Review* 22 [Nov. 1958]: 42).

This same paradox, which Bahá'u'lláh discusses in the Kitáb-i-Íqán, is operant in the history of divine revelation. Religious leaders claim that they long for the advent of the new Revelation from God, but when the Prophet appears, He, like the true artist, is rejected, disdained, persecuted for His too-radical vision and unwelcome advice. He insists that we change our values and perspectives, that we become uncomfortable with our present selves, so we reject Him and cast him out of our midst: "Not one single Manifestation of Holiness hath appeared but He was afflicted by the denials, the repudiation, and the vehement opposition of the people around Him" (*Kitáb-i-Íqán* 5).

It is only much later, long after Their passing, that we come to acknowledge the wisdom and influence of these Divine Emissaries. We then rewrite our histories accordingly, give them a central role, or imagine that, had we been in Their presence and subjected to that judgment, we would have behaved quite differently. Surely we would have been among those few to recognize and follow.

What we fail to appreciate is that the most weighty problem in recognizing the true artist or the true Prophet is that there are no obvious physical or social characteristics that give us clues to their identity. We are forced to discover them through their art. And if their art makes us uncomfortable, if it indicts our circumstances, questions our values, and judges our deeds, how can we respond to them with anything but apprehension, disdain, or—as Samuel Coleridge describes the social rejection of the artist in his poem "Kubla Khan"—with "holy dread":

> And all should cry, Beware! Beware!
> His flashing eyes, his floating hair!
> Weave a circle round him thrice,
> And close your eyes with holy dread,
> For he on honey-dew hath fed,
> And drunk the milk of Paradise.

There is another important similarity between the great artists and the Manifestations besides this irony of the rejection, solitude, and suffering we force them to undergo. Both are, at heart, attempting the same essential task—translating the ephemeral and ineffable world of ideas into some form that we can understand. As a result, both the artist and the Prophet appear among us unexpectedly like alien visitors from another realm come to teach us. What is more, both the artist and the Prophet employ essentially the same techniques. Both refrain from coercing us, but, instead, employ devices that require us to become artists ourselves, first by investing a sufficient amount of creative thought to comprehend their ideas, and then by reinvesting that understanding with our own creative action.

There is no caprice in this. All worthwhile education necessarily involves this same sort of personal effort and individual participation. Otherwise, we are not really learning; we are merely parroting someone else's learning. In short, to recognize the true Prophet or the true artist among us, we must become self-educated, self-motivated, and, to a degree, independent of the standards of society.

But the parallel between the artist and the Manifestation of God is even more explicit. Like the literary artist, the primary medium for the Manifestation is language. Furthermore, the words of the Manifestation are fundamentally artistic in form. To understand the Old Testament myths and prophecies, the New Testament parables, the allusive images of the Qur'án, or the poetic passages of the Báb and Bahá'u'lláh, we must invest the same quality and quantity of study we might invest in trying to come to understand and appreciate the work of Homer, Sophocles, Virgil, Rúmí, Dante, Shakespeare, or Goethe.

B. The Manifestation as Artist

In an essay entitled "The Writings of Bahá'u'lláh" (*Star of the West* 13.5:104–07), Horace Holley discusses how we as an audience must revise the common assertions we make about the artistic process if we are to approach the work of Bahá'u'lláh successfully. Horace Holley begins this discussion by noting how readers commonly assume that a poem is "the poet refined to the utmost degree"—that all the ingredients of a work of art are somehow within the artist. He goes on to note that, in reality, art merely represents the capacity of the artist to respond to an external reality—what Holley calls the "creative impulse."

Therefore, however exact art may be, it can never hope to duplicate the impulse; nor should art be considered identical with the impulse:

> During creation, the author feels an infinite resource opened within him, a resource which the work created never satisfactorily records. The work itself, then, represents merely the author's power of responding to the impulse, not the capacity of the impulse itself. In other words, literature is the record of what the infinite impulse has been able to effect in and through certain limited lives. (*Star of the West* 13.5:104)

Holley goes on to assert that even Shakespeare, whom most students presume "must be supreme in literature for all time," recognized "that all human drama had begun to crumble away with the perception of a greater and a beyond." Therefore, where Shakespeare seemed to sound all the notes that encompass our human experience (so far as we historically had encountered that experience), Bahá'u'lláh brings a literature that "sounds the notes that have been silent in us all" because it encompasses an experience we have yet to undergo or comprehend: "By minds limited to the customary closed circle of experience, [the writings of Bahá'u'lláh] can be read over and over without understanding. The supreme benefit of reading them, indeed, is to learn merely *how* they are to be read" (*Star of the West* 13.5:106). Unlike the artistic process Holley alludes to as occurring with an ordinary human artist—an infinite impulse finding limited expression—the artistic process appropriate to a Manifestation of God is not limited in the same way because the Prophet is not an ordinary human artist. Unlike us, the Prophets are preexistent, are perfect incarnations of all the attributes of God, and Their utterance is a precise expression of the Divine Will.[1]

---

1. See *The Law of Love Enshrined* 59–100 for a more complete discussion of this idea.

'Abdu'l-Bahá describes this relationship when He explains that all human progress and enlightenment comes through the appearance of the Manifestations and that Their utterance is the creative force in our world, the linkage between the "First Mind" (the Divine Will or Holy Spirit) and physical reality:

> The enlightenment of the world of thought comes from these centers of light and sources of mysteries. Without the bounty of the splendor and the instructions of these Holy Beings the world of souls and thoughts would be opaque darkness. Without the irrefutable teachings of those sources of mysteries the human world would become the pasture of animal appetites and qualities, the existence of everything would be unreal, and there would be no true life. That is why it is said in the Gospel: "In the beginning was the Word," meaning that it became the cause of all life. (*Some Answered Questions* 162–63)

Likewise, Bahá'u'lláh in the Kitáb-i-Íqán observes that, because Prophets have the capacity to translate godliness into human experience and to express the Divine Will in human social forms and relationships, the Manifestations could correctly state that They are God:

> Were any of the all-embracing Manifestations of God to declare: "I am God!" He, verily, speaketh the truth, and no doubt attacheth thereto. For it hath been repeatedly demonstrated that through their Revelation, their attributes and names, the Revelation of God, His name and His attributes, are made manifest in the world. (*Kitáb-i-Íqán* 178)

In this vein Christ responds to Philip's request to see the "Father" by explaining, "He that hath seen me hath seen the Father; how can you say [then], Show us the Father?" (John 14:9)[2] Bahá'u'lláh says the same thing in the Súratu'l-Haykal (Súrih of the Temple):

---

2. This and all subsequent references to the Bible refer to the King James version.

> *"Naught is seen in My temple but the Temple of God, and in My beauty but His Beauty, and in My being but His Being, and in My self but His Self, and in My movement but His Movement, and in My acquiescence but His Acquiescence, and in My pen but His Pen, the Mighty, the All-Praised. There hath not been in My soul but the Truth, and in Myself naught could be seen but God."* (qtd. in Shoghi Effendi, *World Order of Bahá'u'lláh* 109)

Here we note that Bahá'u'lláh identifies His person with the attributes of God made manifest and also identifies His revealed writing as the Word of God.

Of course, all the Prophets enunciated this same relationship between Their utterance and the Divine Will. Christ stated, "For I have not spoken of myself; but the Father which sent me, he gave me a commandment, what I should say, and what I should speak" (John 12:49). Muḥammad responded to the caviling of the believers about some of the laws in the Qur'án by telling them, "It is not for me to change it [the Qur'án] as mine own soul prompteth. I follow only what is revealed to me . . ." (10:16).[3]

If the Manifestations are perfect mirrors of Divine attributes and if Their speech is naught but the Word of God, in what sense is Their revealed utterance Their own art? And if this is not Their art but the words of God, then are we correct in studying Their words with the same tools we might use with the work of a human artist?

There are several reasons why the application of the tools of literary analysis to a study of the art of Bahá'u'lláh is valid and useful. First of all, even though the Prophet may be impervious to subtle social or psychological forces that so often shape the thought and themes of an ordinary human artist, the Manifestation gears His utterance to our condition.

---

3. This and all subsequent references to the Qur'án are from the J. M. Rodwell translation.

Let us make this important point a bit clearer. The Prophet is a preexistent emissary from the Spiritual World, a perfect incarnation of all divine attributes. He is infallible, omniscient, and omnipotent.[4] These characteristics and powers are an essential and, consequently, inalienable part of the Prophet's nature. The Prophet is not merely an inspired human being, not a suddenly transformed individual, but an essentially distinct creation, a fact of which the Manifestations are aware from the beginning:

> Verily, from the beginning that Holy Reality is conscious of the secret of existence, and from the age of childhood signs of greatness appear and are visible in Him. Therefore, how can it be that with all these bounties and perfections He should have no consciousness? (*Some Answered Questions* 155)

Clearly, then, the Manifestations are fully capable of transcending all apparent limitations of social status, of education, of culture. They are not products of an age, of an environment, or of inherited personality traits. As we will discuss more completely in our chapter on historical criticism, the Prophets purposefully fashion Their utterance to the distinct historical context in which They appear.

In this "station of distinction," each Prophet carefully devises His art so that it ministers to the needs and capacities of those who must, during His Dispensation, utilize His Revelation. Consequently, we can hardly appreciate what a Manifestation has to say outside the context of human history since, from a Bahá'í perspective, human history (when correctly understood) derives from the advent and influence of successive Prophets. Bahá'u'lláh explains how the Prophet must fash-

4. For a fuller discussion of this topic and for the scriptural basis for these conclusions, see John S. Hatcher, "The Doctrine of 'The Most Great Infallibility' in Relation to the 'Station of Distinction,'" in *The Law of Love Enshrined* 59–100.

ion His teaching technique to the capacity of humankind at the time of His appearance when He states:

> All that I have revealed unto thee with the tongue of power, and have written for thee with the pen of might, hath been in accordance with thy capacity and understanding, not with My state and the melody of My voice. (Hidden Words, Arabic, no. 67)

Likewise in the Kitáb-i-Aqdas Bahá'u'lláh affirms, "These words are to your measure, not to God's. . . . I swear by God, were We to lift the veil, ye would be dumbfounded" (Kitáb-i-Aqdas ¶176). Consequently, because the Prophet employs literary forms and language appropriate to our condition, we can presume that we must approach His art accordingly, using the tools of literary analysis suitable to such forms.

A second reason the application of the tools of literary analysis is valid for studying the revealed art of Bahá'u'lláh is that most tools of literary analysis are concerned less with how the art comes into existence and more with how a systematic examination of art can assist the reader to discover the deeper meaning of a work. For while historical criticism may help us appreciate how meaning can become informed by our appreciation of the circumstances in which the art is produced, other forms of critical examination help us uncover allusions, solve the mysteries of image and symbol, or discern the structure of thought that underlies the sometimes beguiling surface of the art. In short, most of the tools we will employ focus on the artistic properties of language.

C. Assumptions about Bahá'u'lláh's Art

Even though we may be correct in assuming that it is valid and helpful to apply the tools of literary criticism to the art of Bahá'u'lláh, it will be useful for us to consider briefly the special circumstance by which the Divine Will becomes expressed in human language and literary form. For if the powers of the Prophet are perfected, should we not also assume that His art is perfect? And if His art is perfect, can we not rest assured that any effort we invest, however rigorous and imaginative, will never exhaust the potential meanings of the Prophet's craft?[5]

There is a certitude, a conviction we find in studying the work of all masters of literature. We assume that anything we can imagine them doing they were fully capable of executing. Therefore, we have no qualms about trying to discover all manner of hidden meanings and elaborate structural patterns in a Shakespearean tragedy without ever worrying that our time will be wasted or that we may be imposing something on the work that the artist did not intend and that the art does not uphold.

This same sort of conviction is appropriate when we approach the art of Bahá'u'lláh. We can assume that there is always more to what Bahá'u'lláh is doing with His art than we can ever fully comprehend; we are studying the work of divine genius. We can approach the art of Bahá'u'lláh with the same awe and determination with which we might study Sophocles' *Oedipus Rex,* Rúmí's *Mat͟hnaví,* Shakespeare's *Hamlet,* James Joyce's *Ulysses,* or T. S. Eliot's *The Waste Land.* And if we can assume that the art of Bahá'u'lláh is capable of stretching us as far as we wish to go, we need not hesitate to employ all the tools of study at our disposal to help elucidate those meanings, to unleash that power.

If we approach the art of Bahá'u'lláh with this kind of reverence coupled with systematic rigor and inventiveness (in addition to whatever religious motives we have), we become liberated from any misconceptions we might have had about limitations imposed on Bahá'u'lláh by His cultural perspective, by His intellectual background, by His academic training, or by His exposure to other writers. Of course, we can make this presumption only if we have proven to our satisfaction that Bahá'u'lláh's claim to Prophethood is correct.

---

5. Adib Taherzadeh writes, in *Revelation of Bahá'u'lláh* 1:32, that Bahá'u'lláh, in His response to S͟hayk͟h Maḥmud, a Muslim divine of 'Akká, stated that "Every word sent down from the heaven of Divine Revelation . . . is filled with soft-flowing rivers of divine mysteries and wisdom. Bahá'u'lláh also gave in detail, in response to the questioner, several meanings pertaining to the word 'sun,' adding that this word has so many other meanings that if ten secretaries were to record His explanations for a period of one or two years, He would still not exhaust its significance."

Consequently, this is an extremely important assumption because it serves to clarify for us how Bahá'u'lláh might have resorted to existing literary forms or might have alluded to passages from other works and yet still have remained totally in control of His art. He was not the product of an age or a culture or even a certain upbringing. At times He may have employed the literary techniques or styles of His culture, but He did so through conscious choice, not because of unwitting influence or because He was unable to do otherwise.

But it is not merely the special status of the Prophet that merits our assumption that the Prophet's art is perfect art. For example, it might be argued that He is perfect as a Prophet but unexceptional as a poet. After all, His art is whatever it is, regardless of its source. Either it is perfect and subtle, or it is not. Why is it a logical necessity or even an advantage for us to establish first that Bahá'u'lláh has the station of Prophethood before we can properly appreciate His art? Certainly, Bahá'u'lláh seemed content to let the believers decide for themselves about His station. He did not try to convince them of His status solely by virtue of authoritative pronouncement. When Mírzá Yaḥyá, Bahá'u'lláh's younger half-brother, challenged Bahá'u'lláh's claim to be the promised Manifestation the Báb had foretold, Bahá'u'lláh simply exhorted the believers to compare and decide for themselves.

The answer to this question is subtle and necessarily somewhat subjective. If we establish to our satisfaction that Bahá'u'lláh is a Prophet, then there is a distinct difference in the attitude we assume as we approach His art. If we can assume that His utterance has a status and a perfection beyond our ken, then we do not judge the art by our personal standards. We do the reverse: we assume the art has perfection, authority, wisdom, and a myriad mysteries for us to discover if we can elevate our capacity through systematic study of this vast ocean.

This is not to say that the art of Bahá'u'lláh will not endure on its own merits. Over the course of time, Bahá'u'lláh's work will assume its proper place with the "vertical audience." But it does mean that the standards by which we judge this art must often transcend criteria that are precisely quantifiable or empirically demonstrable according to the standards of contemporary scholarship. Therefore, we would do well to consider briefly what we know about the revelation process as it compares to the artistic process of an ordinary human artist so that we can reinforce subjectively what we seem to have deduced doctrinally: that the utterance of the Manifestation is perfect art precisely because He is inherently perfect in all that He does.

D. Revelation as an Artistic Process

To begin with, just as an ordinary human being must struggle to become a noble person, so the ordinary human artist must struggle to develop those skills whereby he or she can express the "creative impulse." The resulting art may have the guise of spontaneity and intuition, but in reality, the artistic process for the ordinary human artist is a process of constant revision and refinement, "a hundred visions and revisions."[6] In fact, as Yeats notes in his poem "Adam's Curse," the artist labors intensely to create an art which has a sense of effortlessness:

> We sat together at one summer's end,
> That beautiful mild woman, your close friend,
> And you and I, and talked of poetry.
> I said, "A line will take us hours maybe;
> Yet if it does not seem a moment's thought,
> Our stitching and unstitching has been naught."
>
> (ll. 1–6)[7]

Even the geniuses among us must struggle to create the guise of spontaneity, for truly spontaneous art is rare indeed. When a Mozart brings forth a finished work with what seems to be little premeditation or effort or revision, he has spent hours contemplating the art before it assumes its final form. He has also devoted hours, days, weeks, years honing those skills whereby the art could issue forth with such apparent ease. The same principle holds true for other arts. If we consider the moves of a ballerina, we might conclude that we are witnessing pure inspiration. And while inspiration may indeed play a significant role in

---

6. T. S. Eliot, "The Love Song of J. Alfred Prufrock," l. 32.

7. W. B. Yeats, in *Norton Anthology of Poetry* 879.

all of these human efforts, what we are really observing is the end product of training coupled with substantial inherent potential, coordinated and empowered by creative impulse (whatever that might be).

The point is that the Prophets have no such training. In fact, the Prophets take great pains to make it absolutely clear that They do not derive the power of Their utterance from any school of influence. They state that They have had no formal training, have studied no works of human authors. For example, the Báb states,

> God beareth Me witness, I was not a man of learning, for I was trained as a merchant. In the year sixty God graciously infused my soul with the conclusive evidences and weighty knowledge which characterize Him Who is the Testimony of God—may peace be upon Him—until finally in that year I proclaimed God's hidden Cause and unveiled its well-guarded Pillar, in such wise that no one could refute it. (*Selections from the Writings of the Báb* 12)

Bahá'u'lláh, though raised among the nobility and having had access to formal training, rejected such schooling and thus later could make precisely the same claim:

> We have not entered any school, nor read any of your dissertations. Incline your ears to the words of this unlettered One, wherewith He summoneth you unto God, the Ever-Abiding. Better is this for you than all the treasures of the earth, could ye but comprehend it. (Kitáb-i-Aqdas ¶104)

Indeed, in the Kitáb-i-Íqán Bahá'u'lláh asserts that none of the Prophets derive Their utterance from any sort of ordinary human methods of learning—They do not need to.

> What blossoms of true knowledge and wisdom hath their illumined bosoms yielded! Were the earth of their hearts to remain unchanged, how could such souls who have not been taught one letter, have seen no teacher, and entered no school, utter such

> words and display such knowledge as none can apprehend? (*Kitáb-i-Íqán* 46)

In other words, the artistic process employed by the ordinary human artist sometimes *seems* spontaneous, but it is inevitably the end result of potential coupled with training and inspiration. The art of the Prophets actually *is* spontaneous.

Bahá'u'lláh vindicates our assumption about the distinction between human artistic inspiration and divine revelation in the Kitáb-i-Aqdas when He affirms that there will be no further revelation until a thousand years have passed: "Whoso layeth claim to a Revelation direct from God, ere the expiration of a full thousand years, such a man is assuredly a lying impostor" (Kitáb-i-Aqdas ¶37). Certainly Bahá'u'lláh is not stating that no one will be spiritually inspired for the next thousand years. He is making the explicit distinction between the inspiration available to an ordinary human being and the special process of revelation unique to the Manifestations of God—a "Revelation direct from God" as opposed to an inspiration received indirectly through the imagination.

Of course, since we possess only a limited understanding of how the human artistic process works, we can presume we know even less about the process of divine revelation. Nevertheless, to substantiate and vindicate further our assumption that the power and authority of Bahá'u'lláh's words derive from this process, let us consider what we can discover about this process.

Bahá'u'lláh alludes to the revelation process in some detail as He describes His experience in the Síyáh-Chál. Since we do not know if He had ever had similar experiences previously, we cannot be certain that this event was the beginning of the active communication to Him of the new Revelation. As we have established, we do know He was always aware of His Prophethood, and yet He seems to portray this experience as if it were something quite new and, to some extent, overwhelming in its intensity, an experience in which the Holy Spirit manifests itself to Him through the image of a veiled maiden:

> . . . He describes, briefly and graphically, the impact of the on-

rushing force of the Divine Summons upon His entire being—an experience vividly recalling the vision of God that caused Moses to fall in a swoon, and the voice of Gabriel which plunged Muḥammad into such consternation that, hurrying to the shelter of His home, He bade His wife, Khadíjih, envelop Him in His mantle. *"During the days I lay in the prison of Ṭihrán,"* are His own memorable words, *"though the galling weight of the chains and the stench-filled air allowed Me but little sleep, still in those infrequent moments of slumber I felt as if something flowed from the crown of My head over My breast, even as a mighty torrent that precipitateth itself upon the earth from the summit of a lofty mountain. Every limb of My body would, as a result, be set afire. At such moments My tongue recited what no man could bear to hear."* (Shoghi Effendi, *God Passes By* 101)

In discussing this process of revelation "direct from God," Shoghi Effendi cites several statements by Bahá'u'lláh which might be taken to imply that an essential change had also taken place in the Prophet. In His epistle to Náṣiri'd-Dín Sháh Bahá'u'lláh seems to imply that as this event occurred, He was suddenly infused with a knowledge that He did not possess heretofore:

> O King! I was but a man like others, asleep upon My couch, when lo, the breezes of the All-Glorious were wafted over Me, and taught Me the knowledge of all that hath been. This thing is not from Me, but from One Who is Almighty and All-Knowing. And He bade Me lift up My voice between earth and heaven, and for this there befell Me what hath caused the tears of every man of understanding to flow. . . . This is but a leaf which the winds of the will of Thy Lord, the Almighty, the All-Praised, have stirred. . . . His all-compelling summons hath reached Me, and caused Me to speak His praise amidst all people. I was indeed as one dead when His behest was uttered. The hand of the will of Thy Lord, the Compassionate, the Merciful, transformed Me. (*Proclamation of Bahá'u'lláh* 57)

But as is discussed at length in "The Doctrine of 'The Most Great Infallibility' in Relation to the 'Station of Distinction,'" in *The Law of Love Enshrined* (59–100), Bahá'u'lláh here is not alluding to any essential change in Himself. He is describing the physical conditions under which He received the Revelation, and He is alluding to the fact that though He had been concealed, He has now received the summons to openly proclaim what He Himself had known all along—that He is the Manifestation of God designated to fulfill the Báb's prophecies and usher in the transformation of human society.

E. The Prophet's Function in This Process

It is noted in *The Law of Love Enshrined* that these dramatic epiphanies in the lives of the Prophets signal the beginning of Their active ministry, not Their transformation from a human condition to a Divine condition. The Prophet does not suddenly become something else. He has always been a Manifestation, and He has always been aware of His station. What seems to be occurring, then, is that the Prophet is given the summons to begin His ministry, a decision, Bahá'u'lláh assures us, that is not of His own devising:

> *"By My Life!"* . . . *"Not of Mine own volition have I revealed Myself, but God, of His own choosing, hath manifested Me."* . . . *"Whenever I chose to hold My peace and be still, lo, the Voice of the Holy Spirit, standing on My right hand, aroused Me, and the Most Great Spirit appeared before My face, and Gabriel overshadowed Me, and the Spirit of Glory stirred within My bosom, bidding Me arise and break My silence."* (qtd. in Shoghi Effendi, *God Passes By* 102)

But does this depiction of revelation imply that the Prophet has no part to play in this process, that He utters precisely the words He hears? Is God the artist and the Prophet but His amanuensis? Or is there in the revelation process some sort of creative participation by the Prophet? Does He translate Divine ideas into human language, albeit perfectly and spontaneously?

Since the Revelation is "direct from God" and instantaneous, we might presume the Prophet does not have an artistic role in the revelation process. For example, Adib Taherzadeh in *The Revelation of Bahá'u'lláh* explains that when Bahá'u'lláh was revealing a work, the words of revelation "poured forth" without revision or change and often with such rapidity that "His amanuensis was often incapable of recording them" (1:23). The amanuensis, usually Mírzá Áqá Ján, would record this dictation in a hurried shorthand. This often illegible script would then be transcribed by the amanuensis, whereupon Bahá'u'lláh would review the finished work, correct any mistakes the amanuensis had made, and approve the copy. Usually, but not always, Bahá'u'lláh would signal this approval by affixing his seal to the work. The work would then be copied and distributed to the believers.

In his discussion about what is happening in this process, Taherzadeh alludes to the mystical union between the Manifestation and God and states that we cannot understand this relationship to any significant degree. He then observes that the

> mystical intercourse between God, as the Father, and His chosen Mouthpiece, the Prophet, as the Mother, gives birth to Divine Revelation which in turn brings forth the Word of God. It is not possible for man to understand the nature of this sacred relationship, a relationship through which God is linked with His Manifestation. (*Revelation of Bahá'u'lláh* 1:21)

Taherzadeh does go on to theorize that the process of revelation is quite distinct from anything that occurs with human artists:

> In order to write, any writer must rely on his knowledge and learning. He will have to meditate on the subject and undertake research. After much work he may produce a book in which always there will be ample room for improvement, and not infrequently he will feel it necessary to rewrite the entire book. This is not so in the case of the Manifestations of God Who do not rely on Their own human accomplishments. (*Revelation of Bahá'u'lláh* 1:23)

In discussing whether or not the Manifestation is in any sense the author of His utterance, Taherzadeh seems to imply a distinction between the inspired idea, which is divine and limitless, and the human language that must needs fall short of conveying the ideal:

> The revealed Word has an inner spirit and an outer form. The innermost spirit is limitless in its potentialities; it belongs to the world of the uncreated and is generated by the Holy Spirit of God. The outer form of the Word of God acts as a channel through which the stream of God's Holy Spirit flows. It has its limitations inasmuch as it pertains to the world of man. *(Revelation of Bahá'-u'lláh* 1:21)

Taherzadeh goes on to note that the language and style of the Prophet relate to the context in which He appears.

The importance of this distinction relates back to Horace Holley's observation. If by "outer form" Taherzadeh is understood to be alluding to the "station of distinction," and if one further infers that these "limitations" are the Manifestation's struggle to deal with the inadequacy of human language, then one might well conclude that the "inner form" is pure, sanctified, and undefiled, but the "outer form," because it "pertains to the world of man," is flawed, subject to contradictory interpretations, or even to unconscious cultural influences outside the Prophet's control.

As we have already concluded, however, the Prophet appears in a distinct historical context but consciously adapts His Revelation to that context. He shapes and fashions each action, each word, even the literary forms He employs to befit these circumstances—whether the words and actions are His, or the result of the Divine Will working through Him, or some combination of the two. And yet, the very nature of the forms He chooses, because they rely heavily on poetic or imagistic language (i.e., symbols, metaphors, and other figurative devices), are fully capable of transcending the limitations that might be associated with ordinary speech. This is, no doubt, what Bahá'u'lláh means at the end of the Kitáb-i-Íqán:

> None apprehendeth the meaning of these utterances except them whose hearts are assured, whose souls have found favour with God, and whose minds are detached from all else but Him. In such utterances, the literal meaning, as generally understood by the people, is not what hath been intended. Thus it is recorded: "Every knowledge hath seventy meanings, of which one only is known amongst the people. And when the Qá'im shall arise, He shall reveal unto men all that which remaineth." He also saith: "We speak one word, and by it we intend one and seventy meanings; each one of these meanings we can explain." (*Kitáb-i-Íqán* 255)

Stated another way, while the Prophet (or God working through the Prophet) employs human language and human literary traditions whose "outer form" relates to the human condition, He does so wittingly and purposefully and perfectly so that there is in His art a perfect fusion of thought and form, a synthesis capable of transcending the limitations of ordinary human speech.

Thus Taherzadeh seems to be correct when he observes that the "outer form of the Word of God acts as a channel through which the stream of God's Holy Spirit flows." Likewise, Taherzadeh is correct in stating that language can never become essence. But we misconstrue Taherzadeh's meaning when he discusses the "outer form" and its "limitations" if by this statement we infer that the revealed word (the Prophet's art) is somehow an inadequate human expression of the Divine Will, that the Prophet is ultimately unable to transcend the human aspects of His condition and circumstance.

No, the revealed word has limitless levels of meaning and limitless applicability for those "whose hearts are assured, whose souls have found favour with God, and whose minds are detached from all else but Him." Taherzadeh himself makes this point clear when he explains, "Not only do the words uttered by the Manifestations have inner meanings but even a single letter contains divine mysteries and significances" (*Revelation of Bahá'u'lláh* 1:34). Hence the distinction Taherzadeh is making is the same distinction one might draw between spiritual reality and physical reality. The essential reality of the visible or physical world is its capacity to metaphorize or give artistic expression to the invisible or spiritual world; the two realities are but dual aspects of a single organic reality: "The spiritual world is like unto the phenomenal world. They are the exact counterparts of each other. Whatever objects appear in this world of existence are the outer pictures of the world of heaven" ('Abdu'l-Bahá, *Promulgation of Universal Peace* 10). But the physical world will never actually *become* the spiritual world. In this same sense, the revealed word may be limitless in its possible meanings and it may represent a perfect union of idea and form, but the "outer form" will never actually *become* the "inner form," even though it may provide us with a perfectly fashioned access to that "inner form."

Is this the Prophet's part in this process, then, to devise forms of language capable of conveying (or at least of alluding to) the "inner form"? While any understanding we have of this process will always necessarily be inexact and incomplete, Shoghi Effendi seems to attribute part of the creative act of fashioning Revelation into language to the individual capacity of the Manifestation. For example, he states that the Kitáb-i-Aqdas "may well be regarded as the brightest emanation of the *mind*[8] of Bahá'u'lláh" (*God Passes By* 213). He also characterizes The Hidden Words as "jewel-like thoughts cast out of the *mind* of the Manifestation of God to admonish and counsel men" (in *Lights of Guidance* 488). Similarly, in discussing the final works produced by Bahá'u'lláh, Shoghi Effendi says

> These Tablets—mighty and final effusions of His indefatigable pen—must rank among the choicest fruits which His *mind* has yielded, and mark the consummation of His forty-year-long ministry. (*God Passes By* 216)

Bahá'u'lláh Himself makes no distinction between which words are His own invention and which words are exact quotes from God, and, in the final analysis, it makes little effective difference for us. Since

8. Emphasis added.

all of Bahá'u'lláh's words are authoritative, infallible, and perfect, for all intents and purposes, the artistry of the Prophet is naught but God's artistry, regardless of exactly how the First Will interacts with the soul of the Manifestation.

F. The Importance of This Distinction

Why does this distinction matter if the words have the same authority regardless of their source? The answer to this question can be stated axiomatically: if we assume that the Manifestation is an ordinary human being (i.e., that the works of Bahá'u'lláh are not revealed, but derived from the same sort of artistic process appropriate to ordinary human writers), then we might reasonably apply the same standards of study to His works that we would employ with every other artist. To account for what Bahá'u'lláh writes or for the style He employs, we might search for clues in the various sorts of external influences we presume may have been present during His upbringing, in the works He may have read, or in the personalities He might have met. Similarly, we might be tempted to search out ulterior motives underlying His themes.

As was noted in *The Law of Love Enshrined,* this sort of secular approach to the work of the Prophet is precisely what was done by J. M. Rodwell in his examination of the Qur'án. Since Muḥammad was neither tutored nor trained in any formal sense, His sudden ability to speak with unsurpassed eloquence in an inimitable style served His followers as a miraculous proof of His claim that He had become anointed with the station of Prophethood. But since Rodwell examines the Qur'án from a narrow Christian bias, he rejects any considerations of a revelation process to account for Muḥammad's capacity.[9] Therefore Rodwell dismisses the possibility of a spiritual explanation

---

9. For Rodwell to consider the possibility that Muḥammad was what He claimed would have imposed on Rodwell the responsibility of deciding whether or not Muḥammad fulfilled Christ's promises about sending "another Comforter" (John 14:16) Who "shall testify of me" (John 15:26).

for Muḥammad's newfound knowledge and artistry, and he seeks instead to discover some material (i.e., non-spiritual) explanation.

Especially troubling to Rodwell was Muḥammad's familiarity with Jewish scripture when this ostensibly unlearned One had no background to warrant such knowledge. For example, when Muḥammad recounts the story of Joseph in exacting detail (Súrih 12), Rodwell concludes that this knowledge "clearly proves that Muḥammad must have been in confidential intercourse with learned Jews" (Rodwell 230 n1). Rodwell's conclusion is somewhat less derogatory than that of Sir William Muir, who concludes that, in recasting the story of Joseph, Muḥammad "entered upon a course of wilful dissimulation and deceit (although the end would justify to him the means employed) in claiming inspiration" (qtd. in Rodwell 239 n1).[10]

If we accept Bahá'u'lláh's own description of the revelation process as elucidated in the Lawḥ-i-Ḥikmat (Tablet of Wisdom), we have quite a different sort of explanation, one that presumes the existence of an intimate spiritual connection between the Prophet and the Primal Will. Bahá'u'lláh states that when He desired to quote from the work of human authors, their work would instantly appear before Him:

> Thou knowest full well that We perused not the books which men possess and We acquired not the learning current amongst them, and yet whenever We desire to quote the sayings of the learned and of the wise, presently there will appear before the face of thy Lord in the form of a tablet all that which hath appeared in the world and is revealed in the Holy Books and Scriptures. (*Tablets of Bahá'u'lláh* 149)

From this account, we can presume that Muḥammad and all the other Prophets had this same capacity, since each Manifestation (according to Bahá'u'lláh) is endowed with essentially the same station and powers.

10. Rodwell here quotes from Sir William Muir, *The Coran, Its Composition and Teaching, and the Testimony It Bears to the Holy Scriptures* (Society for Promoting Christian Knowledge, 1896).

Naturally, it would have been difficult for scholars like Rodwell and Muir, writing in a nineteenth-century Christian academic milieu, to support spiritual explanations for the process of composition employed by Muḥammad. But this same approach is being currently employed in the fields of historical analysis and religious studies with regard to the revealed writings of both the Báb and Bahá'u'lláh. For while contemporary religious study may have largely rid itself of the narrow constraints of a Western Christian bias, such study has largely fallen under the sway of a secular humanistic approach to the study of religions in attempt to segregate "scholarly" analysis from religious apologetics.

While the student of religion can certainly appreciate the desire to segregate homily and polemic from the more objective approach of scientific method to analyze the nature and progress of a religion, the same student can also observe that it is patently unscholarly and illogical to deny a priori the possibility that metaphysical or spiritual forces play a significant, if not a primary, role in the foundation of religions and in shaping the course of religious history. In short, to deny out of hand the possibility that what the Prophet-Founders of religions say is true (i.e., that Their utterances are the result of divine inspiration and guidance) and then to seek other explanations to account for the Prophet's eloquence and influence would seem to be unscholarly. First, such an approach assumes the conclusion that spiritual forces are nonexistent or else that unseen forces could not possibly play a causal role in the Prophet's sudden emergence from obscurity. Second, this initial error in scientific method is compounded by a post hoc fallacy of attributing causality to circumstantial events. That is, the appeal of the religion is attributed to the Prophet's charisma or else to what the scholar believes to be some propitious social or political circumstances.

The facts are that every Prophet has succeeded in spite of incalculable adversity, not because He appears in the right place at the right time. Furthermore, to ignore the lucid and repeated pronouncements by the Prophets and by Their followers about what is really causing the spread of the religion is to risk duplicating the errors of earlier scholars who rejected out of hand the theories of Newton or Einstein about how mysterious, unseen, and ostensibly miraculous forces organize and unify the physical universe. Yet this same groundless cynicism and skepticism afflicts some of the contemporary scholarship which purports to analyze the origins and success of the Bábí and Bahá'í religions. For example, some scholars assume that since no unseen or spiritual force could account for the capacity of this obscure and unlearned merchant, there must be other material explanations for how this lowly man from Shíráz was suddenly possessed of such eloquence and acumen that He was able to attract to His entourage some of the most venerable scholars of Persia. What is of particular interest in the way these scholars portray how the Bábí religion began is that, to avoid following in Muir's footsteps (i.e., chauvinistically asserting that the Báb "dissimulated"), they totally ignore the explicit assertions of the Báb that His utterances derive from a process of divine inspiration:

> God beareth Me witness, I was not a man of learning, for I was trained as a merchant. In the year sixty God graciously infused my soul with the conclusive evidences and weighty knowledge which characterize Him Who is the Testimony of God—may peace be upon Him—until finally in that year I proclaimed God's hidden Cause and unveiled its well-guarded Pillar, in such wise that no one could refute it. (*Selections from the Writings of the Báb* 12)

Instead of discussing the Báb's own statements about this process, as well as the specific accounts by other figures who witnessed the revelation process (e.g., Mullá Ḥusayn), these same scholars assume that the Báb's belief that He had been divinely chosen and inspired gradually took shape in His mind as He saw the influence He was having on others. These same critics assert that, since this simple merchant was a self-educated layman who never had the opportunity to benefit from the scholastic knowledge of the time, His early literary style was less eloquent and sophisticated than His later style, which benefited from the influence of learned followers such as Mullá Ḥusayn. Indeed, some critics ascribe the early success of the Bábí Faith more to the caliber of the early disciples than to the spiritual station and influence of the Báb Himself.

Of course, the fact that these "scholarly" approaches ignore the possibility that there is an unseen force at work in human history does not, in itself, invalidate the sometimes valuable information such studies provide about the circumstances surrounding the history of these religious movements. But when such scholars assume that there must be physical explanations for a process that is defined consistently by the participants and, more especially, by the Prophet-Artist Himself as essentially metaphysical in nature, then these same scholars indict the veracity of the Báb without just cause, significantly inhibit the consideration of style and form as deriving from purposeful artistry rather than from external associational influence, and, more to the point, deny as plausible the essential assertion of all religion—that unseen or spiritual forces exert a profound, even a primary influence on the course of human events. As a consequence of such unfounded assumptions, the field of religious studies has become largely an exploration of religion as a sociological or political process, not as the interplay between the invisible and the visible realities.

Of course, the scholars as historians or as sociologists are by no means obliged to delve into matters of spirituality or theology. They may content themselves with the elucidation of observable factual information surrounding events. But when these same scholars presume to assess the chain of causality responsible for effecting and guiding these events, then they are obliged at least to consider whether or not the explanation given by the participants themselves is feasible (if scholars are to remain faithful to the scientific method). Stated more categorically, the existence of an unseen force at work in human history is no less plausible and no less scholarly as an explanation for events than it is to consider the influence of unseen forces at work in the natural world (e.g., gravity).[11]

---

11. For one indication of a growing body of scientific study to validate a belief in the relationship between metaphysical and physical reality, see Robert G. Jahn and Brenda J. Dunne, *Margins of Reality: The Role of Consciousness in the Physical World* (New York: Harcourt Brace, 1987).

In terms of our consideration of the Prophet as artist, this question assumes immense importance. Bahá'u'lláh in the Kitáb-i-Íqán, His apologia[12] for the Bábí Faith and His most important doctrinal work, states forthrightly that the single most important proof of a Prophet's station is Divine Utterance—His capacity to speak or write spontaneously without revision, yet with unsurpassed eloquence and wisdom. This proof, Bahá'u'lláh observes, excels in importance the fulfillment of prophecy or even the miraculous acts attributed to the Manifestations. Or, stated in terms of Christ's admonition to His own followers about how to recognize the true Prophet ("Wherefore by their fruits ye shall know them," Matt. 7:20), the primary "fruit" of the Manifestation is His capacity to convey the Word of God in its pure form.

In the strictest sense, then, the scholar is correct in the bald assertion that an ordinary writer-artist could not possibly do what the Báb and Bahá'u'lláh were suddenly able to do, not without some "external" assistance. As Bahá'u'lláh repeatedly notes, the Manifestation is not "ordinary"; furthermore, He constantly receives "external" assistance in the form of divine inspiration, divine guidance, and even the very words He utters—the foremost proof of a Prophet's station.

G. Becoming a Creative Reader

If we can accept the utterances of the Prophet as authoritative, whether or not we can know precisely what process brings these words into existence, we may understandably conclude that the comprehension of the Prophet's art should remain a thing of mystery, a purely personal bond between the believer and the Beloved, a relationship that abhors the objective standards of scientific method commonly associated with scholarly study. We may call to mind that many of the spiritual heroes and heroines of the Bahá'í Faith (and of religion in general) are not people of great learning—few of the Dawn-Breakers even had access to many of the revealed writings of the Báb.

---

12. A formal essay in defense of, or in justification of, an idea or set of ideas.

Several statements of Bahá'u'lláh would seem to confirm this conclusion. Bahá'u'lláh states that the capacity to understand those "mysteries" contained in the utterances of the Manifestations is not dependent on traditional learning, but on spiritual capacity and receptivity:

> The understanding of His words and the comprehension of the utterances of the Birds of Heaven are in no wise dependent upon human learning. They depend solely upon purity of heart, chastity of soul, and freedom of spirit. This is evidenced by those who, today, though without a single letter of the accepted standards of learning, are occupying the loftiest seats of knowledge; and the garden of their hearts is adorned, through the showers of divine grace, with the roses of wisdom and the tulips of understanding. (*Kitáb-i-Íqán* 211)

Bahá'u'lláh also notes that the mere recitation of the revealed words will have a salutary effect upon us, whether or not we have a precise understanding of their meaning:

> Whoso reciteth, in the privacy of his chamber, the verses revealed by God, the scattering angels of the Almighty shall scatter abroad the fragrance of the words uttered by his mouth, and shall cause the heart of every righteous man to throb. Though he may, at first, remain unaware of its effect, yet the virtue of the grace vouchsafed unto him must needs sooner or later exercise its influence upon his soul. Thus have the mysteries of the Revelation of God been decreed by virtue of the Will of Him Who is the Source of power and wisdom. (*Gleanings* 295)

Therefore, if one's spiritual life or religious experience is largely a thing of mystery, we might well conclude that it is not necessary to *study* the revealed word in any common academic sense. We might even feel that any sort of scholarly analysis could kill off that spark of intuition and ecstatic delight that attracts us to the realm of the spirit. Certainly, one of the most appealing aspects of religion for many people is its mystery, the promise of an unseen force at work in our lives, an unseen justice that will set our lives in order and, in time, bring about the triumph of good over evil.

But the sense of mystery in the Bahá'í writings is not meant to have the same appeal one might find in the occult or in pseudosciences which imply that our lives are largely beyond our control and, consequently, beyond individual responsibility. The Bahá'í teachings state that we are each personally responsible for our own spiritual development: "For the faith of no man can be conditioned by any one except himself" (*Gleanings* 143). Furthermore, when Bahá'u'lláh exhorts us in the Kitáb-i-Aqdas to "immerse" ourselves in the ocean of His words, He ordains a specific objective for that command—to "unravel its secrets" and to "discover all the pearls of wisdom that lie hid in its depths" (¶182). In the Kitáb-i-Íqán Bahá'u'lláh states this verity more plainly:

> [T]he reading of the scriptures and holy books is for no other purpose except to enable the reader to apprehend their meaning and unravel their innermost mysteries. Otherwise reading, without understanding, is of no abiding profit unto man. (*Kitáb-i-Íqán* 172)

In short, we are mandated to learn practical methods of swimming about in these bountiful waters. Certainly, we are free to employ various methods to "unravel" these "mysteries," but Shoghi Effendi prescribes some specific qualities that must govern the process:

> . . . [Bahá'ís] must study for themselves, conscientiously and painstakingly, the literature of their Faith, delve into its teachings, assimilate its laws and principles, ponder its admonitions, tenets and purposes, commit to memory certain of its exhortations and prayers, master the essentials of its administration, and keep abreast of its current affairs and latest developments. (*Advent of Divine Justice* 49)
>
> His advice to you is to continue deepening your knowledge and understanding of this Revelation, both by means of patient

> and thorough study of Bahá'í writings, and through active association with your fellow-believers and close participation in the activities of your local Bahá'í community. (*Compilation of Compilations* 1: no. 491)

> [T]he friends should arrange proper study classes and deepen their knowledge of the teachings. It is only through such thorough understanding of the literature of the Cause that you can appreciate the real message that Bahá'u'lláh has brought to the world. (*Compilation of Compilations* 1: no. 459)

In sum, Shoghi Effendi portrays the proper study of the art of Bahá'u'lláh as "patient" and "thorough," as a process that must be pursued "conscientiously and painstakingly." Shoghi Effendi goes so far as to observe, "There is no limit to the study of the Cause. The more we read the writings the more truths we can find in them and the more we will see that our previous notions were erroneous" (*Compilation of Compilations* 1: no. 451).

Since Bahá'u'lláh abolished the clergy or any class of divines and has laid the responsibility for study and learning on each individual, all of us are exhorted to become scholars in our own right. But where do we begin? And once we begin, what do we do when we become stumped, when we have no idea what Bahá'u'lláh is saying? What tools or procedures can we use to extricate ourselves from the consternation or bewilderment that each of us will inevitably experience when we encounter passages that we simply do not understand?

First, we can benefit from the preliminary study others have done for us. For even though we may not want others to do our thinking for us, we can gratefully accept the groundwork others have prepared so that we can become more creative and productive in our own study. But perhaps the most useful response we can have to those inevitable moments when we do not understand what we are reading is to organize our thinking. This is the job for which the tools of literary criticism are especially well suited, because at the heart of literary criticism is a fairly simple procedure, an attempt to discover what we do not know by a process of organizing what we do know.

And how do we organize what we do know and identify what we do not know? We begin by asking a series of fairly obvious but nevertheless extremely helpful questions:

1. What is the narrative point of view in this work (Who is speaking to me)?
2. What does historical criticism reveal about this work (In what context are these words spoken)?
3. What does genre criticism reveal about this work (In what literary form is this work written)?
4. What role does figurative language play in this work (What "mysteries," metaphors, symbols, or allusions can I discover in this work)?
5. What does a structural analysis of the work reveal (What pattern of ideas ties together the various parts of this work)?
6. What does a close reading of text reveal about the ultimate meaning of this work (What meaning seems to unify the diverse ingredients in this work after I assemble all the information I have gathered)?

These six questions will form the structural basis for the remaining six chapters of this study. For while there are certainly many other questions we might ask and many other tools of literary criticism we might apply, these six foundational questions constitute a useful beginning for a systematic study of Bahá'u'lláh's artistry: they can instigate further insight into those works we already appreciate, and they can help us proceed from a point of confusion or perplexity to a plateau of fruitful meditation with regard to those works we have difficulty understanding. Stated in terms of our abiding metaphor, the answers we derive from this analysis can help us become more creative readers because they provide some basic swimming lessons until we acquire the confidence to develop our own strokes.

Chapter 2
Narrative Perspective in the Art of Bahá'u'lláh

At one time We spoke in the language of the lawgiver; at another in that of the truth-seeker and the mystic. . . .

—Bahá'u'lláh

In every literary work we read there is a narrative voice speaking to us. It may be the voice of a character telling us his story in the first person, or it may be a disembodied voice of a third-person speaker who focuses our attention elsewhere. But one of the first questions we want resolved as we begin to read is the identity of that narrator, because what we think about the information the speaker tells us depends in large part on what we think about that speaker.

Even though we normally think of narrative perspective as relevant only to belletristic literature (creative literature, fiction, etc.), a study of Bahá'u'lláh's rich array of literary forms reveals an equally varied and creative use of narrative point of view. But before we attempt to assess the effects of Bahá'u'lláh's imaginative use of narrative perspective, let us first define exactly what part narrative point of view can play in the literary arts.

A. Narrative Point of View Defined

Let us presume that an elderly man is hit by a truck. If we hear of this event on the evening news, the story may have little emotional impact on us: "Yesterday at noon an elderly pedestrian was injured by a truck while crossing the street at an intersection. He is listed in critical condition. His name is being withheld pending notification of his family."

Here the point of view is third person, the narrative perspective of a newscaster whose tone is purposefully flat, objective, and calculated to eliminate our own emotional reaction. But if the same event is narrated from the point of view of the truck driver, we get a more powerful emotional response: "It was late in the afternoon. I was tired, and the sun was directly in my eyes. I saw the old man with the cane, but I was sure he would not try to cross when he saw the light changing. I guess he was thinking about something else, because the next thing I knew, I heard the thump of his body against my right front fender. I stepped on the brakes as quickly as I could, and the truck squealed to a stop. I ran over to his mangled body. I tried to help him, but there was no sign of life. There was nothing for me to do."

Here we have first-person narration from a participant, a dramatis personae in the event, though not necessarily the central character. If we shift to the point of view of the old man, we have to become a bit more creative, depending on what degree of consciousness we wish for him to have. He could be recounting the events to a police officer, waking up in a hospital, or assessing his life from the next world after having died.

The point is that each shift in perspective significantly alters our view of reality and the emotion we experience. From the writer's perspective, each shift requires an entirely different sort of creative skill. The effect of narrative perspective (point of view) in literature is thus similar to the effect of camera perspective in cinematography. In a film we see only what the camera allows us to see. The camera's view becomes our own view. The camera lens becomes our eyes. If the camera represents a character surveying a room, then, effectively, we become that character. We assume the emotions and sensibilities of that character. Similarly, if the camera objectively scans a forest from some point in the sky, then we, too, assume that godlike omniscience, that detached perspective.

In literary criticism (literary analysis), the term "point of view" is thus generally employed to discuss the "vantage point from which an author presents a story" (*A Handbook to Literature* 366). More specifically, narrative point of view relates to whether the story is told from a third-person point of view or a first-person point of view:

> If the author serves as a seemingly all-knowing maker, the *point of view* is called omniscient. At the other extreme, a character in the story—major, minor, or marginal—may tell the story as he or she experienced it. Such a character is usually called a first-person narrator. . . . (*Handbook* 366–67)

There are also variants within these categories as well as combinations of these variations.

We might understandably wonder how considerations of narrative point of view have any relevance to a study of Bahá'u'lláh's art. After all, since Bahá'u'lláh is a Manifestation of God, does He not always speak as a Manifestation? How can there be any variation in point of view in His works?

Bahá'u'lláh Himself gives us a clue to the importance of this literary consideration when in Epistle to the Son of the Wolf He observes that He has used various narrative voices or perspectives in His writings: "At one time We spoke in the language of the lawgiver; at another in that of the truth-seeker and the mystic" (15). As we study this aspect of Bahá'u'lláh's art, we begin to observe how He has employed a number of other narrative perspectives. Indeed, one of the most profound and helpful observations we can make about the appearance of the Prophet is that He is a master of dramaturgy because He conceals His true identity in the guise of an ordinary human being. For example, He veils all the attributes, power, and unspeakable glory of God in the persona of a lowly carpenter's son, an unlearned camel driver, a simple merchant, or an exiled prisoner. What is more, in one passage discussing Bahá'u'lláh's ascension, Shoghi Effendi seems to imply that the

Prophet Himself may have some choice as to what persona He will assume when He appears in the physical world:

> Yet, as the appointed Center of Bahá'u'lláh's Covenant and the authorized Interpreter of His teaching had Himself later explained, the dissolution of the tabernacle wherein the soul of the Manifestation of God had *chosen* [italics added] temporarily to abide signalized its release from the restrictions which an earthly life had, of necessity, imposed upon it. Its influence no longer circumscribed by any physical limitations, its radiance no longer beclouded by its human temple, that soul could henceforth energize the whole world to a degree unapproached at any stage in the course of its existence on this planet. (*God Passes By* 244)

But regardless of the extent to which the Prophet devises His own concealment, the point is that the same sort of wit and wisdom we must exercise in discovering the Prophet's identity concealed in the persona of an ordinary human being must also be exercised in discerning the various narrative perspectives Bahá'u'lláh employs among the vast canon of His revealed works.

Therefore, let us examine Bahá'u'lláh's use of various narrative points of view so that we might better understand how His creative use of narrative point of view affects our emotional response to what He is telling us.

B. Narrative Perspective in The Hidden Words

The Hidden Words has two distinct parts—the first in Arabic, the second in Persian. In both parts the narrative perspective is uniformly written from the first-person point of view. As we observed in the narration of the old man being hit by the truck, the usual tonal effect of employing a first-person narrative perspective is to create a sense of familiarity between the speaker and the listener. But we also noted that the narrative tone is greatly affected by the identity of the first-person speaker (i.e., whether it be the news broadcaster, the truck driver, or the accident victim).

Therefore, while the use of the first-person speaker in The Hidden Words does indeed help evoke a sense of intimacy and familiarity between the speaker and the reader (e.g., "I knew my love for thee . . ."), we immediately observe that the first person is *not* Bahá'u'lláh, at least not Bahá'u'lláh speaking from the station of "distinction" (i.e., as an historical figure). The speaker is God—ancient, eternal, timeless, placeless. The perspective is omniscient, calling to mind eternal verities regarding human behavior.

We recognize this perspective from the outset when the speaker identifies Himself as the eternal object of love and striving:

> O SON OF MAN!
> Veiled in My immemorial being and in the ancient eternity of My essence, I knew My love for thee; therefore I created thee, have engraved on thee Mine image and revealed to thee My beauty.
>
> O SON OF MAN!
> I loved thy creation, hence I created thee. Wherefore, do thou love Me, that I may name thy name and fill thy soul with the spirit of life.
>
> O SON OF BEING!
> Love Me, that I may love thee. If thou lovest Me not, My love can in no wise reach thee. Know this, O servant.
> (Hidden Words, Arabic, nos. 3–5)

Of course, the inseparable alliance between the Manifestation and God largely nullifies for us any major distinctions between the voice of the Prophet and the Voice of God. Yet, clearly, the point of view here is more closely aligned with the Prophet speaking from the station of essential unity, rather than from His specific historical perspective (i.e., "the station of distinction").

The tone of this work is strongly influenced by this narrative point of view. The divine presence is speaking intimately to us (sometimes to us individually and sometimes to us collectively as the human race). Some verses are addressed to particular groups of us—to seekers, believers, ecclesiastical leaders, political leaders, servants of God, materialists, egoists, slaves to passion and mammon—and quite naturally the emotional tone of the various verses changes according to the designated addressee. Those attached to self or to the acquisition of material well-being ("Son of Dust," "Essence of Desire," "Bond Slave of the World,") are upbraided or forewarned. The lovers of God ("Son of Spirit," "My Friends," "My Servant,") are comforted, nurtured, reassured, and guided. But whether He is addressing us individually or collectively, this Narrator knows us intimately, knows how we have done so far in our life's journey and what we must now do to redeem ourselves.

From the outset of The Hidden Words Bahá'u'lláh prepares the reader for this omniscient point of view. In His preamble He states that what will follow is a distillation of all spiritual teachings:

> This is that which hath descended from the realm of glory, uttered by the tongue of power and might, and revealed unto the Prophets of old. We have taken the inner essence thereof and clothed it in the garment of brevity, as a token of grace unto the righteous, that they may stand faithful unto the Covenant of God, may fulfill in their lives His trust, and in the realm of spirit obtain the gem of Divine virtue. (*Hidden Words* 3)

The body of The Hidden Words, then, is a collection of aphoristic or axiomatic spiritual verities presented as lyric verses to synthesize all previous Revelations. It is understandable, therefore, that the voice we hear is not that of Bahá'u'lláh as an historical personage. The narrative perspective is that of the unseen world viewing the entirety of human history—our foibles and fallibilities, our failures to heed divine assistance, as well as our noble efforts at transformation and the brightness of our future.

This insight about narrative point of view in The Hidden Words is especially helpful when we encounter in the initial passages statements that could only be applicable to God: "I knew My love for thee; therefore I created thee"; "I loved thy creation, hence I created thee"; "I have breathed within thee a breath of My own Spirit, that thou mayest be My lover" (Hidden Words, Arabic, nos. 3, 4, 19). In short, while it is possible that these same verses could be interpreted to apply to Bahá'u'lláh, most seem to be implying that the narrative voice is God speaking directly to humankind. When the Manifestation is alluded to (as in the Persian Hidden Word number 77), it is from the first-person perspective of the Maid of Heaven reporting on what she has observed about how the Prophet is treated by humankind:

> In the night-season the beauty of the immortal Being hath repaired from the emerald height of fidelity unto the Sadratu'l-Muntahá, and wept with such a weeping that the concourse on high and the dwellers of the realms above wailed at His lamenting. Whereupon there was asked, Why the wailing and weeping? He made reply: As bidden I waited expectant upon the hill of faithfulness, yet inhaled not from them that dwell on earth the fragrance of fidelity. Then summoned to return I beheld, and lo! certain doves of holiness were sore tried within the claws of the dogs of the earth. (Hidden Words, Persian, no. 77)

This is very similar to passages in the Tablet of the Holy Mariner, which likewise describes in allusive and symbolic (i.e., allegorical) terms the relationship between the Heavenly Concourse and the Manifestations. In both cases the narrative perspective is effectively third-person omniscient, and we as audience are allowed to observe from a detached perspective the coordinated effort between the celestial forces and the Prophets as they attempt to teach an unreceptive humankind. The resulting point of view provides us with something like a temporary collective out-of-body experience, that we might appreciate the thankless and often humiliating task assumed by the Prophets in ministering to our needs.

We also see the usefulness of studying narrative point of view when we consider Persian Hidden Word number 19. In spite of 'Abdu'l-Bahá's authoritative assertion that the human soul begins at conception, some have interpreted this verse as an allusion to human preexistence:

> Have you forgotten that true and radiant morn, when in those hallowed and blessed surroundings ye were all gathered in My presence beneath the shade of the tree of life, which is planted in the all-glorious paradise? Awe-struck ye listened as I gave utterance to these three most holy words: O friends! Prefer not your will to Mine, never desire that which I have not desired for you, and approach Me not with lifeless hearts, defiled with worldly desires and cravings. Would ye but sanctify your souls, ye would at this present hour recall that place and those surroundings, and the truth of My utterance should be made evident unto all of you.

If the verse is not alluding to some preexistent condition, then how can the Manifestation say that He has already told us these things? After all, while our identity begins at conception, are we not "emanations from God" ('Abdu'l-Bahá, *Some Answered Questions* 205)?

Here again, as throughout The Hidden Words, the speaker is the Deity, reminding the human race as a collective organism of the guidance that has been given in the past through other Manifestations. If we are attentive, we will be able to perceive the continuity of that guidance and thereby recognize that same voice when it reappears with the advent of a new Manifestation.

In summary, then, The Hidden Words employs the first-person narrative point of view, but that first-person speaker is best understood not as Bahá'u'lláh, the historical author or source of these verses, nor even as a divinely ordained intermediary. There are virtually no allusions to particular personal circumstances or historical personages; there is no breach in this fictive guise. This is the Creator, the Divine Will, speaking with unveiled splendor, candor, and love.

Nowhere is this point of view more evident than in Persian Hidden Word number 29, wherein the progress of humankind is alluded to as an individual who was loved and cared for before birth, who was lovingly nurtured and protected while being raised, and who now, despite being "fully grown," remains unaware of the part God as parent played in his or her development:

O SON OF BOUNTY!
Out of the wastes of nothingness, with the clay of My command I made thee to appear, and have ordained for thy training every atom in existence and the essence of all created things. Thus, ere thou didst issue from thy mother's womb, I destined for thee two founts of gleaming milk, eyes to watch over thee, and hearts to love thee. Out of My loving-kindness, 'neath the shade of My mercy I nurtured thee, and guarded thee by the essence of My grace and favor. And My purpose in all this was that thou mightest attain My everlasting dominion and become worthy of My invisible bestowals. And yet heedless thou didst remain, and when fully grown, thou didst neglect all My bounties and occupied thyself with thine idle imaginings, in such wise that thou didst become wholly forgetful, and, turning away from the portals of the Friend didst abide within the courts of My enemy.

C. Narrative Perspective in Epistle to the Son of the Wolf

Like The Hidden Words, one of Bahá'u'lláh's first major works, Epistle to the Son of the Wolf, one of Bahá'u'lláh's last major works, also employs a first-person perspective, but with a totally different effect. The first-person speaker in Epistle to the Son of the Wolf represents Bahá'u'lláh as an historical persona—the Manifestation in His station of "distinction" appearing at a particular point in the evolution of human society.

It is not hard to understand why Bahá'u'lláh has employed this point of view. Written about a year before Bahá'u'lláh's death in 1892, Epistle to the Son of the Wolf assumes the narrative tone of a personal reflection by One Who, having completed His earthly mission, is soon to return to the realm from which He came. Bahá'u'lláh thus surveys His actions and the scope of His revealed works, citing salient passages as He does so. In particular, Bahá'u'lláh vindicates His behavior in relation to political and ecclesiastical authority, noting repeatedly that He has never sought to usurp their power and has always been a loyal citizen in whatever land He was "forced" to reside.[1]

This is not to say that in this work Bahá'u'lláh conceals the loftiness of His station. While often alluding to Himself as "this Wronged One," He does not speak meekly as an imprisoned citizen, but as the "Divine Voice" summoning the wayward and recalcitrant leaders to the path of God. For example, at the outset Bahá'u'lláh addresses Shaykh Muḥammad-Taqí, the "Son of the Wolf," with respect in spite of the atrocities he and his father had committed against the followers of Bahá'u'lláh. But He also speaks to the Shaykh with a tone of complete authority and command:

> Purify thou, first, thy soul with the waters of renunciation, and adorn thine head with the crown of the fear of God, and thy temple with the ornament of reliance upon Him. (*Epistle* 2)

Bahá'u'lláh then instructs the Shaykh, "Arise, then, and, with thy face set towards the Most Great House, the Spot round which, as decreed by the Eternal King, all that dwell on earth must circle, recite: 'O God, my God, and my Desire, and my Adored One, and my Master, and my Mainstay, and my utmost Hope, and my supreme Aspiration!'" (*Epistle* 2–3)

This prayer, which Bahá'u'lláh advises him to recite, is six pages long and candidly rehearses the very iniquities the Shaykh has committed: "O wretched, wretched that I am! O the cruelties, the glaring cruelties, I inflicted!" (*Epistle* 4). After the prayer, Bahá'u'lláh informs the Shaykh that nothing he or anyone else can do "can harm him that hath clung to the cord of the grace, and seized the hem of the mercy, of the Lord of creation" (*Epistle* 9).

---

1. As is noted in *The Law of Love Enshrined*, the Prophet is fully able to extricate Himself from His circumstances, but usually chooses to allow His physical circumstances to be determined by secular powers and authority, perhaps so that none may later claim His fulfillment of prophecy comes about through His own calculated efforts.

Among the many inferences we draw from this beginning is that there is always hope, even for the most iniquitous of souls. For while we may not expect the Shaykh to heed Bahá'u'lláh's advice (to pray this prayer and seek forgiveness), the avenue for redemption is clearly available to him. The tone here is thus very similar to that of the passage in the Kitáb-i-Aqdas in which Bahá'u'lláh tells His wayward brother Mírzá Yaḥyá that forgiveness is still available to him if he will but act in repentance, though He reminds Mírzá Yaḥyá that such action will be taken solely for his own sake, not because God or Bahá'u'lláh needs or requires his assistance:

> Beware lest the fire of thy presumptuousness debar thee from attaining to God's Holy Court. Turn unto Him, and fear not because of thy deeds. He, in truth, forgiveth whomsoever He desireth as a bounty on His part; no God is there but Him, the Ever-Forgiving, the All-Bounteous. We admonish thee solely for the sake of God. Shouldst thou accept this counsel, thou wilt have acted to thine own behoof; and shouldst thou reject it, thy Lord, verily, can well dispense with thee, and with all those who, in manifest delusion, have followed thee. Behold! God hath laid hold on him [Siyyid Muḥammad-i-Iṣfahání] who led thee astray. Return unto God, humble, submissive and lowly; verily, He will put away from thee thy sins, for thy Lord, of a certainty, is the Forgiving, the Mighty, the All-Merciful. (¶184)

Because Bahá'u'lláh made these explicit historical allusions to the Shaykh in Epistle to the Son of the Wolf, we also discover in this narrative point of view the value of studying this work in light of historical considerations—a matter we will take up in Chapter 3. That is, if the reader is not aware of the character of the recipient of this work and reads Epistle to the Son of the Wolf assuming that Bahá'u'lláh is speaking directly to the generality of humankind, then the often harsh tone and severe recriminations might seem troublesome, even bewildering. Likewise, the repeated allusions to Himself as "this Wronged One" might seem self-pitying if the reader is not aware that Bahá'u'lláh is speaking from the point of view of an Emissary from the spiritual world, enunciating with frankness and candor the irony that He has been made to suffer throughout His ministry by the very people whom He has come to save. For example, in one prayer in Epistle to the Son of the Wolf Bahá'u'lláh speaks as the Prophet nearing the end of His assigned task:

> Glorified art Thou, O Lord my God! Thou seest what hath befallen this Wronged One at the hands of them that have not associated with Me, and who have arisen to harm and abase Me, in a manner which no pen can describe, nor tongue recount, nor can any Tablet sustain its weight. (*Epistle* 35)

If we read into this passage any hint of self-pity or lamentation, we totally misunderstand what is intended. In this same prayer Bahá'u'lláh goes on to beseech God to sustain those who have believed:

> Thou hearest the cry of Mine heart, and the groaning of Mine inmost being, and the things that have befallen Thy trusted ones in Thy cities and Thy chosen ones in Thy land, at the hands of such as have broken Thy Covenant and Thy Testament. I beseech Thee, O my Lord, by the sighs of Thy lovers throughout the world, and by their lamentation in their remoteness from the court of Thy presence, and by the blood that hath been shed for love of Thee, and by the hearts that have melted in Thy path, to protect Thy loved ones from the cruelty of such as have remained unaware of the mysteries of Thy Name, the Unconstrained. Assist them, O my Lord, by Thy power that hath prevailed over all things, and aid them to be patient and long-suffering. (*Epistle* 35–36)

He recounts the trials that have befallen Him, not to wring pity from the Shaykh's heart nor to induce a sense of guilt in the followers who read this panoramic rehearsal of His life's work. Neither is Bahá'u'lláh lamenting His suffering. He states forthrightly that "Troubles have failed to unnerve Me, and the repudiation of the divines hath been powerless to weaken Me. I have spoken, and still speak forth before the face of men . . ." (*Epistle* 85). In other words, though Epistle to the Son of the Wolf is addressed to the Shaykh ostensibly as a vindication of Bahá'u'lláh's ministry, it functions even more powerfully as a unique work among the revealed works of any previous Prophet—an occasion for the Manifestation to summarize and to assay His ministry.

Thus the narrative perspective and tonal qualities of Epistle to the Son of the Wolf find no parallel among the other works of Bahá'u'lláh. Almost symphonic in structure, the emotional strains rise and fall, softening into prayer and praise of the martyrs, becoming analytical when vindicating the events that surround the machinations of the Covenant-breakers, rising to a crescendo of exhortation when admonishing the Shaykh not to forgo his unique opportunity to assist the Cause of God:

> O Shaykh! Enter thou My presence, that thou mayest behold what the eye of the universe hath never beheld, and hear that which the ear of the whole creation hath never heard, that haply thou mayest free thyself from the mire of vague fancies, and set thy face towards the Most Sublime Station, wherein this Wronged One calleth aloud: "The Kingdom is God's, the Almighty, the All-Praised!" We fain would hope that through thine exertions the wings of men may be sanctified from the mire of self and desire, and be made worthy to soar in the atmosphere of God's love. Wings that are besmirched with mire can never soar. Unto this testify they who are the exponents of justice and equity, and yet the people are in evident doubt. (*Epistle* 130–31)

D. Narrative Perspective in the Kitáb-i-Íqán

In contrast to the two examples of Bahá'u'lláh's use of the first-person narrative perspective in The Hidden Words and Epistle to the Son of the Wolf, the Kitáb-i-Íqán is written largely in the third-person point of view. A highly organized doctrinal essay on the fundamental verities of Bahá'í theology (as we will discuss in more detail in Chapter 6 on subject and structure), the Kitáb-i-Íqán functions as an apologia both for the Báb as Qá'im and for the Bábí Faith as a new Revelation.[2] For though the Kitáb-i-Íqán is the most important doctrinal work of Bahá'u'lláh's Revelation, Bahá'u'lláh revealed this work more than a year before His Riḍván announcement in 1863 that He was the promised Manifestation—"Him Whom God shall make manifest"—Whose advent the Báb had foretold.

As a general analysis of divine methodology, the Kitáb-i-Íqán serves to vindicate God's ways to man, to explicate in detail the station and nature of the Prophets, and to explain the reason humanity has so consistently failed to recognize the source of its own salvation. The Kitáb-i-Íqán thus renders a complete analysis of theodicy from a Bahá'í perspective.[3]

While exquisitely organized and largely analytical in tone, the work is not without allusion to Bahá'u'lláh Himself, nor is the narrative tone always impersonal or strictly logical. There is an abundance of irony, and there are many instances of humor as Bahá'u'lláh speaks disparagingly of the vain and patently illogical notions of the so-called "learned" ones—the divines and ecclesiastics of every age and Dispensation. We can observe in the following passages, for example, the tone with which He marvels at the inability of the "scholars" to understand even the most fundamental verities about the process of divine revelation:

> In every age and century, the purpose of the Prophets of God and their chosen ones hath been no other but to affirm the spiritual significance of the terms "life," "resurrection," and "judgment." If one will ponder but for a while this utterance of 'Alí in his heart, one will surely discover all mysteries hidden in the terms "grave," "tomb," "ṣiráṭ," "paradise" and "hell." But oh! how strange and pitiful! Behold, all the people are imprisoned within the tomb

2. See Shoghi Effendi, *God Passes By* 172.

3. That is, an explanation or justification of the concealment of the Prophets and the overall indirection by which God guides and educates humanity, and, more particularly, a vindication of the omniscience and omnipotence of God that accounts for the existence of evil in God's creation.

> of self, and lie buried beneath the nethermost depths of worldly desire! Wert thou to attain to but a dewdrop of the crystal waters of divine knowledge, thou wouldst readily realize that true life is not the life of the flesh but the life of the spirit. (*Kitáb-i-Íqán* 120)

> How strange! These people with one hand cling to those verses of the Qur'án and those traditions of the people of certitude which they have found to accord with their inclinations and interests, and with the other reject those which are contrary to their selfish desires. (*Kitáb-i-Íqán* 168–69)

Sometimes this ironic tone is evoked by a shift in narrative perspective from an objective third-person point of view (in which the structure of the treatise is carried along by the logical sequence of the argument itself) to a more personal and anecdotal style to emphasize a point. But even in these instances Bahá'u'lláh employs not the "I" of Epistle to the Son of the Wolf, but the same sort of collective or editorial "We" Muḥammad employs in the Qur'án:

> One day, a well-known divine came to visit Us. While We were conversing with him, he referred to the above-quoted tradition. He said: "Inasmuch as fasting causeth the heat of the body to increase, it hath therefore been likened unto the light of the sun; and as the prayer of the night-season refresheth man, it hath been compared unto the radiance of the moon." Thereupon We realized that poor man had not been favoured with a single drop of the ocean of true understanding, and had strayed far from the burning Bush of divine wisdom. We then politely observed to him saying: "The interpretation your honour hath given to this tradition is the one current amongst the people. Could it not be interpreted differently?" (*Kitáb-i-Íqán* 39–40)

Here we note that, even though He is clearly amused by the blatant ignorance of this "learned" one, Bahá'u'lláh speaks to the man with utmost kindness and humbly suggests an alternative interpretation rather than pointing out the shallowness or irrationality of the scholar's ideas.

When Bahá'u'lláh occasionally digresses from the quasi-formal tone and structure of this treatise to interpose various reflections on certain points, He is careful to acknowledge His departure from His central theme:

> We have digressed from the purpose of Our argument, although whatsoever is mentioned serveth only to confirm Our purpose. By God! however great Our desire to be brief, yet We feel We cannot restrain Our pen. (*Kitáb-i-Íqán* 70)

For the most part, then, the point of view, when it shifts to the first person, is not the persona of a Prophet; the voice is that of a teacher and true scholar setting forth cogent, vital, and carefully constructed arguments about the most fundamental tenets of Bahá'í belief. Yet the tone is never pedantic. Indeed, as we have noted, Bahá'u'lláh often expresses His disdain for the tiresome practices of divines and scholars.

Bahá'u'lláh as narrator is not totally transparent in this work. Sometimes He alludes to Himself, particularly at the end, where He hints very clearly that He is Mustag͟háth (He Who is Invoked). But for the most part Bahá'u'lláh as an historical figure or even as a divine authority remains in the background, allowing the discourse to speak for itself. It would seem, in short, that He wishes for the certitude alluded to in the title of this book to be derived from the persuasive and lucid logic of the ideas themselves, not from His authority or from His appeal to our emotions. For example, after discussing the distinction between the two stations of the Prophets (the station of essential unity and the station of distinction) Bahá'u'lláh observes:

> From these incontrovertible and fully demonstrated statements strive thou to apprehend the meaning of the questions thou hast asked, that thou mayest become steadfast in the Faith of God, and not be dismayed by the divergences in the utterances of His Prophets and Chosen Ones. (*Kitáb-i-Íqán* 178)

In this context the reader is forced to achieve certitude or conviction by coming to understand and appreciate the abiding logic permeating the relationship between God and man, not from an affirmation of faith derived solely from an assertion of belief. The overall effectiveness of Bahá'u'lláh's use of narrative perspective in the Kitáb-i-Íqán, then, is to objectify the arguments by which one can be led from doubt into the City of Certitude.

E. Narrative Perspective in the Allegorical Works

Thus far we have examined how tone is affected by Bahá'u'lláh's variable use of first-person narration in The Hidden Words and in Epistle to the Son of the Wolf, and by His predominant use of third person in the Kitáb-i-Íqán. We now turn to another use of the third-person perspective in Bahá'u'lláh's allegorical works. A brief examination of Bahá'u'lláh's use of narrative perspective in these creative works should largely eliminate any lingering doubts we might have about the validity of applying tools of literary analysis to the works of Bahá'u'lláh.

Like a parable, an allegory is a fictional construct in which the characters and events represent another reality, most usually an abstract reality. As we will see more completely in our later discussion of allegory as a genre, not all allegories are easy to understand (e.g., Spenser's *The Faerie Queen,* Bunyan's *Pilgrim's Progress,* or Swift's *Gulliver's Travels* in the English literary tradition), but they do have in common a one-to-one relationship between characters or actions and symbolic or metaphorical meaning. They are also similar in narrative perspective in that most employ a third-person point of view; the narrator may be the objective voice of a nameless storyteller or possibly a character, but the focus of attention is always on the story being narrated.

While Bahá'u'lláh employs allegorical ingredients in numerous works (e.g., the structure of The Seven Valleys and The Four Valleys), two of Bahá'u'lláh's better-known works that might be considered full-blown allegories are the Tablet of the Holy Mariner and the Súrah of the Temple. In both of these works Bahá'u'lláh becomes a character, and the narrative perspective is objective. For example, in the Tablet of the Holy Mariner we view a dramatic dialogue between the heavenly concourse and the Holy Mariner (Bahá'u'lláh) as He sails His ark upon "the ancient sea." The Mariner is then commanded to "Teach them that are within the ark that which we have taught thee behind the mystic veil" (*Bahá'í Prayers* 223).

To be accurate, we would have to describe this narrative perspective as a variety of the first-person persona (the heavenly concourse as "We"), but the overall effect as we read the narrative story about the Mariner, the "maids of heaven," and the "favored damsel" sent to assist the Youth and assess His progress is to fashion a perspective beyond that of any one of these characters. This use of the third-person perspective is particularly powerful and evident at the end:

> Glorified be my Lord, the All-Glorious!
>
> Thereupon the maids of heaven hastened forth from their chambers, upon whose countenances the eye of no dweller in the highest paradise had ever gazed.
>
> Glorified be our Lord, the Most High!
>
> They all gathered around her, and lo! they found her body fallen upon the dust. . . . (*Bahá'í Prayers* 228–29)

The narrator is not part of the concourse gathered around the fallen maiden. The perspective is objective so that we can observe the Mariner and His progress or we can switch back to the scene in the spiritual realm to witness how all respond to the difficulties the Mariner (or Youth) is encountering in His mission.

This same sort of creative use of narrative perspective occurs in the Súrah of the Temple (Súratu'l-Haykal), though the narrative perspective in this work is much more complex and shifts in and out of the allegorical framework. As we will discuss in greater detail later, this work is structured primarily on the analogy of the preparation of the Manifestation for His mission on earth to the building of a Temple. When the work is being narrated in this context, the narrator is not Bahá'u'lláh; Bahá'u'lláh is the Temple being constructed. At times, however, this fictional veil is breached, and Bahá'u'lláh will speak very directly about such matters as the perfidy of Mírzá Yaḥyá.

When the allegory is in full force, the narrative perspective, like that in the Tablet of the Holy Mariner, is from the spiritual realm, presumably prior to when Bahá'u'lláh is sent to earth. For example, the Temple (the physical body through which the Prophet will manifest Himself) is endowed with the faculties of the five senses, each of which is blessed with perfection and given its particular mandate:

> O Thou, the Eye of this Temple! Look not to the heaven and what is therein, nor to the earth and whatsoever is thereupon; verily We created Thee for My Beauty—Lo, this is It! Look as it pleaseth Thee and prevent not Thine eye from the Beauty of Thy Lord, the Precious, the Beloved. Through Thee We shall send forth Iron eyes and everseeing sight whereby they shall see the signs of their Creator, and turn away their eyes from that which the worldly wise have comprehended. (*Surat 'ul Hykl* 16)[4]

Here, too, the narrative point of view is, strictly speaking, not third person; the narrative "We" is speaking, presumably as the voice of the celestial powers fashioning a perfect vehicle or human persona through which the Prophet can convey instruction to humankind.

We find this same sort of perspective in the Tablet of Carmel, another allegorical work which portrays a dialogue between "the Concourse on high" and "Carmel." This brief piece consists of three speeches: one by the Concourse, the response by Carmel, and then the instructions to Carmel coming from that same Concourse (the "We" that "made reply"—possibly the Prophet).

Here the narrative perspective is not entirely obvious. It may begin with Bahá'u'lláh speaking and hearing the dialogue between the heavenly Concourse and Carmel (perhaps the earth as bride adorned to receive the bridegroom). What is obvious is Bahá'u'lláh's imaginative use of narrative perspective whereby we witness this imaginative dia-

---

4. All quotations from the Súratu'l-Haykal are from the version translated by Anton F. Haddad, which is titled *Surat 'ul Hykl* and was published in 1900, before the system of transliteration advocated by the Guardian was adopted by the Bahá'í community.

logue as Carmel (perhaps as earth itself) prepares for the honor of having the Kingdom of Heaven established upon her.

F. Bahá'u'lláh's Use of the Persona Device in Prayers

While our purpose here is not to construct a complete or exhaustive list of the variations in point of view employed by Bahá'u'lláh, we can observe that in each work Bahá'u'lláh devises a narrative perspective tailored to the exigencies of the piece. Of particular interest is how Bahá'u'lláh uses a variable *persona*—a persona being a sort of mask or "'second self' created by an author and through whom the narrative is told" (*Handbook* 352). Sometimes a persona is entirely fictional and distinct from the author, as is the character of Gulliver who narrates Jonathan Swift's *Gulliver's Travels,* and sometimes the persona is a more thinly veiled version of the author, as is the character of Dante in *The Divine Comedy* or the narrative voice in Chaucer's *Canterbury Tales.*

As we have already noted, we may at first feel it inappropriate to apply terminology regarding a fictional device to the revealed works of a Prophet, but, as we have already observed, the Manifestation employs these devices when He appears in the guise of a human being. That is, He appears as an ordinary human being, but He is not. He appears powerless, but He is not. He allows Himself to be subject to the caprices and intrigues of religious and political leaders, though, in fact, He is fully capable at any point of extricating Himself from His difficulties and making apparent His true nature and unveiled ascendancy.

As we also observed, He maintains this guise or persona for our instruction and benefit, that we might learn how to discover the Prophet (rather than have obedience to Him imposed on us) and that we might learn gradually rather than be dumbfounded by the sudden brilliance of His Revelation:

> Oh, would that the world could believe Me! Were all the things that lie enshrined within the heart of Bahá, and which the Lord, His God, the Lord of all names, hath taught Him, to be unveiled

> to mankind, every man on earth would be dumbfounded. (*Gleanings* 176)

Part of the subtlety in the revealed works of Bahá'u'lláh, then, derives from the way in which each work implies a distinct persona through the use of these various narrative perspectives. Consequently, as we approach each work, one of the first things we want to consider is the narrative point of view.

Oddly enough, one of the most creative uses of this device can be observed in the revealed prayers of Bahá'u'lláh. Most often we read the prayers of Bahá'u'lláh in our personal worship and meditation, but if we think for a minute about how Bahá'u'lláh has constructed these pieces, we will quickly realize that He has employed a persona for each perspective. After all, these works are narrated from the perspective of the believer, the follower, the supplicant, not from the perspective of the Manifestation. For example, while we know that the Manifestation prays, He would hardly find it necessary to confess His sinfulness, since He is without sin:

> Lord! Thou seest him that kneeleth yearning to arise and serve Thee, the dead calling for eternal life from the ocean of Thy favor and craving to soar to the heavens of Thy wealth, the stranger longing for his home of glory 'neath the canopy of Thy grace, the seeker hastening by Thy mercy to Thy door of bounty, the sinful turning to the ocean of forgiveness and pardon. (*Bahá'í Prayers* 148)

Likewise, the Manifestation hardly needs to confess His powerlessness, and yet He admonishes us that this is precisely what a wise human being should do when faced with the majesty of the revealed word:

> He, indeed, is endued with understanding who acknowledgeth his powerlessness and confesseth his sinfulness, for should any created thing lay claim to any existence, when confronted with the infinite wonders of Thy Revelation, so blasphemous a pretension would be more heinous than any other crime in all the

> domains of Thine invention and creation. (*Prayers and Meditations* 133)

Likewise, since Bahá'u'lláh is the Manifestation, He would hardly find it logical to thank God for having helped Him to recognize Himself, since, as we noted in Chapter 1, the Prophet is aware of His station from the beginning:

> I yield Thee thanks for having enabled me to recognize the Manifestation of Thyself, and for having severed me from Thine enemies, and laid bare before mine eyes their misdeeds and wicked works in Thy days, and for having rid me of all attachment to them, and caused me to turn wholly towards Thy grace and bountiful favors. (*Prayers and Meditations* 110)

In other words, the prayers with which we are most familiar are narrated from our own point of view, a first-person perspective of the follower or believer. To create these works, the Prophet had to create the fiction of a dialogue between us and God wherein He incorporates His own wisdom about what would be most appropriate for us to say in various conditions (e.g., sorrow, sinfulness, joy, gratitude, bereavement, etc.).

However, in *Prayers and Meditations,* a work translated and assembled by Shoghi Effendi, we encounter some prayers in which the Manifestation is speaking in His own voice, prayers He has devised for His own special condition and station, prayers spoken from His own unique perspective. For example, Bahá'u'lláh in one prayer states, "Thou seest me dwelling in this prison-house that lieth behind the seas and the mountains, and knowest full well what I have endured for love of Thee and for the sake of Thy Cause" (*Prayers and Meditations* 106–07). These words might be spoken from the point of view of any faithful believer, and yet as the prayer proceeds, we understand that this is the Prophet Himself in intimate discourse with God and rehearsing what He has endured in the course of His ministry:

> It is Thou Who hast commanded me to tell out the things Thou

> didst destine for them in the Tablet of Thy decree and didst inscribe with the pen of Thy Revelation, and Who hast enjoined on me the duty of kindling the fire of Thy love in the hearts of Thy servants, and of drawing all the peoples of the earth nearer to the habitation of Thy throne.
>
> And when, as bidden by Thee, I arose and called out, by Thy leave, all Thy creatures, the wayward among Thy servants opposed me. Some turned away from me, others disowned my claim, a few hesitated, while others were sore perplexed, notwithstanding that Thy testimony was set forth before the followers of all religions, and Thy proof demonstrated unto all the peoples of the earth, and the signs of Thy might so powerfully manifested as to encompass the entire creation.
>
> I was, moreover, opposed by mine own kindred, although, as Thou knowest, they were dear to me and I had desired for them that which I had desired for mine own self. (*Prayers and Meditations* 107)

Once we recognize the narrative point of view in such a prayer, we are forced to consider what wisdom there was in Bahá'u'lláh's allowing us to become privy to His personal dialogue with God. Certainly, a consideration of narrative perspective forces us to examine the imagery more creatively. For example, the "prison-house" at the beginning might well allude to the Prophet's physical body and human guise through which this otherworldly emissary has consented to operate in order to convey divine guidance to us.

The point is that most revealed prayers have the clear purpose of first providing us with words that depict our condition and then guiding us in our communication with God. From a literary standpoint, Bahá'u'lláh's revealed prayers are thus remarkable in having the believer enunciate his or her present condition, while further setting forth the goals towards which the believer is to strive. But we may well wonder what we are supposed to do with prayers that are specialized for the Prophet and are, therefore, narrated from His own first-person point of view. Do we pray them or study them? And if we study them, what are we to derive from that study? Or, even more to the point, for what reason would the Prophet deem it appropriate for us, His followers, to hear this privileged conversation between Himself and the Divine Will?

There is no single answer to this question. No doubt, there are various sorts of wisdom implicit in allowing us to hear this dialogue, and no doubt the Guardian had a similar motive in deciding that it would be a priority for him to collect, translate, and organize this anthology.[5] But let us consider an obvious rationale. As we peruse some of these prayers and longer meditations that are clearly penned from Bahá'u'lláh's perspective, we discover that we are being given the rather amazing opportunity to eavesdrop. Indeed, we might think of the reader's vantage point with these prayers as being comparable to that of children being allowed to overhear an intimate conversation between their parents and some trusted advisor. From this vantage point, the children hear the parents lament the fact that the offspring do not seem to understand or appreciate that everything the parents say and do is motivated solely by the boundless love they want to bestow.

The benefit children might derive from hearing such a conversation could be weighty indeed. They might come to understand, perhaps for the first time, that even the parents' rules and restrictions are expressions of affection. The children might also come to realize the various kinds of subtle and often unnoticed sacrifice that are inevitably associated with parenting—what Bahá'í poet Robert Hayden has called "love's austere and lonely offices" (*Collected Poems* 41). Perhaps most important of all, the children might understand how much more effective the parents' efforts would be were their progeny receptive to and appreciative of the gifts of love, protection, and education the parents long to give.

There is another equally profound benefit we derive from being given the privilege of hearing this dialogue. Because we now view the life of the Prophet in retrospect with due regard for His majesty and

---

5. The Guardian often lamented that his unrelenting agenda of tasks prevented him from doing all that he so dearly wanted to (e.g., see *Unfolding Destiny* 258); therefore, we can correctly infer that the works he did complete were a priority.

power, we may have the sense that because He is otherworldly and has innate powers beyond our understanding, He was in His brief span on earth impervious to His treatment by others, even to those injuries He suffered from members of His own family or from those personal calumnies inflicted on Him by His most intimate associates and relations. These prayers and meditations reveal that, however perfect and transcendent the Manifestation may be, He does feel the weight of these difficulties—that in a very literal sense His suffering is experienced as an atonement, a ransom for our salvation, and that He persists only in the sure knowledge that He is serving God's purpose.

It is in this context that virtually all of those prayers and meditations penned from Bahá'u'lláh's own point of view emphasize the theme of the trials and afflictions endured by this otherworldly guest at the hands of those to whom He has come as a loving parent, as a Divine Physician, as our personal Lord and Savior:

> Ever since the day Thou didst create me at Thy bidding, O my God, and didst arouse me through the gentle winds of Thy tender mercies, I have refused to turn to any one except Thee, and have, through the power of Thy sovereignty and Thy might, arisen to face Thine enemies, and have summoned all mankind unto the shores of the ocean of Thy oneness and the heaven of Thine all-glorious unity. I have sought, all my days, not to guard myself from the mischief of the rebellious among Thy creatures, but rather to exalt Thy name amidst Thy people. I have, thereby, suffered what none of Thy creatures hath suffered.
>
> How many the days, O my God, which I have spent in utter loneliness with the transgressors amongst Thy servants, and how many the nights, O my Best-Beloved, during which I lay a captive in the hands of the wayward amidst Thy creatures! In the midst of my troubles and tribulations I have continued to celebrate Thy praise before all who are in Thy heaven and on Thy earth, and have not ceased to extol Thy wondrous glory in the kingdoms of Thy Revelation and of Thy creation, though all that I have been capable of showing forth hath fallen short

> of the greatness and the majesty of Thy oneness, and is unworthy of Thine exaltation and of Thine omnipotence. (*Prayers and Meditations* 301–02)

In addition to giving us an intimate insight into the agonies the Prophet must endure, these prayers and meditations also serve as models for how we, too, should respond to similar persecution. What we thus discover in these models is that the Manifestation, though enumerating His difficulties, neither laments His plight nor questions the wisdom of God's Will. Rather, He is utterly joyful in being allowed to serve the advancement of God's creation:

> I am bewildered, therefore, O my God, and know not how to act toward them. Every time I hold my peace, and cease to extol Thy wondrous virtues, Thy Spirit impelleth me to cry out before all who are in Thy heaven and on Thy earth; and every time I am still, the breaths wafted from the right hand of Thy will and purpose pass over me, and stir me up, and I find myself to be as a leaf which lieth at the mercy of the winds of Thy decree, and is carried away whithersoever Thou dost permit or command it. Every man of insight who considereth what hath been revealed by me, will be persuaded that Thy Cause is not in my hands, but in Thy hands, and will recognize that the reins of power are held not in my grasp but in Thy grasp, and are subject to Thy sovereign might. (*Prayers and Meditations* 306–07)

Another insight we might derive from studying the narrative perspective of these prayers is similar to the wisdom we might extrapolate from viewing pictures of 'Abdu'l-Bahá holding prayer beads (as He often did). If 'Abdu'l-Bahá, the perfect Exemplar, must pray and pray so often that He utilizes beads to count the repetitions, then how much more must we who are quite imperfect need this same indispensable nourishment of daily communion? In short, if These exalted Figures are utterly dependent on and submissive to the Will of God, and if prayer is an integral part of their spiritual sustenance even though they are already in a state of perfection, then how much more essential must prayer be to us ordinary human beings who are daily struggling to achieve spiritual development?

G. Some Final Considerations

As with every avenue of analyzing the revealed work of Bahá'u'lláh, an endless amount of study and discussion is possible. But our purpose here will be consistently the same—to provide some examples for each of the tools of literary analysis that we have decided to explore. But we cannot end even so cursory a consideration of narrative perspective without alluding to an anecdote from the life of Bahá'u'lláh that illustrates about as well as anything can the degree to which the Manifestation veils His true capacity in the guise of these various personae.

The story concerns Siyyid Ismá'íl of Zavárih, a believer who, after being invited by Bahá'u'lláh to enjoy some confections, begged to be given instead a glimpse of the spiritual realm that awaited him. After repeatedly informing him of the unwisdom of such a vision, Bahá'u'lláh finally acceded and granted the request. Once the believer had been allowed to glimpse the next world, he found this earthly existence intolerable and immediately took his own life:

> One day, they brought the news of the death of Siyyid Ismá'íl of Zavárih. Bahá'u'lláh said: "No one has killed him. Behind many myriad veils of light, We showed him a glimmer of Our glory; he could not endure it and so he sacrificed himself."[6] Some of us then went to the bank of the river and found the body of Siyyid Ismá'íl lying there. He had cut his own throat with a razor which was still held in his hand. (spoken chronicle of Aḥmad in *Revelation of Bahá'u'lláh* 2:112)

This episode is usually recounted as an example of why the realities of the next world are withheld from us (i.e., we have important

6. Adib Taherzadeh says in *Revelation of Bahá'u'lláh* 2:112n that these are "Not to be taken as the exact words of Bahá'u'lláh. However, they convey the sense of what He said."

work here which we might not do were we intimately aware of the reality that awaits us):

> If any man be told that which hath been ordained for such a soul in the worlds of God, the Lord of the throne on high and of earth below, his whole being will instantly blaze out in his great longing to attain that most exalted, that sanctified and resplendent station. . . . The nature of the soul after death can never be described, nor is it meet and permissible to reveal its whole character to the eyes of men. (Bahá'u'lláh, *Gleanings* 156)

But this story also serves to apprise us of the burden which the Manifestation must constantly endure. Not only is He constantly aware of spiritual reality, He has already experienced it. And yet, for the sake of assisting us, He willingly submits to what Bahá'u'lláh Himself describes as "poverty and afflictions, to hunger, and to the ills and chances of this world" (*Kitáb-i-Íqán* 73).

And yet Bahá'u'lláh also explains that these afflictions, grievous though they be, are a test intended for humanity, not for the Prophet. That is, these events serve to make the people ponder how these Beings can truly have divine powers yet be unable to extricate themselves from Their plight:

> As these holy Persons were subject to such needs and wants, the people were, consequently, lost in the wilds of misgivings and doubts, and were afflicted with bewilderment and perplexity. How, they wondered, could such a person be sent down from God, assert His ascendancy over all the peoples and kindreds of the earth, and claim Himself to be the goal of all creation . . . and yet be subject to such trivial things? (*Kitáb-i-Íqán* 73)

Here is where an understanding of narrative perspective becomes a vital tool in appreciating what the Manifestations must endure to help us. We know these Beings are not automatons; we know They have Their own will, but that They choose to subjugate Their own will in order to serve God. For example, before His arrest, Christ went to the Mount of Olives with His disciples to pray. He foreknew that He would soon be arrested, and He prayed, "Father, if it be possible, let this cup pass from me." But he concludes the prayer by affirming, "nevertheless, not as I will, but as thou [wilt]" (Matt. 26:39). Likewise, after Bahá'u'lláh's two-year sojourn in the mountains of Sulaymáníyyih, Shaykh Sulṭán found Him and pleaded for Him to return. Because, like Christ, Bahá'u'lláh foreknew the suffering that awaited Him, He did not desire to return, but did so because He chose to submit to the Will of God:

> *"From the Mystic source,"* He Himself explains in the Kitáb-i-Íqán, *"there came the summons bidding Us return whence We came. Surrendering Our will to His, We submitted to His injunction."* (Shoghi Effendi, *God Passes By* 126)

Whether or not these incidents indicate that the Prophets are ever really tempted to forgo Their missions, these anecdotes serve well to explain to us that Their gift is not automatic or easy, not matter-of-fact or without suffering and testing. By allowing us to experience Their perspective through prayers penned from the first-person perspective of the Prophets, the Manifestations of God allow us to understand something of the immensity of what They do for us.

Chapter 3
Historical Criticism and the Art of Bahá'u'lláh

[E]ach Manifestation of God hath a distinct individuality, a definitely prescribed mission, a predestined Revelation, and specially designated limitations. Each one of them is known by a different name, is characterized by a special attribute, fulfills a definite Mission, and is entrusted with a particular Revelation.

—Bahá'u'lláh

If our first question concerned the fact that every literary work is presented to us from some particular narrative point of view by means of a distinct narrative voice, our second question focuses on the fact that this narrative voice inevitably speaks within some context. This broad question of context is comprised of several subsidiary questions: To whom is the work addressed? At what time in the life of Bahá'u'lláh was the work revealed? What historical circumstances are related to the work? What historical allusions can we discover in the work?

In general, these questions are closely related to what we discussed in Chapter 1 about the fact that each Manifestation appears in a "station of distinction"—each Prophet operates in the context of an ever-changing and continually evolving human history. Therefore, the study of religion is inseparable from the study of human history. Conversely, human history, when correctly understood, is nothing more or less than tracing evidence of the Divine Will intervening systematically in human affairs to forge an "ever-advancing civilization."

The particular implication of this Bahá'í concept of the relationship between the Divine Will and human history is that each Manifestation must shape His ministry to fit the exigencies of the age in which He appears. Consequently, to understand the divine logic underlying the teaching techniques of an individual Prophet, we must study the historical context in which the Prophet appears: each Prophet alludes to past events and to the teachings of the previous Manifestation; each Prophet speaks of Himself in terms of fulfilling those events; and each Prophet directs the affairs of humankind according to the capacities latent in society at the time of His advent.

However, as we also concluded in Chapter 1, where we might consider the ordinary human artist as a product of history (to varying degrees), the Prophet is the producer of history. The Manifestation is keenly aware of the limitations history has imposed on His audience, and through His loving wisdom He responds accordingly.

A. Some Problems with Traditional Historical Criticism

A Handbook to Literature defines historical criticism as literary study "that approaches a work in terms of the social, cultural, and historical context in which it was produced" (229). However, this same reference work concludes that the "historical critic attempts to recreate the meaning and values of the work for its own time; the critic's objective is not to elucidate the meaning of the work for the present so much as it is to lead the reader into a responsible awareness of the meaning the work had for its own age" (229).

In this definition, which is fashioned to describe historical criticism as it is traditionally applied to human artists, we may detect a problem. Since the Prophet is born into this reality fully aware of history and is likewise cognizant of His part in that history, is it appropriate for His utterance to be discussed solely in terms of what it meant to the people of His age? After all, while the first audience and first followers of the Manifestation may be the contemporaries in His immediate environment, does He not intend for His message to become universal?

Citing a statement by the Báb in the Bayán, Shoghi Effendi seems to confirm this: "In the 'Bayán' the Báb says that every religion of the past was fit to become universal." In this same passage the Báb observes that the reason past religions did not become universal was not due to the inadequacy of the Prophets, but to the failure of humanity to respond appropriately to God's Messenger: "The only reason why they [the religions] failed to attain that mark was the incompetence of their followers" (*Compilation of Compilations* 2: no. 1275).

Of course, the term *universal* is used here in a relative sense. Clearly, the Prophets of the past could not have expected Their religion to have spread throughout the globe when so many peoples of the world remained largely unaware of one another's existence:

> [The Báb] was clearly referring to acceptance among the generality of the populace to whom that Manifestation came, since, as 'Abdu'l-Bahá notes, physical and material constraints of the past meant that "understanding and unity amongst all the peoples and kindreds of the earth were unattainable" when the world was "widely divided." (Hatcher, *Arc of Ascent* 124)

However, in this same passage from the Bayán, the Báb notes that the Revelation of Bahá'u'lláh would not meet with the same fate:

> [The Báb] then proceeds to give a definite promise that this [rejection] would not be the fate of the revelation of "Him Whom God would make manifest," that it will become universal and include all the people of the world. This shows that we will ultimately succeed. (Shoghi Effendi, in *Compilation of Compilations* 2: no. 1275)

In other words, the term "universal" in an age when the planet has become one global community can be understood to include all the peoples and nations of the world, something Bahá'u'lláh Himself confirms:

> The summons and the message which We gave were never intended to reach or to benefit one land or one people only. Mankind in its entirety must firmly adhere to whatsoever hath been revealed and vouchsafed unto it. Then and only then will it attain unto true liberty. The whole earth is illuminated with the resplendent glory of God's Revelation. (*Tablets of Bahá'u'lláh* 89)

Returning to our concern, then, we ask again if it is appropriate in our consideration of historical context to be concerned solely with the meaning the works of Bahá'u'lláh had for His immediate audience, since He expressly intended that His audience be the generality of humankind for the next thousand years?

The answer we discover is that a study of historical context is not only appropriate; in some cases it is essential if we are to arrive at a valid interpretation of Bahá'u'lláh's work. In other words, it is not our goal in this study to use historical criticism solely to "recreate the meaning and values of the work for its own time" instead of studying "the meaning of the work for the present." The utterance of the Prophet is part of His total ministry, all of which is for our instruction. Consequently, to interpret the meaning of His utterances (whether they be oral or written), we must needs become attentive to all of the relevant information about the utterance, including the various implications of historical context.

Citing one example of the importance of studying the historical context in order to understand better the art of Bahá'u'lláh, Shoghi Effendi notes that the Bahá'í must study Islám because the Muslim religion forms the "source and background" of the Bahá'í Faith:

> [Bahá'ís] must strive to obtain, from sources that are authoritative and unbiased, a sound knowledge of the history and tenets of Islám—the source and background of their Faith—and approach reverently and with a mind purged from preconceived ideas the study of the Qur'án which, apart from the sacred scriptures of the Bábí and Bahá'í Revelations, constitutes the only Book which can be regarded as an absolutely authenticated Repository of the Word of God. They must devote special attention

> to the investigation of those institutions and circumstances that are directly connected with the origin and birth of their Faith, with the station claimed by its Forerunner, and with the laws revealed by its Author. (*Advent of Divine Justice* 49)

In another place, however, Shoghi Effendi cautions that the Bahá'í cannot always rely on commonly accepted sources for accurate accounts of that context. He observes that the Bahá'í must study history anew because many sources, particularly those penned by Western historians, have failed to assess properly the role of religions in shaping human history:

> The truth is that Western historians have for many centuries distorted the facts to suit their religious and ancestral prejudices. The Bahá'ís should try to study history anew, and to base all their investigations first and foremost on the written Scriptures of Islám and Christianity. (*Lights of Guidance* 496)

So it is that while the Revelation of Bahá'u'lláh is universal in its scope, it is revealed in the context of a particular set of historical circumstances which we must study if we are to assess correctly the subtleties of tone, style, and allusion that are an intentional part of Bahá'u'lláh's revealed work.

For example, if Bahá'u'lláh's tone is severe in His second epistle to the Emperor Napoleon III, we benefit from knowing that this same emperor had scoffed at Bahá'u'lláh's first tablet, had tossed the epistle "behind his back." Similarly, we observed in the previous chapter the value of knowing that Epistle to the Son of the Wolf is penned to an inveterate enemy of the Bahá'ís.

B. The Layers of Historical Context in the Art of Bahá'u'lláh

As we apply the tools of historical criticism to the art of Bahá'u'lláh, we discover a wide variety of historical considerations appropriate to our study. Proceeding from the broadest to the most specific, we could list the layers of contextual concerns as follows: (1) the art of Bahá'u'lláh as fulfilling the age-old expectations prophesied in past religions about One who would usher in the transformation of humankind on our planet; (2) the art of Bahá'u'lláh as fulfilling the specific expectations of the Islámic and Bábí religions; (3) the art of Bahá'u'lláh as a magnum opus in which each specific work is, when properly understood, an integral and inseparable part of one coherent statement; (4) the art of Bahá'u'lláh as related to the events in Bahá'u'lláh's personal life; and (5) the art of Bahá'u'lláh as related to or informed by the personalities to whom individual works are addressed.

We should not infer from this list that the works of Bahá'u'lláh can or should be classified according to how they relate to one or more of these categories. Understanding any given work may require that we relate that work to only one or to any combination of these types of historical context. But if we examine briefly these "layers" as they are demonstrated in specific works of Bahá'u'lláh, we can better appreciate how a knowledge of historical context can have a significant effect on our understanding of themes that might otherwise remain veiled from us.

1. Bahá'u'lláh's Art as Ushering in the Maturation of Humankind

An essential tenet of the Bahá'í Faith is that, while all Revelations play a strategic role in the advancement of the human race, the appearance of Bahá'u'lláh signifies the long-awaited unification of the planet, a turning point in human history, the maturation of the human race, the point of our collective awareness of human social evolution as a spiritual enterprise. Therefore, where each Manifestation fulfills the concepts of "return" and "resurrection," the Prophets also allude to the special properties of Bahá'u'lláh's Revelation as (1) enunciating our planetary identity and (2) establishing a global system of governance capable of expressing and nurturing that identity.

Shoghi Effendi alludes to this largest historical perspective throughout his discussions of the Bahá'í Revelation. For example, in *The World Order of Bahá'u'lláh* he observes, "The Revelation entrusted by the Almighty Ordainer to Bahá'u'lláh, His followers firmly believe, has been endowed with such potentialities as are commensurate with the maturity of the human race—the crowning and most momentous stage in its evolution from infancy to manhood" (166). In this same discussion Shoghi Effendi asserts that this singular transformation has been alluded to in all past religions:

> The successive Founders of all past Religions Who, from time immemorial, have shed, with ever-increasing intensity, the splendor of one common Revelation at the various stages which have marked the advance of mankind towards maturity may thus, in a sense, be regarded as preliminary Manifestations, anticipating and paving the way for the advent of that Day of Days when the whole earth will have fructified and the tree of humanity will have yielded its destined fruit. (*World Order of Bahá'u'lláh* 166)

For the better part of ten pages in *God Passes By* (93–100), Shoghi Effendi cites allusions to the advent of this Revelation which can be found in the scriptures and traditions of past religions. But more to the point of our discussion, Bahá'u'lláh Himself alludes to the anticipation of this turning point in human history found in past religions when the earth would become "one country, and mankind its citizens" (*Tablets of Bahá'u'lláh* 167):

> *"All the Divine Books and Scriptures have predicted and announced unto men the advent of the Most Great Revelation. None can adequately recount the verses recorded in the Books of former ages which forecast this supreme Bounty, this most mighty Bestowal."* (Bahá'u'lláh, qtd. in *God Passes By* 100)

In another passage Bahá'u'lláh specifically notes that, while all the previous Dispensations could be correctly designated as "God's appointed Day," this particular Dispensation and this particular "Day" has been especially anticipated:

> It is evident that every age in which a Manifestation of God hath lived is divinely ordained, and may, in a sense, be characterized as God's appointed Day. This Day, however, is unique, and is to be distinguished from those that have preceded it. (*Gleanings* 60)

In still another verse Bahá'u'lláh designates this Revelation as the "consummation" of all previous Revelations:

> *"In this most mighty Revelation all the Dispensations of the past have attained their highest, their final consummation." "That which hath been made manifest in this preeminent, this most exalted Revelation, stands unparalleled in the annals of the past, nor will future ages witness its like."* (qtd. in Shoghi Effendi, *Advent of Divine Justice* 77)

Other references to the special nature of this historical period are especially prevalent in two areas of Bahá'u'lláh's works. First, in His tablets to kings and rulers He discusses the obligations imposed on them by this new reality. Second, in His works revealed after the Kitáb-i-Aqdas, many of which elucidate particular laws and concepts of His Most Holy Book, He often alludes to the requirements and potentialities of this milestone in history (i.e., the achievement of a global identity and the need to establish a commonwealth of nations).

In the tablets addressed to the world's religious and political leaders, Bahá'u'lláh specifically discusses the fact that the "time fore-ordained unto the peoples and kindreds of the earth is now come" (*Proclamation of Bahá'u'lláh* 111), a time when there is the opportunity to establish the "Most Great Peace":

> The time must come when the imperative necessity for the holding of a vast, an all-embracing assemblage of men will be universally realized. The rulers and kings of the earth must needs attend it, and, participating in its deliberations, must consider such ways and means as will lay the foundations of the world's Great Peace amongst men. (*Proclamation of Bahá'u'lláh* 115)

However, Bahá'u'lláh does not merely exhort the "Great Powers" to establish such a peace; He specifically explains that such a peace should be secured through the principle of collective security:

> Such a peace demandeth that the Great Powers should resolve, for the sake of the tranquillity of the peoples of the earth, to be

> fully reconciled among themselves. Should any king take up arms against another, all should unitedly arise and prevent him. If this be done, the nations of the world will no longer require any armaments, except for the purpose of preserving the security of their realms and of maintaining internal order within their territories. This will ensure the peace and composure of every people, government and nation. (*Tablets of Bahá'u'lláh* 165)

Because the rulers uniformly rejected or ignored His admonitions, Bahá'u'lláh in a later tablet explains that, having lost this opportunity to seize the "Most Great Peace," they should at least seize the chance for the "Lesser Peace": "Now that ye have refused the Most Great Peace, hold ye fast unto this, the Lesser Peace, that haply ye may in some degree better your own condition and that of your dependents" (*Proclamation of Bahá'u'lláh* 12–13).

In some of these same tablets to the rulers and in the later tablets (those penned after the revelation of the Kitáb-i-Aqdas), Bahá'u'lláh specifically alludes to the procedures, the properties, and the powers that the gradual establishment of a world commonwealth will bring. For example, Bahá'u'lláh speaks of the need to establish a universal auxiliary language in the Kitáb-i-Aqdas (¶189), in the Lawḥ-i-Dunyá (Tablet of the World) (*Tablets of Bahá'u'lláh* 89), in the Ishráqát (*Tablets of Bahá'u'lláh* 127), and in the Lawḥ-i-Maqṣúd (*Tablets of Bahá'u'lláh* 165). He speaks of the need to establish a common script in the Kitáb-i-Aqdas (¶189), in the Ishráqát (*Tablets of Bahá'u'lláh* 127), and in the Lawḥ-i-Dunyá (*Tablets of Bahá'u'lláh* 165–66). He repeatedly talks about how the establishment of a pact of collective security will provide the means to reduce armaments, reduce taxation, and devote more energy to assisting the peoples of the world.

In short, while Bahá'u'lláh is absolutely clear about equating His station as a Prophet with the station of the Prophets who have preceded Him, He is equally clear in these allusions to the special nature of this turning point in human history and to the role of His particular Revelation in ushering in this changed condition. To read these passages without being aware of the Bahá'í paradigm of human history and the crucial role the Revelation of Bahá'u'lláh plays in the total context of that history is to run the risk of interpreting various passages in the works of Bahá'u'lláh as denying some of the most essential tenets of Bahá'í theology—i.e., that the Revelation of God is continuous and that all the Prophets have an equal status, even if They may not have an identical function:

> Each one of them is known by a different name, is characterized by a special attribute, fulfils a definite Mission, and is entrusted with a particular Revelation. Even as He saith: "Some of the Apostles We have caused to excel the others. To some God hath spoken, some He hath raised and exalted. . . ." (*Kitáb-i-Íqán* 176)

2. Bahá'u'lláh's Revelation as Fulfilling Islámic and Bábí Expectations

A somewhat more specific layer of historical context relevant to interpreting the art of Bahá'u'lláh concerns the various allusions Bahá'u'lláh makes to His Revelation as fulfilling prophecies in Islám and in the Bábí Faith. Let us examine some obvious examples of how becoming aware of this context helps provide insight into Bahá'u'lláh's strategic purposes for His works.

Historically, it has been the case that each Manifestation, though intending His message for all peoples that might conceivably be reached during a given Dispensation, carefully fashions His ministry to test the expectations of the followers of the previous Prophet. Furthermore, we can detect this instructional quality in aspects of His physical appearance (i.e., the persona He adopts), in the style of His presentation, in the type of guidance He imparts, and even in the specific answers He gives to questions He is asked. So it is, for example, that Christ confounds the Messianic expectations of the Jews by appearing in humble circumstances instead of as a "king" living among the aristocratic members of Jewish society. He further tests their readiness by speaking in figurative and often enigmatic language (parables) instead of alluding to rabbinical traditions that the Jewish divines might have more easily appreciated. In yet another affront to the messianic expectations of the

Jewish authorities, Christ chooses as His first disciples not scholars or divines, but meek, lowly, and untutored commoners.

Because the Báb and Bahá'u'lláh appear in chronological proximity and consider Themselves part of a twin Revelation, the appearance of Bahá'u'lláh fulfills Islámic prophecies regarding the "Day of Resurrection" and the Bábí prophecies regarding the appearance of Mustagháth (He Who is invoked) or "Him Whom God shall make manifest." Therefore, it is not unusual to find in Bahá'u'lláh's works allusions to Himself in terms of both religious traditions.

For example, the Kitáb-i-Íqán is a doctrinal treatise vindicating the divine plan of God in its entirety, but it specifically addresses proofs that the Báb is the promised Qá'im of Islám. Toward the end of the work, however, Bahá'u'lláh also alludes to His own station and makes it clear that He, like the Báb, is speaking as a Prophet with divine authority.

In effect, Bahá'u'lláh switches audiences or contexts and addresses the "people of the Bayán" (the followers of the Báb), warning them not to repeat the rejection of the Prophet that Bahá'u'lláh has just discussed as having occurred with the appearance of previous Prophets and with the Báb:

> We entreat the learned men of the Bayán not to follow in such ways, not to inflict, at the time of Mustagháth upon Him Who is the divine Essence, the heavenly Light, the absolute Eternity, the Beginning and the End of the Manifestations of the Invisible, that which hath been inflicted in this day. (*Kitáb-i-Íqán* 248)

Here the term Mustagháth (He Who is invoked) alludes to "Him Whom God shall make manifest" (*Selections from the Writings of the Báb* 6), none other than Bahá'u'lláh Himself.

As one studies the Kitáb-i-Íqán, then, one must become aware of the multiple points of view involved in the work as implied in these historical contexts to understand these appellations and allusions. Bahá'u'lláh is sometimes speaking as a follower of the Báb to the Báb's then unconverted uncle. At this point in 1862, Bahá'u'lláh is also speaking as the Manifestation of God: He had already begun His ministry in 1853 but had concealed this fact from the Bábís because of the Báb's request that "Him Whom God shall make manifest" delay this announcement until the year nineteen (1863—i.e., 1844 plus nineteen years) as a favor to the followers of the Báb:

> I, indeed, beg to address Him Whom God shall make manifest, by Thy leave in these words: "Shouldst Thou dismiss the entire company of the followers of the Bayán in the Day of the Latter Resurrection by a mere sign of Thy finger even while still a suckling babe, Thou wouldst indeed be praised in Thy indication. And though no doubt is there about it, do Thou grant a respite of nineteen years as a token of Thy favour so that those who have embraced this Cause may be graciously rewarded by Thee. . . ." (*Selections from the Writings of the Báb* 7)

As this same passage of the Báb indicates, Bahá'u'lláh is also speaking as the Prophet Whose advent fulfills the expected "Latter Resurrection." That is, Bahá'u'lláh explains in the Kitáb-i-Íqán that the term "Day of Resurrection" alludes to the renewal of humankind that occurs whenever a new Manifestation appears:

> Therefore, whosoever, and in whatever Dispensation, hath recognized and attained unto the presence of these glorious, these resplendent and most excellent Luminaries, hath verily attained unto the "Presence of God" Himself, and entered the city of eternal and immortal life. Attainment unto such presence is possible only in the Day of Resurrection, which is the Day of the rise of God Himself through His all-embracing Revelation.
>
> This is the meaning of the "Day of Resurrection," spoken of in all the scriptures, and announced unto all people. (*Kitáb-i-Íqán* 143)

In this sense, the phrase "Day of Resurrection" prophesied throughout the Qur'án alludes to both the Bábí and Bahá'í Revelations (since they are really a twin Revelation), but the term "Latter Resurrection" is employed by the Báb specifically to designate the Dispensation of Bahá'-

u'lláh. The appellation "latter day" (Rodwell) or "Last Day" (Yusuf Ali) appears throughout the Qur'án, and it, as well, would seem to designate primarily the Bahá'í Revelation, though it could also be interpreted to allude to the period in which both Dispensations work together to usher in the transformation—culmination and fulfillment—of human society.

We need not belabor the importance of this second level of historical context. It is sufficient to note how this example demonstrates well the wisdom in Shoghi Effendi's exhortation that the student of Bahá'u'lláh's Revelation must also become aware of the historical context in which the Prophet appears and speaks. In particular, one must become aware of the fundamental components of the Islámic Revelation, the Muslims' specific expectations regarding particular prophecies, and the prophecies of the Báb regarding the appearance of "Him Whom God shall make manifest." The more one studies this historical "judgment," the more one begins to observe how dramatically loaded are Bahá'u'lláh's allusions to such terms as "Latter Day," "Last Day," "Day of Resurrection," "Day of Judgment," "Presence of God," "people of the Bayán," and so on.

While appreciating how Bahá'u'lláh alludes to the expectation of the previous Revelations helps us interpret what He is saying, such an awareness also helps us appreciate the kindness and benevolence of this Divine Educator. He is not content merely to identify Himself and thus judge the followers of the previous Manifestation by forcing His listeners to decide whether or not He speaks the truth. He carefully explains His identity in terms that they should know, and He vindicates His claim with proofs from their own sacred scriptures. In fact, Bahá'u'lláh often elucidates Qur'ánic passages that, until His appearance, would have been largely incomprehensible to the main body of believers. In the Kitáb-i-Íqán, for example, Bahá'u'lláh almost inevitably follows His exegesis of some symbolic term or concept with a passage from the Qur'án. We might presume that such passages (which often begin with "Even as He hath revealed" or "Even as He hath said") are being cited by Bahá'u'lláh to explain or reinforce His own observation with authoritative confirmation. Certainly, that is the tone with which He employs them. But the more one studies the Kitáb-i-Íqán, the more one comes to appreciate that the real effect of these explications is to render a precise understanding of Qur'ánic verses that would otherwise remain abstruse, veiled, or (as has more often been the case) completely misinterpreted by the divines.

The end result of Bahá'u'lláh's allusions to Qur'ánic prophecy is that the Kitáb-i-Íqán, in addition to proving the station of the Báb and the divine wisdom in the plan of God, also effectively unseals some of the most significant (albeit elusive and elliptical) concepts in the Qur'án. This is, no doubt, the reason Shoghi Effendi asserts that the Kitáb-i-Íqán "broke the 'seals' of the 'Book' referred to by Daniel, and disclosed the meaning of the 'words' destined to remain 'closed up' till the 'time of the end'" (*God Passes By* 139).

There are any number of other works by Bahá'u'lláh that also demonstrate why it is important to become aware of how Bahá'u'lláh relates His ministry to the specific religious context in which He appears. For example, The Hidden Words takes its title from the tradition that Fáṭimih, the daughter of Muḥammad, was comforted after her father's death by a book revealed to the Imám 'Alí by the Angel Gabriel, a work which Shí'ih Islám calls *The Hidden Book of Fáṭimih* (the original title for The Hidden Words). Knowing this background may not significantly alter one's interpretation of The Hidden Words, but such information certainly helps the reader become aware of how carefully the Prophet relates what He does and says to everything that has preceded Him. He thereby builds on the foundation established by prior Manifestations and reconfirms our appreciation that all the Prophets work together in intimate association and accord to foster our spiritual progress.

3. Bahá'u'lláh's Revelation as a Magnum Opus

A third and even more specific context which is useful to consider in studying how Bahá'u'lláh's art relates to context is in the relationship that each individual work has to Bahá'u'lláh's Revelation as a whole. As we study the works of Bahá'u'lláh, we begin to realize that no single work encompasses the entirety of the Revelation, nor does any single work stand alone. Each work is revealed with the presumption that the reader has access to or at least is aware of the Revelation as a whole.

From this perspective, all of the works can be considered as divisions of one magnum opus. Consequently, it can be a fruitful process to study how each work relates to the overall plan of the Revelation. Of course, one might argue that many of the works of Bahá'u'lláh are yet to be edited and translated into English; therefore, how can we presume to consider such an approach when we do not have in hand but a portion of the revealed writings of Bahá'u'lláh?

Indeed, in the statistical report for Riḍván of 1983, the Bahá'í World Center issued the following report:

> Work has continued on the collation and classification of the Sacred Texts. The original Tablets of Bahá'u'lláh and 'Abdu'l-Bahá and the original letters of Shoghi Effendi now housed at the World Centre number approximately 15,000. Authenticated copies of Tablets and letters available at the World Centre for which no originals have been received include some 46,000 items. Of these originals and copies, approximately 15,000 are Tablets of Bahá'u'lláh. . . . (*Seven Year Plan* 22.)

While we might be amazed that there is so much more to know, the fact is that we can still presume that we have access to the foundational shape of the Revelation as a whole. Shoghi Effendi translated into English most of Bahá'u'lláh's major works (except for the Kitáb-i-Aqdas), and he also translated some of the most significant passages from Bahá'u'lláh's other important tablets, passages which are assembled in *Gleanings from the Writings of Bahá'u'lláh* or else incorporated in Shoghi Effendi's discussions of special topics in works such as *The World Order of Bahá'u'lláh* and *The Advent of Divine Justice*. Consequently, now that the Kitáb-i-Aqdas is translated and notated in its entirety, we can derive a fairly accurate sense of the entirety of Bahá'u'lláh's art. For example, this same report notes that even those works that remain to be translated "have been studied and important passages from them extracted and classified."

Let us consider, then, the skeletal framework of Bahá'u'lláh's Revelation as a single work revealed in parts. In such a context, The Hidden Words might constitute an obvious beginning. Composed in 1858,

The Hidden Words consists of 153 poetic statements of spiritual verities (71 in Arabic and 82 in Persian), which, as we have noted, synthesize and distill all the spiritual teachings of previous Revelations. By summarizing previously revealed truth, The Hidden Words thus serves as an appropriate beginning to a ministry that will usher in the consummation and fulfillment of all that has gone before during the Adamic or Prophetic Cycle.

Having reminded the believer of what foundation has been laid in the past, Bahá'u'lláh is then ready to reveal what is new, and at the heart of this new knowledge is the Kitáb-i-Íqán, revealed three years later in 1862. A virtual textbook on the process of divine revelation, the Kitáb-i-Íqán elucidates the process by which God educates humankind through successive Manifestations. This treatise also explains why humankind has consistently failed to recognize and follow these Infallible Guides. In effect, the Kitáb-i-Íqán establishes the intellectual basis for all religious belief.

Two years later, after forewarning His followers in the Tablet of the Holy Mariner of the impending trials that would afflict Him individually and the Bahá'í community as a whole, Bahá'u'lláh informs the believers of what most have already assumed—that He, indeed, is the Promised Manifestation prophesied by the Báb. The gathering around the figure of Bahá'u'lláh can no longer be considered a casual love feast—He is the Prophet of God, and all must choose (and thus be judged) as to whether or not they will follow. But this judgment is not for the near ones only. In Adrianople Bahá'u'lláh announces to the world at large that the long-awaited Revelation has come. In a series of epistles and tablets to the world's religious and political leaders, Bahá'u'lláh sets forth in forceful and direct language His identity as a Divine Emissary, the new paradigm of human governance that must be fashioned to accommodate a world commonwealth, and the specific course of action world leaders must take to usher in this new era. Excerpts from these tablets appear in the collection entitled *The Proclamation of Bahá'u'lláh,* though not all of the works contained in this volume were penned during this one interval. But the epistles to the world begin at this point, and Bahá'u'lláh continues to address the notables of the world throughout the coming years.

It is 1873 when Bahá'u'lláh reveals the work that constitutes the climax of this magnum opus, the Kitáb-i-Aqdas, the "Mother Book," the Most Holy Book. With the revelation of this work, the Bahá'í religion can no longer be considered merely an outpouring of intellectual insight. Ideas become fused with action: a plan emerges for creating and implementing social systems to translate the new knowledge into the fabric of a global community. Setting forth specific laws and establishing the model for future legislation, the Kitáb-i-Aqdas also establishes the foundation for the institutions of the Bahá'í Faith itself.

Many of the best-known works of Bahá'u'lláh revealed after the Kitáb-i-Aqdas reflect and elaborate on the laws and principles set forth in it. The collection *Tablets of Bahá'u'lláh* contains some of the best known of these: the Bis͟hárát (Glad-Tidings), the Ṭarázát (Ornaments), the Tajallíyát (Effulgences), the Kalimát-i-Firdawsíyyih (Words of Paradise), the Is͟hráqát (Splendors), and various others.

While a multitude of other weighty works highlight the final decade of Bahá'u'lláh's ministry, Epistle to the Son of the Wolf is an important conclusion to the Revelation as a whole. Penned as an autobiographical retrospective of Bahá'u'lláh's life and ministry (among other things), Epistle to the Son of the Wolf reflects on and analyzes the major events that shaped the Prophet's life and cites passages from Bahá'u'lláh's own writings that respond to these events.

In this sense, Epistle to the Son of the Wolf functions as a concluding chapter to the Revelation, though it is not the end point. Finally, of course, Bahá'u'lláh revealed the Kitáb-i-'Ahd, the Book of the Covenant. Written entirely in Bahá'u'lláh's own hand, this last brief tablet of Bahá'u'lláh constitutes His will and testament. By appointing 'Abdu'l-Bahá the head of the Bahá'í Faith after Bahá'u'lláh's passing (though powerfully alluding to future attempts which would be made to vitiate this clear Covenant), the Kitáb-i-'Ahd thus concludes Bahá'u'lláh's Revelation and establishes the crucial link between His own ministry and the administrative order that He set forth in His revealed writings.

Once we become familiar with even this most fundamental sort of "shape" to Bahá'u'lláh's Revelation, we can then study other individual works and passages in relation to this pattern of organic unity. It is a helpful process because Bahá'u'lláh often writes as if He assumes that the reader knows what He has previously said and builds on those previous statements. For example, in Epistle to the Son of the Wolf Bahá'u'lláh frequently precedes a quote from His own revealed works with the attribution, "We said . . . " or "And further We have said. . . ." Or, for example, in His tablet to Kaiser Wilhelm I, He alludes to the fact that after Napoleon III had cast aside Bahá'u'lláh's tablet to him, the once mighty emperor "went down to dust in great loss":

> Do thou remember the one whose power transcended thy power (Napoleon III), and whose station excelled thy station. Where is he? Whither are gone the things he possessed? Take warning, and be not of them that are fast asleep. He it was who cast the Tablet of God behind him, when We made known unto him what the hosts of tyranny had caused Us to suffer. Wherefore, disgrace assailed him from all sides, and he went down to dust in great loss. (*Proclamation of Bahá'u'lláh* 39)

Likewise, in the Kalimát-i-Firdawsíyyih (Words of Paradise), Bahá'u'lláh cites for Ḥájí Mírzá Ḥaydar-'Alí (to whom the work is addressed) a passage He had previously revealed regarding the behavior of the Bahá'ís:

> We have said: "My imprisonment doeth Me no harm, nor do the things that have befallen Me at the hands of My enemies. That which harmeth Me is the conduct of my loved ones who, though they bear My name, yet commit that which maketh My heart and My pen to lament." Such utterances as these have again and again been revealed, yet the heedless have failed to profit thereby, since they are captive to their own evil passions and corrupt desires. (*Tablets of Bahá'u'lláh* 70)

This view of Bahá'u'lláh's works as one unified statement is thus not our own invention. Clearly, Bahá'u'lláh expects the reader to study the entire "ocean," not merely a few tributaries that flow into that vast body.

The more intimate we become with the art of Bahá'u'lláh, the more we come to appreciate this context of the Revelation as having continuity and integrity. And the more we come to discover this overall unity to the Revelation, the more we appreciate that no single work can be fully studied apart from this context any more than a single passage can be analyzed out of the context of the work in which it appears.

4. Bahá'u'lláh's Life as Historical Context

Still another more specific context which establishes the backdrop against which the art of Bahá'u'lláh can be more fruitfully studied and understood is the life of Bahá'u'lláh, because many works are Bahá'u'lláh's response to events in His life or events in the lives of the believers. In this connection, the student of Bahá'u'lláh's art can benefit immensely from such studies as Shoghi Effendi's *God Passes By* and Adib Taherzadeh's four-volume work, *The Revelation of Bahá'u'lláh,* both of which discuss the revealed works of Bahá'u'lláh in relation to biographical events that sometimes inspired the work.

For example, the passage cited above in which Bahá'u'lláh says "My imprisonment doeth Me no harm" was originally spoken in the early part of Bahá'u'lláh's imprisonment in 'Akká. Several Bahá'ís had become incensed by and infuriated with the fact that Siyyid Muḥammad of Iṣfahán was working in league with the government to identify Bahá'í pilgrims who had come to visit Bahá'u'lláh. They then took it upon themselves to kill this enemy of Bahá'u'lláh, in spite of Bahá'u'lláh's clear instructions that Siyyid Muḥammad of Iṣfahán (the "Anti-Christ" of the Bahá'í Revelation) was not to be molested.[1] To understand this context is to realize the full implication of this passage—that even though the believers thought they were doing a courageous service, when they violated the explicit instructions of Bahá'u'lláh, they soon discovered their deeds would have precisely the opposite effect from what they had intended. The community was once again under tight scrutiny, the motives of the believers were questioned, their reputations were tarnished, and confinement was intensified.

1. See Shoghi Effendi, *God Passes By* 189.

An earlier example of a work that was instigated by events surrounding Bahá'u'lláh's life is the Lawḥ-i-Kullu'ṭ-Ṭa'ám (Tablet of All Food). This tablet was revealed around 1854, prior to Bahá'u'lláh's sojourn in the mountains of Kurdistán. Mírzá Yaḥyá had already begun to instigate trouble among the disorganized and confused Bábís. No matter what Bahá'u'lláh attempted to do by way of revivifying the languishing remnants of the Bábí community,[2] Mírzá Yaḥyá made it appear that Bahá'u'lláh was attempting to usurp Mírzá Yaḥyá's position as "nominee" of the Báb.[3]

But instead of leading the community, Mírzá Yaḥyá concealed himself for fear of being discovered to be a Bábí, and coupled with Mírzá Yaḥyá's nonfeasance was a malfeasance instigated by Siyyid Muḥammad of Iṣfahán to discredit Bahá'u'lláh:

> A clandestine opposition, whose aim was to nullify every effort exerted, and frustrate every design conceived, by Bahá'u'lláh for the rehabilitation of a distracted community, could now be clearly discerned. Insinuations, whose purpose was to sow the seeds of doubt and suspicion and to represent Him as a usurper, as the subverter of the laws instituted by the Báb, and the wrecker of His Cause, were being incessantly circulated. His Epistles, interpretations, invocations and commentaries were being covertly and indirectly criticized, challenged and misrepresented. An attempt to injure His person was even set afoot but failed to materialize.
>
> The cup of Bahá'u'lláh's sorrows was now running over. All His exhortations, all His efforts to remedy a rapidly deteriorating situation, had remained fruitless. The velocity of His

2. After the Báb's execution in 1850, after the further persecutions resulting from the attempt on the life of the Sh̲áh in 1853, and after Bahá'u'lláh's subsequent imprisonment and exile in 1853.

3. The one appointed by the Báb to administer the affairs of the community until the appearance of "Him Whom God shall make manifest." Instead of assuming the duties that this mantle conferred, Mírzá Yaḥyá concealed himself and later professed to be the Prophet ("Him Whom God shall make manifest") instead of the "nominee."

> manifold woes was hourly and visibly increasing. (Shoghi Effendi, *God Passes By* 117)

It was in this context that Bahá'u'lláh departed from Ba<u>gh</u>dád so that, according to His own words in the Kitáb-i-Íqán, He could avoid becoming a source of discord:

> The one object of Our retirement was to avoid becoming a subject of discord among the faithful, a source of disturbance unto Our companions, the means of injury to any soul, or the cause of sorrow to any heart. Beyond these, We cherished no other intention, and apart from them, We had no end in view. (*Kitáb-i-Íqán* 251)

But before He determined that this was the best course of action for Him to follow, an event occurred which further intensified the jealousy that Mírzá Yaḥyá and Siyyid Muḥammad already had for Bahá'u'lláh. A certain Ḥájí Mírzá Kamálu'd-Dín, a believer of "culture and knowledge" who had "attained the presence of the Báb in Ká<u>sh</u>án" had traveled to Ba<u>gh</u>dád to "meet and receive enlightenment from Mírzá Yaḥyá" (*Revelation of Bahá'u'lláh* 1:56). In particular, Ḥájí Mírzá Kamálu'd-Dín asked Mírzá Yaḥyá for a commentary on a verse in the Qur'án stating that "All food was allowed to the children of Israel except what Israel made unlawful for itself." Ḥájí Mírzá Kamálu'd-Dín became distraught and disillusioned when Mírzá Yaḥyá's interpretation of this verse demonstrated "incompetence and superficiality" (Shoghi Effendi, *God Passes By* 116).

The discouraged Bábí then turned to Bahá'u'lláh for enlightenment, whereupon Bahá'u'lláh revealed the Lawḥ-i-Kullu'ṭ-Ṭa'ám (Tablet of All Food). Upon receiving this tablet, Ḥájí Mírzá Kamálu'd-Dín became so enlightened and enraptured that he immediately recognized Bahá'u'lláh as "Him Whom God shall make manifest." However, Bahá'u'lláh cautioned him not to divulge "his discovery of God's hidden Secret"(Shoghi Effendi, *God Passes By* 117) to anyone, and the devoted believer returned to his town, where he remained a faithful Bahá'í until his death.

The Lawḥ-i-Kullu'ṭ-Ṭa'ám, in addition to explicating the passage from the Qur'án, is thick with allusions to this time and these events. A passage translated by Shoghi Effendi allows us to observe the very real pain to which the Manifestation willingly subjects Himself for our instruction:

> *"Oceans of sadness have surged over Me, a drop of which no soul could bear to drink. Such is My grief that My soul hath well nigh departed from My body." "Give ear, O Kamál! . . . to the voice of this lowly, this forsaken ant, that hath hid itself in its hole, and whose desire is to depart from your midst, and vanish from your sight, by reason of that which the hands of men have wrought. God, verily, hath been witness between Me and His servants." . . . "Woe is Me, woe is Me! . . . All that I have seen from the day on which I first drank the pure milk from the breast of My mother until this moment hath been effaced from My memory, in consequence of that which the hands of the people have committed."* (qtd. in *God Passes By* 118)

As Taherzadeh discusses in *The Revelation of Bahá'u'lláh,* there is a great deal more to this Arabic tablet than these lamentations. The work discusses "the mystery and the vastness of the spiritual world of God which are without limit and far beyond the understanding of men" (1:57). But our very limited point here is to note how our understanding of the work is inextricably connected to our appreciation of the events in Bahá'u'lláh's life that served as a backdrop for the revelation of the work.

5. Individual Recipients and Historical Context

Most of Bahá'u'lláh's works are written to particular individuals as a result of particular circumstances. For example, in the last chapter of this study we will come to appreciate that our knowledge of the occasion for a given tablet and the character of the recipient provide some of the most telling keys in helping us unlock the treasures of that brief but weighty piece.

Another tablet that illustrates this vital connection between the nature of a work and the recipient is the Kitáb-i-Badí'. Though as yet untranslated into English, the importance of this work is alluded to by Shoghi Effendi, and its background and contents are discussed at length by Taherzadeh (*Revelation of Bahá'u'lláh* 2:370–87). According to the Guardian, the Kitáb-i-Badí' is an apologia written in defense of the Bahá'í Faith in the same way that the Kitáb-i-Íqán is an apologia for the Faith of the Báb. More specifically, the Kitáb-i-Badí' is written "to refute the accusations levelled against Him by Mírzá Mihdíy-i-Rashtí" (*God Passes By* 172).

However, the tone of this work is vastly different from that of the Kitáb-i-Íqán because the Kitáb-i-Badí' responds to accusations leveled by an inveterate enemy of Bahá'u'lláh whose sole purpose in life became the destruction of the Bahá'í community, whereas the Kitáb-i-Íqán responds to the sincere queries of a true seeker, the Báb's uncle who, as a result of receiving the Kitáb-i-Íqán, became a faithful believer.

The circumstances surrounding Bahá'u'lláh's writing of this defense of His claim to be "Him Whom God shall make manifest" occur in Adrianople when this same Mírzá Mihdí moved to Constantinople, ostensibly as a Bábí.[4] In fact, Mírzá Mihdí was anything but a faithful follower of the Báb and soon aligned himself with the insidious Siyyid Muḥammad and became his functionary in the attempt to undermine Bahá'u'lláh's reputation and leadership.

One instance of the perfidy of Mírzá Mihdí involved a letter he sent to Áqá Muḥammad-'Alí, a "devoted companion of Bahá'u'lláh" (Taherzadeh, *Revelation of Bahá'u'lláh* 2:371), accusing Bahá'u'lláh of having improperly laid claim to the station of the Prophet foretold by the Báb. The faithful Áqá Muḥammad-'Alí immediately took the letter to Bahá'u'lláh, Who, during the next three days, dictated to Áqá Muḥammad-'Alí a work twice the length of the Kitáb-i-Íqán.

This work discusses at length the Báb's prophecies concerning "Him Whom God shall make manifest" and "demonstrates that the

4. This "Mírzá Mihdí" should not be confused with Bahá'u'lláh's son who was known by this same name and by the surname "the purest Branch," an appellation bestowed on him by Bahá'u'lláh.

advent of the Revelation of Bahá'u'lláh was the ultimate aim of the Báb" (Taherzadeh, *Revelation of Bahá'u'lláh* 2:373). As Taherzadeh goes on to note, the Kitáb-i-Badí' exercised an important influence on the Bábí community by explaining what had been considered abstruse passages in the writings of the Báb:

> The book exerted a great influence upon the members of the Bábí community, especially those who were confused and vacillating. It resolved many of their doubts and perplexities and enabled them to recognize the exalted station of Bahá'u'lláh as "He Whom God shall make manifest." For those who are well versed in the Writings of the Báb, this book may be regarded as a key to many of the mysteries which are to be found in the Revelations of the Báb and Bahá'u'lláh. (2:373)

Taherzadeh further notes that one of the most "outstanding features" of the Kitáb-i-Badí' is the "way in which Bahá'u'lláh refutes the objections and accusations of Mírzá Mihdí with such convincing proofs that the reader becomes overwhelmed by the irrefutable power of His reasoning" (2:373–74).

For the purposes of our discussion, however, we should note that another important feature of this work is the fact that Bahá'u'lláh does not simply use the occasion of the letter as an opportunity to speak on these subjects. He dictates the work as if it were being written by Áqá Muḥammad-'Alí himself. His fundamental procedure is to quote a passage of accusation from the letter of Mírzá Mihdí and then follow that with a lengthy discourse utterly refuting the accusation. By the end of the work, every single inference of Mírzá Mihdí has been answered. However, the tone of this work is not the dispassionate and logical style of Bahá'u'lláh's "argument" that constitutes the body of the Kitáb-i-Íqán. Bahá'u'lláh strongly condemns the actions of Mírzá Mihdí and Siyyid Muḥammad, stigmatizing them with harsh epithets and warning them that their actions will soon result in their own downfall.

As has been previously noted, the importance of the relationship between the recipient and the nature of Bahá'u'lláh's art is equally clear in a work like Epistle to the Son of the Wolf, in which the tone and content are carefully geared to the character and background of Shaykh Muḥammad Taqíy-i-Najafí. An even more obvious example of this relationship between recipient and the structure and style of a work is The Seven Valleys. Penned in the form of a mystical treatise to Shaykh Muḥyi'd-Dín, a student of Ṣúfí philosophy, The Seven Valleys gently guides the recipient to the true path of spiritual ascent. The work is an emblem of kindness because Bahá'u'lláh later proscribed the ascetic life (monasticism) in general and mendicancy (often a part of the life of a Ṣúfí or dervish) in particular.

The Seven Valleys is neither derisive nor accusatory in tone. It urges the recipient towards a higher vision than that which Sufism professes. Employing the form, the language, the poetic tradition of mystical writers in the Ṣúfí tradition, Bahá'u'lláh pens a most exquisite poetic statement about the path of true mysticism. Indeed, to appreciate the love implicit in this response, we do well to consider the rather harsh condemnation of Sufism written by noted Bahá'í scholar, Mírzá Abu'l-Faḍl:

> [Bahá'u'lláh] has clearly demonstrated to intelligent men, that corruptions of Divine Religions, and the appearances of ruinous, discordant beliefs, divisions, sects and heresies, have been invented worships resulting from Sufism and asceticism. For when, like a paralysis, such practices afflicted any religion or people, enthusiasm, fervor, high understanding and perception were destroyed, and lethargy, inactivity and seclusion established instead. This finally led to heretical worships and beliefs, and the corruption and destruction of the religion. (*Bahá'í Proofs* 93–94)

There are numerous other works we could cite that would serve well to demonstrate for students of Bahá'u'lláh's art the value of becoming aware of the vital relationship between recipient and work. In the next chapter we will briefly note how this relationship plays a part in our understanding of the Lawḥ-i-Ḥikmat (Tablet of Wisdom, addressed to Nabíl-i-Akbar[5]), the Kalimát-i-Firdawsíyyih (Words of Para-

5. Áqá Muḥammad-i-Qá'iní.

dise, addressed to Ḥájí Mírzá Ḥaydar-'Alí), and the Lawḥ-i-Burhán (Tablet of the Proof, addressed to Shaykh Muḥammad Báqir[6]).

C. Historical Context and the Tablet of the Holy Mariner

While we will in Chapter 7 significantly employ the tools of historical criticism to help resolve some of the mysteries of the Tablet of Aḥmad, let us conclude this introduction to some of the various applications of historical criticism by demonstrating its usefulness in action. One of the most profound and obvious demonstrations of the power of this tool to enlighten our study can be found in our attempt to understand the Tablet of the Holy Mariner.

The Tablet of the Holy Mariner is a work best known for its abstruse symbols and veiled poetic language. Very little about this work is obvious or direct. It is presented as a narrative, a story, an allegory, or a parable. We might presume, therefore, that the best method for explicating the essential theme and purpose of this tablet would be to approach it subjectively and imaginatively. For example, we might begin our study by trying to guess who the characters represent and what events are foretold, because we know from 'Abdu'l-Bahá's statement about the work that the symbols in the tablet demonstrate Bahá'u'lláh's ability to see into the future:

> Study the Tablet of the Holy Mariner that ye may know the truth and consider that the Blessed Beauty hath fully foretold future events. Let them who perceive take warning. Verily in this is a bounty for the sincere! (*Selections from the Writings of 'Abdu'l-Bahá* ¶233.15)

6. Stigmatized by Bahá'u'lláh as the "Wolf."

From 'Abdu'l-Bahá's observation, we might conclude that the events foreshadowed are yet to occur and that we should "take warning" by studying the tablet to prepare ourselves for those events.

If we approach the work without regard to historical context, we are liable to arrive at all manner of intriguing interpretations. For example, we might conclude from the following passage that the work is prophesying the advent of the next Manifestation of God, that this Prophet will be a woman, and that she will be rejected by humanity: "And she fell upon the dust and gave up the spirit. It seemeth she was called and hearkened unto Him that summoned her unto the Realm on High" (*Bahá'í Prayers* 228). But when we consider the historical context in which the work was revealed, we discover something quite different. In his discussion of the Tablet of the Holy Mariner, Shoghi Effendi explains that, while the work seems incredibly allusive and abstruse to us, its meaning was immediately apparent to the believers who first heard it chanted that fateful day when it was revealed on the outskirts of Baghdád in 1863:

> It was on the fifth of Naw-Rúz (1863), while Bahá'u'lláh was celebrating that festival in the Mazra'iy-i-Vashshásh, in the outskirts of Baghdád, and had just revealed the "Tablet of the Holy Mariner," whose gloomy prognostications had aroused the grave apprehensions of His Companions, that an emissary of Namíq Páshá arrived and delivered into His hands a communication requesting an interview between Him and the governor. (*God Passes By* 147)

At this time, the Bahá'í community (still known as the "Bábí" community) was experiencing relative tranquillity. Bahá'u'lláh had transcribed and promulgated the writings of the Báb, and He had organized the formerly chaotic and confused Bábís into an exemplary community of believers of noble repute and character. Bahá'u'lláh had even managed to win the complete affection of the governor of Baghdád. As Bahá'u'lláh's reputation had spread abroad, sages, clerics, nobles, and peasants of every sort traveled vast distances to visit the Most Holy House,[7] that they might sit at the feet of Bahá'u'lláh and listen to His discourses.

But in the background, the jealous 'ulamá (Muslim clergy) had managed to convince the Sháh and the Sulṭán that Bahá'u'lláh was a pernicious influence and that He should be removed even farther away from Persia. Already the governor had received orders from the Sulṭán to have Bahá'u'lláh sent to Constantinople, but the governor had twice refused to inform Bahá'u'lláh, much less command Him to leave.

Naturally, Bahá'u'lláh, "omniscient at will" (Shoghi Effendi, *Unfolding Destiny* 449), was aware of these machinations and the effect they would ultimately have. Consequently, "during the last years of His sojourn in Baghdád," Bahá'u'lláh alluded to a "period of trial and turmoil that was inexorably approaching, exhibiting a sadness and heaviness of heart which greatly perturbed those around Him" (Shoghi Effendi, *God Passes By* 147). According to the second volume of Nabíl's narrative, Bahá'u'lláh began to prepare the believers for this period. He once shared with them a dream that alluded to these difficulties:

> A dream which He had at that time, the ominous character of which could not be mistaken, served to confirm the fears and misgivings that had assailed His companions. *"I saw,"* He wrote in a Tablet, *"the Prophets and the Messengers gather and seat themselves around Me, moaning, weeping and loudly lamenting. Amazed, I inquired of them the reason, whereupon their lamentation and weeping waxed greater, and they said unto me: 'We weep for Thee, O Most Great Mystery, O Tabernacle of Immortality!' They wept with such a weeping that I too wept with them. Thereupon the Concourse on high addressed Me saying: '. . . Erelong shalt Thou behold with*

7. A foremost place of pilgrimage for Bahá'ís, this abode, though now inaccessible to Bahá'ís, is given great esteem in the tablets of Bahá'u'lláh, one of which is addressed to the House. It is clear that in the future it will be a place of great honor and import.

> *Thine own eyes what no Prophet hath beheld. . . . Be patient, be patient.' . . . They continued addressing Me the whole night until the approach of dawn."* (Shoghi Effendi, *God Passes By* 147)

To one familiar with the Tablet of the Holy Mariner, this dream seems very similar to the images of lamentation we find in that work. But the relationship between these intimations of impending events and the revelation of the Tablet of the Holy Mariner become even more obvious when we discover the exact circumstances in which the tablet was revealed and shared with the followers of Bahá'u'lláh.

It had become the custom for Bahá'u'lláh and the believers to take sojourns to the countryside. One such occasion was at Naw-Rúz in 1863:

> Bahá'u'lláh had pitched His tent in a field on the outskirts of Baghdád, known as the Mazra'iy-i-Vashsháh—a place rented by His faithful brother Mírzá Músá. Bahá'u'lláh was celebrating this festival with a number of His companions, who were likewise living in tents in the open countryside. Outings at this time of year when the spring season had just begun and the weather was mild were extremely pleasant, and Bahá'u'lláh always enjoyed nature and beautiful scenery and loved to be in the country. (Taherzadeh, *Revelation of Bahá'u'lláh* 1:228)

On the fifth day of Naw-Rúz, Bahá'u'lláh's amanuensis, Mírzá Áqá Ján, emerged from Bahá'u'lláh's tent, "gathered the believers around him and chanted that mournful Tablet to them." The Bahá'í historian Nabíl was present at this astounding event and described it as follows:

> "Oceans of sorrow surged in the hearts of the listeners when the Tablet of the Holy Mariner was read aloud to them. . . . It was evident to every one that the chapter of Baghdád was about to be closed, and a new one opened, in its stead. No sooner had that Tablet been chanted than Bahá'u'lláh ordered that the tents which had been pitched should be folded up, and that all His companions should return to the city. While the tents were being re-

moved He observed: *'These tents may be likened to the trappings of this world, which no sooner are they spread out than the time cometh for them to be rolled up.'* From these words of His they who heard them perceived that these tents would never again be pitched on that spot." (qtd. in Shoghi Effendi, *God Passes By* 147)

Before the tents were removed, a messenger from Baghdád arrived, informing Bahá'u'lláh that He must meet with the governor the next day. On the following day Bahá'u'lláh was given the letter "inviting" Him to go to Constantinople to be a "guest" of the Ottoman government.

And yet this further exile was not itself the affliction foretold in the Tablet of the Holy Mariner, a fact confirmed by Bahá'u'lláh in the Tablet of the Howdah, another tablet revealed en route to Constantinople:

> Sighting from His howdah the Black Sea, as He approached the port of Sámsún, Bahá'u'lláh, at the request of Mírzá Áqá Ján, revealed a Tablet, designated Lawḥ-i-Hawdaj (Tablet of the Howdah), which by such allusions as the *"Divine Touchstone," "the grievous and tormenting Mischief,"* reaffirmed and supplemented the dire predictions recorded in the recently revealed Tablet of the Holy Mariner. (Shoghi Effendi, *God Passes By* 157)

But while the events prophesied in the Tablet of the Holy Mariner had not yet occurred, they would quickly begin to unfold. Upon His arrival in Sámsún, Bahá'u'lláh was treated with respect, but "seven days after His arrival, He, as foreshadowed in the Tablet of the Holy Mariner, was put on board a Turkish steamer and three days later was disembarked, at noon, together with His fellow-exiles, at the port of Constantinople" (Shoghi Effendi, *God Passes By* 157). According to the Guardian, "A period in which untold privations and unprecedented trials were mingled with the noblest spiritual triumphs was now commencing" (*God Passes By* 157).

During His brief stay in Constantinople, Bahá'u'lláh refused to meet with Sulṭán 'Abdu'l-'Azíz to pay His respects as was the custom.

Consequently, four months later Bahá'u'lláh and His entourage were removed to the city of Adrianople, where they would dwell for some four years.

To one who has studied the period of exile in Adrianople, the veiled allusions of the Tablet of the Holy Mariner are hardly mysterious. During this period Bahá'u'lláh suffered the most grievous wounds inflicted by His perfidious brother Mírzá Yaḥyá, who had already caused Him such anguish as to precipitate Bahá'u'lláh's two-year withdrawal to Sulaymáníyyih (1854–56). In Adrianople Mírzá Yaḥyá, persistently urged on by Siyyid Muḥammad of Iṣfahán,[8] not only made spurious accusations against Bahá'u'lláh to government officials, but went so far as to have Bahá'u'lláh poisoned. Though He survived the attempt on His life, Bahá'u'lláh was given up for dead and became so seriously ill that the disease left Him, Shoghi Effendi says, "with a shaking hand till the end of His life" (*God Passes By* 165).

In his discussion of "The Rebellion of Mírzá Yaḥyá," Shoghi Effendi details the panoply of horrors perpetrated by this jealous half-brother, but the culmination of these events was the "Most Great Separation," an event instigated by Bahá'u'lláh. After years of forbearance, patience, and incredible demonstrations of love towards Mírzá Yaḥyá, Bahá'u'lláh determined the time had come to officially separate Himself from this thankless one, an act which He had forestalled as long as possible for the sake of the community.[9]

Bahá'u'lláh declared that the believers must decide for themselves whom to follow: those who wished to do so could follow Mírzá Yaḥyá, and those who wished could follow Him. Those who remained with Mírzá Yaḥyá were thenceforth designated as Azalís (followers of Ṣubḥ-i-Azal) or "People of the Bayán" (meaning those who are still following

8. Stigmatized as the Antichrist of the Bahá'í Revelation.

9. Mírzá Yaḥyá had made numerous complaints to the government, stating that he was the rightful leader of the Bábí religion and that Bahá'u'lláh was trying to usurp his authority. Had Bahá'u'lláh taken action against Mírzá Yaḥyá, such actions might have been construed by the government as confirming Mírzá Yaḥyá's accusations.

the Bayán),[10] while those who remained followers of Bahá'u'lláh were designed henceforth as Bahá'ís (followers of Bahá).

Needless to say, we could discuss these events and their importance endlessly without exhausting their significance. The point is that the kind of persecution of the Manifestation alluded to in the Tablet of the Holy Mariner, while it may also represent the suffering of Bahá'u'lláh in general (as well as the historical treatment of all the Prophets), clearly foreshadows this particular period in Adrianople when Bahá'u'lláh would undergo trials so personally afflictive, so incredibly grievous, that they ultimately resulted in the further exile of Bahá'u'lláh and His kindred to what was presumed to be their deaths in the ghastly prison city of 'Akká.

Shoghi Effendi confirms this interpretation of the Tablet of the Holy Mariner when he states:

> . . . [The Tablet of the Holy Mariner] is one of the most significant Tablets revealed by Bahá'u'lláh during the last days of His stay in Baghdád, and refers to the sad, though momentous events which were to transpire soon after His arrival in Adrianople. Its main significance lies in the fact that in it Bahá'u'lláh clearly foreshadows the grave happenings, which eventually led to the defection of Subḥi-Azal, and to the schism which the latter thought to create within the ranks of the faithful. (qtd. in *Lights of Guidance*, no. 1609)

We can thus appreciate with this example the essential importance of studying the historical context in which the works of Bahá'u'lláh were revealed. Without such information, the meaning of the Tablet of the Holy Mariner might remain hidden, or else we might unwittingly read into it various sorts of inappropriate meanings. Of course, having this information does not close off other more expan-

---

10. The Báb explicitly cautioned His followers that anyone who continued to follow the Báb after the appearance of "Him Whom God shall make manifest" (Bahá'u'lláh) was not really following Him (the Báb).

sive interpretations of the work. In this allegorical piece the Prophet shares with us a sense of the communication between the Prophet and the Divine Concourse through the intermediary of the Holy Spirit, personified for Bahá'u'lláh by the veiled maiden.

But if the events have already occurred, why does 'Abdu'l-Bahá exhort us to study the work so that we might observe how Bahá'u'lláh has foretold the future? The answer may be that our study is not intended to reveal to us what will happen in our future. Perhaps our consideration of this tablet helps confirm for us the fact that Bahá'u'lláh had the power of infallibility and omniscience. Still, we might wonder why 'Abdu'l-Bahá also cautions, "Let them who perceive take warning. Verily in this is a bounty for the sincere!" (*Selections from the Writings of 'Abdu'l-Bahá* ¶233.15) If we are not being warned about future perils, then what are we being warned of?

The answer to this question may lie in the passage immediately preceding 'Abdu'l-Bahá's admonition wherein 'Abdu'l-Bahá cautions against stirring up mischief:

> Beware lest any soul privily cause disruption or stir up strife. In the Impregnable Stronghold be ye brave warriors, and for the Mighty Mansion a valiant host. Exercise the utmost care, and day and night be on your guard, that thereby the tyrant may inflict no harm.
>
> Study the Tablet of the Holy Mariner that ye may know the truth. . . . (*Selections from the Writings of 'Abdu'l-Bahá* ¶233.14–15)

In effect, we should not imagine that anything we do is beyond the knowledge of God and His Prophets, even though our mischief may not be immediately apparent to others. We could still end up like Mírzá Yaḥyá.

Of course, to study the tablet and to realize how Bahá'u'lláh's prophecies were fulfilled might also induce in us an assurance that His other prophecies will also come true. For example, we might conclude that, in light of His clear foreknowledge of these events, we should heed Bahá'u'lláh's dire predictions as discussed by Shoghi Effendi regarding the impending turmoil that is an inescapable part of our own future.[11]

In conclusion, the usefulness of applying the tools of historical criticism as an aid to understanding various levels of meaning in the works of Bahá'u'lláh is clear. Equally clear is the fact that each work will dictate the fundamental parameters of historical analysis. But as we benefit from applying the tools of historical criticism, we should likewise come to appreciate the groundwork done by scholars who have provided us with the means of pursuing our study, whether these be the commentaries and interpretations of Shoghi Effendi, the biographies of Hasan M. Balyuzi, the observations of Adib Taherzadeh, or the various other studies (compilations, glossaries, concordances, dictionaries, and software) which make our study so much more productive. In effect, we come to appreciate the role scholars will have in this Dispensation, not as religious leaders or as authoritative interpreters of holy text, but as helpmates to other believers.

11. See Shoghi Effendi's discussion of "The Fire of Ordeal" in *World Order of Bahá'u'lláh* (46 ff.), of "American Bahá'ís in the Time of World Peril" in *Citadel of Faith* (122 ff.), and of the "tempest, unprecedented in its violence" in *Promised Day Is Come* (¶2 ff.).

Chapter 4
Genre and Style in the Art of Bahá'u'lláh

The summons and the message which We gave were never intended to reach or to benefit one land or one people only. Mankind in its entirety must firmly adhere to whatsoever hath been revealed and vouchsafed unto it. Then and only then will it attain unto true liberty. The whole earth is illuminated with the resplendent glory of God's Revelation.

—Bahá'u'lláh

After we have asked ourselves who is speaking to us and under what circumstances, we can next question the form that speech takes. This question is particularly relevant to a study of Bahá'u'lláh's art because His vast writings encompass so many varied genres or literary forms. In fact, Bahá'u'lláh Himself indicates that He has selected these forms according to the purpose of each work. In the Súratu'l-Haykal (Súrih of the Temple) Bahá'u'lláh observes "We have caused the signs to descend after nine conditions. . . ." (*Surat 'ul Hykl* 33).[1] Adib Taherzadeh

1. All quotations from the Súratu'l-Haykal are from the version translated by Anton F. Haddad, which is entitled *Surat 'ul Hykl* and was published in 1900, before the system of transliteration advocated by the Guardian was adopted by the Bahá'í community.

and others have interpreted this passage as meaning that "in this Dispensation the verses of God have been revealed in nine different styles or categories" (*Revelation of Bahá'u'lláh* 1:42). Interestingly, Bahá'u'lláh in this same passage goes on to observe that He could have employed even more "conditions" or styles had He wished:

> Say, Verily, We have caused the signs to descend after nine conditions, each of which is proof of the Dominion of God, the Protector, the Self-existent,—any one of these conditions is sufficient to convince whomsoever is in heaven and earth, but the majority of the people are heedless. Had we willed We would have revealed the signs after other conditions whose number could not be reckoned. (*Surat 'ul Hykl* 33–34)

According to Taherzadeh, the Bahá'í scholar Jináb-i-Fáḍil-i-Mázindarání after "careful study of the Writings" speculated that those nine styles were the following:

1. Tablets with the tone of command and authority.
2. Those with the tone of servitude, meekness and supplication.
3. Writings dealing with interpretation of the old Scriptures, religious beliefs and doctrines of the past.
4. Writings in which laws and ordinances have been enjoined for this age and laws of the past abrogated.
5. Mystical writings.
6. Tablets concerning matters of government and world order, and those addressed to the kings.
7. Tablets dealing with subjects of learning and knowledge, divine philosophy, mysteries of creation, medicine, alchemy, etc.
8. Tablets exhorting men to education, goodly character and divine virtues.
9. Tablets dealing with social teachings.

(*Revelation of Bahá'u'lláh* 1:43)

While these categories are helpful, especially in light of our discussion about tone in relation to point of view, we can observe a certain lack of parallelism in this list. For example, the first two categories are based on tonal considerations, whereas the remaining seven are concerned with the subject or theme of the works. Furthermore, if Bahá'u'lláh is alluding to nine different styles, then this list would not seem an appropriate catalog. For example, "mystical writings" might sometimes be conveyed with highly rhetorical and poetic images while at other times they might be delivered in a more straightforward expository style. The same sort of distinction might hold true for Bahá'u'lláh's works on "social teachings." The Kitáb-i-Aqdas might be considered Bahá'u'lláh's most important repository of social teachings, and yet, stylistically, it contains rapid transitions from one style to another, from poetic explication to homiletic exhortation, from simple and unembellished enunciation of law to philosophical explication of spiritual concepts.

But it is certainly not our purpose here to refute the speculation of Jináb-i-Fáḍil-i-Mázindarání or to replace his list with another of our own. Whether Bahá'u'lláh employed nine styles or ninety, the significance is the same: Bahá'u'lláh was capable of expressing Himself in whatever style was needed to reach people from every conceivable background and condition. In fact, Bahá'u'lláh's allusion to nine styles or "conditions" is most likely His symbolic way of stating that, for the purpose of this unique point in human history when all peoples are to be brought together under the shelter of one faith, God through His Prophet has provided *ample* or *sufficient* access. The vast array of styles Bahá'u'lláh has employed thus symbolizes how in this Revelation access to God's divine plan is at long last provided simultaneously for all the diverse peoples of the earth. Bahá'u'lláh's Revelation thus consummates all previous Revelations.

Hence the number *nine* in this passage from the Súratu'l-Haykal may have the same symbolic value as do the nine portals in the design of the Mashriqu'l-Adhkár.[2] The nine doors symbolize that each world religion has provided a pathway to the same God, and the design of the

2. An Arabic appellation designating a Bahá'í House of Worship; literally translated, it means the "Dawning-place of the Praise of God."

temple as a whole indicates that in the shelter of this Dispensation all the diverse pathways will become united.

Of course, there have been more than eight previous religions. The nine portals thus represent *all* previous Revelations, not just nine specific religions. In this same sense, the Greatest Name *Bahá* has the numerical value of nine, symbolizing perfection or completeness and indicating that all previous Revelations have their consummation in the Revelation of Bahá'u'lláh. That is, in this Dispensation all peoples of the earth will at long last realize the essential unity of humankind as well as the fundamental unity and integrity of all previous Revelations.

With this less literal interpretation of Bahá'u'lláh's allusion to the "styles" of His art in mind, we can appreciate that, while it is not essential for us to discover nine specific "conditions," it may prove extremely helpful in our study of Bahá'u'lláh's art to observe the variety of genres He employs. As we survey this rich array of literary styles and forms, we can begin to understand more fully how this variety of genre is yet another indication of how Bahá'u'lláh shaped His art to respond to the central objective of this Dispensation—to provide ample means of gaining access to God for all the diverse peoples of the world, some avenue that transcends the constraints of a single cultural or religious perspective.

This interpretation of Bahá'u'lláh's allusion to the nine styles, forms, or "conditions" is supported by the general symbolic nature of the Súratu'l-Haykal. As we noted in Chapter 2, the Súratu'l-Haykal allegorically compares the fashioning of the Prophet (Himself) to the building of a Temple—the "temple" in this context being a commonplace metaphor for the human body or the physical aspect of the Prophet when He appears among us. Therefore, the styles of utterance with which we gain entrance to this temple (i.e., recognize the Prophet) are explained in terms of portals to the sacred shelter of the Mashriqu'l-Adhkár.

In this chapter we will sample a few of these "portals," some of the more obvious categories of literary forms or genres. But before we examine how an awareness of genre can help us in our study of Bahá'u'lláh's art, let us first review some basic information about how the study of genre is most often employed by students of literature.

The term *genre* means "class" or "category." The term can allude to broad categories such as prose, poetry, and drama. It can also allude to more particular categories within these broad classifications. For example, within the category of poetry we may study the epic mode and the lyric mode. Likewise, the lyric mode could be studied as constituting a variety of even more specific categories of poetry such as the sonnet, the ode, the elegy, the haiku, and so on.

In this general sense, the use of generic terms assumes that certain groups of literary works share certain common characteristics. During the course of literary history, these definitions sometime assume prescriptive power so that a writer might feel obliged to follow certain rules or traditions that have evolved for a genre. For example, it has sometimes been debated whether or not Shakespeare's tragedies strictly follow the Aristotelian formula enunciated in the *Poetics.* Literary critics have written volumes attempting to identify what Shakespeare intended to be *hamartia* (the tragic flaw) in the character of Hamlet. In the same vein, some critics have rejected a view of Arthur Miller's *Death of a Salesman* as tragedy because the main character, Willy Loman, never seems to achieve true Aristotelian "recognition"—he never acknowledges that his own moral choices have brought about his tragic downfall.

This sort of prescriptive use of genre, sometimes designated as "formalism" or "formalist criticism," is not our purpose here. That is, "formalism" assumes that there are "groups of formal or technical characteristics among works of the same generic kind regardless of time or place of composition, author, or subject matter; and that these characteristics, when they define a particular group of works, are of basic significance in talking about literary art" (*Handbook* 212). But some recent trends in literary criticism, particularly in what has become known as "deconstructionist criticism," take issue with "formalism" for reasons that are relevant to our own study.

That is, genre criticism found great favor with the "New Critics" earlier in this century because it upholds an objectivist approach to the critical analysis of literature. This approach advocates *explication de texte* (a close reading of text) as the best tool for getting at meaning in a work, as opposed to the tools of historical context or biographical perspective which we discussed earlier. Stated more plainly, formal genre criticism assumes the work itself creates its own microcosm which is accessible to the resourceful and creative reader. In fact, some critics employing the tenets of objectivist criticism reject what information we might be able to glean from the circumstance of the work's creation because that information might sway us to interpret the work according to this external information rather than according to the fictive world the artist has constructed.

It is an important issue and a sensitive one. For example, are the characters in a Hemingway novel just thinly veiled masks for Hemingway and his companions, or do these figures have a life of their own in the context of the created world Hemingway fashioned? Similarly, when we read the work of a poet such as Robert Frost, do we automatically assume that the first-person speaker must be Frost himself and interpret the poem according to what we can learn about Frost at that point in his life? In short, can we allow for the possibility that the artist is capable of employing imagination effectively so as to create a reality essentially different from that which he or she has experienced?

Of course, if we cannot allow for the possibility that the artist has the capacity to understand the perspective and personality of characters distinct from (and sometimes diametrically opposed to) the artist's own perspective or the perspective of other characters within the same work, then we certainly will have trouble explaining someone like Shakespeare who creates characters that are precisely antithetical to each other. For example, how could the same artist simultaneously create the naive and trusting Othello and (in the same play) the diabolical, cynical, and ostensibly "motivelessly malignant" Iago?

Traditionally, there has been a tension between these two critical approaches, the objectivist and the historical. As with most such controversies in which two views lie at polar extremes, truth lies somewhere in the middle. Sometimes it is extremely helpful and even essential to know the historical background of the author or the age that forms the context for the artist's creation. At other times, such information can interfere with our appreciation of the integrity of the world the artist has brought to life as the fruit of a creative imagination expressed through a well-honed craft.

In this sense, each work of art is a unique construct for each individual examining that work. Likewise, each work of art dictates its own rules and requirements. In effect, interpretation is a personal experience which, while it may be informed by the knowledge of what others perceive, cannot be dictated by the formal standards set forth by scholars of literature. Certainly, Bahá'u'lláh seems to vindicate this observation by eliminating formal or authoritative interpretations of His work[3] and by commanding that each individual become a scholar in his or her own right.

There is one further observation we must acknowledge before we attempt our broad survey of some of the categories or forms employed by Bahá'u'lláh: a great deal of profound and weighty scholarship on genre remains to be done. In particular, there needs to be a study of Bahá'u'lláh's use of Persian and Arabic literary models. For our present purposes, let us note some representative examples of those genres employed by Bahá'u'lláh that seem to transcend cultural orientation so that we can observe how such study helps us penetrate the often demanding and challenging surfaces of Bahá'u'lláh's works.

1. The Mystical Treatise

One of the most distinctive portals for those attracted to poetic style and mystical insight is Bahá'u'lláh's use of the mystical treatise. Two of the best-known examples of this style are The Seven Valleys and The Four Valleys. For the Persian Bahá'í steeped in the poetic traditions of Rúmí and other gifted masters, the particular figurative images, allusions, and symbols in these works are virtually intuited. In effect, the subtle cultural training in the mystical poetic tradition gives someone familiar with this background an advantage. Therefore, where many Persians might know full well the tradition behind the search for the "Friend," the Western reader of The Seven Valleys needs some background about mysticism as a way of life and as a literary tradition.

3. Except for those by 'Abdu'l-Bahá and Shoghi Effendi.

In most religious traditions the mystic is a solitary figure. He spends much of his time fasting, rapt in prayer, or following some other form of independent spiritual exercise. He may not perceive religious institutions as detrimental to his solitary life, but usually he wants no part of organized society and pursues instead a course of personal spiritual illumination and transformation through extensive periods of devotions, meditation, and solitude.

The goal of the mystic is the attainment of or experience of proximity to God—or to some universal source of spiritual energy. Though clearly such nearness has allegorical implications, the mystical quest is usually pursued as a sensually based experience, not simply as achieved insight, as enlightenment, or as heightened spiritual awareness. Consequently, it is not uncommon that the central focus of mysticism is to undergo in ever more intense fashion the sensual experience associated with the ecstasy of nearness:

> This goal of union or reunion with God or with some divine force or essence might be described in terms of Nirvana to the Hindu, of being in the presence of the "Good" to the neo-Platonist, of having a vision of Christ to the Christian, of attaining the presence of the "Friend" to the Ṣúfí: one hesitates to give specific parameters to such an experience because it is entirely subjective and therefore variously portrayed. But at the heart of the mystical experience is the sensation of being utterly detached from mortal concerns or selfish desires and of experiencing a union (perhaps "reunion" would be more appropriate) with the spiritual forces of the universe. (Hatcher, *Arc of Ascent* 63)

How the mystic achieves this condition varies from religion to religion and from culture to culture. In some tribal religions hallucinogens are used. In some ascetic orders the mystic may employ various forms of deprivation to achieve a sense of detachment and reunion—extended periods of prayer, fasting, isolation, or meditation. Some Ṣúfís arrive at a state of ecstasy by means of whirling dances (hence the term *whirling darvís͟h*). But it is fairly common to all the varieties of mysticism that the process occurs in successive stages of increasing intensity until some final and more or less complete state of ecstasy is attained. In this state of ecstasy the mystic often has a sense of immense insight, universal knowledge, ineffable tranquillity, and detachment from the physical world and the physical self. Therefore, it is most often the objective of the mystical treatise to describe the successive stages of the process whereby this ecstatic condition is achieved.

In The Seven Valleys Bahá'u'lláh responds to questions asked Him by S͟hayk͟h Muḥyi'd-Dín, who was a student of Sufism and the judge of a town near the Persian border northeast of Bag͟hdád. In this work Bahá'u'lláh employs the form and language of Sufism to describe the seven "valleys" that represent seven successive stages of spiritual ascent, a seven-part structural scheme very similar to that used by the noted poet 'Aṭṭár (Farídu'd-Dín 'Aṭṭár, ca. 1150–1230) in his famous *Mantiqu'ṭ-Ṭayr* (Language of the Birds). Even the stages themselves are similar. 'Aṭṭár divides the mystic journey into Search, Love, Knowledge, Detachment, Unification, Bewilderment, and Annihilation; Bahá'u'lláh divides the spiritual journey into the valleys of Search, Love, Knowledge, Unity, Contentment, Wonderment, and True Poverty and Absolute Nothingness.

In writing The Seven Valleys Bahá'u'lláh thus presumes that the reader understands something about mysticism in general and Ṣúfísm in particular. Certainly, without some background knowledge, the power of the work may be greatly diminished for the reader. For example, it is helpful to know that Sufism is divided into two main groups—those who affirm the necessity of working within religious institutions, of abiding by the law of the Qur'án and the fundamental requisites of Islámic law, and those who, though regarding themselves as Muslims in a general sense, believe themselves beyond the need of law or ecclesiastical authority. A *darvís͟h* or *faqír* may belong to any of the numerous orders of Islámic mystics, but he can usually be classified as subscribing to one of these two orientations towards religious authority:

> A member of the former [those who live by Qur'ánic law] is known as a traveler *(sálik)* on the pathway *(ṭaríqat)* to heaven. The later are *ázád*, free, or *majd͟húb*, rapt, abstracted, attracted.
>
> (Gail, *Bahá'í Glossary* 15)

While Shoghi Effendi observes that the Bahá'í Faith, like all religions, is "fundamentally mystic in character," he also notes that the "chief goal" of the Bahá'í Faith is the spiritual development of the individual through the "acquisition of spiritual virtues and powers" (qtd. in *Compilation of Compilations* 2: no. 1763). This relationship between the mystical aspects of belief and the expression of that insight in reformed character and social action is the most important key to understanding what distinguishes Bahá'u'lláh's treatment of mysticism in The Seven Valleys. Bahá'u'lláh employs the genre of the mystical treatise or allegory, but throughout the work He subtly (almost subliminally) instructs the reader in twin themes: the need for the individual to gain access to spiritual ascent through the intermediary of the Prophet (the Friend) and the obligation of the enlightened individual to apply his mystic vision or insight to the improvement of society.

We can appreciate this subtle turn when we realize that mysticism is frequently proscribed by ecclesiastical authority because it tacitly (and sometimes explicitly) advocates the circumvention of traditions, laws, and ecclesiastical authority. One's relationship with God is viewed as purely private, personal, and not, therefore, subject to such constraints. Indeed, it is in this same vein that Bahá'u'lláh in the Kitáb-i-Aqdas proscribes asceticism and monasticism (¶36). In later tablets He also returns to this subject. For example, in the Bis͟hárát (Glad-Tidings) Bahá'u'lláh affirms that the service of the pious is needed in the world (*Tablets of Bahá'u'lláh* 24):

> The pious deeds of the monks and priests among the followers of the Spirit—upon Him be the peace of God—are remembered in His presence. In this Day, however, let them give up the life of seclusion and direct their steps towards the open world and busy themselves with that which will profit themselves and others. We have granted them leave to enter into wedlock that they may bring forth one who will make mention of God, the Lord of the seen and the unseen, the Lord of the Exalted Throne.

Stated with utmost simplicity, then, Bahá'u'lláh in The Seven Valleys employs the literary form and the fundamental philosophy/theology of mysticism to demonstrate some of the shortcomings of mysticism: (1) the assumptions that spiritual ascent can take place individually, autonomously, ascetically (2) the assertion that one does not need a formal religious institution or the laws of a Prophet for personal transformation, and (3) the notion that sensually based ecstasy is itself the sole objective of one's spiritual journey or longing.

To realize the loving indirection with which Bahá'u'lláh has taught this student of Ṣúfísm is to understand more completely the teaching technique of the Prophet in general, as well as the sort of gentleness and respect with which any teacher of religious truth should approach a true seeker. Bahá'u'lláh affirms the loftiest aspirations of the true mystic (spiritual growth), redefines "the Friend" as a specific allusion to the Manifestation of God (instead of some self-proclaimed divine), and asserts that, after the ecstasy of reunion with the Friend, the seeker is obliged to redirect his steps towards work in the world.

2. The Lyric Mode

Much of Bahá'u'lláh's work could be described as having poetic characteristics, and Bahá'u'lláh penned exquisite poems, only a few of which are as yet translated into English. But among the works presently available in English is at least one major tablet, The Hidden Words, which could be correctly classified as a collection of lyric poems.

While the term *lyric* can only be broadly defined, it is most often the lyric mode we think of when we designate a writer as a poet. Sometimes we refer to authors of verse narratives, epics, and dramatic works as poets (e.g., Homer, Virgil, Milton, Sophocles, Shakespeare, etc.). But usually when we think of poets, we have in mind those who write in the lyric mode: poets of the Ṣúfí tradition such as Rúmí (Jalálu'd-Dín, 1207–1273), 'Aṭṭár (Farídu'd-Dín 'Aṭṭár, ca. 1150–1230), and Ḥáfiẓ (Shamsu'd-Dín Muḥammad, d. ca. 1389); or poets in the English tradition such as Wordsworth, Coleridge, Keats, or, more recently, poets such as Dylan Thomas or W. H. Auden.

What distinguishes the lyric mode from other poetic forms is the fact that the lyric verse is relatively brief, usually very compressed, and tightly focused on one theme. Usually the lyric is also typified by its evocative appeal to sensual perception, something it most often accomplishes through the imaginative use of sound effects and inventive sensual imagery.

Bahá'u'lláh's use of the lyric mode in The Hidden Words accords with the definition and standards we have just cited. Such an observation does not imply that the work lacks unity. As we noted previously, Bahá'u'lláh Himself states that the work synthesizes and distills all the spiritual teachings formerly "revealed unto the Prophets of old." But the thematic unity of the work seems to revolve around the inextricable relationship between belief and action, between one's outward title or declared intention and one's daily performance:

> Guidance hath ever been given by words, and now it is given by deeds. Every one must show forth deeds that are pure and holy, for words are the property of all alike, whereas such deeds as these belong only to Our loved ones. (Hidden Words, Persian, no. 76)

In this vein, the work concludes with a series of verses which exhort Bahá'u'lláh's "servants" to "give forth goodly and wondrous fruits" (Hidden Words, Persian, no. 80), affirming that the "best of men are they that earn a livelihood by their calling and spend upon themselves and upon their kindred for the love of God, the Lord of all worlds" (Hidden Words, Persian, no. 82).

Therefore, we can see in this work various strands of themes woven throughout like the melodic lines of a symphony. But the work has no precise plan or order. In each individual Hidden Word Bahá'u'lláh has "taken the inner essence" of a particular spiritual verity and has "clothed it in the garment of brevity. . . ." And the form that this "garment of brevity" assumes is lyric verse.

Shoghi Effendi confirms this observation, stating that the individual verses were revealed gradually as Bahá'u'lláh "paced, wrapped in His meditations, the banks of the Tigris" (*God Passes By* 140), and that the individual verses "have no sequence." He goes on to describe these poems as "jewel-like thoughts cast out of the mind of the Manifestation of God to admonish and counsel men" (*Unfolding Destiny* 456).

This is not to say we cannot benefit from going through the work in sequence, but we can also approach this work as we would any collection of lyric poems, turning to particular verses out of sequence to find what seems to minister to our spiritual needs at the moment. And as we approach these lyric poems, we should take appropriate note of the diversity of these pieces. Some are succinct and unembellished axioms: "The best beloved of all things in My sight is Justice" (Hidden Words, Arabic, no. 2); "If thou lovest Me, turn away from thyself . . ." (Hidden Words, Arabic, no. 7). Some are long and imagistic, even allegorical in form:

> In the night-season the beauty of the immortal Being hath repaired from the emerald height of fidelity unto the Sadratu'l-Muntahá, and wept with such a weeping that the concourse on high and the dwellers of the realms above wailed at His lamenting. Whereupon there was asked, Why the wailing and weeping? (Hidden Words, Persian, no. 77)

Others are in the form of brief but intriguing analogies:

> Sow the seeds of My divine wisdom in the pure soil of thy heart, and water them with the water of certitude, that the hyacinths of My knowledge and wisdom may spring up fresh and green in the sacred city of thy heart. (Hidden Words, Persian, no. 33)

The most consistent distinction we can detect between the major division of the work into the Arabic and Persian verses is that the Arabic verse is more forthright, less imagistic, whereas the Persian verses, deriving as they do from the Persian poetic tradition, are more embellished, more imagistic. A more particular observation we should consider as we approach these lyric pieces is the caveat we require when examining the work of any other lyric poet—since each verse is an autonomous work of art, each Hidden Word demands its own special study of the allusions, symbols, and imagery that contain the keys to unlocking the meaning concealed beneath the beguilingly accessible surfaces of these poems.

It should not surprise us that Bahá'u'lláh could be considered a poet; all the Prophets employ techniques that are essentially poetic in nature. More particularly, however, we should remember that one of the skills that distinguished Bahá'u'lláh among the Ṣúfís during His two-year sojourn in the mountains of Sulaymáníyyih was His ability to compose poetry:

> Amazed by the profundity of His insight and the compass of His understanding, they were impelled to seek from Him what they considered to be a conclusive and final evidence of the unique power and knowledge which He now appeared in their eyes to possess. "No one among the mystics, the wise, and the learned," they claimed, while requesting this further favor from Him, "has hitherto proved himself capable of writing a poem in a rhyme and meter identical with that of the longer of the two odes, entitled Qaṣídiy-i-Tá'íyyih composed by Ibn-i-Fáriḍ. We beg you to write for us a poem in that same meter and rhyme." This request was complied with, and no less than two thousand verses, in exactly the manner they had specified, were dictated by Him, out of which He selected one hundred and twenty-seven, which He permitted them to keep, deeming the subject matter of the rest premature and unsuitable to the needs of the times. It is these same one hundred and twenty-seven verses that constitute the Qaṣídiy-i-Varqá'íyyih, so familiar to, and widely circulated amongst, His Arabic speaking followers (Shoghi Effendi, *God Passes By* 123).[4]

We can conclude from this episode that we are quite correct in studying works such as The Hidden Words with the same tools we might

4. See *Revelation of Bahá'u'lláh* 1:63 for a discussion of the theme of the Qaṣídiy-i-Varqá'íyyih.

employ to study the poetry of any of the great poets. We can further surmise that as the other poems of Bahá'u'lláh are translated into other languages, we will be able to acquire a more ample appreciation of the Prophet as poet.

3. The Doctrinal or Philosophical Essay

A third genre we can discover in the art of Bahá'u'lláh is the doctrinal or philosophical essay. These works are often similar in tone and mode to 'Abdu'l-Bahá's discussions in *Some Answered Questions,* in which subjects of theology, philosophy, cosmology (study of the nature of the universe), teleology (study of design in nature), ontology (metaphysical study of being), exegesis (scriptural interpretation), and various other doctrinal matters are discussed. Characterized by an almost detached tone, a highly logical structure, and a carefully designed argument, these discussions are often supported by or illustrated liberally with marvelous analogies and are often punctuated with humor.

A. The Kitáb-i-Íqán (Book of Certitude)

Certainly, the most important example of the doctrinal or philosophical essay among the works of Bahá'u'lláh is the Kitáb-i-Íqán. Revealed in the course of two days and structured into two parts, this essay is described by Shoghi Effendi as occupying "a position unequaled by any work in the entire range of Bahá'í literature, except the Kitáb-i-Aqdas, Bahá'u'lláh's Most Holy Book" (*God Passes By* 139). He further observes that it occupies a position of "unsurpassed preeminence among the doctrinal . . . writings of the Author of the Bahá'í Dispensation" (*God Passes By* 140).

Shoghi Effendi alludes to the Kitáb-i-Íqán generically as an *apologia* revealed "in defense of the Bábí Revelation" (*God Passes By* 172)—an apologia being a formal essay in defense of or justification of an idea or set of ideas.[5] Shoghi Effendi describes the Kitáb-i-Íqán stylistically

5. Shoghi Effendi in this same passage states that the Kitáb-i-Badí' was Bahá'u'lláh's apologia for His own Revelation.

as a "model of Persian prose, of a style at once original, chaste and vigorous, and remarkably lucid, both cogent in argument and matchless in its irresistible eloquence," a work which was penned in "fulfillment of the prophecy of the Báb, Who had specifically stated that the Promised One would complete the text of the unfinished Persian Bayán. . . ."[6] Shoghi Effendi states that thematically this essay sets forth "the Grand Redemptive Scheme of God" (*God Passes By* 138–39).

The importance of recognizing these most obvious and fundamental aspects of the generic makeup of the Kitáb-i-Íqán becomes apparent when we consider the goal of this work as implied by its title and by its origin. The title of the work translates as "The Book of Certitude," and it was written prior to Bahá'u'lláh's announcement to the Bábís that He was the promised Manifestation ("Him Whom God shall make manifest"). As we have mentioned previously, it was revealed in answer to specific questions put to Bahá'u'lláh by the then unconverted uncle of the Báb.

From these circumstances, we may safely infer that the purpose of the work is to induce certitude or conviction by explicating and vindicating the rationale that underlies the divine plan by which God educates humankind through a succession of Prophets, or Manifestations. This is a particularly significant observation as we consider the generic nature of this work, because we might understandably assume that a work fashioned to inspire conviction or to confirm belief would be an emotionally charged exhortation, perhaps a highly poetic or mystical piece. That is, we normally think of religious faith and conviction as an emotional attitude, almost the antithesis of conclusions derived from logical argumentation. But since Bahá'u'lláh chose to employ the form of a logically structured argument, we must conclude that He considered the soundest foundation for certitude to be a firm grasp of

6. Shoghi Effendi goes on to state that the work is written "in reply to the questions addressed to Bahá'u'lláh by the as yet unconverted maternal uncle of the Báb, Ḥájí Mírzá Siyyid Muḥammad, while on a visit, with his brother, Ḥájí Mírzá Ḥasan-'Alá, to Karbilá" (*God Passes By* 138). In *Bahá'u'lláh: The King of Glory* 164–65, Hasan Balyuzi lists these questions, as do we in our discussion of the Kitáb-i-Íqán in Chapter 6.

the logical methodology by which God brings creation into being and promotes human advancement.

Shoghi Effendi summarizes in some detail the major subjects or themes that constitute the argument of the Kitáb-i-Íqán,[7] but for our purposes here, it is sufficient to note that the work as a whole begins with one overriding question and then proceeds to answer that question in two ways. Stated plainly, the question concerns how the plan of an Omnipotent Being (God) could become frustrated or diverted. In other words, if God sends Prophets and intends for humanity to recognize and follow these Guides, why are the Prophets historically rejected and persecuted, and why does human history seem to be largely ignorant of the very process (progressive revelation) devised to foster human development?

The general answer offered in the Kitáb-i-Íqán is that the Plan of God is never harmed by human rejection of this felicitous remedy. As the patient, humankind must suffer the consequences of refusing the prescription of the Divine Physician, but in time the patient will come to understand the truth, accept the prescribed remedy, and become cured.

The particular answer is given in terms of the two major considerations: (1) people have rejected the Prophets because they have understood prophetic language as being literal rather than symbolic or metaphorical, particularly when these same people have become misled by religious leaders who have a vested interest in attempting to forestall the acceptance of the new Revelation; (2) people have consistently misunderstood the station of the Prophets by deifying Them (e.g., Christ), by believing Them to be solely the product of social or political circumstances (e.g., Moses and the Báb), or else by considering one particular Prophet to be the final Revelation in human history (e.g. Christ and Muḥammad).

As we will observe in Chapter 6 in our discussion of structure, the significance in recognizing the generic makeup of the Kitáb-i-Íqán as a logically structured essay is that we can study the work more effec-

7. See *God Passes By* 139. These are discussed in Chapter 6.

tively. In particular we will discover the usefulness of analyzing the logical framework of the tablet through the construction of a formal outline to trace the progress of Bahá'u'lláh's argument.

B. The Súriy-i-Vafá (Tablet to Vafá)

A much briefer but no less effective example of the essay style is the Súriy-i-Vafá. Since the tablet is a letter to an individual, this work has some of the characteristics we will consider with regard to Bahá'u'lláh's epistolary style. For example, the Súriy-i-Vafá contains a highly rhetorical preamble alluding to the character and condition of the recipient. In this case the recipient is Muḥammad Ḥusayn, "one of the early believers of Shíráz, surnamed 'Vafá' (Fidelity) by Bahá'u'lláh" (*Tablets of Bahá'u'lláh* 179, n1).[8]

The subject of the preamble is firmness in the Covenant. In particular, Bahá'u'lláh warns Vafá that, while he has been "faithful to the Covenant of God and His Testament at a time when all men have violated it and have repudiated the One in Whom they had believed" (*Tablets of Bahá'u'lláh* 181), he must strive to attain a more secure state: "It behoveth thee, however, to exert thine utmost to attain the very essence of fidelity" (181).

Bahá'u'lláh does not leave it to Vafá to figure out what such a condition would entail: "This implieth to be well assured in thy heart and to testify with thy tongue to that whereunto God hath testified for His Own exalted Self . . . " (181). Bahá'u'lláh then gives Vafá general instructions about how this condition of fidelity and certitude can be achieved (e.g., through detachment, through service, through attentiveness to the words that the Manifestation is about to impart to him):

> Hearken thou unto the Words of thy Lord and purify thy heart from every illusion so that the effulgent light of the remembrance of thy Lord may shed its radiance upon it, and it may attain the station of certitude. (183)

8. See Taherzadeh, *Revelation of Bahá'u'lláh* 4:205–13, for further discussion of this tablet and of Vafá, a survivor of the persecutions in Nayríz.

Following the preamble is a discourse in which Bahá'u'lláh responds to specific questions which Vafá has sent to him, stating that the ability to ask God questions is a special bounty for those living in "this Day":

> Know thou moreover that thy letter reached Our presence and We perceived and perused its contents. We noted the questions thou hast asked and will readily answer thee. It behoveth everyone in this Day to ask God that which he desireth, and thy Lord will heed his petition with wondrous and undeniable verses. (183)

The subjects about which Vafá has inquired seem to be four in number: (1) the "subject of the return," (2) the "worlds of God," (3) the "ordinances of God," and (4) "Paradise." Structurally, the essay proceeds to respond somewhat systematically to these questions, though Bahá'u'lláh devotes a greater part of the discussion to explicating the first question, the meaning of "return," especially in reference to "the Day of Resurrection" alluded to throughout the Qur'án. Specifically, Bahá'u'lláh discusses with this faithful believer the test imposed on believers to recognize the new Prophet, and, even more particularly, He cautions Vafá not to fall prey to the same blindness that has afflicted "the people of the Bayán" (the Bábís who failed to recognize Bahá'u'lláh). Bahá'u'lláh states that, had these people truly recognized "the Point of the Bayán" (the Báb), they would have subsequently recognized "Him Whom God shall make manifest" (Bahá'u'lláh):

> Beware, beware lest thou behave like unto the people of the Bayán. For indeed they erred grievously, misguided the people, ignored the Covenant of God and His Testament and joined partners with Him,[9] the One, the Incomparable, the All-Know-

9. The phrase "join partners with God" has a powerfully negative connotation, both in the Bahá'í writings and in the Qur'án, designating one who presumes to assume an equal status with God, as opposed to complete obedience and subservience to His Will.

> ing. Verily they failed to recognize the Point of the Bayán, for had they recognized Him they would not have rejected His manifestation in this luminous and resplendent Being. (*Tablets of Bahá'u'lláh* 185)

The answers to the other questions are succinct, unembellished, and powerfully logical, similar in style to 'Abdu'l-Bahá's tablet to Auguste Forel.

The main departure from this tone and structure is a brief but wrenching digression at the end of His discussion of the "worlds of God" (similar to the same sort of digression in The Seven Valleys).[10] In the midst of His discussion Bahá'u'lláh states, "We have refrained from dwelling upon this theme owing to the sorrow that hath encompassed Us from the actions of them that have been created through Our words . . ." (*Tablets of Bahá'u'lláh* 188).

Obviously, this is a topical allusion the intensity of which is pitched by the subsequent emotionally charged plea, "Where is the one who can help Me and shield Me from the words of these faithless souls?" (188). This unexpected switch from the tone of logical discourse to personal reflection, however, reinforces the theme of this work—the necessity for each believer to achieve certitude independent of others. "Where is the man of insight," He asks, "who will behold the Words of God with his own eyes and rid himself of the opinions and notions of the peoples of the earth?" (188). He then entreats Vafá, "Warn thou the servants of God not to reject that which they do not comprehend" (188), a most intriguing command in the context of a tablet designed to remove doubts by discussing the divine logic underlying the esoteric questions Vafá has asked.

The important inference one might draw from this interruption in the "argument" is that Bahá'u'lláh has deigned to answer the queries

10. In the Valley of Wonderment, Bahá'u'lláh interrupts the narrative tone of the pilgrim's progress to state the following: "In sum, there is no end to the description of these stages, but because of the wrongs inflicted by the peoples of the earth, this Servant is in no mood to continue" (*Seven Valleys* 35).

of those who have demonstrated fidelity and who ask questions that stem from a sincere quest for knowledge or as a further confirmation of their faith. But before one can become worthy of that blessing, one must first have the sort of conviction or faith whereby fidelity is not based on the standards of proof "current amongst men."[11]

c. The Lawḥ-i-Ḥikmat (Tablet of Wisdom)

Another good example of Bahá'u'lláh's use of the expository essay genre or style is the Lawḥ-i-Ḥikmat (Tablet of Wisdom). Like the Kitáb-i-Íqán and the Súriy-i-Vafá, this work is an epistle in response to specific questions put to Bahá'u'lláh by a believer—Áqá Muḥammad-i-Qá'iní, whose title was Nabíl-i-Akbar.[12] More elaborate and lengthy than the Súriy-i-Vafá, the Lawḥ-i-Ḥikmat follows basically the same format of a formal and highly rhetorical preamble to the recipient, followed by a logically structured discussion of Nabíl's question regarding "the beginning of creation."

Because the subject is so encompassing, the essay necessarily moves from topic to topic in what may seem to be a somewhat random or associational process. But as we will see in Chapter 6, the structural links and transitions are clear, and the various specific topics are profoundly weighty and powerful. Indeed, Adib Taherzadeh notes that in "one of His Tablets, Bahá'u'lláh states that in each verse of the Tablet of Ḥikmat an ocean is concealed" (*Revelation of Bahá'u'lláh* 4:39).[13]

Penned in a style which Taherzadeh calls "the language of an intellectual philosopher" (*Revelation of Bahá'u'lláh* 4:34), the Lawḥ-i-Ḥikmat provides succinct resolution to eternal questions. Interspersed

---

11. This phrase appears in numerous tablets of Bahá'u'lláh to designate the learning or opinion which is commonly held by the scholars and divines. The phrase connotes any widely held opinion that establishes as a standard ideas that ignore the existence or influence of a divine reality.

12. An eminent mujtahid who became a Bahá'í after hearing a discourse by Bahá'u'lláh, Nabíl-i-Akbar was later designated by 'Abdu'l-Bahá as a "Hand of the Cause" and by Shoghi Effendi as one of the "Apostles" of Bahá'u'lláh.

13. Taherzadeh cites the source of this statement as *Á<u>th</u>ár-i-Qalam-i-A'lá* 7:113.

among these lofty observations and profound elucidations about ontological questions are personal admonitions to Nabíl:

> [S]peak forth in such wise as to set the hearts of true believers ablaze and cause their bodies to soar. (*Tablets of Bahá'u'lláh* 142)

> Be thou as a throbbing artery, pulsating in the body of the entire creation, that through the heat generated by this motion there may appear that which will quicken the hearts of those who hesitate. (143)

> Teach thou the Cause of God with an utterance which will cause the bushes to be enkindled. . . . (143)

Thus, while the Kitáb-i-Íqán as an essay is largely devoid of personal allusion (either to the recipient or to Bahá'u'lláh as Prophet), these briefer doctrinal essays are less formal and demonstrate how Bahá'u'lláh has lovingly bestowed on these stalwart believers the bounty of special insights, though He then exhorts these same believers to use this special bounty as a means for enlightening others. In short, their fidelity has merited reward, but the foremost reward is the capacity for additional service. Being allowed to serve the Cause of God is itself the highest bounty the Prophet can bestow (a theme to which we will return in our discussion of the Tablet of Aḥmad in Chapter 7).

Certainly, Bahá'u'lláh is well aware that the tablet will be disseminated as part of His Revelation, and in that sense the tablet is for everyone. But the honor of receiving the tablet implies that Nabíl is especially blessed because he will receive the bounty of understanding and applying this wisdom before others have had that opportunity. It also implies that the sincerity and humility of Nabíl's questions, together with the nobility of his character, instigated the Prophet to bestow this knowledge upon all humankind:

> Had it not been for the love I cherish for thee, I would not have uttered a single word of what hath been mentioned. Appreciate the value of this station and preserve it as thou wouldst thine eye

> and be of them that are truly thankful. (*Tablets of Bahá'u'lláh* 149)

In effect, Nabíl's nobility has won for humanity the bounty of this gift of further insight. And the reader is indeed struck by the startling jewels of insight that emerge from this piece:

> Indeed expositions and discourses in explanation of such things [the nature and origin of creation] cause the spirits to be chilled. (142)

> The sages aforetime acquired their knowledge from the Prophets, inasmuch as the latter were the Exponents of divine philosophy and the Revealers of heavenly mysteries. (144–45)

> Thou knowest full well that We perused not the books which men possess and We acquired not the learning current amongst them, and yet whenever We desire to quote the sayings of the learned and of the wise, presently there will appear before the face of thy Lord in the form of a tablet all that which hath appeared in the world and is revealed in the Holy Books and Scriptures. (149)

Of course, there is a clear and logical sequence to the work as a whole. It begins with a discussion of the eternality of creation as an essential and inextricable (though contingent) expression of the Divine Will. It then proceeds to demonstrate that all progress in human understanding derives from the continual outpouring disseminated through the appearance of the Prophets.

Interestingly, just as Bahá'u'lláh indicates that the insight He provides through this tablet is a special bounty, so His ending of the discourse seems to come at the command of the Divine Will:

> When the discourse reached this stage, the dawn of divine mysteries appeared and the light of utterance was quenched. May

> His glory rest upon the people of wisdom as bidden by One Who is the Almighty, the All-Praised. (151)

This passage seems to indicate that Bahá'u'lláh has revealed as much to Nabíl as He is allowed to. In this sense, the passage might well call to mind Persian Hidden Word number 77: "At that moment a voice was heard from the inmost shrine: 'Thus far and no farther.'" According to Shoghi Effendi, this Hidden Word indicates that more information will have to await a future revelation.[14]

4. Gnomic Verse

If these brief doctrinal essays seem to reflect the light of the Kitáb-i-Íqán, it might correctly be observed that other later tablets have a similar relationship to the Kitáb-i-Aqdas. While these tablets partake of the ancient Persian gnomic literary tradition (*andarz* literature), gnomic verse as a generic form seems to exist in many cultures and literary traditions, particularly among cultures in their earlier tribal conditions.

For example, the book of Proverbs in the Bible, purporting to be the wisdom of Solomon, is a collection of spiritual and social gnomes, or axioms. It begins with a brief preamble stating that these proverbs are offered

> To know wisdom and instruction; to perceive the words of understanding; To receive the instruction of wisdom, justice, and judgment, and equity; To give subtlety to the simple, to the young man knowledge and discretion. A wise [man] will hear, and will increase learning; and a man of understanding shall attain unto wise counsels: To understand a proverb, and the interpretation; the words of the wise, and their dark sayings. (Prov. 1:2–6)

It is then followed by the proverbial statements themselves which have no precise order, though they do begin with, "The fear of the Lord [is] the beginning of knowledge."

---

14. See *World Order of Bahá'u'lláh* 59, 116.

This pattern of a preamble about how knowledge is gained (by people sharing wisdom with each other—i.e., consultation), followed by a catalog of axiomatic statements of spiritual insights and moral commands is a generic form clearly similar to what has become called "gnomic" verse in Anglo-Saxon poetry.[15] One of the best of these is a title-less poem from the Exeter Manuscript which follows this formula so precisely, we might suspect some attempt has been made to imitate Proverbs, except that the poem derives from the pre-Christian heritage of this Scandinavian people (i.e., it was only after exposure to Christianity that these people would have had access to the Old Testament):

> Speak to me in plain words,
> Let not thy thoughts be hidden,
> thy inmost wisdom withheld—
>
> I will not reveal my secrets
> if you keep from me your mind's craft.
> Sage ones should share their insight.
>
> First let us praise God well
> since He loaned us this life and brief joy;
> and he will remind us of these gifts.[16]

Bahá'u'lláh uses a similar formula with those tablets we might classify as belonging to this gnomic, or *andarz,* tradition. Many of these have a preamble followed by a catalog of admonitions, insights, laws, and ordinances. Interestingly, Bahá'u'lláh's Aṣl-i-Kullu'l-Khayr (Words of Wisdom), though it has no preamble, states in the second verse, "The essence of wisdom is the fear of God, the dread of His scourge and punishment, and the apprehension of His justice and de-

---

15. Four such poems survive, all essentially the same in structure and approximately the same length—about sixty-five lines.

16. These stanzas are from my poem "The Witan Consults on Stoicism," published in *A Sense of History* 32. It is based upon a translation of an Anglo-Saxon poem appearing as folios 88b–89a in *The Exeter Book* manuscript.

cree" (*Tablets of Bahá'u'lláh* 153), a verse quite similar to the beginning passages in both Proverbs and in the Anglo-Saxon gnomic poem from the Exeter Book.

But our purpose here is not to set forth some exacting analysis of this genre or to assert that it is some inevitable cultural phenomenon. Nevertheless, it is interesting to note that Bahá'u'lláh employs what may well be a traditional form to help elucidate and reiterate axiomatic principles of law already revealed in the Kitáb-i-Aqdas, a fact that the Guardian is careful to point out in a discussion of these same tablets:

> The formulation by Bahá'u'lláh, in His Kitáb-i-Aqdas, of the fundamental laws of His Dispensation was followed, as His Mission drew to a close, by the enunciation of certain precepts and principles which lie at the very core of His Faith, by the reaffirmation of truths He had previously proclaimed, by the elaboration and elucidation of some of the laws He had already laid down, by the revelation of further prophecies and warnings, and by the establishment of subsidiary ordinances designed to supplement the provisions of His Most Holy Book. These were recorded in unnumbered Tablets, which He continued to reveal until the last days of His earthly life, among which the "Ishráqát" (Splendors), the "Bishárát" (Glad Tidings), the "Ṭarázát" (Ornaments), the "Tajallíyát" (Effulgences), the "Kalimát-i-Firdawsíyyih" (Words of Paradise), the "Lawḥ-i-Aqdas" (Most Holy Tablet), the "Lawḥ-i-Dunyá" (Tablet of the World), the "Lawḥ-i-Maqṣúd" (Tablet of Maqṣúd), are the most noteworthy. These Tablets—mighty and final effusions of His indefatigable pen—must rank among the choicest fruits which His mind has yielded, and mark the consummation of His forty-year-long ministry.
>
> (*God Passes By* 216)

While most of the eight tablets cited here by Shoghi Effendi follow this gnomic pattern (a preamble followed by a catalog or list of axioms), there is substantial variety among these works. The Aṣl-i-Kullu'l-Khayr (Words of Wisdom) has no preamble; the preamble for the other tablets is sometimes brief, as in the Bishárát (Glad-Tidings); sometimes a couple of pages, as in the Ṭarázát (Ornaments), as in the Tajallíyát (Effulgences), and in the Lawḥ-i-Maqṣúd (Tablet of Maqṣúd); and sometimes a long discourse, as in the Kalimát-i-Firdawsíyyih (Words of Paradise) and the Lawḥ-i-Dunyá (Tablet of the World). There is also great variation in the number of items in each catalog: there are fifteen "Glad-Tidings" in the Bis͟hárát, six "Ornaments" in the Ṭarázát, four "Effulgences" in the Tajallíyát, eleven "Leaves" in the Kalimát-i-Firdawsíyyih, five "fundamental principles for the administration of the affairs of men" in the Lawḥ-i-Dunyá, nine "Splendors" in the Is͟hráqát, twenty-two verses in the Aṣl-i-Kullu'l-K͟hayr,[17] and approximately sixteen divisions in the Lawḥ-i-Maqṣúd.[18]

We also find variety in length, in style, and in subject among these cataloged utterances. Some are brief statements of specific laws or principles. Others catalog definitions of human virtues. Some are more lengthy and homiletic, discussing various aspects of divine wisdom or theological doctrine. For the most part, however, each catalog is fairly consistent in theme within the particular tablet. For example, Bahá'u'lláh prefaces the list of five principles in the Lawḥ-i-Dunyá with the statement:

> Whilst in the Prison of 'Akká, We revealed in the Crimson Book [the Kitáb-i-'Ahd] that which is conducive to the advancement of mankind and to the reconstruction of the world. The utterances set forth therein by the Pen of the Lord of creation include the following which constitute the fundamental principles for the administration of the affairs of men. . . . (*Tablets of Bahá'u'lláh* 89)

Most of these maxims, aphorisms, or dictums focus on human virtue, on spiritual attributes, or on particular laws that are conducive to our

17. These are more or less autonomous "words of wisdom"; they are variously designated as the "source" of something, the "essence" of something, or as the true meaning of something (i.e., "true remembrance," "true reliance," or "true loss").

18. Most of these begin with "The Great Being saith."

edification; therefore, the wisdom in grouping them in these tablets might be mnemonic (i.e., to help the believer associate them with each other in a particular context so that they might be more easily remembered).

One final observation we might note in our brief assessment of this genre concerns the various recipients of these eight tablets. The Bis͟hárát is to the "people of the earth" (21), the Ṭarázát to "thou who hast quaffed the wine of Mine utterance" (34),[19] the Tajallíyát to Ustád 'Alí-Akbar (48),[20] the Kalimát-i-Firdawsíyyih to Ḥájí Mírzá Ḥaydar-'Alí,[21] the Lawḥ-i-Dunyá to the "people of God" (88), the Is͟hráqát to Jalíl-i-K͟hu'í,[22] the Lawḥ-i-Maqṣúd to Mírzá Maqṣúd,[23] and the Aṣl-i-Kullu'l-K͟hayr to those who would be "thankful unto the Lord, Thy God, and glory therein amidst all peoples" (157)—presumably the faithful believers.

The point is that the tone of these works seems to imply that the recipient is a believer, has familiarity with some of the essential teachings of the Faith, and is aspiring to be a faithful believer. And since these are revealed after the Kitáb-i-Aqdas, they seem to be reminders, tokens, or somewhat more expansive statements of what has already been revealed. The tone of these pieces, therefore, is often mild, encouraging, comforting, as if Bahá'u'lláh is bestowing a boon on those who have demonstrated fidelity and are thus ready for additional insight.

---

19. The final pages of this piece constitute a postscript to "the people of the Bayán" and to Mírzá Hádí Dawlat-Ábádí.

20. "He designed the Mas͟hriqu'l-Ad͟hkár of 'Is͟hqábád, and his design was approved by 'Abdu'l-Bahá. Ustád 'Alí-Akbar offered up his life as a martyr in Yazd in 1903" (*Tablets of Bahá'u'lláh* 48).

21. An "outstanding Persian Bahá'í teacher and author" (*Tablets of Bahá'u'lláh* 57, n1) who later became known by the Western pilgrims as "the Angel of Mount Carmel."

22. An early believer in Ád͟hirbáyján, Persia.

23. An early believer who lived in Damascus and Jerusalem at the time the tablet was revealed.

5. Epistolary

Perhaps the majority of Bahá'u'lláh's works are addressed to particular individuals. As we have noted, many respond to particular questions or groups of questions asked of the Prophet. Bahá'u'lláh's response to these questions serves to remind us that it is not only permissible to ask information from Bahá'u'lláh; it is incumbent on us to inquire if we are to advance in our understanding.

In this broad sense, the majority of Bahá'u'lláh's writings could be considered as letters of a sort. But among the tablets addressed to individuals are those that take a distinct form as an epistle. And while the art of letter writing is rapidly disappearing in the modern age, epistolary style has a long-standing history as an art form, and it has been a common practice to publish the collected letters of prominent individuals. In fact, the epistolary novel (a novel comprised of fictional letters by the various characters) became a popular genre with such eighteenth-century English writers as Samuel Richardson and Tobias Smollett. It has been less frequently employed in modern literature except by such writers as John O'Hara and John Barth. What we discover as we consider the vast array of epistles penned by Bahá'u'lláh is that it can be a useful exercise to group them together according to recipient.

A. Epistles to Believers

We have already mentioned several of the tablets and epistles to particular followers: the Tablet of Aḥmad, the Súriy-i-Vafá, and the Lawḥ-i-Ḥikmat. Among the most obvious components in these and similar tablets are (1) a praise of the individual believer's potential, (2) a caution against falling prey to pride, cynicism, or the thousand tests that would inevitably beset them, and (3) some specific charge or duty they must now fulfill as a result of being favored with a tablet from the Prophet of God. For example, part of Bahá'u'lláh's familiar charge to Aḥmad in the Tablet of Aḥmad is the following:

> O Aḥmad! Forget not My bounties while I am absent. Remember My days during thy days, and My distress and banishment in this remote prison. And be thou so steadfast in My love that thy

> heart shall not waver, even if the swords of the enemies rain blows upon thee and all the heavens and the earth arise against thee.
>
> Be thou as a flame of fire to My enemies and a river of life eternal to My loved ones, and be not of those who doubt.
>
> (*Bahá'í Prayers* 211)

In the Lawḥ-i-Ḥikmat He exhorts Nabíl:

> O My Nabíl! Let nothing grieve thee, rather rejoice with exceeding gladness inasmuch as I have mentioned thy name, have turned My heart and My face towards thee and have conversed with thee through this irrefutable and weighty exposition. Ponder in thy heart upon the tribulations I have sustained, the imprisonment and the captivity I have endured, the sufferings that have befallen Me and the accusations that the people have levelled against Me. Behold, they are truly wrapped in a grievous veil. (*Tablets of Bahá'u'lláh* 151)

Bahá'u'lláh praises Vafá in the Súriy-i-Vafá: "Blessed art thou O Vafá, inasmuch as thou hast been faithful to the Covenant of God. . . ." But then He cautions him to achieve even more, "to exert thine utmost to attain the very essence of fidelity" (181).

B. Epistles to the Kings and Rulers

The epistles to the kings and rulers vary in style and content according to the character of the recipient, something that demonstrates Bahá'u'lláh's remarkable sensitivity to the personality of the individual recipients of these epistles. Begun in Adrianople after Bahá'u'lláh had proclaimed His identity to the Bábí community, these epistles formally and systematically proclaim to the world's religious and political leaders the advent and purpose of God's new Revelation. It is because of Bahá'u'lláh's revelation of these epistles that the house from which they issued forth was titled "the house of Amru'lláh" (the house of "God's command").[24]

---

24. See Shoghi Effendi, *God Passes By* 162.

The nature and power of these epistles is astounding; their very existence should inspire our wonder. What reaction did Bahá'u'lláh expect from the mighty and the powerful to whom He addressed these letters? Did He expect them to recognize His authority and accede to His advice? Did the leaders and rulers have any clear proof, or even a reasonable clue that Bahá'u'lláh was Someone to Whom they should pay careful attention? What effect did these letters have on the lives of these individuals?[25]

The first thing we might notice is that these epistles are tonally distinct from one another; these are not form letters. However, there are some common ingredients among them. Each begins with a clear indication that the writer speaks with divine authority:

> Thus have the mighty verses of Thy Lord been again sent down unto thee. . . . [second epistle to Napoleon III] (*Proclamation of Bahá'u'lláh* 17)

> O Czar of Russia! Incline thine ear unto the voice of God. . . . (27)

> O Queen in London! Incline thine ear unto the voice of thy Lord, the Lord of all mankind . . . (33)

> O King of Berlin! Give ear unto the Voice calling from this manifest Temple: Verily, there is none other God but Me, the Everlasting, the Peerless . . . (39)

> Hearken ye, O Rulers of America and the Presidents of the Republics therein, unto that which the Dove is warbling on the Branch of Eternity: There is none other God but Me . . . (63)

25. Excerpts from some of the more important of these epistles appear in *The Proclamation of Bahá'u'lláh;* a discussion of what happened to these figures after they received these epistles and what happened as a result of their rejection of Bahá'u'lláh's advice is found in Shoghi Effendi, *The Promised Day Is Come.*

One noteworthy distinction we can observe in the style among these epistles is that Bahá'u'lláh seems more indirect and gentle with the two rulers who had been the most cruel to Him personally and the most inveterate enemies of the Faith in general: the Sháh of Persia (Náṣiri'd-Dín Sháh) and the head of the Ottoman Empire (Sulṭán 'Abdu'l-'Azíz). In both instances we might assume that this mild tone is due to their familiarity with Bahá'u'lláh as a prisoner and as a Bábí. Consequently, Bahá'u'lláh must now present Himself in a new light—as having acquired a new status. Therefore, He carefully explains to them why He now possesses an authority quite beyond their own. For example, He first reminds the Sulṭán that He (Bahá'u'lláh) did not seize the opportunity to present Himself to the Sulṭán to ask for assistance (as was the custom):[26]

> Hearken, O King, to the speech of Him that speaketh the truth, Him that doth not ask thee to recompense Him with the things God hath chosen to bestow upon thee, Him Who unerringly treadeth the straight Path. (*Proclamation* 47)

And to Náṣiri'd-Dín Sháh Bahá'u'lláh explains that the authority with which He speaks is the authority of God:

> O King! I was but a man like others, asleep upon My couch, when lo, the breezes of the All-Glorious were wafted over Me, and taught Me the knowledge of all that hath been. This thing is not from Me, but from One Who is Almighty and All-Knowing. (*Proclamation* 57)

Another common ingredient among these epistles is some specific personal sign or evidence that Bahá'u'lláh is not an ordinary person. To Napoleon He reveals His awareness that the French monarch had cast behind his back "the Book of God" when it was sent to him

26. See Shoghi Effendi, *God Passes By* 158 ff.

"by Him Who is the Almighty, the all-Wise" (*Proclamation* 20). Even more mysteriously, this exiled Prisoner from a distant land quotes words that Napoleon had uttered in private to the Czar of Russia:

> O King! We heard the words thou didst utter in answer to the Czar of Russia, concerning the decision made regarding the war (Crimean War). Thy Lord, verily, knoweth, is informed of all. Thou didst say: "I lay asleep upon my couch, when the cry of the oppressed, who were drowned in the Black Sea, wakened me." This is what we heard thee say, and, verily, thy Lord is witness unto what I say. (*Proclamation* 19–20)

To Czar Alexander II, Bahá'u'lláh is more gentle in tone, noting that when He (Bahá'u'lláh) was imprisoned in the Síyáh-Chál, "one of thy ministers extended Me his aid"(*Proclamation* 27).[27] Therefore Bahá'u'lláh's proof to this monarch relates to the Czar's piety: "We, verily, have heard the thing for which thou didst supplicate thy Lord, whilst secretly communing with Him"(*Proclamation* 27). Incredibly, Bahá'u'lláh goes on to remind the Czar that the prayer was answered.

Bahá'u'lláh lets Emperor Francis Joseph know that He is aware of the emperor's pilgrimage to Jerusalem and explains to him the irony of his visit:

> O Emperor of Austria! He who is the Dayspring of God's Light dwelt in the prison of 'Akká, at the time when thou didst set forth to visit the Aqṣá Mosque (Jerusalem). Thou passed Him by, and inquired not about Him, by Whom every house is exalted, and every lofty gate unlocked. (*Proclamation* 43)

Perhaps the most potent opening in these epistles is in Bahá'u'lláh's tablet to Pope Pius IX. Bahá'u'lláh alludes to Christian prophecy regarding the return of Christ, stating that the Second Coming has occurred, and asserting that the Pope is in danger of committing the

27. See Shoghi Effendi, *God Passes By* 104.

same sin at this, the Second Coming, as did the Pharisees and the Sanhedrin at the first coming of Christ:

> He, verily, hath again come down from Heaven even as He came down from it the first time. Beware that thou dispute not with Him even as the Pharisees disputed with Him (Jesus) without a clear token or proof. (*Proclamation* 83)

Bahá'u'lláh continues in this vein, pointing out the irony that Christ lived among the poor while the Pope lives "in palaces," and reminding the Pope of the parallels between this advent and that of Christ.

There are many other common ingredients that characterize these epistles to the mighty rulers of the earth. To some Bahá'u'lláh gives specific guidance. For example, He is frank in His assessment of their leadership. He compliments Queen Victoria on the abolition of slave trade and for having "entrusted the reins of counsel into the hands of the representatives of the people" (*Proclamation* 34), and yet He cautions her that, however fine her actions may be, "Man's actions are acceptable after his having recognized (the Manifestation),"[28] and He reveals a special prayer for her to say.

For some He makes dire predictions and prophecies. He tells Napoleon III, "thy kingdom shall be thrown into confusion, and thine empire shall pass from thine hands, as a punishment for that which thou hast wrought. Then wilt thou know how thou hast plainly erred" (*Proclamation* 20–21). He forewarns Kaiser Wilhelm I that Germany, though now in prosperity, will twice experience warfare and carnage:

> Be warned, be of them who reflect. . . . O banks of the Rhine! We have seen you covered with gore, inasmuch as the swords of

---

28. Here Bahá'u'lláh is alluding to the principle He enunciated in the preamble to the Kitáb-i-Aqdas that it is incumbent upon all to (1) recognize the Prophet and (2) follow His commands, and that neither of these actions is "acceptable without the other" (Kitáb-i-Aqdas ¶1).

> retribution were drawn against you; and you shall have another turn. And We hear the lamentations of Berlin, though she be today in conspicuous glory. (*Proclamation* 39)

He repeatedly cautions 'Abdu'l-'Azíz "not to entrust thine affairs of state entirely into another's hands. None can discharge thy functions better than thine own self" (*Proclamation* 51).

There are many other observations we might make about Bahá'u'lláh's announcement of His station to these historical figures. Among the most interesting studies of these epistles is Shoghi Effendi's discussion of the subsequent history of these figures in *The Promised Day Is Come*. Especially enlightening is Shoghi Effendi's discussion of the specific predictions made by Bahá'u'lláh in these tablets and of how these prophecies become fulfilled in the lives of these recipients.

c. Epistles to Adversaries of the Bahá'í Religion

We have already alluded to the epistles written to leaders who were enemies of the Faith of Bahá'u'lláh. These Bahá'u'lláh addresses with respect and decorum, though with fearlessness and undaunted authority. He instructs them, but not with a tone of derision or condescension such as that with which He addresses Napoleon III. But to those individuals who are personally responsible for the most severe attacks on the Bábís and Bahá'ís, Bahá'u'lláh writes epistles with a tone of astounding majesty and condemnation. In these instances, the voice of the Prophet resounds with lightning-like flashes of rhetorical power, with the tone of omnipotent authority and final judgment. Perhaps more to the point, Bahá'u'lláh explains to the recipients of these epistles that it is they who need Him, not the other way around. He announces that if they truly understood His station, they would fall prostrate at His feet and beg forgiveness.

And yet, while He admonishes them to do precisely that (to humble themselves before God)—and in some cases He goes so far as to reveal prayers for them to recite to accomplish this—He makes it clear that He is perfectly willing to leave them to their own devices because the Will of God will be done regardless. Nothing they can do will deter that process.

One of the best examples of this tone is the Lawḥ-i-Burhán (Tablet of the Proof). The epistle is addressed to S͟hayk͟h Muḥammad Báqir, whom Bahá'u'lláh denounced and stigmatized as the "Wolf" for having pronounced the death sentence on two famous brothers, Mírzá Muḥammad-Ḥasan and Mírzá Muḥammad-Ḥusayn.[29] Considering the title of this work, we might expect this tablet to be a doctrinal essay, a logically organized argument to vindicate Bahá'u'lláh's claims. Instead, this epistle is a highly rhetorical harangue, unreservedly severe in tone and devastating in its impact.

The allusion to "proof," we discover in the second paragraph, concerns the fact that these brothers, these emblems of devotion and purity, were slaughtered without proof, as were the Prophets of old: "Indeed thou hast produced, in this day, the same proofs which the foolish divines advanced in that age" (*Tablets of Bahá'u'lláh* 206). The ironic implication is that the cleric does indeed have the "proof" of who these martyrs really were and what their cause truly represented— the cleric's power will come to naught and he will be made to lament eternally his actions: "Thou hast torn in pieces a remnant of the Prophet Himself, and imagined that thou hadst helped the Faith of God" (*Tablets of Bahá'u'lláh* 206).

While there is substantive discussion in this epistle, the dominant impact results from Bahá'u'lláh's rhetorical style and wilting tone, all of which convey one simple idea—if S͟hayk͟h Muḥammad Báqir had the faintest appreciation of the depravity he had exhibited, "thou wouldst have cast thyself into the fire, or abandoned thine home and fled into the mountains, or wouldst have groaned until thou hadst returned unto the place destined for thee by Him Who is the Lord of strength and of might" (*Tablets of Bahá'u'lláh* 205).

This is truly an amazing work, certainly among the most potent examples of the Prophet permitting us momentarily to hear the full power of His voice and to glimpse the full authority of His station.

---

29. Shoghi Effendi in *God Passes By* describes these brothers as "the 'twin shining lights,' respectively surnamed 'Sulṭánu's͟h-S͟huhadá' (King of Martyrs) and 'Maḥbúbu's͟h-S͟huhadá' (Beloved of Martyrs), who were celebrated for their generosity, trustworthiness, kindliness and piety" (200).

The terms he uses to stigmatize this rapacious "wolf" would be enough to cause the limbs of any sensate human being to tremble: "O thou who art even as nothing!" (*Tablets of Bahá'u'lláh* 205); "O thou who hast gone astray!" (207); "O foolish one!" (207); "O thou who hast turned away from God!" (209). Instead of producing proof of His own station, Bahá'u'lláh assumes it and demands that Shaykh Muḥammad Báqir produce proof that he was following a divine calling and not the "promptings of thine own desires": "Produce thou a sign, if thou art one of the truthful" (207).

What is implicit in this statement (as the recipient is fully aware) is that the martyrdom of the two brothers was instigated by "the She-Serpent" (the Imám-Jum'ih of Iṣfahán) because he owed the brothers money. The last pages of the epistle are devoted to enunciating the judgment that will befall this "perverse hater":

> Gainsayest thou the signs of thy Lord which no sooner were sent down from the heaven of His Cause than all the books of the world bowed down before them? Meditate, that thou mayest be made aware of thine act, O heedless outcast! Ere long will the breaths of chastisement seize thee, as they seized others before thee. (*Tablets of Bahá'u'lláh* 214)

Bahá'u'lláh concludes this epistle with a simple but starkly powerful statement of an incontrovertible verity:

> Thus have We adorned the heaven of Our Tablet with the suns of Our words. Blessed the man that hath attained thereunto and been illumined with their light, and woe betide such as have turned aside, and denied Him, and strayed far from Him. (216)

6. Allegory

As defined by *A Handbook to Literature,* allegory is a "form of extended metaphor in which objects, persons, and actions in a narrative, either in prose or verse, are equated with meanings that lie outside the narrative itself" (10). Stated more simply, allegory "represents one thing in the guise of another," most often an abstraction in the "guise" of a "concrete image" (10).

The main distinction between allegory and other uses of symbol and/or metaphor is that the writer of allegory most often creates an object or character that functions to represent one clear meaning (as opposed to the more ambiguous possibilities of symbolism and metaphor). For example, in the famous allegorical medieval morality play *Everyman,* the central character Everyman represents all humankind, as his name implies. In the same play the character Good Deeds clearly represents the good deeds that Everyman has performed. We need not wonder what these characters and their actions represent because there is usually little ambiguity intended in this one-to-one relationship between the literal narrative and the abstractions represented, even though it is not always a simple task to determine what that abstraction is. Furthermore, allegory most often can be translated into numerous layers of increasingly more expansive meanings or applications. For example, in Edmund Spenser's famous *Faerie Queene,* the character of Una may represent (1) truth, (2) the Church of England, or (3) the quality of belief available to one who has freed himself from sin.

All of Christ's parables are allegories, as is the Biblical story of Adam and Eve—although it might be hard to find two students of religion who will agree on exactly what this allegory means.[30] This ambiguity does not disqualify a work as allegory, nor should the lack of a precise or obvious meaning be viewed as a defect. Nevertheless, allegory is most often less ambiguous than symbol or metaphor because the writer translates an entire system of abstract ideas into a narrative framework (e.g., Dante's *Comedia Divina,* Spenser's *The Faerie Queene,* or Bunyan's *Pilgrim's Progress).*

a. The Seven Valleys

We have already discussed The Seven Valleys as an example of a mystical treatise, but we can hardly discuss Bahá'u'lláh's use of allegory without beginning with this obvious use of an allegorical structuring de-

30. In Hatcher, *Arc of Ascent* 35–43, Adam is interpreted as the physical aspect of the human reality, and Eve as the soul or spiritual aspect.

vice. Each of the seven main divisions of The Seven Valleys represents a successive stage in the process of individual or collective spiritual development; spiritual progress is portrayed as a journey through seven successive valleys.

In allegorical terms, there is a one-to-one relationship between each valley and a more-or-less definable stage of spiritual progress: (1) search, (2) love, (3) knowledge, (4) unity, (5) contentment, (6) wonderment, and (7) true poverty and absolute nothingness. As we read through the work, we may quickly forget this framework as we become immersed in Bahá'u'lláh's complex presentations of the challenges and rewards each valley presents to us, but the allegorical arrangement always exercises its abiding influence on unifying the theme of work as a whole.

In some places the allegory is obvious and unavoidable: we ride through the Valley of Search on the steed of Patience; we ride through the Valley of Love on the steed of Pain. But because there are so many layers of imagery in this work, we are often oblivious to the simple image of spiritual ascent as an arduous journey over sometimes treacherous terrain.

Within the work are several parables which are allegorical in nature. In the Valley of Search Bahá'u'lláh presents the story of the "Majnún of Love" searching for his beloved Laylí, a narrative calculated to portray the "standard" or quality of the seeker after truth—the seeker should be enthralled, resolute, and relentless. Likewise, in the Valley of Knowledge Bahá'u'lláh narrates the story of the lover being pursued in the night by what he thinks to be his angel of death, a narrative which has as its primary objective the explanation of true knowledge as the capacity to see the end in the beginning—i.e., to understand divine justice underlying the ostensible injustices of this life.

b. The Tablet of the Holy Mariner

As we have already discussed in Chapter 3 on historical criticism, the Tablet of the Holy Mariner foreshadows in allegorical terms the trials that would beset Bahá'u'lláh in Adrianople at the hands of Mírzá Yaḥyá, a rebellion that would "precipitate the gravest crisis in the history of the

Faith" (Shoghi Effendi, *God Passes By* 148).[31] While Shoghi Effendi's statement about the overall significance of the Tablet of the Holy Mariner may give us a general sense of what the work is about, we are still left with the problem of figuring out *how* the tablet conveys this meaning through allegory.

Here, too, Shoghi Effendi gives us a head start. He explains that the figure of "The Holy Mariner is a reference to Bahá'u'lláh Himself and the Ark mentioned in that Tablet is the Ark of His Cause" (qtd. in *Lights of Guidance* 483–84). Shoghi Effendi also notes that "the Youth" in this same tablet "means Bahá'u'lláh, Himself" (*Unfolding Destiny* 462).

Needless to say, these authoritative clues to interpretation of the allegorical narrative of the Tablet of the Holy Mariner get us started, but as with any allegory, much remains to be done by way of translating the entire narrative story into its spiritual meaning. For example, if the Holy Mariner is Bahá'u'lláh and He is commanded to "Bid thine ark of eternity appear before the Celestial Concourse," we might infer this to mean that the Divine Will is signaling the Prophet that it is now time for Him to reveal His Faith, to "launch it upon the ancient sea" (*Bahá'í Prayers* 221), and then to "teach them that are within the ark that which we have taught thee behind the mystic veil" (223)—to share with the believers the knowledge that Prophet has learned in His preexistent state in the spiritual world.

Certainly, the tumult of the seas might represent the forthcoming crisis that the machinations of Mírzá Yaḥyá would bring about in his vain attempt to disrupt the progress of the Bahá'í Faith. It might further allude to the deterioration of society as a whole, much as the story of Noah is also an allegorical narrative employing many of these same figurative devices to depict the difficulties the Prophet faces in trying to teach a perverse and stubborn humanity.[32] Certainly, in both

31. Shoghi Effendi observes the following about the Tablet of the Holy Mariner: "Its main significance lies in the fact that in it Bahá'u'lláh clearly foreshadows the grave happenings, which eventually led to the defection of Ṣubḥ-i-Azal, and to the schism which the latter thought to create within the ranks of the faithful" (qtd. in *Lights of Guidance* 484).

32. Shoghi Effendi states, "The Ark and the Flood we believe are sym-

allegories the ark itself represents the Prophet's Covenant, which is able to protect all the faithful believers when trials afflict them.

However, parts of the story are quite challenging. In dreamlike imagery the occupants of the vessel "passed the grades of worldly limitations" (*Bahá'í Prayers* 223), but in their hubris they desire "to ascend unto that state which the Lord hath ordained to be above their stations" (223). As a result, the "guardian angels" are commanded to "return them to their abode in the world below" (224).

The allegory thus shifts around on us, much as in a dream, even though the overall meaning is fairly clear. Having become intoxicated with the serenity of the ark and the presence of the Mariner, some aspire to greater heights, to stations of power. In particular, of course, this seems to be an allusion to Mírzá Yaḥya as he becomes tempted by Siyyid Muḥammad of Iṣfahán to try to usurp the authority of Bahá'-u'lláh.

At this point in the allegorical narrative, the perspective shifts to the heavenly concourse and to a "maid of heaven" (*Bahá'í Prayers* 224) who looks out "from her exalted chamber" (224) and summons "one maiden from her handmaidens" (225) to "descend into space" (225) to reconnoiter in order to assess the fidelity of "these idle claimants" (229). She reports that the "Youth hath remained alone and forlorn in the land of exile in the hands of the ungodly" (228). When the heavenly concourse understand what has transpired "they bared their heads, rent their garments asunder, beat upon their faces" (229).

This abrupt and unresolved ending to the tablet no doubt had a most devastating effect on the hearts and minds of the believers assembled outside Bahá'u'lláh's tent as they listened to Mírzá Áqá Ján recite the just-revealed tablet. Most instantly understood that the interlude of growth, development, and felicity in the presence of the Blessed Beauty was about to come to a sudden end.

---

bolical" (qtd. in *Lights of Guidance* 508). Accordingly, we might presume that the pairs of animals brought on board the ark symbolize the male and female aspects of various human attributes, inasmuch as it was a commonplace in ancient poetic traditions to have animals symbolize human qualities. See, for example, the Anglo-Saxon *Physiologus* or the Middle English *Bestiary* (c. 1240) adopted from an eleventh-century Latin *Physiologus* by Theobaldus.

c. The Súratu'l-Haykal

Another excellent example of allegory that can be found in the art of Bahá'u'lláh is demonstrated by the allegorical framework of the document titled Súratu'l-Haykal (meaning, "Súrih of the Temple"). This work is designated by Shoghi Effendi as "one of the most challenging works of Bahá'u'lláh" (*World Order of Bahá'u'lláh* 109). The tablet, which is some sixty-three pages in length, focuses on the allegorical act of fashioning a temple. As we noted in Chapter 2, this allegory works on a number of different levels. On the simplest level, the temple represents the physical body of the Prophet, the human persona through whom Bahá'u'lláh will communicate to humankind. In the tablet, the divine concourse at the behest of the Divine Will fashions the temple by endowing it with the powers and faculties that the Prophet will need to carry out His mission.

> O Thou, the Eye of this Temple! Look not to the heaven and what is therein, nor to the earth and whatsoever is thereupon; verily We created Thee for My Beauty—Lo, this is It! (*Surat 'ul Hykl* 16)

> O Thou, the Tongue of this Temple, Verily We have created Thee in My Name, the Merciful, and taught Thee that which was stored in el-Beyan (the revelation), and made Thee to speak for the sake of My great commemoration in the contingent world. . . . (17)

> O Heart of this Temple! Verily we have made Thee the rising place of My science and the manifestation of My wisdom to whomsoever is in heaven and earth. (43)

As we attempt to interpret these allegories, then, we begin to appreciate how demanding and yet richly rewarding this poetic process can be for the creative reader, and we will examine it further in Chapter 5. Allegory can work on so many levels and can compress so much meaning into a simple narrative framework, that we readily appreciate why the Prophet (or any good teacher) would find allegory an amazingly effective tool for teaching concepts of spirituality. We also discover how allegory is particularly useful in alluding prophetically to forthcoming events.

7. Supplications and Meditations

In Chapter 2, which examined the narrative perspective, we discussed how Bahá'u'lláh has subtly demonstrated a creative use of persona in the body of His prayers and meditative writings. As we noted in that discussion, we might not normally think of prayers as a form of creative writing—we normally accept them as thoroughly utilitarian devices, not works of art to be analyzed. If we feel sick, we pray a prayer for healing. If a loved one dies, we recite prayers for the departed. If we feel gratitude, we praise God. In short, we usually think of the prayers of Bahá'u'lláh as intimate communication between ourselves and God. Consequently, the figure of Bahá'u'lláh is purposefully transparent in this arrangement: the voice and perspective are our own.

Almost as actors in a play, we read our lines and discover ourselves as suppliants praising God in a language we could not have invented, however much we might have longed to have such literary powers. And as we vocalize our innermost thoughts, we hear our human voices enunciating amazing things about ourselves, truths we may not have realized until the words emerge from our lips: that we have sinned and yet are forgiven, that we have been awakened from the sleep of heedlessness, that we have recognized the Manifestation of God and will be rewarded for that recognition.

Of course, nowhere are we deterred from using our own words, but we soon discover that the prayers Bahá'u'lláh has provided for us invariably convey our thoughts and feelings, our hopes and desires, our fears and longings more profoundly than any we ourselves might devise. We also discover another benefit by using the prayers revealed for us. Because we do not have to ponder what words might best communicate our thoughts, we are freed to meditate on the ideas contained in the verses and bask in this nearness. The activity of prayer is thus transformed from a cerebral act of contemplation to a spiritual experience of meditation and reunion.

We may not be aware that we are being trained in this process, yet we do not feel coerced or catechized—we experience comfort, ease, and, in time, transformation. We soon realize that the prayers of Bahá'-u'lláh have a power that surpasses anything we might have conceived, that the Prophet has a wisdom about us that exceeds our own understanding ("Thou art more friend to me than I am to myself").

A. Prayers for General Use

Certainly the most important prayers for daily use are the three obligatory prayers. Ordained by Bahá'u'lláh in the Kitáb-i-Aqdas, these prayers are described by Shoghi Effendi as having "a special potency and significance" (qtd. in *Directives from the Guardian* 55).

The three obligatory prayers vary in style and length, but there is no variation among them in rank or degree (i.e., the longer prayer is not portrayed as having any greater potency or effectiveness than the shorter prayer). One might understandably wonder, then, why Bahá'-u'lláh bothered to reveal three prayers when one would seem sufficient.

Here again we discover the wisdom in Bahá'u'lláh's use of variable literary forms to minister to the needs of the various personalities, cultural orientations, and religious practices of the peoples of the world. The short prayer, though devoid of ritual movements and required only once during the day, is not the obvious choice of all. The medium prayer (with its symbolic washing of hands and face, standing and sitting) and the long prayer (also with symbolic gestures and movements) are widely used by Bahá'ís even though such usage is freely chosen. For the Bahá'í from a Muslim background who is accustomed to praying five times a day, a single short prayer might not seem sufficient. Likewise, for those approaching the Bahá'í Faith from a background of formal ritualistic worship, the symbolic gestures might feel familiar and comforting.

The generality of prayers by Bahá'u'lláh have no special requirements regarding how they should be said and are thus easily adapted to various cultures and modes of worship; one may chant or intone the prayers, recite or sing them. What distinguishes the prayers Bahá'u'lláh has revealed for daily or general use are the creative exercises that often lie slightly concealed within these supplications.

For example, when we get up in the morning, we may recite a prayer for the morning. And yet, if we study the prayer, it may have very little to do with a specific period of the day. Instead, the early part of the day may be an allusion to the early part of the Dispensation of Bahá'u'lláh. Thus, as a follower of the new Prophet in this early period of "His Day," the believer is expressing gratitude for having been allowed to become awakened from spiritual heedlessness, for having been blessed with the capacity to recognize the "Daystar" of illumination, the new Manifestation, and for holding fast to the Cord of His Covenant:

> I give praise to Thee, O my God, that Thou hast awakened me out of my sleep, and brought me forth after my disappearance, and raised me up from my slumber. I have wakened this morning with my face set toward the splendors of the Daystar of Thy Revelation, through Which the heavens of Thy power and Thy majesty have been illumined, acknowledging Thy signs, believing in Thy Book, and holding fast unto Thy Cord. (*Bahá'í Prayers* 118)

In other words, few of the prayers of Bahá'u'lláh are as simple as they at first seem. As with the rest of Bahá'u'lláh's art, we must become creative readers of these prayers if we are to reap their full benefit.

b. Occasional Prayers

In addition to the great variety of prayers Bahá'u'lláh revealed for general use are prayers which Bahá'u'lláh revealed for particular occasions. This category might include prayers commemorating events on the Bahá'í calendar, such as prayers for the Intercalary Days, prayers for the Fast, and the prayer for Naw-Rúz. This category might also include the "Tablet of Visitation" (the prayer to be said on the occasion of visits to the Shrines of Bahá'u'lláh and the Báb),[33] as well as the Prayer for Marriage and the Prayer for the Dead.

---

33. These are also frequently used in commemorating the anniversaries associated with Bahá'u'lláh and the Báb.

There are various other particular prayers and categories of prayers we might refer to as occasional (the obligatory prayers, the Fire Tablet, the Tablet of Aḥmad, and so on). But since our classifications here are constructed solely for the practical purposes of this exercise and not to imply some rigid or authoritative division, let us content ourselves with an examination of a few distinguishing characteristics of these prayers.

One common thing we notice among the occasional prayers is a homiletic or instructional quality. The believer may find himself enunciating the purpose of the event and learning the spiritual qualities to be derived from observing the occasion. For example, in the prayer for Intercalary Days, Bahá'u'lláh has the suppliant announce that "the fast which Thy most exalted Pen hath enjoined . . . is approaching" (*Bahá'í Prayers* 236). The suppliant then speaks of the value of obeying the law of God: "all such as have during that period clung to the cord of Thy commandments, and laid hold on the handle of Thy precepts . . ." "They have bowed themselves before Thy Cause, and received Thy Book with such resolve as is born of Thee, and observed what Thou hadst prescribed unto them, and chosen to follow that which had been sent down by Thee" (*Bahá'í Prayers* 237).

In other words, the believer is being prepared and girded to accept with understanding the command to fast. Interestingly, however, the believer recites this in the third person—not "we" but "they." The implication in this seems clear: those who are the true believers and faithful followers will obey, and the suppliant must himself determine if he or she is to be included in that number.

This same subtle instructional or homiletic quality is found in the Tablet of Visitation. The believer states the essential equation of the eternal Covenant, that to know the Prophet is to know God: "I bear witness that he who hath known Thee hath known God, and he who hath attained unto Thy presence hath attained unto the presence of God" (*Bahá'í Prayers* 231). The believer also acknowledges the sacrifice borne by the Manifestation: "May my spirit be a sacrifice to the wrongs Thou didst suffer, and my soul be a ransom for the adversities Thou didst sustain" (232–33). Similarly, the marriage prayer revealed by Bahá'u'lláh, besides being a supplication for a blessing, contains a succinct statement of the purpose of marriage.

In the prayers for the Fast, we discover the same variety of length and style we find in the obligatory prayers. We also find the frank enunciation of the purposes of the Fast. In this sense, these longer occasional prayers that are to be recited during the Fast, on pilgrimage, or on other special occasions have a meditative quality that is important to understand, as is the Bahá'í concept of meditation itself.

The process of meditation is lauded as an essential spiritual exercise in the Bahá'í writings:

> Through meditation the doors of deeper knowledge and inspiration may be opened. Naturally, if one meditates as a Bahá'í he is connected with the Source; if a man believing in God meditates he is tuning in to the power and mercy of God. . . . (Shoghi Effendi, qtd. in *Compilation of Compilations* 2: no. 1774)

At the same time, Shoghi Effendi is careful to point out that the Bahá'í concept of meditation does not imply some prescribed or recognized process—it is entirely individual in nature:

> There are no set forms of meditation prescribed in the teachings, no plan, as such, for inner development. The friends are urged—nay enjoined—to pray, and they also should meditate, but the manner of doing the latter is left entirely to the individual. (*Compilation of Compilations* 2: no. 1770)

Bahá'u'lláh seems to allude to the process of meditation primarily as a process of "reflection": "the lofty heights of detachment must needs be attained, and the meditation referred to in the words 'One hour's reflection is preferable to seventy years of pious worship' must needs be observed . . ." (*Kitáb-i-Íqán* 238). 'Abdu'l-Bahá in *Paris Talks* describes meditation as a sort of internal dialogue or internal consultation, perhaps between the rational faculties and the soul itself:

> It is an axiomatic fact that while you meditate you are speaking with your own spirit. In that state of mind you put certain questions to your spirit and the spirit answers: the light

> breaks forth and the reality is revealed.
>
> You cannot apply the name 'man' to any being void of this faculty of meditation; without it he would be a mere animal, lower than the beasts. (*Paris Talks* 54:9–10)

It is in this sense that Shoghi Effendi describes one of the purposes of the Fast as being a self-evaluation arrived at through "meditation and prayer":

> [Fasting] is essentially a period of meditation and prayer, of spiritual recuperation, during which the believer must strive to make the necessary readjustments in his inner life, and to refresh and reinvigorate the spiritual forces latent in his soul. (*Directives from the Guardian* 25)

In other words, there are no works of Bahá'u'lláh specifically designated as meditational works. Consequently, we might reject the idea of "meditations" as a separate or distinct genre. Rather, we see how many works of Bahá'u'lláh (particularly some of the longer prayers) evoke reflection or meditation because of the homiletic or instructional nature of what they say and because of their length.

c. Prayers and Tablets of Special Potency

Another possible sub-genre of prayers might consist of certain tablets designated as having a special power.[34] This category may overlap other classifications since the obligatory prayers (which could also well be considered "occasional") are among these. But among prayers specifically designated as having a special potency are the fasting prayers, the Long Healing Prayer, the obligatory prayers, the Tablet of Aḥmad, the

---

34. Here we are not making an exact distinction between works designated as "tablets" and those designated as "prayers." The book *Prayers and Meditations* and the prayer book *Bahá'í Prayers* contain both. Therefore the Tablet of Aḥmad and the Fire Tablet do not have the same form as most prayers; there is no invocation to God nor any closing listing the attributes of God (i.e., "Thou, in truth, art immensely exalted above all else . . ." *Bahá'í Prayers* 91).

Tablet of the Holy Mariner, and the so-called Fire Tablet.[35] While we could profitably expend considerable effort probing the special attributes of each of these works, let us here take note of one particular device common to many of them: the use of repetition.

The use of repetition for spiritual instruction might at first seem mindless, a remnant of religion's ritualistic past, but properly understood and utilized, repetition can become a source of comfort, contemplation, or spiritual conditioning. For example, in the longest prayer for the Fast, each paragraph contains two sentences, the first beginning with "I beseech Thee, O my God. . . ." Each paragraph concludes with the refrain

> Thou seest me, O my God, holding to Thy Name, the Most Holy, the Most Luminous, the Most Mighty, the Most Great, the Most Exalted, the Most Glorious, and clinging to the hem of the robe to which have clung all in this world and in the world to come. (*Prayers and Meditations* 288)

The remainder of the first sentence varies with each successive paragraph or stanza, but the framework of repetition functions to encase each new request for some manner of spiritual assistance or transformation, as one might display a jewel in an exquisite container.

Almost the exact same kind of repetition occurs with the Long Healing Prayer. Each verse repeats the same sentence, except that some of the epithets for God change with each verse. The effect of this repetition is that the suppliant becomes aware of the multitude of epithets or attributes that are appropriate to God. The Tablet of the Holy Mariner exemplifies a similar method of incremental repetition. Interspersed with repeated praise of God is the narrative of the allegory.

---

35. Bahá'í scholar Adib Taherzadeh states that the prayer or tablet known in the West as the Fire Tablet is "possessed of great powers, and the believers often recite it at times of difficulties and suffering" (*Revelation of Bahá'u'lláh* 3:226). At the end of the tablet Bahá'u'lláh Himself states, "Should all the servants read and ponder this, there shall be kindled in their veins a fire that shall set aflame the worlds" (*Bahá'í Prayers* 221).

In a discussion of the reason for repetition in the prayers of Bahá'u'lláh, the Research Department at the Bahá'í World Center notes that the use of repetition in prayer may have much the same effect that it has as "an important characteristic of music":

> It is interesting to note, therefore, that in the original Arabic of the Long Healing Prayer, the Prayer for the Dead and the Prayer for the Fast beginning, "I beseech Thee, O my God," the refrains are composed of rhyming words which give them a lyrical, musical quality which promotes their evocative power. (Memorandum dated 21 November 1995 from the Research Department of the Universal House of Justice)

Of course, these are not the only prayers that utilize repetition. In the Kitáb-i-Aqdas Bahá'u'lláh ordains that believers repeat the "Greatest Name" *(Alláh-u-Abhá)* ninety-five times each day. Likewise, there are other prayers that are to be repeated for special purposes.[36] In this regard, it is worthwhile to note again that many of the photographs of 'Abdu'l-Bahá, especially those pictures for which he posed, show him holding prayer beads (beads commonly used for counting the number of repetitions of a verse). And because nothing in the Revelation of Bahá'u'lláh is mindless or without rational explanation, we could certainly benefit from pondering some of the benefits the suppliant gains from the process of repetition. Of course, for one in grief or pain, repetition can have an incredibly soothing effect, like a mantra or melody that calms the nerves and consoles the spirit, as the repetitions in the Prayer for the Dead demonstrate.

D. Prayers for Individuals

One final sub-genre of prayer we might consider are those prayers revealed for specific individuals to recite. We have already mentioned

---

36. For example, women "in their courses" repeat a certain verse ninety-five times in lieu of obligatory prayers, and another verse is to be recited eighteen times by one who has missed an obligatory prayer.

some of these: the prayer devised for Shaykh Muḥammad Taqíy-i-Najafí (the "son of the Wolf"), the one for Queen Victoria, and the prayer for Nabíl-i-Akbar.

Bahá'u'lláh's prayer revealed for Queen Victoria to recite is particularly interesting. Bahá'u'lláh exhorts the Queen to "Turn thou unto God" and repeat a prayer which begins with her frank admission that she is "but a vassal" of God, Who is, "in truth, the King of Kings." Later in the prayer Bahá'u'lláh has her request from God that He "rend asunder the veils" that have impaired her recognition of the Manifestation. Here again, Bahá'u'lláh as Divine physician praises her nobility, but frankly points out her shortcomings and prescribes the remedy, albeit in a most loving and gentle tone:

> Deprive me not, O my Lord, of the fragrances of the Robe of Thy mercy in Thy days, and write down for me that which Thou hast written down for thy handmaidens who have believed in Thee and in Thy signs, and have recognized Thee, and set their hearts towards the horizon of Thy Cause. (*Proclamation of Bahá'u'lláh* 35)

But if Bahá'u'lláh devises creative prayers for those of noble bearing, He is no less inventive in the prayers He reveals for those who have proved themselves to be utterly depraved and iniquitous, whose station might seem beyond hope or help. We have already cited a portion of Bahá'u'lláh's prayer for Shaykh Muḥammad Taqíy-i-Najafí (the Son of the Wolf), a startling six-page confession of the Shaykh's guilt which he is to recite to purify his soul "with the waters of renunciation, and adorn [his] head with the crown of the fear of God" (*Epistle to the Son of the Wolf* 2), as he turns his face toward "the Most Great House"[37] and recites the prayer. During the course of this prayer, Bahá'u'lláh has the Shaykh admitting to "the cruelties, the glaring cruelties, I inflicted" (*Epistle* 4). In full contrition the Shaykh is to cry out, "Woe is me, woe

37. The House of Bahá'u'lláh in Baghdád designated by Bahá'u'lláh in the Kitáb-i-Aqdas as a place of pilgrimage and considered a holy shrine by Bahá'ís.

is me, for my remoteness from Thee, and for my waywardness, and mine ignorance, and my baseness, and my repudiation of Thee and my protests against Thee!"(4)

But the prayers of Bahá'u'lláh revealed for individuals are not solely for non-believers and enemies; Bahá'u'lláh also revealed special prayers for some of the faithful. One notable example occurs in the Lawḥ-i-Ḥikmat, which is addressed to Nabíl-i-Akbar (a Bahá'í noted for his learning, designated by 'Abdu'l-Bahá a Hand of the Cause of God, and named by Shoghi Effendi as one of the "Apostles" of Bahá'u'lláh). In this prayer the believer, having been given the gift of this esoteric knowledge, asks for assistance in utilizing this gift of wisdom to teach the Cause of God:

> Unloose my tongue therefore to proclaim that which will captivate the minds of men and will rejoice their souls and spirits. Strengthen me then in Thy Cause in such wise that I may not be hindered by the ascendancy of the oppressors among Thy creatures nor withheld by the onslaught of the disbelievers amidst those who dwell in Thy realm. Make me as a lamp shining throughout Thy lands that those in whose hearts the light of Thy knowledge gloweth and the yearning for Thy love lingereth may be guided by its radiance. (*Tablets of Bahá'u'lláh* 152)

e. Prayers for the Manifestation

In the Chapter 2 discussion of point of view, we examined the unique opportunity Bahá'u'lláh provides by allowing us to study the prayers between Himself and God. We do not need to repeat those observations here, but we might note one additional insight that helps us appreciate further why Bahá'u'lláh has provided us with these works.

As we discussed in Chapter 1, even though the Manifestations possess a spiritual station far beyond that of ordinary human beings (as well as extraordinary powers that we can only vaguely comprehend), these exalted Beings still rely on prayer for sustenance. Stated in blunt terms, the Prophet does not seem to impose on us any spiritual exercise that He does not utilize Himself. Stated more creatively, prayer provides the vital connection between this world and the next, the essential umbilicus through which we receive our daily nourishment in our womb-like preparation for our birth into the spiritual realm. By bequeathing us these works, Bahá'u'lláh demonstrates that even in His lofty station He, too, requires this constant connection, this firm cord.

8. Homiletic and Orational Works

Yet another style of Bahá'u'lláh's art is found most often as distinctive passages that appear as parts of larger works. These are passages of a homiletic or orational style[38] wherein the Prophet suddenly speaks with the inimitable eloquence of Divine Authority, with the unleashed power and omniscience of His unique perspective as God's viceroy.

Tonally, these passages effectively convey to us a complete sense of the Prophet's station of essential unity, as if, for a moment, He steps out of His guise as an historical or human persona and allows us to hear what we can hardly bear—the limitless range of Divine Authority channeled through the form of human language.

Shoghi Effendi does not specifically designate which works he would categorize as homilies, but he does allude to Bahá'u'lláh's use of this genre as being an important style employed by Bahá'u'lláh during the rich outpouring of writing that He undertook during the Baghdád period:

> . . . the "Javáhiru'l-Asrár" and a host of other writings, in the form of epistles, odes, homilies, specific Tablets, commentaries and prayers, contributed, each in its own way, to swell the *"rivers of everlasting life"* which poured forth from the *"Abode of Peace"* and lent a mighty impetus to the expansion of the Báb's Faith in both Persia and 'Iráq, quickening the souls and transforming the character of its adherents. (*God Passes By* 141)

38. A homily is a form of sermon or moralizing discourse, though it is sometimes distinguished from the sermon because it tends to give what *A Handbook to Literature* terms "practical moral counsel rather than discussion of doctrine" (241).

Possibly the best-known example of such a form is the Tablet of Carmel. In this brief but powerful allusion to the future ascendancy of the Bahá'í Administrative Order, Bahá'u'lláh gives authoritative utterance (albeit in allegorical or symbolic language) to the future progress of His Cause. Appropriately, Bahá'u'lláh revealed the tablet in resounding tones while standing atop Mount Carmel.[39] In one of the most memorable parts of this work, the Divine Will commands Carmel (perhaps as an allegorical personification of the earth itself) to call out to Zion:

> "Call out to Zion, O Carmel, and announce the joyful tidings: He that was hidden from mortal eyes is come! His all-conquering sovereignty is manifest; His all-encompassing splendor is revealed. Beware lest thou hesitate or halt. Hasten forth and circumambulate the City of God that hath descended from heaven, the celestial Kaaba round which have circled in adoration the favored of God, the pure in heart, and the company of the most exalted angels. . . ." (*Tablets of Bahá'u'lláh* 4)

Another orational piece of similar power and rhetorical tone is a tablet entitled Muballigh (the "teacher" or "proclaimer"), originally part of a tablet revealed in honor of Ḥájí Muḥammad-Ibráhím. Taherzadeh refers to this as a dialogue between "the voice of Truth and the voice of those who are bereft of true understanding . . ." (*Revelation of Bahá'u'lláh* 4:153). In this dialogue questions are asked regarding Islámic prophecies about the promised Day of God,[40] and the Voice of Divine Authority gives the answer that all has been fulfilled:

> Among them are those who have said: "Have the verses been sent down?" Say "Yea, by Him Who is the Lord of the heavens!" "Hath the Hour come?" "Nay, more; it hath passed, by Him Who is the

39. The spot is now designated by an obelisk on the promontory of the mountain, marking the site upon which in the future a Bahá'í House of Worship is to be constructed.

40. Variously alluded to as the Day of Resurrection or Day of Judgment.

> Revealer of clear tokens! Verily, the Inevitable is come, and He, the True One, hath appeared with proof and testimony. The Plain is disclosed, and mankind is sore vexed and fearful. Earthquakes have broken loose, and the tribes have lamented, for fear of God, the Lord of Strength, the All-Compelling." Say: "The stunning trumpet-blast hath been loudly raised, and the Day is God's, the One, the Unconstrained." And they say: "Hath the Catastrophe come to pass?" Say: "Yea, by the Lord of Lords!" "Is the Resurrection come?" "Nay, more; He Who is the Self-Subsisting hath appeared with the Kingdom of His signs." (*Tablets of Bahá'u'lláh* 117–18)

The questions and answers continue until Bahá'u'lláh concludes by observing, "The Tablet is ended, but the theme is unexhausted. Be patient, for thy Lord is patient" (119).[41]

Two other examples of this orational or homiletic tone can be found in passages that take the form of a series of admonitions. One functions as a code of conduct that Bahá'u'lláh sent as advice to one of His sons,[42] though we find the work repeated in Epistle to the Son of the Wolf, where Bahá'u'lláh states that He is commanded to convey this same advice to Shaykh Muḥammad Taqíy-i-Najafí:

> At this moment the shrill voice of the Most Sublime Pen hath been raised, and hath addressed Me saying: "Admonish the Shaykh even as Thou hast admonished one of Thy Branches (sons), that haply the breezes of Thine utterance may attract and draw him nigh unto God, the Lord of the worlds." (*Epistle* 93)

The passage is succinct, unveiled, memorable in its simplicity, but stunning in its forceful catalog of human virtue:

---

41. Interestingly, Bahá'u'lláh observes in the Ishráqát that these verses "We sent down previously," and He quotes these same verses again in *Epistle to the Son of the Wolf* 131.

42. Bahá'u'lláh states this in *Epistle to the Son of the Wolf* 93, though He does not say which son.

> Be generous in prosperity, and thankful in adversity. Be worthy of the trust of thy neighbor, and look upon him with a bright and friendly face. Be a treasure to the poor, an admonisher to the rich, an answerer to the cry of the needy, a preserver of the sanctity of thy pledge. Be fair in thy judgment, and guarded in thy speech. Be unjust to no man, and show all meekness to all men. Be as a lamp unto them that walk in darkness, a joy to the sorrowful, a sea for the thirsty, a haven for the distressed, an upholder and defender of the victim of oppression. Let integrity and uprightness distinguish all thine acts. Be a home for the stranger, a balm to the suffering, a tower of strength for the fugitive. (*Epistle* 93–94)

Of course, since this piece is a catalog of conduct, we might conceivably classify it as another example of gnomic verse; again we must take note of the unscientific and imprecise nature of our categories. At the same time, we can sense in the orational quality of this mandate with its lack of elaboration or explanation a definable tone and style.

A second passage also containing a series of admonitions that functions as a code of conduct is sometimes referred to as the Tablet of the True Seeker, even though it is, in fact, a part of the Kitáb-i-Íqán. The passage appears at the end of the Kitáb-i-Íqán, after Bahá'u'lláh has for some two hundred pages demonstrated why the learned have in every age so often been the most active deterrents to the recognition of the Prophet.

Like the Muballigh, the Tablet of the True Seeker begins with a catalog of attributes. After noting that the truly learned are not necessarily those who have formal training, but those who "are initiated into the divine mysteries," Bahá'u'lláh elucidates the attributes or qualities of those who would be *truly* learned, at the conclusion of which He observes that these are "among the attributes of the exalted, and constitute the hall-mark of the spiritually-minded." A portion of this remarkable synthesis of the virtues of the true seeker reads as follows:

> But, O my brother, when a true seeker determineth to take the step of search in the path leading to the knowledge of the An-

> cient of Days, he must, before all else, cleanse and purify his heart, which is the seat of the revelation of the inner mysteries of God, from the obscuring dust of all acquired knowledge, and the allusions of the embodiments of satanic fancy. He must purge his breast, which is the sanctuary of the abiding love of the Beloved, of every defilement, and sanctify his soul from all that pertaineth to water and clay, from all shadowy and ephemeral attachments. He must so cleanse his heart that no remnant of either love or hate may linger therein, lest that love blindly incline him to error, or that hate repel him away from the truth. Even as thou dost witness in this day how most of the people, because of such love and hate, are bereft of the immortal Face, have strayed far from the Embodiments of the divine mysteries, and, shepherdless, are roaming through the wilderness of oblivion and error. (*Kitáb-i-Íqán* 192–93)

Certainly, this passage serves as one of the most useful, lucid, and thorough descriptions of those qualities that should distinguish the character of every Bahá'í. And though Bahá'u'lláh's discussion of this theme continues, He does pause after this catalog to observe, "Our purpose in revealing these convincing and weighty utterances is to impress upon the seeker that he should regard all else beside God as transient, and count all things save Him, Who is the Object of all adoration, as utter nothingness" (*Kitáb-i-Íqán* 195).

9. Documents of the Covenant

The last category we will mention in our brief exploration of some of the genres or styles evident in the art of Bahá'u'lláh concerns those works specialized to establish the succession of authority for the religion of Bahá'u'lláh. These documents relating to the Covenant are, to a certain extent, dissimilar stylistically but united in purpose.

The Kitáb-i-Aqdas is among the most obvious examples of documents of the Covenant, establishing as it does the laws and institutions that must needs become the physical or social expression of Bahá'u'lláh's Revelation. Furthermore, Bahá'u'lláh makes it absolutely clear that obedience to His law is the most important sign of our recognition of His station and our subsequent participation in the Covenant. At the same time, while the Kitáb-i-Aqdas bequeaths to the believers specific laws and the foundation for a code of behavior, it also establishes the chain of authority whereby the administration of the religion (and, implicitly, the administration of human affairs in general) will be conferred upon the several institutions alluded to in this document: the Center of the Covenant, the Guardian, the House of Justice, and the "learned ones" (Kitáb-i-Aqdas ¶173).

In this sense, the documents of Bahá'u'lláh with which we are presently concerned are those that specifically allude to Bahá'u'lláh's ordination of 'Abdu'l-Bahá as His lawful successor, as the "Center" of His Covenant, as the "Interpreter" of His words, and as the "Exemplar" of Bahá'í attributes.

Shoghi Effendi lists three primary works that accomplish this task—the Súriy-i-Ghuṣn (Tablet of the Branch), the Kitáb-i-Aqdas (Most Holy Book), and the Kitáb-i-'Ahd (Book of His Covenant):

> Whether in the Kitáb-i-Aqdas, the most weighty and sacred of all the works of Bahá'u'lláh, or in the Kitáb-i-'Ahd, the Book of His Covenant, or in the Súriy-i-Ghuṣn (Tablet of the Branch), such references as have been recorded by the pen of Bahá'u'lláh—references which the Tablets of His Father addressed to Him mightily reinforce—invest 'Abdu'l-Bahá with a power, and surround Him with a halo, which the present generation can never adequately appreciate. (*World Order of Bahá'u'lláh* 133–34)

After glimpsing the terms Bahá'u'lláh uses to describe 'Abdu'l-Bahá in these works, we can more fully appreciate that, however much we may regard every revealed law as part of Bahá'u'lláh's Covenant, His appointment of 'Abdu'l-Bahá as His successor was the single most important act in securing the unbroken chain of infallible authority and guidance.

A. The Súriy-i-Ghuṣn (Tablet of the Branch)

The Súriy-i-Ghuṣn is the first of these works chronologically, and, in one sense, the most marvelous. For in addition to anticipating the explicit designation of 'Abdu'l-Bahá as successor in the Kitáb-i-'Ahd, the Súriy-i-Ghuṣn portrays the exemplary character and strategic importance of 'Abdu'l-Bahá.

Penned by Bahá'u'lláh during the Adrianople period (ca. 1867), the Súriy-i-Ghuṣn alludes to 'Abdu'l-Bahá with most weighty and revealing epithets: "He is eulogized as the *'Branch of Holiness,'* the *'Limb of the Law of God,'* the *'Trust of God,' 'sent down in the form of a human temple'*" (Shoghi Effendi, *God Passes By* 177). Elsewhere in this same tablet 'Abdu'l-Bahá is exalted as Bahá'u'lláh's "'*most great favor*' unto men, as His *'most perfect bounty'* conferred upon them."[43]

Of course, the title of the work contains the most emphatic symbol of what the work is really about—'Abdu'l-Bahá as the sacred offshoot of the Divine Lote-Tree, the Most Great Branch that will save and shelter all who abide beneath its shade:

> There hath branched from the Sadratu'l-Muntahá this sacred and glorious Being, this Branch of Holiness; well is it with him that hath sought His shelter and abideth beneath His shadow. (qtd. in Shoghi Effendi, *World Order of Bahá'u'lláh* 135)

However, later in this same passage Bahá'u'lláh more explicitly ascribes to 'Abdu'l-Bahá the station of authority with which He will be formally invested in Bahá'u'lláh's will and testament:

> Verily the Limb of the Law of God hath sprung forth from this Root which God hath firmly implanted in the Ground of His Will, and Whose Branch hath been so uplifted as to encompass the whole of creation. . . . Render thanks unto God, O people, for His appearance; for verily He is the most great Favor unto you, the most perfect bounty upon you; and through Him every mouldering bone is quickened. Whoso turneth towards Him hath turned towards God, and whoso turneth away from Him hath turned away from My beauty, hath repudiated My Proof, and transgressed against Me. He is the Trust of God amongst you,

43. See Shoghi Effendi, *God Passes By* 242.

> His charge within you, His manifestation unto you and His appearance among His favored servants. . . . We have sent Him down in the form of a human temple. Blest and sanctified be God Who createth whatsoever He willeth through His inviolable, His infallible decree. They who deprive themselves of the shadow of the Branch, are lost in the wilderness of error, are consumed by the heat of worldly desires, and are of those who will assuredly perish. (qtd. in Shoghi Effendi, *World Order of Bahá'u'lláh* 135)

In light of these clear allusions to the authority and station of 'Abdu'l-Bahá, it is not at all surprising that Bahá'u'lláh would some thirty years later formally confer upon 'Abdu'l-Bahá the station of successorship.

But what is also apparent in the Súriy-i-Ghuṣn is the wondrous love Bahá'u'lláh has for this cherished son, a theme to which Shoghi Effendi alludes in his discussion of the Súriy-i-Ghuṣn in *The World Order of Bahá'u'lláh:*

> *"O Thou Who art the apple of Mine eye!"* Bahá'u'lláh, in His own handwriting, thus addresses 'Abdu'l-Bahá, *"My glory, the ocean of My loving-kindness, the sun of My bounty, the heaven of My mercy rest upon Thee. We pray God to illumine the world through Thy knowledge and wisdom, to ordain for Thee that which will gladden Thine heart and impart consolation to Thine eyes." "The glory of God rest upon Thee,"* He writes in another Tablet, *"and upon whosoever serveth Thee and circleth around Thee. Woe, great woe, betide him that opposeth and injureth Thee. Well is it with him that sweareth fealty to Thee; the fire of hell torment him who is Thine enemy." "We have made Thee a shelter for all mankind,"* He, in yet another Tablet, affirms, *"a shield unto all who are in heaven and on earth, a stronghold for whosoever hath believed in God, the Incomparable, the All-Knowing. God grant that through Thee He may protect them, may enrich and sustain them, that He may inspire Thee with that which shall be a wellspring of wealth unto all created things, an ocean of bounty unto all men, and the dayspring of mercy unto all peoples."* (135–36)

Perhaps the most touching insight into Bahá'u'lláh's boundless love for this dutiful son is found in the Lawḥ-i-Arḍ-i-Bá (Tablet of the Land of Bá). A letter dictated by Bahá'u'lláh to 'Abdu'l-Bahá, Who was at the time visiting Beirut, the Lawḥ-i-Arḍ-i-Bá is penned in a style of great formality. Bahá'u'lláh refers to 'Abdu'l-Bahá as "the Most Mighty Branch of God" and God's "ancient and immutable Mystery." It becomes quickly apparent, however, that this brief epistle is really a love note to His son, a touching plaint by a loving Father Who dearly misses the cherished presence of His beloved son. At the end of the tablet, Bahá'u'lláh prays to God for 'Abdu'l-Bahá's speedy return:

> Blessed, doubly blessed, is the ground which His footsteps have trodden, the eye that hath been cheered by the beauty of His countenance, the ear that hath been honoured by hearkening to His call, the heart that hath tasted the sweetness of His love, the breast that hath dilated through His remembrance, the pen that hath voiced His praise, the scroll that hath borne the testimony of His writings. We beseech God—blessed and exalted be He—that He may honour us with meeting Him soon. He is, in truth, the All-Hearing, the All-Powerful, He Who is ready to answer. (*Tablets of Bahá'u'lláh* 227–28)

The style and tenor of these earlier allusions to the station of 'Abdu'l-Bahá are not legalistic. They are filled with emotion and a sort of personal affection that we witness in very few of the works of Bahá'u'lláh thus far translated into English. For while Bahá'u'lláh here designates Himself as Prophet, as the Sadratu'l-Muntahá, the persona is that of a father who is affectionate, vulnerable, and, on some level, always terribly alone.[44]

---

44. Here I refer to the fact that the labor of the Prophet is, when properly appreciated, a thoroughly lonely task, because few of even the most intimate disciples truly understand His station. No doubt, Bahá'u'lláh felt incredible comfort, therefore, in knowing that His own son, the first to believe in Him, was flawlessly faithful, reliable, and devoted.

B. The Kitáb-i-Aqdas (Most Holy Book)

Chronologically, the next major work concerned directly with the Covenant of Bahá'u'lláh is the Kitáb-i-Aqdas, revealed in 1873. Indeed, in a very real sense, the Kitáb-i-Aqdas encapsulates, enshrines, and codifies the Covenant of Bahá'u'lláh. This most crucial work of the Revelation of Bahá'u'lláh contains the foundation of all Bahá'í law and administration, restates the successorship enunciated in the Súriy-i-Ghuṣn, and speaks directly about the advent of the next Manifestation. Stylistically, the Kitáb-i-Aqdas establishes its own unique category:

> Structurally [the Kitáb-i-Aqdas] proceeds like a variegated tapestry into which Bahá'u'lláh has woven His vision of a global civilization. Within this vision are very specific images of the "refined" individual, the product of an harmonious and well-ordered family, itself an integral part of a spiritually based and highly organized local community.
>
> Woven into the fabric of this vision of future society are laws, scattered like luminescent jewels. Some laws seem to appear almost randomly, as if to shock us into thought. Some establish a theme after which will follow a discourse or meditative exemplum. Other laws conclude a moral commentary, as if to punctuate a theme. (Hatcher, *Law of Love Enshrined* 173)

The point is that, however rich and varied are the styles and genres employed by Bahá'u'lláh, the Kitáb-i-Aqdas will, we can be sure, challenge many a creative student to decipher its intricate style and structure. Perhaps the most significant thing we can observe at this point in the study of this work is that, however formless, random, and difficult it may appear, we can be certain that, in light of all that we have thus far observed regarding the art of Bahá'u'lláh, this most weighty of all His works possesses a perfect unity of form and function.[45]

---

45. One valuable attempt to illustrate this union between the fundamental structure of the Kitáb-i-Aqdas and its unifying theme is William Hatcher's article "*The Kitáb-i-Aqdas:* The Causality Principle," in *Law of Love Enshrined* 101–57.

The one passage dealing explicitly with succession within the Dispensation of Bahá'u'lláh at first seems less explicit than the passages in either the Súriy-i-Ghuṣn or the Kitáb-i-'Ahd:

> When the ocean of My presence hath ebbed and the Book of My Revelation is ended, turn your faces toward Him Whom God hath purposed, Who hath branched from this Ancient Root. (¶121).

Since Bahá'u'lláh had other children, the passage might not seem explicitly to refer to 'Abdu'l-Bahá, even though it follows an exhortation about trustworthiness, truthfulness, and servitude, qualities which certainly typify this eldest son. However, as we will shortly observe, Bahá'u'lláh in the Kitáb-i-'Ahd clarifies this ambiguity, as does 'Abdu'l-Bahá in various other tablets.[46]

Also related to the Covenant of Bahá'u'lláh as regards succession is the explicit passage in the Kitáb-i-Aqdas alluding to the advent of the next Manifestation of God. As we have already noted, Bahá'u'lláh in the Súratu'l-Haykal alludes to the advent of this individual, expressing His concern for what that Prophet would face. In the Kitáb-i-Aqdas Bahá'u'lláh assures His followers that they need not concern themselves with this matter before the passing of a thousand years: "Whoso layeth claim to a Revelation direct from God, ere the expiration of a full thousand years, such a man is assuredly a lying impostor" (¶37). However, Bahá'u'lláh is also warning Bahá'ís that such an individual would indeed arise, would cause confusion, and would attract a following:

> We pray God that He may graciously assist him [the one making such a claim] to retract and repudiate such claim. Should he repent, God will, no doubt, forgive him. If, however, he persisteth in his error, God will, assuredly, send down one who will deal mercilessly with him. Terrible, indeed, is God in punishing! (¶37)

46. See *Selections from the Writings of 'Abdu'l-Bahá* ¶186.1–8.

Bahá'u'lláh goes on to state that, "Erelong shall clamorous voices be raised in most lands. Shun them, O My people, and follow not the iniquitous and evil-hearted" (¶37).

Of course, scriptural prophecy is often symbolic, as Bahá'u'lláh observes in discussing prophetic terminology in the Kitáb-i-Íqán. Consequently, to make sure no one interprets this directive about the passage of a thousand years as having some veiled or symbolic meaning, Bahá'u'lláh states, "Whosoever interpreteth this verse otherwise than its obvious meaning is deprived of the Spirit of God and of His mercy which encompasseth all created things" (¶37).

c. The Kitáb-i-'Ahd (Book of the Covenant)

First and foremost among those works establishing the Covenant of Bahá'u'lláh is the Kitáb-i-'Ahd, the Book of My Covenant,[47] as Bahá'u'lláh Himself sometimes referred to this work. The Kitáb-i-'Ahd is the Will and Testament of Bahá'u'lláh, written in His own hand probably a year before His passing[48] and entrusted to 'Abdu'l-Bahá during Bahá'u'lláh's last illness. This work is described by Shoghi Effendi as unique in religious history:

> [T]his unique and epoch-making Document, designated by Bahá'u'lláh as His "Most Great Tablet," and alluded to by Him as the "Crimson Book" in His "Epistle to the Son of the Wolf," can find no parallel in the Scriptures of any previous Dispensation, not excluding that of the Báb Himself. (*God Passes By* 238).

The uniqueness of the work lies in what it does more than how it does it. The Kitáb-i-'Ahd represents the first time in religious history on this planet in which the Manifestation has in a written document designated successorship and the specific parameters of the authority of that successor:

47. See Shoghi Effendi, *God Passes By* 238.
48. See Taherzadeh, *Covenant of Bahá'u'lláh* 142.

> For nowhere in the books pertaining to any of the world's religious systems, not even among the writings of the Author of the Bábí Revelation, do we find any single document establishing a Covenant endowed with an authority comparable to the Covenant which Bahá'u'lláh had Himself instituted. (Shoghi Effendi, *God Passes By* 238)

The work itself is brief, only a few pages in length. It is clear, accessible, and contains a minimum of "veiled language" or imagery. Approximately the first half of the work functions as a preamble and is structured around a series of weighty observations, admonitions, dictums, and commands:

> Earthly treasures We have not bequeathed, nor have We added such cares as they entail. (*Tablets of Bahá'u'lláh* 219)

> We exhort you, O peoples of the world, to observe that which will elevate your station. Hold fast to the fear of God and firmly adhere to what is right. (219)

> O ye that dwell on earth! The religion of God is for love and unity; make it not the cause of enmity or dissension. (220)

> Conflict and contention are categorically forbidden in His Book. This is a decree of God in this Most Great Revelation. (221)

> Blessed are the rulers and the learned among the people of Bahá. They are My trustees among My servants and the manifestations of My commandments amidst My people. (221)

After bequeathing advice about how the believers should comport themselves, Bahá'u'lláh turns to the weightiest matter of all—His testament. Speaking directly to His descendants (the Aghṣán) and to the descendants of the Báb (the Afnán), Bahá'u'lláh commands them to turn to

'Abdu'l-Bahá, the "Most Mighty Branch,"[49] after Bahá'u'lláh has ascended:

> The Will of the divine Testator is this: It is incumbent upon the Aghṣán, the Afnán and My Kindred to turn, one and all, their faces towards the Most Mighty Branch. (*Tablets of Bahá'u'lláh* 221)

This is the one and only provision of the will itself. All else is subordinated to this purpose. And yet, what follows is wonderfully revealing of Bahá'u'lláh's omniscience about the events that would follow His passing. Immediately after announcing that 'Abdu'l-Bahá is His lawful successor, Bahá'u'lláh explains that it was 'Abdu'l-Bahá Whom He had designated from the beginning. Bahá'u'lláh explains that He had indicated 'Abdu'l-Bahá in the Kitáb-i-Aqdas with the phrase "Who hath branched from this Ancient Root":

> Consider that which We have revealed in Our Most Holy Book: "When the ocean of My presence hath ebbed and the Book of My Revelation is ended, turn your faces toward Him Whom God hath purposed, Who hath branched from this Ancient Root." The object of this sacred verse is none other except the Most Mighty Branch ['Abdu'l-Bahá]. Thus have We graciously revealed unto you our potent Will, and I am verily the Gracious, the All-Powerful. (*Tablets of Bahá'u'lláh* 221–22)

This statement is important for several reasons. First, Bahá'u'lláh states here with unmistakable clarity that He as Prophet is Omnipotent ("All-Powerful"), a fact that is too often ignored in discussions of the powers and capacities of the Manifestation. Second, we know that this docu-

49. This term allows no other interpretation because "Most Mighty" or "Greatest" designates Bahá'u'lláh's eldest son, 'Abdu'l-Bahá. The term "Greater Branch" is used a few lines later to refer to the next oldest living son, Muḥammad-'Alí.

ment "was probably written at least one year before the Ascension of Bahá'u'lláh" (Taherzadeh, *Covenant of Bahá'u'lláh* 142) because it is alluded to as "the Crimson Book" in Epistle of the Son of the Wolf, which was written in 1891. But in this passage Bahá'u'lláh makes it clear that He had made His decision to designate 'Abdu'l-Bahá as His successor at least as far back as 1873, when He revealed the Kitáb-i-Aqdas. This passage in the Kitáb-i-'Ahd thus anticipates any claim that the decision was made hastily or during a condition of failing health—it cannot be dismissed as the unreliable utterance of a dying man.

Of course, Bahá'u'lláh was fully aware of what would follow: the grievous attempts by Muḥammad-'Alí to vitiate the Covenant,[50] the occupation of Bahjí by the family of Muḥammad-'Alí, and the attempts by the followers of Muḥammad-'Alí (the "Nakeseens") to steal various tablets, seal rings, and other property that rightfully belonged to 'Abdu'l-Bahá and to the Bahá'í community. Consequently, Bahá'u'lláh specifically warns against committing these very acts. He states that the station of the Greater Branch (Muḥammad-'Alí) is "beneath that of the Most Great Branch" (*Tablets of Bahá'u'lláh* 222). He warns the Aghṣán that they have no "right to the property of others" (222). He exhorts all His kindred to "fear God," to possess "upright character," and to bring forth "pure and goodly deeds" (222). Perhaps most ironic of all, Bahá'u'lláh warns, "Let not the means of order be made the cause of confusion, and the instrument of union an occasion for discord" (222).

The profound effect of these admonitions from our own historical perspective is that we can observe how Bahá'u'lláh made sure that no one in the future could excuse any manner of infidelity with regard to this firmly established Covenant. Furthermore, when Bahá'u'lláh's cautionary statements are later seen to be precise predictions of what would later occur, the faithful could have no doubt as to what was going on.

---

50. Shoghi Effendi in *God Passes By* observes the following about Mírzá Muḥammad-'Alí: "He it was who had the impudence and temerity to tell 'Abdu'l-Bahá to His face that just as 'Umar had succeeded in usurping the successorship of the Prophet Muḥammad, he, too, felt himself able to do the same" (249).

Generically, then, these documents of the Covenant are sublimely succinct, simple, and clear. They leave no room for interpretation or alteration. When the Kitáb-i-'Ahd was unsealed and read on the ninth day after the Ascension of Bahá'u'lláh, no one, not even Muḥammad-'Alí himself, found reason to question its obvious intent.[51]

51. Shoghi Effendi observes that this "unique and epoch-making Document" was "unsealed, on the ninth day after His ascension in the presence of nine witnesses chosen from amongst His companions and members of His Family; read subsequently, on the afternoon of that same day, before a large company assembled in His Most Holy Tomb, including His sons, some of the Báb's kinsmen, pilgrims and resident believers" (*God Passes By* 238).

Chapter 5
The Ḥúrís of Inner Meaning: Solving the Mysteries of Figurative Language

By God! This Bird of Heaven, now dwelling upon the dust, can, besides these melodies, utter a myriad songs, and is able, apart from these utterances, to unfold innumerable mysteries. Every single note of its unpronounced utterances is immeasurably exalted above all that hath already been revealed, and immensely glorified beyond that which hath streamed from this Pen. Let the future disclose the hour when the Brides of inner meaning will, as decreed by the Will of God, hasten forth, unveiled, out of their mystic mansions, and manifest themselves in the ancient realm of being.

—Bahá'u'lláh

Thus far we have posed relatively simple and straightforward questions: Who is speaking to me? In what context? In what form? As a result of the answers we have derived from these questions, we have become more creative and productive in our attempt to study the art of Bahá'u'lláh. Our fourth question is not so easy, and yet it is probably the most important. The question can be posed in many forms, but the essence of the query is this: What mysteries are concealed in Bahá'u'lláh's language and how can we solve them?

What we are really considering in this fourth area of literary analysis are the figurative devices Bahá'u'lláh has employed (i.e., metaphor, symbol, allusion, allegory, etc.), because figurative language is the primary means by which the Prophet conceals or veils the meaning of His words. But before we can discuss how to approach these poetic devices and solve these mysteries, let us first consider why the Prophets resort to this sort of indirect language in the first place. That is, why would a Messenger from God, whose purpose it is to instruct human beings, choose to conceal His meaning and create these mysteries? What benefits are derived from this indirection, from the use of parables, symbols, metaphors, and other poetic devices that seem to be an inevitable part of the Prophet's literary technique?

A. Why the Prophets Are Poets

Physical reality is not what it seems; it appears to be the "real" world, but it is actually a metaphorical or symbolic expression of the "real" world (i.e., spiritual reality):

> Know thou that the Kingdom [Spiritual Reality] is the real world, and this nether place is only its shadow stretching out. A shadow hath no life of its own; its existence is only a fantasy, and nothing more; it is but images reflected in water, and seeming as pictures to the eye. ('Abdu'l-Bahá, *Selections from the Writings of 'Abdu'l-Bahá* ¶150.2)

In this sense, physical reality has no inherent meaning except for its capacity to render concrete or visible representation of the unseen spiritual reality which it dramatizes: "Whatever objects appear in this world of existence are the outer pictures of the world of heaven" ('Abdu'l-Bahá *Promulgation of Universal Peace* 10).

This relationship is discussed in some detail in *The Purpose of Physical Reality: The Kingdom of Names,* in which the physical world is compared to a classroom where our souls (spiritual entities) are prepared for entrance into a life in the spiritual world by being gradually introduced to spiritual faculties and concepts. The physical world thus gives artistic expression to spiritual reality, just as our physical bodies are capable of expressing the condition of our souls.

From this perspective, physical reality is not evil or corrupt, but an ingenious device through which the Divine Will trains us to understand the nature of the spiritual world we will all soon enter. In other words, because the spiritual world is purposefully veiled from direct comprehension during our physical existence, physical reality becomes the language through which the unseen reality is made apparent to us. Therefore, the more we study this "language" (the laws and relationships governing physical reality), the more we have access to that unseen reality.

Language itself functions in this same manner: we understand one reality in terms of another. That is, language, like physical reality, is once removed from the reality it represents. The word *eye* alludes to a certain organ in our head, but the word *eye* is not the organ itself. Furthermore, when we study the etymology of words, we often discover a similar kind of metaphorical relationship. For example, one Anglo-Saxon word for eyes is *heafodgimmas* (gems or jewels of the head). When the word was originally devised, the *scop* or wordsmith was, no doubt, aware of the poetic nature of his creation—this comparison between the gift of sight and the receiving of some precious treasure. Over time, however, the poetic or metaphorical nature of this relationship became lost or forgotten, and the word lost its poetic power and functioned as a direct reference to eyes.

All language functions this way: we understand one reality in terms of another. Then, gradually, as we build upon our experience, we are capable of alluding to things directly. For example, we infer the meaning of *love* by having a variety of concrete experiences related to this *abstract* reality. As we acquire more and more of these experiences, we can begin to distinguish among various types of love. We can also allude directly to these various abstractions without the need of a physical referent. That is, we may no longer need to understand the unseen *love* in terms of the seen (i.e., a *loving* experience).

We can observe this same relationship in the utterances of the Manifestation. The essential task of the Prophets is to educate us, and the principal tool through which this education is accomplished is utterance or language. In this sense, language is a tool specialized for the spiritual enlightenment of humankind. For this reason language or utterance has an exalted status among the Messengers of God. Indeed, one might observe that Bahá'u'lláh's primary doctrinal work, the Kitáb-i-Íqán, is a study of language in relation to education.

Furthermore, the most significant type of language with which the Prophets educate us is figurative language because it enables these Divine Emissaries to discuss with us the unseen reality in terms of the seen. Because the Prophets are aware that we are incapable of experiencing spiritual reality directly, They discuss that reality in terms of the physical reality which we can experience. Therefore, the Prophets become poets because poetry is based primarily on figurative language, and at the heart of figurative language is the expression of one reality in terms of another. By means of this analogical process, all ideas and concepts can find expression.

B. The Components of Figurative Language

Language can be broadly divided into two methods of describing reality: a literal or direct method, and a figurative or indirect method. For example, the word *dog* may denote a certain species of quadruped. This word in its present form is literal or direct. Upon seeing or hearing this word, we may concoct in our mind's eye a mental image of a *dog*, and usually that image will derive from our own experience.

For example, the word may be connotatively charged so that this mental image is affected by our cultural orientation. If we live in an area where dogs are considered to be a nuisance (unclean, perhaps, or dangerous), the word *dog* may evoke an unpleasant emotion. The word *dog* may even be used pejoratively as a metaphor for an undesirable person. However, if we have a pet dog that we love, the word *dog* may evoke a totally opposite response.

But regardless of what connotative response the word may evoke, the writer or speaker can alter our response by directly shaping that image in our mind. This can be done by adding descriptors. The dog may be portrayed as *big,* or *bouncy,* or *floppy,* or *cuddly,* etc. However, the mental image can also be shaped indirectly by employing various types of figurative devices wherein one reality is compared to another. The dog might be likened to a *circus clown* or to a *dust mop.* Thus where literal language employs a direct process of describing reality, figurative language describes one reality in terms of another. In other words, figurative language is capable of creating poetic or metaphorical equivalents for reality (what T. S. Eliot called "objective correlatives"), most of which employ a comparison or equation between these two essentially different realities.

With literal or direct description, we (as audience) remain more or less passive. We are told what to think or imagine, and we comply. We create in our mind's eye a dog that is big, or bouncy, or floppy, or cuddly. But figurative language creates an indirect process in which we as audience are required to become active participants in the process of completing the description. For example, if we are to conceive of this dog as a circus clown or as a dust mop, we must consider imaginatively what qualities are shared in common by these two different realities. In effect, we contribute our own creative efforts to this process of conceiving a mental image of the dog. Therefore, while there is no precise or simple definition of figurative language, most often it involves the indirection of an analogical relationship whereby one reality is used to gain an understanding of or access to another reality. In this sense, figurative language is more of a process than a collection of specific rhetorical devices. Even the terms with which scholars discuss figurative language vary. In discussing poetry, a critic might use the term *imagery* to designate the various figures of speech a poet employs (e.g., simile, metaphor, apostrophe, synecdoche, trope, etc.). But at the heart of all figurative language is the process of building on what we already know by comparing the known to the unknown.

For example, in a prayer often recited by Bahá'í children, the child asks God to "make of me . . . a brilliant star." Obviously, this is not a literal request; the child is not asking to become a celestial object in the night sky. What, then, is the prayer really about? In what sense does the child wish to become a "star"?

Deciphering this simple but slightly "veiled" or "concealed" image is not difficult. In every culture since the dawn of time, stars have served as a means by which people can find guidance in the night, whether on land or on the sea. Particularly "brilliant" stars (such as the North Star) may quickly orient the lost traveler so that the correct path is followed. The child is thus asking for God's help in becoming a clear source of guidance to those who are lost in the darkness.

Of course, we can more fully appreciate the power of this simple image if we become aware of the frequent use of "nighttime" and "darkness" in the Bahá'í scriptures in alluding to those historical periods of spiritual decline that immediately precede the ascent of a new Revelation. In such periods, the Bahá'í scriptures assert, the spiritual luminaries of the previous Dispensation no longer provide light or guidance. It is in this figurative context that the earliest Bábís are alluded to with the poetic epithet "dawn-breakers" because they recognize the new "daystar" of guidance (the Báb) before others are yet awake. We might infer, then, that the child is asking to acquire those qualities that will be all the more luminous in the context of a period of spiritual heedlessness, a "nighttime" of spiritual decadence and immorality.

When we consider how much information is compressed in this one-word metaphor, we may well call to mind the tradition cited by Bahá'u'lláh in the Kitáb-i-Íqán when He speaks of the various levels of meaning that figurative language is capable of containing: "'We speak one word, and by it we intend one and seventy meanings; each one of these meanings we can explain'" (255). We can also observe how much less effective the same prayer would be were a child to make this request literally instead of figuratively: "Give me those qualities of spirit and help me follow a course of conduct that will serve as a standard whereby others might be so impressed that they would take note of my noble character and try to emulate this standard in their own lives."

As we analyze the components of figurative language, we begin to detect the essential method it employs, as well as the requirements it makes upon us as an audience. First, we note that most figurative language is analogical; it implies a comparison between two essentially different categories of reality: a dog is compared to a clown; a child desires to become like unto a star. The reader must discover some area of similitude between two essentially different categories of existence.

The result of this analogical relationship is a process that contains three fundamental parts: (a) the *tenor* (that which we are describing), (b) the *vehicle* (that which is compared to the *tenor*), and (c) the *meaning* (that area of similarity these two different realities share). Thus, in the child's prayer, the child would be the tenor, the star would be the vehicle, and the way in which both entities can become a source of guidance to those who are struggling to find their way in a period of darkness would be the meaning.

Some figurative visualizations may help us understand more clearly how these three components work. One helpful visualization is based on a diagram of an electrical circuit. If we imagine our soul as the battery or power source, then we can conceive of our meditative or contemplative faculty as the electrical current generated by that source. If we further imagine that the completion of thought is analogous to the completion of the circuit, then the process by which we try to discover the similitude between two essentially unlike things can be likened to resistors in an electrical circuit. Therefore we might think of (a) the tenor and (b) the vehicle as resistors, and (c) discovering the meaning of this comparison (i.e., the similitude between tenor and vehicle) as the completion of the circuit (see Fig. 5.1). The more difficult the analogy is to comprehend, the more mental effort (creative energy) we will need to invest to discover the meaning. Or, stated in

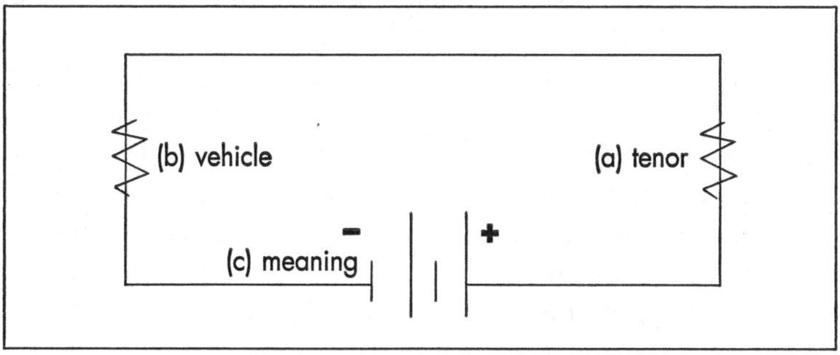

FIG. 5.1. CIRCUIT ANALOGY.

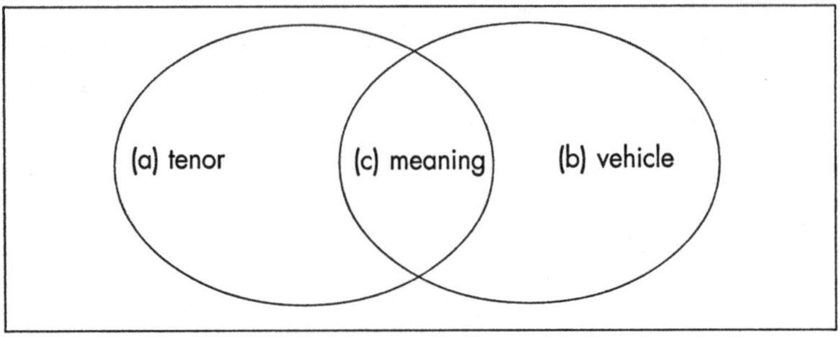

FIG. 5.2. FIGURATIVE IMAGE AS SET THEORY.

terms of our analogy, the greater the resistance, the greater the electrical power must be in order to complete the circuit.

We might not need to invest an immense amount of creative energy to solve the mystery of how a child could be like a brilliant star, but we might need to invest considerably more effort in solving other figurative images. Accordingly, when a figurative image becomes trite or commonplace (usually through overuse), it may lose its figurative power. Or, stated in terms of our analogy, a short circuit may occur; meaning will be achieved without any creative thought. Communication will still occur, but it will take place directly instead of indirectly; the figurative or poetic power of thought has been circumvented.

For example, if the same child were to refer to a popular singer as a "star," we would not feel the need to consider the metaphorical implications of the word *star.* What once was a figurative image has now become literal and direct; the word *star* in this context literally denotes a publicly acclaimed entertainer. We have a short circuit.

Another useful visual aid that we might employ for explaining how the analogical process works is derived from symbols used in explaining set theory. If we envision the tenor as set *a,* and the vehicle as set *b,* then the intersection of these two sets *(c)* represents those characteristics that the two realities have in common, the shared attributes or the meaning. Thus if we visualize the child as *a* and the star as *b,* then the meaning *c* represents the common, or shared, qualities: both give off light and guidance in a period of darkness (see Fig. 5.2).

Still another visualization that might prove useful in helping us understand how figurative language works is possibly the most useful—viewing figurative imagery as an algebraic expression. In algebra we try to discover the value (or meaning) of an unknown variable by expressing a relationship between the unknown variable and a known variable. For example, if we know that the tenor *a* is a child and that the vehicle *b* is a star, then we are trying to solve for *c*. The variable *c* is thus our unknown, our concealed value, our hidden mystery, the pearl in the shell of this figurative statement, the "ḥúrí"[1] of inner meaning:

> Notwithstanding all that We have mentioned, how innumerable are the pearls which have remained unpierced in the shell of Our heart! How many the ḥúrís of inner meaning that are as yet concealed within the chambers of divine wisdom! None hath yet approached them;—ḥúrís, "whom no man nor spirit hath touched before." (Bahá'u'lláh, *Kitáb-i-Íqán* 70–71)

Having stated an image in terms of a mathematical or algebraic problem, we are then faced with the further challenge of how to solve the problem in order to discover the value of the unknown variable. In the case of the child being compared to a star, we might most easily accomplish this task by employing the algebraic formula for determining ratios. The ratio is thus stated as follows: a star is to its light as a child is to *x* (see Fig. 5.3). The problem of stating the image in these terms is

$$\frac{\text{star}}{\text{starlight}} : \frac{\text{child}}{\text{(unknown)}}$$

FIG. 5.3

1. The term *ḥúrí* alludes to a Maiden of Heaven as portrayed in the Qur'án. The word means literally "white one." Islamic tradition holds that the sanctified souls will consort with these maidens in paradise, though Bahá'u'lláh clearly uses the term (the veiled maiden) as a metaphor for the hidden (veiled) meanings or "mysteries" that become understood (unveiled) by those who study the writings. Thus, most generally, the term alludes to symbols, metaphors, and other sorts of figurative language.

that such an arrangement presumes we already know the qualities of the star that are being likened to the comparable or analogous attributes of the child. Furthermore, the unknown variable is not always the meaning *c*. When Bahá'u'lláh alludes to Himself as a Lote-Tree, we know that the tenor *a* is Bahá'u'lláh, that the vehicle *b* is Lote-Tree, and that the meaning *c* concerns an affirmation of the Prophet's station or function. But the way we gain access to the meaning of this allusion is by discovering the meaning or value of the allusive vehicle "Lote-Tree"; unless we understand what this object is, we cannot discover how it is being compared to the Prophet.

For example, when Bahá'u'lláh states that He has unsealed the "Choice Sealed Wine," we may know that the meaning *c* is that He has given us something wonderful, and we know that the vehicle *b* (wine) represents that something. But it is the tenor *a* that is veiled or concealed by the image.

Of course, not all figurative images are one-word similes and metaphors. As we will see, figurative language includes extended analogies (i.e., parables and allegories) or conceptual comparisons (*conceits*[2]). Figurative language can employ an object closely associated with something to stand for the whole (metonymy), as in the following passage in which Bahá'u'lláh speaks of His "Robe," possibly an allusion to the Bahá'í religion:

> This Hem of His Robe hath ever been and remaineth unsullied, though many have, at the present time, purposed to besmirch it with their lying and unseemly calumnies. (*Epistle* 67)

Figurative language can employ a part of something to stand for the whole (synecdoche), as when Bahá'u'lláh alludes to God's power in terms of God's "hand":

2. *Conceit* is a literary term designating a type of poetic metaphor that is particularly imaginative or inventive.

> How can the hand of Him Who is the King in truth, Who caused the countenance of Moses to be made manifest, and conferred upon Him the robe of Prophethood—how can the hand of such a One be chained and fettered? (*Kitáb-i-Íqán* 136)

But our purpose here is not to render a complete or exacting analysis of all the types of figurative language employed by Bahá'u'lláh. Rather, we want to understand better how to analyze, interpret, and thereby more adequately appreciate the variety of ways Bahá'u'lláh has employed this literary technique in communicating to us the fundamental properties of spiritual reality and our relationship to that reality.

Nevertheless, before we proceed to discuss the usefulness of this device and examine it in action, we should become aware of at least two other prominent forms of figurative devices found in the works of Bahá'u'lláh. The first is *allusion,* a "brief reference to a historical or literary figure, event, or object" (*Handbook* 13). For example, in Chapter 7 we will attempt a fairly complete literary analysis of the Tablet of Aḥmad, and we will discover, among other things, that Bahá'u'lláh's allusion to Aḥmad in the tablet is extremely important. In effect, we can hardly understand the full impact of this work until we uncover this allusion by studying a little bit about the life of Aḥmad.

Like analogical devices, allusion leaves something unsaid, some mystery for us to solve. We must discover what special meaning the allusion or reference connotes, and sometimes we need to discover how it has come to acquire this special meaning. Often the allusion will also be figurative. For example, Bahá'u'lláh's reference to the "Choice Sealed Wine" alludes to a passage from the Qur'án, and yet the wine itself could be considered a metaphor for divine guidance.

A similar figurative device is the symbol. Like the analogical devices we have mentioned, a symbol links two realities together. Often, though not always, objects in physical reality will be employed to symbolize (or allude to) attributes of spiritual reality. For example, water may symbolize divine assistance: "Quench the thirst of heedlessness with the sanctified waters of My grace . . ." (*Gleanings* 323).

The main distinction between a symbol and an analogical device is that no comparison is necessary for a symbol to work. For example, when a flag is used as a symbol of a country or the cross is used as a symbol of Christianity, we are not really comparing one reality to another (i.e., the flag is not *like* a country; the cross is not *like* Christianity). The symbol alludes directly to the referent that it symbolizes. The symbol thus has only two parts: the symbol and the referent (that which is symbolized).

And yet there is a third part to this process of communication, and it is quite similar to the process we have described regarding the deciphering of a metaphor. It is sometimes valuable and necessary for us to discover *how* the symbol came to allude to the referent. Certainly, we can appreciate more fully the reverence with which a Christian regards the cross once we know the story of Christ's martyrdom and what this sacrificial act signifies in terms of the Christian concept of atonement and the forgiveness of sins.

This process of discovering how the symbol came about is sometimes described as "recovering the allusion." It is not always necessary; we need not know how the color red came to symbolize "stop" before we appreciate its meaning and respond accordingly. But the same sort of creative energy we invest in trying to solve the mysteries of analogical devices is often required for uncovering meaning when the poet employs symbolism.

C. The Power of Figurative Language

Figurative language is commonly employed by the Prophets because it is the best means of expressing what cannot be expressed directly or literally. For example, a child looks at a star in the night sky. The child may be incapable of conceptualizing infinity, understanding the properties of a star, or comprehending the distance light travels to reach us. But through poetry the child can verbalize an ineffable subjective experience of these realities:

> Twinkle, twinkle, little star!
> How I wonder what you are
> up above the world so high
> like a diamond in the sky!

The child communicates otherwise inexpressible emotions by comparing the unknown reality in terms of a reality the child has experienced—the spectral fire of colors emitted when light refracts from the facets of a diamond.

This same power of figurative language is exemplified when 'Abdu'l-Bahá employs a poetic image to exhort us not to fear death. He compares the sense of exhilaration we will feel at death when our soul is released from its association with the body to the joy a bird might feel upon being released from a cage:

> To consider that after the death of the body the spirit perishes is like imagining that a bird in a cage will be destroyed if the cage is broken, though the bird has nothing to fear from the destruction of the cage. Our body is like the cage, and the spirit is like the bird. We see that without the cage this bird flies in the world of sleep; therefore, if the cage becomes broken, the bird will continue and exist. Its feelings will be even more powerful, its perceptions greater, and its happiness increased. In truth, from hell it reaches a paradise of delights because for the thankful birds there is no paradise greater than freedom from the cage. That is why with utmost joy and happiness the martyrs hasten to the plain of sacrifice. (*Some Answered Questions* 228)

'Abdu'l-Bahá thus employs a simple but effective analogy to portray an unknown spiritual experience in terms of something we can immediately understand or imagine. While the analogy is not difficult, it is extremely valuable and comforting in its ability to translate an ineffable experience into a physical analogue, an analogy that implies both a rational proof that death does not affect the soul's progress and a consolation that we need not fear that transition to our future existence. Furthermore, in the guileless simplicity of this figurative explanation we come to appreciate poet Robert Hayden's observation that poetry is a means of saying the unsayable.

Another power of figurative language is its limitless potential.

With direct or literal language we may quickly run out of adjectives to describe something, or else the direct language soon loses its credibility. A young man tells a woman she is beautiful. The words have been used so often, they have lost their power and credibility. The young man must now invent some means of reinvesting his words with power to communicate his emotion. He resorts to comparison—"You are as beautiful as . . ."—and poetry is born. The young man will never run out of comparisons of the infinitude of possible relationships from which he can draw in order to convey his thoughts and feelings, providing, of course, he is creative enough and patient enough to discover these analogies.

Still another power of figurative language is the fact that it is limitless vertically as well as horizontally: there is an infinitude of possible comparisons we could employ to describe the same tenor, and a single comparison can render limitless levels of application. For example, the child prays to become spiritually luminous; yet we are all children of God, so the prayer is no less applicable to adults. Adults also should direct their lives so as to become sources of guidance and inspiration for others. In other words, we can envision the prayer being appropriate to any number of different individuals or groups, and we can interpret the specific qualities that would cause us to become sources of guidance in ever more refined and encompassing ways.

Certainly, figurative language has many other powers worth noting, but for our purposes it is sufficient to mention two other significant attributes of this indirect process. First, figurative language is capable of compressing an astounding amount of information into a brief space. We have already noted this quality in the child's prayer. When the Prophet employs images that have a whole history of usage, a truly amazing amount of information can be imparted. We need only think of how much information is implied when Bahá'u'lláh alludes to 'Abdu'l-Bahá as "the Most Great Branch" or to Himself as "the long-lost Joseph" or "the traceless Friend."

Perhaps the most profound power figurative language has as a teaching device is its capacity to force us to think for ourselves. And, as Bahá'u'lláh so often reminds us, independent thought epitomizes the condition of justice in human reality:

> The best beloved of all things in My sight is Justice; turn not away therefrom if thou desirest Me, and neglect it not that I may confide in thee. By its aid thou shalt see with thine own eyes and not through the eyes of others, and shalt know of thine own knowledge and not through the knowledge of thy neighbor.
> (Hidden Words, Arabic, no. 2)

Of course, we can allow someone else to interpret Bahá'u'lláh's art for us, but if we blindly accept an interpretation someone else has discovered, then we have not really learned much; we have merely memorized the learning someone else has acquired. It is precisely this requirement that we think for ourselves that redefines the role of scholars in this Dispensation as servants to the servants of God, not as a specialized class of divines. In commenting on this very issue, the Universal House of Justice, in letters written on its behalf, made the following observations:

> In the study of the Revelation of God, an individual's proficiency in one of the physical or social sciences, in law, philology, or other fields of specialization will often throw valuable light on issues being examined, and such contributions are greatly to be appreciated. . . . However, no one specialization among the many branches of scholarly research can confer upon its practitioners an authoritative role in the common effort of exploring the implications of so staggering and all-encompassing a body of truth.
>
> Collateral with His summons to the pursuit of knowledge, Bahá'u'lláh has abolished entirely that feature of all past religions by which a special caste of persons such as the Christian priesthood or the Islamic 'ulamá came to exercise authority over the religious understanding and practice of their fellow believers. (letter dated 20 March 1996 to an individual)
>
> The House of Justice wishes to avoid use of the terms "Bahá'í scholarship" and "Bahá'í scholars" in an exclusive sense, which

> would effectively establish a demarcation between those admitted into this category and those denied entrance into it. It is clear that such terms are relative, and that what is a worthy scholarly endeavour by a Bahá'í, when compared to the activities of those with whom he is in contact, may well be regarded as of vastly lesser significance when measured against the accomplishments of the outstanding scholars which the Faith has produced. The House of Justice seeks the creation of a Bahá'í community in which the members encourage each other, where there is respect for accomplishment, and common realization that every one is, in his or her own way, seeking to acquire a deeper understanding of the Revelation of Bahá'u'lláh and to contribute to the advancement of the Faith. (letter dated 19 October 1993 to an individual, quoted in *Scholarship* 7)

In fact, it is precisely this class that Bahá'u'lláh criticizes in the Kitáb-i-Íqán as having rejected the Manifestations because these "scholars" were incapable of understanding the poetic nature of divine utterance. It is in this same context that Christ responds to His own disciples' question about His own use of figurative language (i.e., parables) by explaining to them that He is trying to force His audience out of religious literalism, to make them think for themselves rather than merely parrot the thoughts of others:

> And the disciples came, and said unto him, Why speakest thou unto them in parables? He answered and said unto them, Because it is given unto you to know the mysteries of the kingdom of heaven, but to them it is not given. For whosoever hath, to him shall be given, and he shall have more abundance: but whosoever hath not, from him shall be taken away even that he hath. Therefore speak I to them in parables: because they seeing see not; and hearing they hear not, neither do they understand. And in them is fulfilled the prophecy of Esaias, which saith, By hearing ye shall hear, and shall not understand; and seeing ye shall see, and shall not perceive. (Matt. 13:10–14)

D. Experimenting with a Matrix

One of the more useful exercises in learning how to interpret figurative language is to create a matrix into which we can place the three components of analogical devices. Let us attempt several experiments with the matrix to determine how helpful this process can be in assisting us to elucidate the poetic language of divine utterance.

1. Experiment Number 1

> O MY SERVANT!
> Thou art even as a finely tempered sword concealed in the darkness of its sheath and its value hidden from the artificer's knowledge. Wherefore come forth from the sheath of self and desire that thy worth may be made resplendent and manifest unto all the world. (Hidden Words, Persian, no. 72)[3]

The general purpose of this verse seems to be an exhortation that we make use of our potential. But to unleash the full meaning of this poetic statement, we need to examine how the components convey this idea.

The most obvious parts of this image are the vehicles: "sword," "sheath," and "artificer." Therefore, let us begin our experiment by placing these vehicles in the second column of our matrix (see Table 5.1, p. 182). Our next step is to supply the tenors in the first column. Bahá'u'lláh has already provided us with two of these when He states that the sword is "Thou" (i.e., the "Servant"—presumably ourselves as believers) and that the "sheath" is the "self." We may presume that the "artificer" is God or, more appropriately, the Prophet who functions as God's artist or, in this case, as God's sword smith (see Table 5.2, p. 182). Even though our main concern with regard to the meaning of the image is to discuss how all the components can be assembled into one unified poetic statement, let us now try to insert the specific values in the third column for each particular relationship.

3. This same verse is used to explain some of the properties of metaphor in Hatcher, *Purpose of Physical Reality* 100.

TABLE 5.1

(a) Tenor	(b) Vehicle	(c) Meaning
	sword	
	sheath	
	artificer	

TABLE 5.2

(a) Tenor	(b) Vehicle	(c) Meaning
tongue (speech)	sword	
self	sheath	
God	artificer	

First, we should note that the believer is not just any sword; he is a "finely tempered" sword. In other words, this sword is capable of rendering great service. And while we might find it strange that the Prophet would want to compare His followers to instruments of warfare, we must remember that, symbolically, a sword is also capable of cutting through the veils that obscure the truth, something a believer is empowered to do by virtue of having been enlightened by the Prophet's revealed utterance. Therefore, the sword might be interpreted more particularly as a certain capacity of the believer—the special insight, wisdom, or knowledge that the Prophet has bestowed on the believer, or more precisely, the tongue which gives the believer the capacity to teach the Faith.

But this sword, though full of potential, is not being used for any purpose at all. It is concealed in a sheath as a soldier on parade might pridefully wear his weapon for purposes of ceremonial display. Consequently, the sheath represents something negative, that part of the "self" that would prevent this gift of knowledge from being used to full advantage. Indeed, throughout the Bahá'í writings, the "self" is portrayed as the inveterate enemy of those who aspire to spiritual growth and development or those who would assist others. For example, in another poetic exhortation Bahá'u'lláh calls upon His followers to

> Burn away, wholly for the sake of the Well-Beloved, the veil of self with the flame of the undying Fire, and with faces joyous and beaming with light, associate with your neighbor. (*Gleanings* 316)

In these passages "self" is thus not a form of self-respect, but veils that conceal one's nobler aspirations to serve God and to serve one's fellowman.

In terms of the "sheath of self," then, the believer has withheld or concealed his potential to serve—to help rend asunder the veils of confusion that perplex and prevent others from recognizing the Manifestation of God. Instead, the believer displays his knowledge as a sign of status or else busies himself with the attaining of wealth, position, or comfort. In this sense the precious tool bequeathed the believer by the Prophet is hidden from the Creator because the "self" effectively prevents this knowledge from being employed for those purposes the artificer intended (see Table 5.3, p. 184). Like any poetic utterance, this passage is capable of various interpretations and many levels of meaning, but the emphasis in this verse occurs in the second sentence, in which the "servant" is exhorted to change, to make his "worth" "resplendent and manifest unto all the world." In other words, the servant is already fully fashioned and ready for use, brimming with power and potential. The speaker/artificer is thus not suggesting that the servant needs to become something else. By renouncing self-interest, the power that has already been bestowed but that resides dormant in the sheath of self will become unleashed and manifest to others.

2. Experiment Number 2

Using this same matrix, let us attempt a similar exercise with a Hidden Word that might prove somewhat more complex:

> O SON OF MY HANDMAID!
> Quaff from the tongue of the merciful the stream of divine mystery, and behold from the dayspring of divine utterance the unveiled splendor of the daystar of wisdom. Sow the seeds of My divine wisdom in the pure soil of the heart, and water them

TABLE 5.3

(a) Tenor	**(b) Vehicle**	**(c) Meaning**
tongue (speech)	sword	God through His Prophet has given the believer all the capacities needed to render great service in defense of God's Cause and in elucidating its truths.
self (silence)	sheath	Instead of using these tools for service, the believers have paid more attention to selfish desires and thereby have neglected service to God.
God (Prophet)	artificer	God through His Prophet/ Artificer has endowed the believers with the gift of knowledge and has given them guidance about how to apply this knowledge for the advancement of human society.

> with the waters of certitude, that the hyacinths of knowledge and wisdom may spring up fresh and green from the holy city of the heart. (Hidden Words, Persian, no. 78)

With this verse we find several metaphors working together to describe a series of actions. Here the vehicles are fairly apparent, the general sense of what the poem means is relatively clear, but the precise tenors are not.

Here, too, Bahá'u'lláh is addressing the believer, a servant, the "son of my handmaid!"—one who has already recognized the Prophet as the source of divine guidance. The general sense of the command thus seems to be that if we take certain actions, the wisdom we gain from the Prophet will produce specific results in our lives and in the spiritual development of our souls. What may not be clear is what those actions are and how they will bring forth the desired results.

As with our first exercise, let us once more begin by establishing what information is readily apparent. The first sentence compares drinking from a stream with becoming attentive to the utterances of the Prophet. If we drink from this stream, the sentence goes on to say, we will comprehend "the unveiled splendor of the daystar of wisdom."

It is with the second sentence that the poetic utterance becomes more abstruse. Here we encounter a variety of verbs and nouns as vehicles: "sow," "seeds," "pure soil," "water," "hyacinths," "spring up," "fresh and green," and "holy city." We can also observe that for most of these vehicles Bahá'u'lláh has provided the tenor; therefore, let us insert these values in our matrix and see what remains to be discovered (see Table 5.4).

While some of this seems clear enough, we can see from our matrix that we lack precise tenors for the principal action "sow" and for the "springing up" of the flowers. While "sowing" in this context could represent some specific action (such as reading or memorizing the words of the Prophet), it obviously alludes to some means by which the heart of the believer is exposed to these same utterances that are portrayed as a "stream of divine mystery" in the first sentence of the verse. The springing up of "knowledge and wisdom" could likewise have a variety of meanings, but in a most general sense this verb seems to imply some means by which the knowledge takes root and evolves or progresses or becomes apparent to others.

TABLE 5.4

(a) Tenor	(b) Vehicle	(c) Meaning
?	sow	
divine wisdom	seeds	
heart	pure soil	
certitude	water	
knowledge and wisdom	hyacinths	
?	spring up	
?	fresh and green	
heart	holy city	

Thus, if we recast this sentence in somewhat more literal terms, we might end with something like the following: Meditate on the utterances of the Prophet with a pure heart (without ulterior motive); nourish the wisdom these utterances impart with conviction, steadfastness, and devotion (certitude) so that the knowledge contained in these utterances will bring about the subsequent transformation of your soul and the elevation of your character will be manifested in your actions.

Naturally, we find it noisome to translate the poetry out of the verse; certainly, we find it impossible to do it well. This is one important lesson we can learn from our experiment, that the Prophet employs poetic language precisely because it is capable of communicating what ordinary speech is incapable of expressing, or at least is incapable of expressing effectively. Certainly, we could profitably spend a considerable amount of creative energy explicating more completely many of the components in this brief passage. For example, Bahá'u'lláh often employs the hyacinth as a symbol of wisdom that flowers or flourishes in the human heart:

> Be as resigned and submissive as the earth, that from the soil of your being there may blossom the fragrant, the holy and multicolored hyacinths of My knowledge. (*Gleanings* 322)

> Sow the seeds of My divine wisdom in the pure soil of thy heart, and water them with the water of certitude, that the hyacinths of My knowledge and wisdom may spring up fresh and green in the sacred city of thy heart. (Hidden Words, Persian, no. 33)

> Wherefore sow the seeds of wisdom and knowledge in the pure soil of the heart, and keep them hidden, till the hyacinths of divine wisdom spring from the heart and not from mire and clay. (Hidden Words, Persian, no. 36)

The hyacinth is a simple but elegant flower. It gives off a most delightful fragrance, and Bahá'u'lláh utilizes this same image because it succinctly and immediately conveys the idea of beauteous results.

Let us now attempt to complete our matrix by filling in the third column to see how these figurative components work together to communicate Bahá'u'lláh's message to us (i.e., that the utterances of the Manifestations, when studied, memorized, or otherwise considered and then implemented, have the capacity to effect personal transformation (see Table 5.5, p. 188).

3. Experiment Number 3

Similar to the extended simile or metaphor is the parable, one of the favorite teaching devices employed by Christ. As we noted in our discussion of genre, the parable is an allegorical story. As we also noted, in allegory all objects and actions have a metaphorical significance, though the story usually focuses on conveying one major theme or concept (i.e., it usually has a moral). To illustrate how our matrix can help illuminate the meaning of a parable, let us study briefly one of the better-known parables of Christ which employs the same imagery of planting seeds that we observed in Persian Hidden Word number 78:

> And he spake many things unto them in parables, saying, Behold, a sower went forth to sow; And when he sowed, some seeds fell by the way side, and the fowls came and devoured them up: Some fell upon stony places, where they had not much earth: and forthwith they sprung up, because they had no deepness of earth: And when the sun was up, they were scorched; and because they had no root, they withered away. And some fell among thorns; and the thorns sprung up, and choked them: But others fell into good ground, and brought forth fruit, some an hundredfold, some sixtyfold, some thirtyfold. Who hath ears to hear, let him hear. (Matt. 13:3–9)

Perhaps the first thing we notice with this parable as we compare it to Persian Hidden Word number 78 is that, to a certain extent, Christ has made His meaning more veiled or concealed by not revealing any of the tenors and by not hinting at the overall meaning. We thus begin our matrix with a list of some thirteen vehicles and no obvious tenors

TABLE 5.5

(a) Tenor	(b) Vehicle	(c) Meaning
study and contemplate	sow	expose your heart or innermost self to
divine wisdom	seeds	the insights and wisdom contained in the Prophet's words, wisdom that is expansive and thus capable of producing further understanding
heart	pure soil	that part of yourself that is receptive to spiritual insights (the heart as opposed to the intellect)
certitude	water	Nourish this exposure to divine utterance with that conviction which is achieved by prayer, study, and deeds.
knowledge and wisdom	hyacinths	so that these initial insights will develop and transform your character and lead to further understanding
become apparent	spring up	may become apparent so that others may see in you the effects of this spiritual process
new and startling	fresh and green	wisdom (such as the concept of progressive revelation or the unity of the planet) that offers some new vision of ourselves
from the heart	from the holy city	from our pure motives, our desire to assist humankind, not from our desire to achieve prominence or notoriety

(see Table 5.6). Of course, we may be helped in discerning the overall meaning of this parable by our conclusions about Bahá'u'lláh's use of imagery in Persian Hidden Word number 78: the Word of God (i.e., the utterances of the Prophet) is likened to seeds to be planted in the human heart. But we also can discover one major difference that leads us almost immediately to a sense of the overall meaning here. Persian Hidden Word number 78 is addressed to a faithful believer ("Son of My Handmaiden") in the form of advice; the believer must do the "sowing." Christ's parable is an objective, third-person analysis of what happens to divine utterance as it is sown by the Prophet and then received by people whose "soils" (hearts) are in various conditions. Specifically, Christ lists four places where the seeds fall: the "way side," "stony places," "thorny places," and "good ground."

We can presume that the fourth place (good ground) represents that "pure soil" of the "Son of My Handmaiden" in Persian Hidden Word number 78. Thus, like the seeds in Bahá'u'lláh's image which bring forth hyacinths, the seeds in Christ's parable that fall upon this "good ground" also bring forth results—various quantities of fruit. The overall meaning would thus seem to be that, while the word of

TABLE 5.6

(a) Tenor	**(b) Vehicle**	**(c) Meaning**
?	sower	?
?	seeds	?
?	way side	?
?	fowls	?
?	stony places	?
?	sun	?
?	scorched	?
?	no root	?
?	thorny places	?
?	thorns choked	?
?	good ground	?
?	fruit	?
?	(quantity)	?

God is available to all alike, it has the most profound and lasting results with those recipients whose hearts are pure. With this meaning in mind, we are now able to fill in a bit more of our matrix (see Table 5.7).

Before we try to resolve the remaining unknown variables, we might find it valuable to observe another overall tenor here. This parable occurs in the context of a discussion about parables themselves; it

TABLE 5.7

(a) Tenor	**(b) Vehicle**	**(c) Meaning**
Manifestation (Christ)	sower	comes to change humankind by conveying the Word of God (seeds)
divine utterance	seeds	Words are sown or scattered so that they are available to all alike.
?	way side	?
?	fowls	?
?	stony places	?
?	sun	?
?	scorched	?
?	no root	?
?	thorny places	?
?	thorns choked	?
pure hearts of the believers	good ground	those who are able to transcend accepted opinion and think for themselves
results (i.e., changed character?)	fruit	As a tree bears fruit, so belief in the heart of the faithful will bring forth good acts.
amount or type of results	(quantity)	Each person has a different capacity, a distinct gift to give.

is followed by the already-mentioned response of Christ to His disciples' question about His use of this device. When Christ responds, "it is given unto you to know the mysteries of the kingdom of heaven," He is implicitly comparing his disciples to "good soil." In effect, the parables themselves may be the overall tenor in this analogy, the "seed" scattered among the people. Those with spiritual receptivity can figure them out and become changed (i.e., produce hyacinths and fruit), but those whose hearts have "waxed gross" and whose ears are "dull of hearing" and whose "eyes . . . have closed" (Matt. 13:15) are the other sorts of soil represented in this parable.

But, regardless of whether we tie the comparison of planting seeds to Christ's use of parables or more generally to the divine utterances of the Prophets, the meaning of the various sorts of soil is clear; they represent the many different things that prevent the seeds from taking root. Therefore, let us attempt to understand the specific condition represented by the other types of soil.

The first type of soil is the stony place. Here there is soil for the seed to grow, but the soil has no depth. Thus, if the ascent of the sun represents the growing intensity of the revelation, then the scorching and subsequent withering of these plants might represent a faith unable to withstand the stark truth that the new Revelation discloses. Of course, for the early Bábís there were the tests of physical persecution (just as there were for the early Christians). And yet the test here is from a positive source (the sun), not from those forces that would destroy this belief (i.e., the thorns and weeds of the thorny place). Hence it would seem more likely that the lack of depth would signify a faith that had been derived from an initial attraction to the words of the Prophet—a faith which could not withstand the subsequent utterances.

Bahá'u'lláh describes such a believer in great detail in the Kitáb-i-Íqán when He speaks of how each Prophet brings teachings that inevitably test the belief of those who initially profess allegiance (e.g., Christ abrogated certain Jewish laws, Muḥammad changed the Qiblih from Jerusalem to Mecca, etc.). Bahá'u'lláh compares these changes, which test believers and non-believers alike, to the smoke and clouds of prophecy which veil the mind of man from perceiving the identity of the Prophet: "The symbolic term 'smoke' denotes grave dissensions, the abrogation and demolition of recognized standards, and the utter destruction of their narrow-minded exponents" (*Kitáb-i-Íqán* 76).

In short, the Revelation, while a source of enlightenment, is not designed to make us comfortable. On the contrary, the Prophet is the trainer of our souls, and His exercises are devised to stretch us beyond our present condition, beyond what we are presently capable of doing with ease. Consequently, if we have no depth of belief, or do not develop it, we will not be able to bear the mounting intensity of the Revelation as its light illuminates our most hidden thoughts and secret desires.

The thorny place is relatively simple to understand. Here the seeds also take root, but the plant grows among hostile or contrary plants (thorns and weeds) which choke off this fragile new life. The vehicle *thorn* might thus represent other ideas or beliefs that people have in the soil of their hearts, ideas which they are not willing to root out or disregard. One immediately calls to mind Christ's own observation:

> No man can serve two masters: for either he will hate the one, and love the other; or else he will hold to the one, and despise the other. Ye cannot serve God and mammon. (Matt. 6:24)

Bahá'u'lláh observes the same spiritual axiom in Persian Hidden Word number 31:

> O SON OF EARTH!
> Wouldst thou have Me, seek none other than Me; and wouldst thou gaze upon My beauty, close thine eyes to the world and all that is therein; for My will and the will of another than Me, even as fire and water, cannot dwell together in one heart.

and in Persian Hidden Word number 52:

> O CHILDREN OF NEGLIGENCE AND PASSION!
> Ye have suffered My enemy to enter My house and have cast out My friend, for ye have enshrined the love of another than Me in your hearts. . . .

Whatever the specific "thorn" may be—whether an unwillingness to change one's behavior to comply with Divine Law or to relinquish the love of some contrary interests—the thorn seems to represent something within the heart of the individual, not an outside force that poses a threat to the believer.

The hardest "soil" to understand is the "way side." Here some alien or external force snatches up the seed before it has a chance to take root. Of course, the "way side" is not a particularly good place to plant seed in the first place, so possibly this part of the parable alludes to those utterances of the Prophet that are taken out of context and snatched up by birds.

Because they are devourers, destroyers, or usurpers of the word, we would most understandably interpret these symbolic birds as allusions to the divines or ecclesiasts, those who prevent the words from reaching the people, who distort or misrepresent the words to the people, or who otherwise hamper the "seeds" from taking root in the hearts of the people. These are the same ones whom Bahá'u'lláh describes at length in the Kitáb-i-Íqán:

> Leaders of religion, in every age, have hindered their people from attaining the shores of eternal salvation, inasmuch as they held the reins of authority in their mighty grasp. Some for the lust of leadership, others through want of knowledge and understanding, have been the cause of the deprivation of the people. (15)

Of course, the bearing of "fruit" in Christ's parable, like the blooming "hyacinth" in Bahá'u'lláh's metaphor, represents fruition of faith. It ties in with Christ's later metaphor comparing Himself to a vine, God to the vinedresser (husbandman), and the believers to branches that bear fruit that is then changed into the choice wine of Christ's Revelation. The fact that the various plants (believers) produce different quantities of fruit (deeds) parallels Bahá'u'lláh's own statement that each individual has a "pre-ordained measure" of capacity and that our individual exercise of free will determines to what extent we will transform this latent capacity into realized acts:

> Know thou that all men have been created in the nature made by God, the Guardian, the Self-Subsisting. Unto each one hath been prescribed a pre-ordained measure, as decreed in God's mighty and guarded Tablets. All that which ye potentially possess can, however, be manifested only as a result of your own volition. Your own acts testify to this truth. (*Gleanings* 149)

Certainly, we could do a great deal more by way of explicating the components of this parable, but we have done enough to fill in our matrix and derive from these components a fairly clear sense of the overall meaning (see Table 5.8).

4. Experiment Number 4

For our fourth experiment with the matrix, let us examine the parable from the Valley of Knowledge in The Seven Valleys that Bahá'u'lláh uses to explain that one important property of knowledge is to endow the believer with the ability to see the "end in the beginning":

> There was once a lover who had sighed for long years in separation from his beloved, and wasted in the fire of remoteness. From the rule of love, his heart was empty of patience, and his body weary of his spirit; he reckoned life without her as a mockery, and time consumed him away. How many a day he found no rest in longing for her; how many a night the pain of her kept him from sleep; his body was worn to a sigh, his heart's wound had turned him to a cry of sorrow. He had given a thousand lives for one taste of the cup of her presence, but it availed him not. The doctors knew no cure for him, and companions avoided his company; yea, physicians have no medicine for one sick of love, unless the favor of the beloved one deliver him.
>
> At last, the tree of his longing yielded the fruit of despair, and the fire of his hope fell to ashes. Then one night he could live no more, and he went out of his house and made for the marketplace. On a sudden, a watchman followed after him. He broke into a run, with the watchman following; then other watchmen came together, and barred every passage to the weary

TABLE 5.8

(a) Tenor	**(b) Vehicle**	**(c) Meaning**
Manifestation (Christ)	sower	comes to change humankind by conveying the Word of God (seeds)
divine utterance	seeds	Words are sown or scattered so that they are available to all alike.
words out of context?	way side	words of the Prophet that are not "sown" but are taken out of context and used against the Prophet
divines or ecclesiasts	fowls	try to prevent words from reaching the people
followers who have no depth of understanding	stony places	followers who may be initially attracted but who, upon being exposed to more, are unable to withstand the challenge the Revelation imposes
the light or intensity of the Revelation	the sun	Like the sun rising during the day, the intensity of the Revelation increases as the Dispensation progresses.
belief is unable to withstand test	scorched	Beliefs are tested as the believers are faced with denying their long-held beliefs and customs.
no depth of understanding	no root	The beliefs are not confirmed by study or willingness to change one's innermost desires.
believers who cannot relinquish conflicting desires	thorny places	believers who cherish ideas and desires that are in conflict with the teachings of the Prophet and who are not willing or able to relinquish these affections

TABLE 5.8 [CONTINUED]

(a) Tenor	(b) Vehicle	(c) Meaning
contrary ideas dominate purer instincts	thorns choked plant	The more one is tested and required to relinquish affection for contrary desires, the more those "thorns" kill off belief.
pure hearts of the believers	good ground	those who are able to transcend accepted opinion and think for themselves
results, changed character?	fruit	As a tree bears fruit, so belief in the heart of the faithful will bring forth good acts.
amount or type of results	(quantity)	Each person has a different capacity, a distinct gift to give.

> one. And the wretched one cried from his heart, and ran here and there, and moaned to himself: "Surely this watchman is 'Izrá'íl, my angel of death, following so fast upon me; or he is a tyrant of men, seeking to harm me." His feet carried him on, the one bleeding with the arrow of love, and his heart lamented. Then he came to a garden wall, and with untold pain he scaled it, for it proved very high; and forgetting his life, he threw himself down to the garden.
>
> And there he beheld his beloved with a lamp in her hand, searching for a ring she had lost. When the heart-surrendered lover looked on his ravishing love, he drew a great breath and raised up his hands in prayer, crying: "O God! Give Thou glory to the watchman, and riches and long life. For the watchman was Gabriel, guiding this poor one; or he was Isráfíl, bringing life to this wretched one!" (*Seven Valleys* 13–14)

Bahá'u'lláh gives us an extremely helpful head start in our effort to interpret this allegory by providing the heart of the overall meaning—

that true knowledge enables us to appreciate the ultimate outcome of our efforts:

> Now if the lover could have looked ahead, he would have blessed the watchman at the start, and prayed on his behalf, and he would have seen that tyranny as justice; but since the end was veiled to him, he moaned and made his plaint in the beginning. Yet those who journey in the garden land of knowledge, because they see the end in the beginning, see peace in war and friendliness in anger. (*Seven Valleys* 15)

The problem or mystery for us thus becomes discerning *how* the story comes to signify this meaning and appreciating more precisely what else seeing "the end in the beginning" might signify. We can begin the process of interpretation by first placing the more obvious vehicles in the second column (see Table 5.9). Obviously, there are other compo-

TABLE 5.9

(a) Tenor	**(b) Vehicle**	**(c) Meaning**
	lover	
	beloved	
	love-sick	
	despair	
	watchman chases him	
	passages barred	
	frightened and suffering	
	scales wall	
	forgetting life, he jumps	
	sees beloved	
	watchman was Gabriel or Isráfíl	

nents we could include as vehicles. For example, we might try to interpret the specific ills that afflict the lover, why the beloved is carrying a lamp in the night, what her ring symbolizes, and so on. But let us confine our experiment to the more obvious vehicles and insert into our matrix some of the more apparent tenors.

If the lover is the seeker after knowledge, then perhaps the beloved is the Manifestation (or the knowledge of some spiritual truth which the Manifestation can provide). Perhaps the watchman in the night might be the tests that come to us in times of "darkness" (spiritual deprivation or heedlessness). These tests appear as adversity, but they actually set us in motion towards the object of our quest, even though we do not realize it at the time. Hence the watchman whom the seeker presumed at first to be 'Izrá'íl (his angel of death), he later realizes was, in actuality, "Gabriel, guiding this poor one; or he was Isráfíl, bringing life to this wretched one!" *(Seven Valleys* 14).[4]

The other watchmen who bar "every passage to the weary one" (14) might represent the laws of the Prophet which function to deter the seeker from choosing a course of action that, while appearing to be an escape from tribulation, actually prevents him from attaining his objective. Here again, the seeker presumes the opposite—that these "watchmen" are obstructing his escape from danger. Only at the end of his struggle will he come to appreciate how these watchmen are safeguarding him and assisting him by urging him towards the object of his desire.

The leap over the wall is perhaps the most perplexing vehicle. This desperate act might represent a leap of faith or some self-imposed dramatic change in the seeker's life in response to this testing. If the

4. In Islámic lore the angel Isráfíl is supposed to blow a trumpet announcing Judgment Day, but to interpret the character of the watchman according to such a scholarly anagogical perspective is to go beyond the bounds of the more basic interpretation of our present experiment. Nevertheless, it is very important to realize that this story, like all Bahá'í scripture, can also be interpreted according to various ascending levels of meaning. From a more expansive perspective, for example, the lover might represent humankind; his perilous search, the course of history; and the various watchmen who bar passages of escape, the successive Manifestations.

parable is seen as a more encompassing view of our spiritual journey, the leap could represent our passage into the next world where, at last, all the things we endured in this life are suddenly seen as the perfect preparation for our future growth and development in the world of the spirit.

Of course, the reunion with the beloved represents the seeker's attainment of true knowledge, the very thing the seeker desired in the first place. All his experience which had appeared as torment, as trial, and as restriction he now understands in retrospect as divine assistance in his quest, as the surest path to freedom and understanding. Thus, as we fill in the tenors in the first column, we discover that, in light of Bahá'u'lláh's succinct summary of the parable's theme, we can easily fill in the third column as well (see Table 5.10). The further theme or meaning in this would seem to be that, having triumphed, the true seeker does not need to go through this process again. Having once under-

TABLE 5.10

(a) Tenor	**(b) Vehicle**	**(c) Meaning**
one seeking truth or the identity of the Prophet	lover	Like a lover deprived of his beloved, the true seeker can find comfort nowhere but in the presence of spiritual truth.
Manifestation of divine knowledge and wisdom	beloved	As the object of the lover's longing is nearness to the beloved, so the true seeker's obsession is with discovering the source of divine guidance.
longing for the comfort of divine presence and inspiration	love-sickness	Nothing else will suffice for the one who sincerely desires the Divine Presence.
tests and difficulties that beset the seeker	watchman chases	As one seeks to discover spiritual truth, one is assisted by experiences that seem to be tests but that turn out to be guidance.

TABLE 5.10 [CONTINUED]

(a) Tenor	**(b) Vehicle**	**(c) Meaning**
The seeker is protected from diversions from what he seeks, perhaps by laws of God.	passages barred	God will guide and protect the true seeker in such a way that no diversion will suffice, and those actions that would be harmful to the seeker are mysteriously shut off, perhaps by laws, or else by fortuitous events.
There are points when the seeker feels abandoned and the quest seems unendurable.	frightened and suffering	However faithful or constant the seeker may be, there will be times when one's personal strength will seem insufficient, when one is humbled and is tempted to despair.
The seeker responds to fear by instigating some daring course of action.	scales wall	However inadequate the seeker may feel, the true seeker will be chastened to follow the right path by being forced to alter his response to life and by being strengthened to initiate some radical change.
Becoming detached from the things of this world, the seeker dares to act.	forgetting life, he jumps	Once the seeker has faced the worst that life can do, he may become daring.
The seeker discovers the spiritual solace he has been seeking.	sees beloved	Like being reunited with a loved one, the seeker suddenly realizes that what he thought of as random injustice was naught but guidance in disguise.
Seeker understands the purpose of tests and of physical reality in general.	watchman was Gabriel or Isráfíl	The seeker realizes that all his suffering and pain were but a means to a just, benign, and felicitous end—he understands that divine guidance will always be available for the true seeker, even when it seems absent.

stood the essential benignity of divine law and of God's creation as a whole, the true seeker will no longer become disturbed or perplexed by personal adversity (the seeming injustice he encounters). He will know, in short, that the overall outcome of all social conflict and all human perversity will be the eventual triumph of God's plan. On a personal level the parable serves to gird the believer in times of testing by providing the same comforting assurance Bahá'u'lláh imparts in the following passage:

> O My servants! Sorrow not if, in these days and on this earthly plane, things contrary to your wishes have been ordained and manifested by God, for days of blissful joy, of heavenly delight, are assuredly in store for you. Worlds, holy and spiritually glorious, will be unveiled to your eyes. You are destined by Him, in this world and hereafter, to partake of their benefits, to share in their joys, and to obtain a portion of their sustaining grace. To each and every one of them you will, no doubt, attain. (*Gleanings* 329)

Likewise, our interpretation of the watchmen as laws would seem to be supported by one of Bahá'u'lláh's statements regarding "true liberty" (as opposed to that "license" which has the guise of liberty):

> Say: True liberty consisteth in man's submission unto My commandments, little as ye know it. Were men to observe that which We have sent down unto them from the Heaven of Revelation, they would, of a certainty, attain unto perfect liberty. Happy is the man that hath apprehended the Purpose of God in whatever He hath revealed from the Heaven of His Will, that pervadeth all created things. (*Gleanings* 336)

In summary, then, we begin to see how much meaning Bahá'u'lláh has compressed in this simple story. To understand and appreciate the larger implications of this allegory, we must turn to the overall theme of theodicy that Bahá'u'lláh addresses in the Kitáb-i-Íqán, something we will partially address in our discussion of structure in the next chapter.

E. Patterns of Imagery in the Art of Bahá'u'lláh

Now that we have a fundamental understanding of how and why the Prophets conceal the pearls of inner meaning within the shells of symbol and metaphor, of allegory and allusion, we can go a step farther. We can sample some of the ways Bahá'u'lláh employs imagery in His art. In particular, we can discover some of the patterns of images in the works of Bahá'u'lláh that cause various themes to echo and reverberate throughout the vast ocean of His words. This cursory exercise will help us appreciate how Bahá'u'lláh often repeats certain vehicles and symbols and how He will frequently draw a number of vehicles or symbols from the same context. This exercise will also help us realize that, once we become aware of a repeated symbol or vehicle, we can then become attuned to the power of that device to convey a symphony of thought in a handful of carefully chosen notes.

1. How Patterns Become Established

Patterns of images can become established in a variety of ways. For example, Christ often employs bread as a metaphorical vehicle. He explains to the Jews that the manna they received in the wilderness was really the spiritual teachings come down from God. He then expands that metaphor to explain that He is also the same sort of spiritual nourishment come down to them from God (i.e., the Word made flesh):

> Our fathers did eat manna in the desert; as it is written, He gave them bread from heaven to eat. Then Jesus said unto them, Verily, verily, I say unto you, Moses gave you not that bread from heaven; but my Father giveth you the true bread from heaven. For the bread of God is he which cometh down from heaven, and giveth life unto the world. Then said they unto him, Lord, evermore give us this bread. And Jesus said unto them, I am the bread of life: he that cometh to me shall never hunger; and he that believeth on me shall never thirst. (John 6:31–35)

Christ also uses the gift of bread in this same sense in the Lord's Prayer when He commands the faithful to pray, "Give us this day our daily bread" (Luke 11:3). In effect, He is exhorting the believers to reflect on and become nourished by Christ's teachings on a daily basis. Christ employs this same symbol dramatically when He miraculously feeds the four thousand with an endless supply of bread (Matt. 15). He again uses bread in this same symbolic sense to represent His own flesh (i.e., the Word made flesh) at the dramaturgical ritual He performs at the Last Supper (Luke 22:19).[5]

The value of becoming attentive to Christ's repeated use of bread imagery, particularly as regards the concept of the "bread of life," is that we no longer see these as separate statements or events. We understand and appreciate the continuity of this divine theme as it runs throughout His ministry. We instantly connect the feeding of the Jews in the wilderness with the Lord's Prayer, with the feeding of the four thousand, and with the Last Supper. Furthermore, we connect the whole concept of physical nourishment with the "Word made flesh" as spiritual nourishment.

Of course, it is quite possible that we might sense the meaning of these passages on some unconscious level without having to study the nature of figurative language. Yet the learned Pharisees were certainly perplexed by the poetic devices in Christ's words:

> I am the living bread which came down from heaven: if any man eat of this bread, he shall live for ever: and the bread that I will give is my flesh, which I will give for the life of the world. The Jews therefore strove among themselves, saying, How can this man give us his flesh to eat? Then Jesus said unto them, Verily, verily, I say unto you, Except ye eat the flesh of the Son of man, and drink his blood, ye have no life in you. Whoso eateth my flesh, and drinketh my blood, hath eternal life; and I will raise him up at the last day. (John 6:51–54)

Furthermore, the Roman Catholic Church itself later established the doctrine of transubstantiation, the belief that the wine and bread literally become the blood and flesh of Christ, thus duplicating what the

---

5. In effect, the disciples act out their belief that Christ as the Word of God is the spiritual nourishment they need on a daily basis.

Pharisees had done by way of interpreting literally the poetic utterances of the Prophet.

The more attentive we become to the figurative devices commonly employed by a Prophet, the more we can train ourselves to avoid the pitfalls of literalism. For example, Bahá'u'lláh employs several memorable figures of speech when alluding to Himself and to His mission: He is the Nightingale of Paradise whose melodic voice calls out in the dark of night; He is the Divine Lote-Tree, the Sadratu'l-Muntahá, the guidepost marking the true path; He is the "Divine and infallible Physician" (*Gleanings* 213) Who diagnoses the illness of humankind and prescribes the remedy.

While some of these symbolic epithets are easy enough to penetrate, others require more effort on our part. For example, in some of His more mystical writings Bahá'u'lláh alludes to Himself as the "long-lost Joseph." On the simplest level, Bahá'u'lláh is identifying Himself as one who has been concealed or hidden even as the identity of Joseph was concealed from his brothers. However, the figure of Joseph has a power quite beyond this obvious meaning. Clustered around this story are allusions drawn from the lengthy account of Joseph in Genesis, from the more compressed but more direct narration of the same story in the Qur'án, and from the Báb's lengthy explication of the Súrih of Joseph in the Qayyúmu'l-Asmá'.

As the story is told in Genesis, we are presented with what seems to be a detailed literal account of how Joseph is sold into slavery by his brothers, comes to power in Egypt, and later dramatically reveals himself to these same brothers when he saves them from starvation. In the Súrih of Joseph in the Qur'án, Muḥammad identifies Joseph as an Apostle, a Prophet. Even though Joseph does not reveal a "book," Bahá'u'lláh indicates that Joseph has a lofty station as a "lesser" Prophet:

> The names of those cited in Bahá'u'lláh's Prayer in the Dispensation are quite correct as you gave them, (Abraham, Moses, Joseph, John the Baptist, Christ, Muḥammad, Imám Ḥusayn, the Báb, and Bahá'u'lláh.)
>
> The Prophets "regarded as one and the same person" include the lesser Prophets as well, and not merely those who

> bring a "Book." The station is different, but They are Prophets and Their nature thus different from that of ours. (Shoghi Effendi, *Directives from the Guardian* 57)

Muḥammad's retelling of the story in the Qur'án thus emphasizes Joseph as an emissary of God, but it ends enigmatically with the implication that the story has an important symbolic value quite beyond its obvious meaning: "This is no new tale of fiction, but a confirmation of previous scriptures, and an explanation of all things, and guidance and mercy to those who believe" (Qur'án 12:111).

As students of Bahá'í history are well aware, Mullá Ḥusayn was intrigued and perplexed by the meaning of this enigmatic assurance in the Súrih of Joseph; consequently, he had determined that, should he encounter one who he thought might indeed be the promised Qá'im, the final confirmation for him would be that the true Qá'im would, unasked, reveal for him the meaning of this Súrih.

Of course, the Báb did exactly that on that fateful evening of May 22, 1844, as He chanted the opening verses of the Qayyúmu'l-Asmá', the work "characterized by Bahá'u'lláh as *'the first, the greatest, and mightiest of all books'* in the Bábí Dispensation" (Shoghi Effendi, *Promised Day Is Come* ¶65). While we need not go into detailed discussion of the Báb's work, we can note several major clues as to the importance of the figure of Joseph as a symbolic allusion to Bahá'u'lláh.

First, Shoghi Effendi explains that the abiding purpose of the Qayyúmu'l-Asmá' is "to forecast what the true Joseph (Bahá'u'lláh) would, in a succeeding Dispensation, endure at the hands of one who was at once His arch-enemy and blood brother" (*God Passes By* 23). In this sense, the rejection and persecution of Bahá'u'lláh by His own brother, Mírzá Yaḥyá, fulfills the Prophecy implicit in the Qur'án. In addition to this parallel, Bahá'u'lláh alludes to images of the unmasking of Joseph to his brothers as parallel to the advent of a new Manifestation. In effect, the same figure whom the brothers had betrayed and had left for dead they now recognize as their savior. In this sense, the followers of Muḥammad and the followers of the Báb are tested and judged just as the brothers of Joseph are tested.

This interpretation is confirmed when we consider that Joseph and his brothers go on to establish the nation of Israel. That is, they are literally the sons of Jacob (who is renamed as "Israel"), and thus they collectively represent the chosen followers of God in every dispensation. Therefore the brothers' journey into Egypt to seek assistance during the famine symbolically alludes to the search for the new Manifestation during a period of spiritual dryness (i.e., when humankind is in need of spiritual nourishment or divine bestowals). The fact that the brothers do not initially recognize Joseph, especially in his station as ruler, effectively portrays both the difficulty for the followers of a previous Dispensation in recognizing a new Manifestation, as well as the shock that a people experience upon recognizing the true power and station of the concealed Prophet who formerly lived among them.

For example, Bahá'u'lláh employs an allusion to Joseph in the Valley of Love in The Seven Valleys:

> Until thou enter the Egypt of love, thou shalt never come to the Joseph of the Beauty of the Friend; and until, like Jacob, thou forsake thine outward eyes, thou shalt never open the eye of thine inward being; and until thou burn with the fire of love, thou shalt never commune with the Lover of Longing. *(Seven Valleys* 9)

With the knowledge of the story that is behind this allusion, the reader can derive much of the full impact of this poetic statement. Jacob, the father of Joseph, perceives the spiritual power of his son, and we, like Joseph's brothers and their father, must be tested before we, too, can be allowed to behold the "Beauty of the Friend" (i.e., recognize Bahá'u'lláh as a Manifestation of God).

By reviewing the background of the phrasal epithet "long-lost Joseph," we come to appreciate the veiled power of this simple appellation. Understanding this background also enables us to spot other allusions to this same story, as in The Four Valleys when Bahá'u'lláh alludes to the story of Joseph with the lines: "Methinks at this moment,

I catch the fragrance of His garment blowing from the Egypt of Bahá; verily He seemeth near at hand, though men may think Him far away" (*Seven Valleys* 59).

Another example of how various metaphorical terms can be grouped or clustered around a single context is Bahá'u'lláh's allusion to alchemy. In a number of places Bahá'u'lláh alludes to the Word of God as the Divine Elixir. Possibly, we sense in this image that the "elixir" is a life-giving potion, but unless we uncover more precisely how this image works, we are deprived of the remarkable symbolic power of this seemingly simple term.

If we research the term *elixir,* we discover that it derives from the study of alchemy, a speculative philosophy of ancient and unknown origins that attempted to determine the nature of matter and man's relationship to materiality. As it evolved from century to century and from culture to culture, it became a literal attempt to transmute base metals into gold, ultimately becoming in western Europe during the medieval era the foundation for modern chemistry.

During its heyday in medieval Europe alchemy became largely a pseudoscience employed by charlatans to bilk unsuspecting investors out of great sums of money, something Chaucer depicts satirically in "The Canon's Yeoman's Tale." But theoretically and poetically alchemy retained its philosophical roots as a symbol of human spiritual transformation. Let us examine briefly how alchemy came to assume this important symbolic significance.

The fundamental theory behind alchemy is that, by combining certain ingredients (usually various combinations of base metals) and then heating these ingredients in various proportions, one could change copper, lead, or some other base metal into gold. However, according to the theory of this mysterious science, the key to success was dependent on discovering the mysterious unknown substance which, when combined with these other ingredients, would function as a catalyst to effect the desired transmutation.

This unknown ingredient was designated by the term *elixir* and sometimes by the epithet *the philosopher's stone.* Consequently, over the course of time many writers, philosophers, and theologians alike came to see in this literal search for the mysterious elixir a symbol of the search for personal moral or spiritual transformation. For some Christian writers, the elixir more specifically symbolized the saving grace bestowed on humankind by Christ's martyrdom whereby Christ's death paid the ransom for the sins of the world.

In the writings of Bahá'u'lláh we discover a number of symbolic terms derived from alchemy: figurative uses of *elixir, philosopher's stone,* and the concept of *transmutation*. However, we also discover, interestingly enough, allusions to the literal significance of this process. For example, Bahá'u'lláh in the Kitáb-i-Aqdas alludes to the literal accomplishment of this transmutation as one sign that humanity has achieved maturation:

> The first sign of the coming of age of humanity referred to in the Writings of Bahá'u'lláh is the emergence of a science which is described as that *"divine philosophy"* which will include the discovery of a radical approach to the transmutation of elements. This is an indication of the splendors of the future stupendous expansion of knowledge. (*Kitáb-i-Aqdas* n194)

Furthermore, in the Kitáb-i-Íqán Bahá'u'lláh states forthrightly that He was perfectly capable of performing this transmutation, though He laments that, even were He to carry out such a miraculous feat, it would not change the hearts of those who were against Him:

> But of what avail! All this generation could offer Us were wounds from its darts, and the only cup it proffered to Our lips was the cup of its venom. On our neck We still bear the scar of chains, and upon Our body are imprinted the evidences of an unyielding cruelty. (190)

Thus, while we will in time no doubt discover more and more about the literal significance of this process, our awareness of the background associated with the study of alchemy helps us as readers appreciate Bahá'u'lláh's symbolic use of these terms. Bahá'u'lláh speaks of the "potency of the Divine Elixir, which, swift as the twinkling of an eye, transmuteth the souls of men!" (*Kitáb-i-Íqán* 157). In one prayer Bahá'-

u'lláh alludes to the "most exalted Word" as "the Divine Elixir unto all who are in Thy realm, the Elixir through whose potency the crude metal of human life hath been transmuted into purest gold" (*Prayers and Meditations* 54). In a tablet Bahá'u'lláh exhorts the believers to "memorize phrases and passages" from the "heavenly Scriptures" because "these holy verses are the most potent elixir" (*Tablets of Bahá'u'lláh* 200). In still another passage Bahá'u'lláh compares a "'true believer'" to the "'philosopher's stone'" (*Kitáb-i-Íqán* 79).

2. Sample Patterns Derived from Repetition

Now that we understand the importance of learning to uncover the allusions in the symbols, metaphors, and other poetic devices employed by Bahá'u'lláh, we are ready to discover how these same devices often appear in patterns in which certain figurative devices are repeated. With the concordances and computer retrieval programs that are presently available, any reader is capable of quickly discovering these patterns. By surveying some examples of how images become repeated throughout the art of Bahá'u'lláh, we can discover quite easily how useful such an exercise can be in broadening our perspective about the hidden treasures of meaning in Bahá'u'lláh's art.

a. *Drinking Imagery*

Let us begin with a simple but effective recurring metaphor, Bahá'u'lláh's frequent reference to drinking as a vehicle for the act of receiving divine guidance, inspiration, or assistance. For example, Bahá'u'lláh often employs the vehicle of drinking to represent the process of receiving (partaking of) the divine utterances of the Prophets. In these figurative images Bahá'u'lláh will usually indicate the tenor, and sometimes He will also indicate what the fountain source of the liquid represents, as well as the container. Let us examine several examples of the metaphorical verb *quaff* to demonstrate the variety of concepts Bahá'u'lláh clothes in the garment of this simple image:

> The Sealed Wine is disclosed in this day before the faces of men. Seize it in the name of thy Lord, and *quaff* thy fill in remembrance of Him Who is the Mighty, the Incomparable.
>
> (*Epistle* 88)

This is the Day whereon the rushing waters of everlasting life have gushed out of the Will of the All-Merciful. Haste ye, with your hearts and souls, and *quaff* your fill, O Concourse of the realms above! (*Gleanings* 30)

The people of the left hand sigh and bemoan. The people of the right abide in noble habitations: they *quaff* the Wine that is life indeed, from the hands of the All-Merciful, and are, verily, the blissful. (*Gleanings* 40–41)

This is the flowing water ye were promised in the Qur'án, and later in the Bayán, as a recompense from your Lord, the God of Mercy. Blessed are they that *quaff* it. (*Gleanings* 46)

Hearken to the delightsome words of My honeyed tongue, and *quaff* the stream of mystic holiness from My sugar-shedding lips. (Hidden Words, Persian, no. 33)

Help us then to *quaff*, O my God, from the fingers of mercy the living waters of Thy loving-kindness, that we may utterly forget all else except Thee, and be occupied only with Thy Self. (*Prayers and Meditations* 30)

Make them, then, to *quaff* from the hand of Thy grace the wine of Thy mercy, that it may assure their hearts, and cause them to turn away from the left hand of idle fancies and vain imaginings to the right hand of confidence and certitude. (*Prayers and Meditations* 111–12)

Make me to *quaff*, O my Lord, from the fingers of Thy bounteousness the living waters which have enabled every one that hath partaken of them to rid himself of all attachment to any one save Thee. . . . (*Prayers and Meditations* 240)

> From the crystal springs of Thy love suffer me to *quaff,* O my Glory, and beneath the shadow of Thine everlasting providence let me abide, O my Light! (*Prayers and Meditations* 258)

> Seize ye the chalice of constancy through the power of His Name, *quaff* then therefrom by virtue of the sovereignty of God, the Powerful, the Omnipotent. (*Tablets of Bahá'u'lláh* 247)

> By the righteousness of the true God, if ye remain steadfast upon this line which standeth upright between the two lines, ye shall, in very truth, *quaff* the living waters from the Fountain of this wondrous Revelation as proffered by the hand of His Remembrance. . . . (*Selections from the Writings of the Báb* 58)

Among these examples we observe a variety of tenors represented by the vehicles for the drink and for the source of the drink. The drink may be a "Sealed Wine," "waters of everlasting life," the "Wine that is life," the "flowing water ye were promised in the Qur'án," the "stream of mystic holiness," the "waters of loving-kindness," the "wine of mercy," or the "living waters." The vehicle representing the source of these drinks may be "My sugar-shedding lips," the "crystal springs of Thy love," "the chalice of constancy," or the "Fountain of this wondrous Revelation." Likewise, the container may be proffered by "the hands of the All-Merciful," the "fingers of mercy," the "hand of Thy grace," or the "fingers of Thy bounteousness."

Needless to say, we could list countless other uses of this same essential figurative image. For example, in this context we might continue investigating drinking imagery by noting Bahá'u'lláh's use of metaphorical verbs such as "drink" or "taste"; metaphorical sources for these liquids, such as "cup," "fountain," or "ocean"; and metaphorical liquids such as "water," "wine," or "stream." For even though this is a relatively simple metaphor, one whose meaning we instinctively understand without much contemplation, we can enhance the power of these expressions by observing the variable use of this simple metaphorical construction.

b. Olfactory Imagery

Another simple but effective use of metaphor also occurring with significant frequency consists of images associated with smell or fragrance. Here again the image is not difficult to understand, but there is a significant power in this poetic figure to express a difficult idea with a commonly accessible comparison—the idea of being able to sense abstract qualities even though we cannot precisely identify the source of that awareness.

For example, Bahá'u'lláh implies that the seeker can detect the fragrance of the Divine Presence through the perfume of the Prophet's utterance:

> Happy is the lover that hath inhaled the divine fragrance of his Best-Beloved from these words, laden with the perfume of a grace which no tongue can describe. (Kitáb-i-Aqdas ¶4)

> Every fair-minded person is led, by the fragrance of these words, unto the garden of understanding, and attaineth unto that from which most men are veiled and debarred. (*Epistle* 146)

These images are important, because the meaning (the similarity between tenor and vehicle) implies that being able to recognize the Prophet and to recognize the divine authority in the utterance of the Prophet, is not something we can always do scientifically or mechanically. If we have spiritual sensitivity, we become aware of this spiritual power in the same way we become aware of a fragrant scent in the air.

This same sort of subtlety of spiritual influence pertains to the power of the good deeds of a believer—i.e., these deeds that are endowed with a fragrance that is capable of enduring forever:

> Strive thou, that haply thou mayest achieve a deed the fragrance of which shall never fade from the earth. (*Epistle* 115)

Of course, if the spiritual attributes have a fragrant smell, acts have their own characteristic aroma:

> Time and again have We admonished Our beloved ones to avoid, nay to flee from, anything whatsoever from which the odor of mischief can be detected. (*Tablets of Bahá'u'lláh* 94)

Explaining the verity that "'knowledge is a light which God sheddeth into the heart of whomsoever He willeth'" (*Kitáb-i-Íqán* 184), Bahá'-u'lláh employs olfactory imagery to denounce a pompous work by a supposedly learned scholar, the title of whose exposition was *"Guidance unto the Ignorant":* "From this title We perceived the odor of conceit and vainglory, inasmuch as he hath imagined himself a learned man and regarded the rest of the people ignorant" (185).

Like the metaphors associated with drink, these olfactory images are not usually elaborate or difficult to understand. In fact, we barely notice them as images because they relate so immediately and powerfully to the concept they portray. Yet they are still extremely effective because they depict so convincingly the human capacity for detecting a quality or an attribute immediately and intuitively even when there is no visible or obvious empirical evidence to support one's inferences.

For example, if someone is performing an ostensibly noble service, but for purposes of self-aggrandizement, we sense the dissimulation. The act gives off its own distinct smell. Similarly, the simplest deed from someone pure in heart also has its own special fragrance. Of course, not everyone is endowed with the capacity to detect these smells. If one's sense of smell has become perverted or dysfunctional, then this subtle spiritual sensibility is likewise encumbered: "Yea, to the beetle a sweet fragrance seemeth foul, and to the man sick of a rheum a pleasant perfume is as naught" (*Seven Valleys* 20). Here we see that the beetle becomes a vehicle for a person who is in a state of spiritual perversity or degeneration. Consequently, the things that attract such a one are exactly the opposite of what they should be. Similarly, to someone like the beetle who is dwelling "close to the earth" (the earth being a frequent symbol in Bahá'u'lláh's works of sensuality and appetency), the things that seem attractive are, in reality, "foul-smelling"; conversely, that which is truly fragrant repels such a one.

For example, to the ecclesiasts infatuated with their own learning and lofty stature, the appearance of the Manifestation is abhorrent.

And to someone who is caught up in sensuality, the laws of the Manifestation regarding moderation, fidelity, or abstinence from licentiousness or intoxication might seem unjust restrictions on personal freedom, when, in reality, Bahá'u'lláh notes that from these very laws "the sweet-smelling savor of My garment can be smelled" (Kitáb-i-Aqdas ¶4).

c. The Cycle of the Day

Like most of the Manifestations before Him, and like most poets as well, Bahá'u'lláh selects the majority of His vehicles from the world of nature. Vehicles drawn from nature are particularly useful because they have a universal power since experiences in the natural world are relatively common to all peoples and cultures. Furthermore, because the Bahá'í writings affirm that the natural world inherently reflects spiritual attributes, the poet or Prophet need not invent metaphorical relationships.

For example, because the primary concern of Bahá'u'lláh's revealed writing is in the growth and development of humankind, both individually and collectively, His art often draws on metaphors that are taken from growing things and, more particularly, from the cyclical process by which plants evolve. These patterns of growth are most often employed as vehicles for the evolutionary changes in other categories of organic progression. Indeed, it is commonplace in scripture to compare the stages in human life to the seasons of a year or the cycle of a Dispensation to the progress of a day. For example, Bahá'u'lláh explains the rationale for progressive revelation with a helpful analogy—what might be more appropriately designated a conceit—that compares the gradualness by which the day brightens with the light of of the sun to the progressive enlightenment of humankind effected by successive divine Revelations:

> Know of a certainty that in every Dispensation the light of Divine Revelation hath been vouchsafed unto men in direct proportion to their spiritual capacity. Consider the sun. How feeble its rays the moment it appeareth above the horizon. How gradually its warmth and potency increase as it approacheth its zenith,

> enabling meanwhile all created things to adapt themselves to the growing intensity of its light. How steadily it declineth until it reacheth its setting point. Were it, all of a sudden, to manifest the energies latent within it, it would, no doubt, cause injury to all created things. . . . In like manner, if the Sun of Truth were suddenly to reveal, at the earliest stages of its manifestation, the full measure of the potencies which the providence of the Almighty hath bestowed upon it, the earth of human understanding would waste away and be consumed; for men's hearts would neither sustain the intensity of its revelation, nor be able to mirror forth the radiance of its light. Dismayed and overpowered, they would cease to exist. (*Gleanings* 87–88)

Similarly, Bahá'u'lláh often alludes to the Bahá'í Dispensation as a special "Day" in the lifetime of human society on this planet:

> Great indeed is this Day! The allusions made to it in all the sacred Scriptures as the Day of God attest its greatness. The soul of every Prophet of God, of every Divine Messenger, hath thirsted for this wondrous Day. All the divers kindreds of the earth have, likewise, yearned to attain it. No sooner, however, had the Day Star of His Revelation manifested itself in the heaven of God's Will, than all, except those whom the Almighty was pleased to guide, were found dumbfounded and heedless. (*Proclamation of Bahá'u'lláh* 112)

Here again the student of Bahá'u'lláh's writing can benefit immensely from surveying the frequency and variety of metaphors associated with "day," "night," "morning," and other allusions to the cycles of religious history depicted in terms of the smaller cycle of a day.

d. Tree Imagery

Another of the more succinct but powerful images drawn from nature is Bahá'u'lláh's use of plants or trees as figurative allusions to the Manifestation. As we mentioned in Chapter 4, the Manifestation is variously designated as the "Divine" or "Sacred Lote-Tree," the Sadratu'l-

Muntahá, to which Shoghi Effendi refers as the "'Tree beyond which there is no passing'" (*God Passes By* 94). Literally, this is "the tree which, in ancient times, the Arabs planted to mark the end of a road" (Momen, *Basic Bahá'í Dictionary* 200). Thus its symbolic meaning might be an allusion to the object of one's quest or journey (the goal of one's search) or possibly to the limit of what one can know until the next Prophet appears.

In general, the tree is employed to symbolize the continuity of Revelation from one Prophet to the next. Bahá'u'lláh also employs the same symbolic terms to designate the station of 'Abdu'l-Bahá and His relationship to the Manifestation. For example, in the *Will and Testament of 'Abdu'l-Bahá,* the Guardian (Shoghi Effendi) is referred to as "the youthful branch branched from the two hallowed and sacred Lote-Trees and the fruit grown from the union of the two offshoots of the Tree of Holiness" (11); Shoghi Effendi was descended from both the Báb and Bahá'u'lláh. This same vehicle is used to express other familial relationships to Bahá'u'lláh and the Báb. The descendants of Bahá'u'lláh are referred to as the *Aghṣán,* or Branches, of the Sacred Lote-Tree, and the descendants of the two brothers of the Báb's wife and of the Báb's maternal uncles are designated as the *Afnán,* or Twigs, of the sacred Lote-Tree. Most often these appellations allude to the male descendants; whereas frequently the female descendants are referred to as *varaqat,* or leaves, of the Sacred Lote-Tree.

Often Bahá'u'lláh will employ the tree image to refer to the Anísá, the "Tree of Life," as in the Tablet of Aḥmad, in which Bahá'u'lláh alludes to the Báb as the "Tree of Life that bringeth forth the fruits of God, the Exalted, the Powerful, the Great" (*Bahá'í Prayers* 210). Here the tenor for "Tree of Life" is the Prophet as the continuous source of fruit for humanity. Thus in The Hidden Words when Bahá'u'lláh alludes to a time past ("that true and radiant morn") when "ye were all gathered in My presence beneath the shade of the tree of life, which is planted in the all-glorious paradise" (Hidden Words, Persian, no. 19), He is not alluding to some preexistent state of the human soul, a concept contrary to explicit Bahá'í teachings. Instead, He seems to be speaking as the eternal voice of the Divine Presence alluding to previous Dispensations when humanity was similarly called to recognize the

Voice of God coming from the source of the celestial Tree. In fact, Shoghi Effendi authoritatively interprets this passage as alluding even more specifically to the Covenant:

> Extolled by the writer of the Apocalypse as "the Ark of His (God) Testament"; associated with the gathering beneath the *"Tree of Anísá"* (Tree of Life) mentioned by Bahá'u'lláh in the Hidden Words; glorified by Him, in other passages of His writings, as the *"Ark of Salvation"* and as *"the Cord stretched betwixt the earth and the Abhá Kingdom,"* this Covenant has been bequeathed to posterity in a Will and Testament which, together with the Kitáb-i-Aqdas and several Tablets, in which the rank and station of 'Abdu'l-Bahá are unequivocally disclosed, constitute the chief buttresses designed by the Lord of the Covenant Himself to shield and support, after His ascension, the appointed Center of His Faith and the Delineator of its future institutions. (*God Passes By* 239)

Thus in the Adamic myth (as depicted in the Old Testament) the tree in the Garden represents both the point beyond which humankind cannot pass, as well as the continuity of God's assistance through the Manifestations: "The tree of life is the highest degree of the world of existence: the position of the Word of God, and the supreme Manifestation" ('Abdu'l-Bahá, *Some Answered Questions* 124).

The same image obviously also relates to the voice of God transmitted to Moses through the Burning Bush. For example, Bahá'u'lláh alludes to Himself as a second Moses[6] when in a tablet to Napoleon III He states: "Give ear, O King, unto the Voice that calleth from the Fire which burneth in this verdant Tree, on this Sinai which hath been raised above the hallowed and snow-white Spot, beyond the Everlasting City: 'Verily, there is none other God but Me, the Ever-Forgiving, the Most Merciful!'" (*Proclamation of Bahá'u'lláh* 18)

Again, we can profitably invest a great deal of energy researching the various uses of this recurring image to allude to the continuity of

---

6. "He [Bahá'u'lláh] was the One Moses conversed with in the Burning Bush" (*Lights of Guidance* no. 1552).

God's grace as demonstrated through the advent of Prophets. Indeed, Muḥammad also employs the same imagery when He prophesies the advent of the Báb: "From a blessed tree is it lighted, the olive neither of the East nor of the West, whose oil would well nigh shine out, even though fire touched it not!" (Qur'án 24:35)

e. Garden Imagery

Another frequently used image drawn from nature employs the vehicle of gardens. In fact, gardens have inevitably provided for the poet such a rich resource for metaphorical vehicles that entire volumes have been devoted to discussing the use of garden imagery in literature.[7] The garden is a useful image because it ties in so effectively with some of the other images used by Bahá'u'lláh to allude to the Bahá'í Revelation.

Sometimes Bahá'u'lláh will use the garden image in a general sense, as in the following metaphor which employs *garden* as a vehicle for the tenor *understanding:*

> Every fair-minded person is led, by the fragrance of these words, unto the garden of understanding, and attaineth unto that from which most men are veiled and debarred. (*Epistle* 146)

Here words are compared to the flowers in the garden of understanding, implying, we might conclude, that the beauty of the creative word of God attracts people to study, to meditate thereon, and thus to achieve greater understanding.

One of the most powerful uses of the garden metaphor is to represent the Revelation itself. For example, in the Hidden Words we find the following passage:

> Proclaim unto the children of assurance that within the realms of holiness, nigh unto the celestial paradise, a new garden hath

7. For example, see Julie Scott Meisami, "Allegorical Gardens in the Persian Poetic Tradition: Nezami, Rumi, Hafez," *International Journal of Middle East Studies* 17 (1985): 229–60.

> appeared, round which circle the denizens of the realm on high and the immortal dwellers of the exalted paradise. (Hidden Words, Persian, no. 18)

In the context of this same metaphor, Bahá'u'lláh often alludes to the development of spiritual attributes in terms of flowers being grown and nourished within this garden:

> With the hands of loving-kindness I have planted in the holy garden of paradise the young tree of your love and friendship, and have watered it with the goodly showers of My tender grace; now that the hour of its fruiting is come, strive that it may be protected, and be not consumed with the flame of desire and passion. (Hidden Words, Persian, no. 34)

> Ye are the trees of My garden; ye must give forth goodly and wondrous fruits, that ye yourselves and others may profit therefrom. (Hidden Words, Persian, no. 80)

Sometimes the garden more generally seems to symbolize the ongoing Revelation of God, as with the Garden of Eden in the Adamic myth or in the following passage from The Seven Valleys in which Bahá'u'lláh compares Himself to a tormented thrush: "many a talon claweth at this thrush of the eternal garden" (41).

The student of Bahá'í history may also associate Bahá'u'lláh's use of the garden image with the episode at the Conference at Badasht. According to Shoghi Effendi, the purpose of the conference was to sound the "clarion-call" of "a new Dispensation," the Revelation of the Báb (*God Passes By* 32). However, Bahá'u'lláh, Who "steadily, unerringly, yet unsuspectedly, steered the course of that memorable episode" (32), arranged for three gardens—one for Quddús, one for Ṭáhirih, and one for Himself.

The climactic episode of the conference occurs when Bahá'u'lláh claims to be ill, invites the contending Quddús and Ṭáhirih to His tent, whereupon, in a symbolic act designed to proclaim that a new Revelation has begun, Ṭáhirih unveils herself so that all may behold her beauteous countenance. The attendees then all assume new names individually; they also determine that the advent of the Báb signals a new religion, not merely a reformation of Islám.

Shoghi Effendi indicates that all of this is prearranged, that Bahá'-u'lláh has coordinated this dramaturgy to act out before the assembled believers the significance of who they are and what their new identity means.[8] In what we might look upon as a sort of allegorical play, Quddús, who speaks for the conservative contingent that wishes to remain Muslim, feigns anger at Ṭáhirih, who advocates a break with Islámic laws and traditions. In this context, the garden of Quddús represents the Revelation of Muḥammad; the garden of Ṭáhirih represents the Revelation of the Báb; and the third garden, the garden of Bahá'u'lláh, where this episode takes place and the quarrel is resolved, represents the Revelation of Bahá'u'lláh (which would serve to clarify for these Bábís, and for humanity in general, the unity and continuity of all religious history).

f. Wine and Vineyard Imagery

Christ speaks of the "new wine" which must needs be placed in a new wine skin as an allusion to the relationship between spiritual teachings and the implementation of those teachings in social and ecclesiastical structures.[9] Christ also explains divine justice in relation to the kingdom of heaven through the parable of the workers in the vineyard—those who labor to gather the fruit that will produce the wine (Matt. 20:1–16). Later, in attempting to explain His relationship to His followers and to God, Christ again employs vineyard imagery: "I am the true vine, and my Father is the husbandman. Every branch in me that beareth not fruit he taketh away: and every branch that beareth fruit, he purgeth it, that it may bring forth more fruit" (John 15:1–2).

---

8. See Shoghi Effendi, *God Passes By* 31–33, for a discussion of the conference, and see Nabíl, *The Dawn-Breakers* 294, n1, for a confirmation that the quarrel was prearranged.

9. This is discussed at length in *The Arc of Ascent: The Purpose of Physical Reality II.*

This idea of the purging or pruning of the branch would seem to allude to the testing to which a follower will be subjected so that he or she might bring forth the fruit of good deeds. Furthermore, the analogy implies that meaningful action or deeds can only be accomplished when one is aware of the source of those deeds and, consequently, remains faithful to the Covenant. Thus every follower is a branch of the "true vine," the Manifestation of God. But a branch cannot thrive or produce fruit unless it remains connected to the vine. It is through that bond or connection that its nourishment is received because "the branch cannot bear fruit of itself, except it abide in the vine" (John 15:4).

Applying the matrix to this analogy, we might end up with something like Table 5.11. Is the wine produced by the fruit of these branches the same wine that they imbibe at the Last Supper? Christ seems to

TABLE 5.11

(a) Tenor	**(b) Vehicle**	**(c) Meaning**
Christ	vine	He is the source of their relationship to God.
believers	branches	Their reality derives from their connection to Christ.
spiritual achievements	fruit	They can only produce spiritual results so long as they remain faithful to Christ's teachings and Christ's covenant.
suffering and tests	purgeth (pruning)	Only through tests and suffering will the believers achieve further growth and thereby produce even more spiritual results.
God	husbandman	God is ultimately in control of the whole process whereby the believers are made capable of transforming themselves and others.

explicate the symbolism of that wine somewhat differently; the wine at the Last Supper seems to represent Christ's blood, the covenant by which Christ's sacrifice atones for the sins of humanity. And yet, in reality, this wine may still allude to the same image. The fruit of religion is the continuation of God's grace to humankind. In this sense, the wine produced from the fruit by laborers in the vineyard symbolizes the ongoing process by which God brings forth an "ever-advancing civilization" through the continuous appearances of the Manifestations.

Vineyard imagery is similarly employed by Bahá'u'lláh. In Epistle to the Son of the Wolf, Bahá'u'lláh states that "Carmel, in the Book of God, hath been designated as the Hill of God, and His Vineyard. It is here that, by the grace of the Lord of Revelation, the Tabernacle of Glory hath been raised" (145). Likewise, 'Abdu'l-Bahá employs such epithets as "celestial Vineyard" (*Selections from the Writings of 'Abdu'l-Bahá* ¶42.5) and "vineyard of God" (*Tablets of Abdul-Baha Abbas* 1:21) when referring to the Bahá'í Faith. In the same vein, he may address an individual Bahá'í as a "gardener of Truth" in the "divine vineyard" (*Tablets of Abdul-Baha* 3:536) or as a "skillful laborer in the vineyard of God" (*Tablets of Abdul-Baha* 1:121).

Of course, the wine image may seem an ironic and troublesome metaphor because Bahá'u'lláh, like Muḥammad before Him, proscribes the drinking of wine. In other words, we might wonder why Bahá'u'lláh would employ as a vehicle for a positive process what is on a literal level a negative and proscribed experience, becoming intoxicated by imbibing wine.

The enigmatic nature of this relationship between the vehicle *(producing and drinking wine)* and the tenor *(implementing the spiritual transformation of the planet and becoming exhilarated by the love of God)* is one means by which the Prophet forces us to think. If we accept the words literally, they make no sense. Hence it is not a literal wine we imbibe that intoxicates us with the carefree joy and detachment which one enthralled with the love of God exhibits; it is a spiritual elixir (to explain one metaphor in terms of another).

Interestingly, Bahá'u'lláh seems to realize that not everyone would be immediately able to penetrate the metaphorical nature of this image. Therefore, Bahá'u'lláh takes the trouble to caution the believers that this is a metaphorical use of wine and should not be taken literally:[10]

> [T]hink not that the wine We have mentioned in Our Tablet is the wine which men drink, and which causeth their intelligence to pass away, their human nature to be perverted, their light to be changed, and their purity to be soiled. Our intention is indeed that wine which intensifieth man's love for God, for His Chosen Ones and for His loved ones, and igniteth in the hearts the fire of God and love for Him, and glorification and praise of Him. (*Compilation of Compilations* 2: no. 1785)

He further explains the specific meaning of this metaphor as it appears in His own writings as well as in the Qur'án:

> We meant by this Wine, the River of God, and His favour, the fountain of His living waters, and the Mystic Wine and its divine grace, even as it was revealed in the Qur'án, if ye are of those who understand. He [Muḥammad] said, and how true is His utterance: "A wine delectable to those who drink it." And He had no purpose in this but the wine We have mentioned to you, O people of certitude! (*Compilation of Compilations* 2: no. 1785)

Therefore, even though Christ did not specifically proscribe the drinking of wine, it is equally clear that His use of the metaphor is likewise symbolic. Wine symbolizes divine sustenance, a source of inspiration capable of exhilarating and transforming whoever imbibes it. Perhaps even more relevant, this wine is made from the fruit of the branches, fruit that is picked by the laborers working in the vineyard. If the branches are the believers, their fruit would be their spiritual understanding translated into deeds, and the gathering of that fruit by the

---

10. Considering what had been done with the literal interpretation of previous scriptures, Bahá'u'lláh understandably anticipates that His own followers could well fall prey to this same sort of literalism.

laborers would signify some coordination of those actions, possibly an allusion to the construction of religious and social institutions by those who work within the administrative order.[11] Of course, the use of wine and vineyard imagery has a particularly powerful usage in Bahá'u'lláh's allusion to His Revelation as representing the "Choice Sealed Wine" prophesied in the Qur'án. More particularly, His revelation of the Kitáb-i-Íqán seems to be that "sealed wine," and the revelation of the Kitáb-i-Aqdas represents the unsealing of that choice vintage.[12]

g. City and Fortress Imagery

Another image that we find frequently employed by Bahá'u'lláh in relation to the correlation between spiritual perception and daily action or between spiritual truth and an administrative order is the image of a city. One of the most familiar scriptural uses of this image, of course, is the concept of the City of God descended from heaven, alluded to as the New Jerusalem in the New Testament.

Bahá'u'lláh explains that the tenor for this image is the Word of God: "That City is none other than the Word of God revealed in every age and dispensation" (*Kitáb-i-Íqán* 199). However, sometimes this metaphor is employed in the writings of Bahá'u'lláh to allude in particular to the Revelation of Bahá'u'lláh, something we would assume occurs in the following passage:

> A Great City hath descended from heaven, and Zion trembleth and exulteth with joy at the Revelation of God, for it hath heard the Voice of God on every side. (*Epistle* 145)

Likewise, in the Tablet of Carmel when Bahá'u'lláh alludes to circumambulating the "City of God," He seems to be alluding to the Bahá'í Administrative Order that would be established on the mountain:

---

11. In the context of the Bahá'í institutions, for example, this could specifically allude to the institutions of the "rulers" and the "learned"— i.e., the elected and appointed branches of the Bahá'í Administrative Order.

12. For full discussions of this imagery, see Hatcher, *Arc of Ascent* 202–34, and Hatcher and Hatcher, *The Law of Love Enshrined* 101–12.

> Hasten forth and circumambulate the City of God that hath descended from heaven, the celestial Kaaba round which have circled in adoration the favored of God, the pure in heart, and the company of the most exalted angels. (*Gleanings* 16)

Indeed, 'Abdu'l-Bahá explains that the New Jerusalem in the Book of Revelation is alluding to this process in general and to the Bahá'í Revelation in particular:

> The heavenly Jerusalem is none other than divine civilization, and it is now ready. (*Promulgation of Universal Peace* 102)

> The Law of God is also described as the Holy City, the New Jerusalem. (*Some Answered Questions* 68)

In this sense, it is possible that when Bahá'u'lláh employs this city metaphor in other contexts, He is at the same time alluding to the Bahá'í Revelation, particularly as it implies the laws and institutions which have descended from heaven. For example, in the Kitáb-i-Íqán when Bahá'u'lláh alludes to the "city of the divine presence" (55) and in Epistle to the Son of the Wolf when He alludes to the "city of Bahá," He seems to be referring specifically to His own Revelation:

> We have admonished Our loved ones to fear God, a fear which is the fountain-head of all goodly deeds and virtues. It is the commander of the hosts of justice in the city of Bahá. (*Epistle* 135)

Another frequent use of the city metaphor is as an allusion to the concept of certitude. Bahá'u'lláh frequently exalts the station of certitude and, conversely, often admonishes the believers to pass beyond the stages of doubt. Of course, true conviction cannot be commanded, because it is a property of assurance derived from personal proof (whether theoretical or empirical). Certitude is thus induced by repeated confirmations of various sorts. Therefore Bahá'u'lláh frequently alludes to the attainment of conviction not as an emotional condition of blind faith nor strictly as a matter of the heart. Attaining certitude is portrayed in terms of entering a place of refuge, a stronghold, a fortified city. More broadly, this image conveys a sense of certitude acquired by committing ourselves to a new way of life:

> None have believed in Him except them who, through the power of the Lord of Names, have shattered the idols of their vain imaginings and corrupt desires and entered the city of certitude. (*Gleanings* 12)

> When the channel of the human soul is cleansed of all worldly and impeding attachments, it will unfailingly perceive the breath of the Beloved across immeasurable distances, and will, led by its perfume, attain and enter the City of Certitude. (*Kitáb-i-Íqán* 197)

In Chapter 4 we noted Bahá'u'lláh's repeated use of this same vehicle as a symbol of the human heart. With that usage in mind we can appreciate the following poetic exhortation: "Open, O people, the city of the human heart with the key of your utterance" (*Gleanings* 304). Here the believer as teacher is exhorted to gain access to the city of the heart of a seeker by using kind words as a metaphorical key to open the door to that city.

h. Garment or Clothing Imagery

Employed primarily to allude to the personal acquisition of spiritual attributes, clothing imagery appears throughout the writings of Bahá'u'lláh because it is a simple and easily understood expression of an extremely complex process. Clothing imagery readily lends itself to this purpose of portraying personal transformation because, in a social sense, clothing itself is so often used as a symbol of social status or function.[13]

---

13. The nineteenth-century English author Thomas Carlyle employed this symbolism to advantage in his elaborate satirical essay *Sartor Resartus* ("the tailor re-patched"), which concludes that outward human forms (institutions, professions, etc.) are but a sort of clothing we wear and, as such, are temporary and unreliable.

Indeed, it is common in virtually every society or culture for clothing to be used to designate rank and vocation. Often this symbolism is systematically devised and officially sanctioned, as is the case with some religions and with governmental agencies such as the police or the military.

Thus, in the same way that Bahá'u'lláh, in the laws of the Kitáb-i-Aqdas, gives importance to the literal cleanliness and refinement of one's clothing and outward appearance, so Bahá'u'lláh employs the vehicle of clothing to represent various spiritual conditions.[14] Furthermore, clothing is useful because it can be employed to represent either a positive or a negative condition. Consequently, Bahá'u'lláh employs such terms as *garment, robe,* and *veils* as metaphors for a wide range of tenors. One positive use, for example, is Bahá'u'lláh's use of clothing imagery to allude to the station or role of the Prophet: "They are all invested with the robe of prophethood, and are honored with the mantle of glory" (*Gleanings* 51). In this same vein Bahá'u'lláh portrays the tenor of the perfection of the Manifestation in terms of the vehicle of a stainless or unsullied garment:

> This Hem of His Robe hath ever been and remaineth unsullied, though many have, at the present time, purposed to besmirch it with their lying and unseemly calumnies. (*Epistle* 67)

Likewise, Bahá'u'lláh often alludes to the attributes and power of His Revelation as constituting a robe that His followers can wear:

> Divest not yourselves of the Robe of grandeur, neither suffer your hearts to be deprived of remembering your Lord, nor your ears of hearkening unto the sweet melodies of His wondrous,

14. For example, Bahá'u'lláh states, "Cleave ye unto the cord of refinement with such tenacity as to allow no trace of dirt to be seen upon your garments. Such is the injunction of One Who is sanctified above all refinement. Whoso falleth short of this standard with good reason shall incur no blame. God, verily, is the Forgiving, the Merciful" (Kitáb-i-Aqdas ¶74).

> His sublime, His all-compelling, His clear, and most eloquent voice. (*Gleanings* 107)

In a more general metaphorical statement of the acquisition of virtue, Bahá'u'lláh admonishes His followers in the Kitáb-i-Aqdas:

> Adorn your heads with the garlands of trustworthiness and fidelity, your hearts with the attire of the fear of God, your tongues with absolute truthfulness, your bodies with the vesture of courtesy. (¶120)

In other positive uses of clothing imagery in portraying various spiritual powers, attributes, and actions, Bahá'u'lláh speaks of the "Robe of grandeur" (*Gleanings* 107), the "robe of forbearance and justice" (*Gleanings* 305), the "robe of virtue" (*Gleanings* 334–35), the "robe of Thy remembrance" (*Prayers and Meditations* 16), the "raiment of Thy love," (*Prayers and Meditations* 63), the "garment of assurance" (qtd. in *Bahá'í World Faith* 206), the "garment of truthfulness" (*Compilation of Compilations* 2: no. 2038), and the "vesture of courtesy" (Kitáb-i-Aqdas ¶120).

In one of these clothing images, Bahá'u'lláh demonstrates how one metaphor can work within another metaphor; clothing becomes both an outward sign of an inner condition, but it also becomes a suit of armor to protect the believer from attack:

> Clothe yourselves, O people, with the garment of assurance, in order that He may protect you from the dart of doubts and superstitions, and that ye may be of those who are assured in those days wherein none shall ever be assured and none shall be firmly established in the Cause, except by severing himself from all that is possessed by the people and turning unto the holy and radiant Outlook. (qtd. in *Bahá'í World Faith* 206)

The acquisition of virtue thus takes on the same symbolism as does the arming of the hero in the classical epic tradition or the arming of the knight in the medieval chivalric romance tradition.

In another use of clothing imagery, Bahá'u'lláh will often describe the condition of the vesture (whether or not it is clean or fragrant) to convey various tenors. Bahá'u'lláh states that His laws are like the sweet fragrance of His garment:

> Say: From My laws the sweet-smelling savor of My garment can be smelled, and by their aid the standards of Victory will be planted upon the highest peaks. (Kitáb-i-Aqdas ¶4)

Likewise, Bahá'u'lláh, in a more elaborate and complex conceit, states that all "sweet-smelling" things in this day derive their fragrance from the perfume of His "garment":

> This is the Day whereon every sweet smelling thing hath derived its fragrance from the smell of My garment—a garment that hath shed its perfume upon the whole of creation. (*Gleanings* 30)

Thus when the believer becomes a Bahá'í and puts on the robe of a believer (or, indirectly, the robe bequeathed by the Prophet), he is obliged to keep that vesture clean:

> We have admonished all the loved ones of God to take heed lest the hem of Our sacred vesture be smirched with the mire of unlawful deeds, or be stained with the dust of reprehensible conduct. (*Gleanings* 240)

Finally, Bahá'u'lláh sometimes uses this same vehicle to represent negative attributes. In this context believers are admonished to disrobe themselves of unseemly qualities, to divest themselves of the "veil of worldly vanity and desire" (*Gleanings* 295), the "garment of unbelief" (*Gleanings* 26), the "garment of vainglory" and the "attire of haughtiness" (Hidden Words, Persian, no. 47), to "divest thy body and soul of the old garment, and array thyself with the new and imperishable attire" (*Kitáb-i-Íqán* 158).

F. Some Conclusions about Imagery

The heart of what we have attempted in this chapter is (1) to arrive at a clearer understanding of what figurative language is and how it works; (2) to discuss some of the reasons the Prophets find figurative language to be the best medium through which to communicate Their ideas; (3) to study some of the components of various figurative devices; (4) to experiment with interpreting figurative devices so that we do not find this veiled language so intimidating; and (5) to become aware of patterns of imagery that permeate and unify the varied themes found in the utterances of Bahá'u'lláh.

Of course, not all of the hidden meanings that Bahá'u'lláh alludes to as "ḥúrís" are figurative devices, but most often they are. Certainly, Bahá'u'lláh would not have devoted so much of the Kitáb-i-Íqán, His most important doctrinal work, to explicating the symbolic or figurative nature of prophetic utterance if He did not think this a critical insight for anyone wishing to understand how the Manifestations teach us and why their utterances so often challenge our common approach to religious learning.

However, we do well to keep in mind one important caveat about interpreting figurative images. The reader may well ponder whether or not he or she has discovered the meaning intended by the author (i.e., the *real* or *true* meaning). It is for this reason that ecclesiasts of the past have been so reluctant to leave this task of interpreting scripture in the hands of the believers and instead have controlled what scripture was allowed to mean. Indeed, the leaders of many religions have felt it dangerous to permit believers even to have access to the scriptures; instead, the generality of believers were taught only the authoritative "glossing" or interpretation of scripture. It is because of this background that the medieval English writer Geoffrey Chaucer used the word "glosing" (lying) ironically as a pun for "glossing" (authoritative interpretation of scripture).

As we noted earlier, Bahá'u'lláh exhorts us to study and to interpret His words. He further alleviates our concerns about discovering the "correct" meaning (i.e., the meaning "intended" by the Prophet) when He notes that there is no *single* meaning: by its very nature scripture contains a variety of meanings and a variety of levels of meaning, each one of which is valid and each one of which is fully intended by the Prophet:

> Thus it is recorded: "Every knowledge hath seventy meanings, of which one only is known amongst the people. And when the Qá'im shall arise, He shall reveal unto men all that which remaineth." He also saith: "We speak one word, and by it we intend one and seventy meanings; each one of these meanings we can explain." (*Kitáb-i-Íqán* 255)

Chapter 6
Subject and Structure in the Art of Bahá'u'lláh

'Abdu'l-Bahá has likened the power of concentration to a cubic crystal. He said, "If you place a ruby, the hardest stone, in a seven times heated furnace, the heat will have no effect, but if you place that ruby in a cubic crystal in the rays of the midday sun, it will be dissolved." This He has likened to the power of concentration in man.

—May Maxwell

We have thus far posed four successive questions, and we have experimented with four tools of literary criticism to answer those questions: (1) Who is speaking to me? (a study of narrative point of view); (2) In what circumstances is the narrator speaking to me? (a study of historical criticism); (3) What is the literary form of the work? (a study of genre criticism); and (4) What mysteries or hidden meanings are concealed in the poetic language of the work? (a study of figurative imagery). We are now ready to pose a fifth question: How are the ideas in the work structured or organized?

This query might seem to duplicate the question we posed in our discussion of genre in Chapter 4, since the genre of a work will sometimes dictate the basic parameters of form or structure. But in this chapter we are concerned with something more basic, more fundamental—the flow of thought, the way in which the ideas in the work are grouped together, the pattern by which the work proceeds from thought to thought, from subject to subject. For example, The Seven Valleys has what would seem to be an obvious structure derived from its generic type—seven divisions which represent seven stages of spiritual development. And yet, as we study the work, we discover that each valley has its own individual structure, its own special pattern of ideas.

The fundamental skill we need for this task is similar to what we used in our examination of imagery—the ability to discover the similarity among diverse ingredients. Our approach to discovering the pattern of ideas consists of three relatively simple steps. First, we attempt to identify the fundamental groups of ideas in a work. In effect, we catalog the ideas or subjects that are presented. Second, we determine the subordination among these ideas by constructing an outline. This second part of our procedure is especially valuable for those works that have no foundational or obvious sort of structure derived from genre.[1] The third part of our analysis consists of trying to discover unified purpose in a work as that purpose is revealed through the various patterns of ideas.

While we could derive useful information by applying this exercise to any number of the works of Bahá'u'lláh, we will confine our experiment to only two, the Lawḥ-i-Ḥikmat and the Kitáb-i-Íqán. The Lawḥ-i-Ḥikmat (Tablet of Wisdom) has no obvious inherent structure, while the Kitáb-i-Íqán (Book of Certitude) has an exacting structure. However, our experiment should prove equally valuable with both works because both are similarly intense, intellectual pieces: the Lawḥ-

1. For example, Shoghi Effendi knew that before a useful translation of the Kitáb-i-Aqdas could be accomplished, there first needed to be a Synopsis and Codification. When we compare the Synopsis and Codification to the Kitáb-i-Aqdas itself, we quickly discover the Guardian's rationale for this conclusion; there is no obvious structure to the Kitáb-i-Aqdas. The Synopsis and Codification thus accomplishes the same thing that our first two procedures do; it groups these laws into categories and then creates an outline demonstrating the general relationship among them.

i-Ḥikmat deals with the "fundamentals of true philosophy" (Shoghi Effendi, *God Passes By* 219), and the Kitáb-i-Íqán vindicates the eternal plan of God. In short, we can be assured that each of the two works is unified around a central thematic purpose.

A. The Lawḥ-i-Ḥikmat (Tablet of Wisdom)

The Lawḥ-i-Ḥikmat is approximately sixteen pages long in translation. In Chapter 4, we classified the work generically as an expository essay, even though the work is an epistle addressed to Nabíl-i-Akbar. According to Bahá'u'lláh's opening passages, this epistle would seem to be a gift of knowledge, "a breath of life unto those who dwell in the realm of creation" (*Tablets of Bahá'u'lláh* 137), revealed in honor of this learned Hand of the Cause: "In this Epistle mention is made of him who magnifieth the Name of God, his Lord, and who is named Nabíl in a weighty Tablet" (137).[2] As we indicated in Chapter 4, though Bahá'u'lláh states that the tablet is intended for all people, He indicates that the work is addressed to Nabíl-i-Akbar as a tribute to him, as if this believer's fidelity, learning, and efforts to teach the Cause have won for humankind the bounty of the wisdom imparted through this tablet. But if this is something more than a love note of encouragement to a devoted and learned follower, in what sense is it an "irrefutable and weighty exposition" (151), "a Tablet wherein the Pen of the Unseen hath inscribed the knowledge of all that hath been and shall be—a knowledge that none other but My wondrous Tongue can interpret" (149)? What special or esoteric information does it impart? What star-

2. This epistle was revealed for Nabíl-i-Akbar in honor of his visit with Bahá'u'lláh in 'Akká, prior to Bahá'u'lláh's move to Mazra'ih: "This Tablet in Arabic, revealed before Bahá'u'lláh's move to Mazra'ih, stands out amongst the Writings of Bahá'u'lláh for its philosophical terminology and its references to ancient Greek philosophers, as well as profound explanations of the influence of the Word of God, the cause and origin of creation, the mysterious workings of nature, and many other weighty topics. Nabíl-i-Akbar, its recipient, was a man of great knowledge and learning" (Taherzadeh, *Revelation of Bahá'u'lláh* 4:33).

tling new insights does it unveil? Finally, is there some subtle theme that unifies the seemingly diverse parts of this work?

1. Listing Groups of Ideas

In the second paragraph of the Lawḥ-i-Ḥikmat Bahá'u'lláh states in most general terms that the objective of this epistle is "to acquaint thee with that which will serve as a reminder unto the people, that they may put away the things current amongst them and set their faces towards God, the Lord of the sincere" (137). But what does Bahá'u'lláh wish to remind the people about, and what are the "things current amongst them" that people should "put away"?

In the first several paragraphs Bahá'u'lláh exhorts humanity during this period of decadence ("in these days when the countenance of Justice is soiled with dust") to have an upright character, to be "shining examples unto all mankind": "Let your eye be chaste, your hand faithful, your tongue truthful and your heart enlightened" (138). But in spite of these positive exhortations, there is a powerful undercurrent of sadness and sorrow throughout the seven paragraphs of what seems to be a preamble to the main body of this epistle. However, this lament does not appear as self-pity; Bahá'u'lláh is saddened by the treatment Nabíl-i-Akbar has experienced in attempting to teach others. Therefore, He exhorts Nabíl not to become discouraged:

> By My life! Thy grievances have plunged Me into sorrow. Regard not the children of the world and all their doings but fix thy gaze upon God and His never-ending dominion. Verily, He calleth to thy remembrance that which is the source of delight for all mankind. (139)

Bahá'u'lláh then charges Nabíl-i-Akbar to "establish the word of truth" and thereby "dispel falsehood from the face of the earth" (139).

It would seem, then, that Bahá'u'lláh here alludes both to a lack of accord among the believers ("Ye were created to show love one to another and not perversity and rancour") and to the disdain with which Náṣiri'd-Dín Sháh and the 'ulamá had received the Revelation of Bahá'u'lláh. Bahá'u'lláh concludes these allusions with this general observation about His frustration at trying to bring Divine teachings to a populace so thoroughly entrenched in pride and iniquity: "In such circumstances as thou seest, how can the Celestial Bird soar into the atmosphere of divine mysteries when its wings have been battered with the stones of idle fancy and bitter hatred, and it is cast into a prison built of unyielding stone?" (139–40).

Immediately after this plaint, Bahá'u'lláh begins what would seem to be at first glance the heart of His discourse. He presents a series of terse, elliptical, and ostensibly unrelated comments on a variety of subjects: (1) the origin and nature of creation, (2) "some accounts of the sages" (i.e., the station of various philosophers and other men of learning), (3) the influence of the Prophets on the great philosophers, (4) the means by which Bahá'u'lláh (and presumably every other Prophet) gains access to the words written by others (even when the Manifestations have not had an opportunity to read these words), (5) the process by which "a luminary of knowledge" has been "set up" in every land, and, finally, (6) a teaching prayer (presumably revealed for Nabíl to use).

2. Outlining the Lawḥ-i-Ḥikmat

As diverse and ostensibly disjointed as the subjects of these various parts might at first appear, careful attention to the relationships among these ideas can reveal an underlying pattern. In particular, an outline of the tablet demonstrates that there is a unity, an awareness of which will help explain the lofty status Bahá'u'lláh ascribes to the Lawḥ-i-Ḥikmat. For ease of reference in citing passages, the outline will refer to paragraph numbers rather than page numbers.

Outline of the Lawḥ-i-Ḥikmat

I. Bahá'u'lláh describes this "Epistle" as having been revealed in honor of Nabíl-i-Akbar:
   A. It is a "breath of life" whose purpose is to "acquaint thee with that which will serve as a reminder unto the people that they may put away the things current amongst them and set their faces towards God. . . ." (¶1–2)
   B. In these times of moral decadence, injustice, and

faithlessness, people must become "shining examples unto all mankind," must avoid "promoting . . . personal interest," and must "love . . . fellow-creatures." (¶3–5)

II. Bahá'u'lláh tells Nabíl not to grieve if the "children of the world" seem to pay no heed to Him, but to "establish the word of truth with eloquence and wisdom and to dispel falsehood from the face of the earth." (¶6)
   A. Bahá'u'lláh alludes to a tablet revealed to a ruler and mentions how it was ignored.[3] (¶7)

III. Bahá'u'lláh discusses theories of creation and the origin of existence, and He alludes to the well-known Islámic tradition "I was a Hidden Treasure." (¶8–14)[4]
   A. The concept of a "first cause" is discussed. (¶8)
   B. Creation results from "the interaction between the active force and that which is its recipient." (¶9)
   C. The "irresistible Word of God" is the "Cause of the entire creation." (¶9–10)
   D. The "objections" which the "unbelievers" might voice to these concepts "turn upon themselves." (¶11)
   E. Though the Word of God is a sufficient cause for the contingent world, that world is "being renewed and regenerated at all times." (¶12)
   F. To study the contingent world is to witness the divine imprint, a sufficient cause for its existence, because "Nature in its essence is the embodiment of My Name." (¶13–14)

IV. There is no important need to turn to the knowledge of former or "more recent" times—the knowledge of this Revelation "will in truth suffice all mankind." (¶15)

---

3. Taherzadeh identifies this tablet as the one Bahá'u'lláh gave to Badí' to deliver to Náṣiri'd-Dín Sháh.

4. See Taherzadeh, *Revelation of Bahá'u'lláh* 4:39, and H. M. Balyuzi, *'Abdu'l-Bahá* (London: George Ronald, 1971) 14.

A. He who understands that humankind has been reborn and that "God . . . wieldeth supreme ascendancy and absolute authority over this new creation" is among the truly learned. (¶16)
B. "Walk high above the world of being through the power of the Most Great Name" so that you may "become aware of the immemorial mysteries" and thereby be a "throbbing artery, pulsating in the body of the entire creation." (¶17)
C. At the house of Majíd[5] you (Nabíl) were allowed to understand the mysteries of creation; now you must use your voice to teach others. (¶19–20)

V. Strict materialists who reject God are "bereft of knowledge and wisdom"; therefore they dispute among themselves, while the leaders among them believed in God. (¶21)
A. The "people of the East" marveled at the accomplishments of the West, presuming that these resulted from material causes; they were oblivious to the influence of God. But those who were "the source and the wellspring of Wisdom" were well aware of the "moving Impulse" behind their knowledge and accomplishments. (¶22)
B. We will now mention "some accounts of the sages," that people may become aware that God is the source of all knowledge. For, however wise "contemporary men of learning" may be, anyone with a "discriminating eye" will acknowledge that these individuals are merely building on the foundation established by "sages of the past," who

5. Prior to becoming a Bahá'í, Nabíl-i-Akbar had been an eminent mujtahid, one of the most learned men in Persia. During a meeting with Bahá'u'lláh at the home of 'Abdu'l-Majíd-i-Shírází in Kázimayn, Nabíl-i-Akbar talked with Bahá'u'lláh about the mysteries of creation. See Taherzadeh, *Revelation of Bahá'u'lláh* 4:46 and 1:91–95.

themselves "acquired their knowledge from the Prophets." (¶23–24)

1. Empedocles "was a contemporary of David." (¶25)
2. Pythagoras "lived in the days of Solomon." (¶25)
3. Even though the "essence and the fundamentals of philosophy have emanated from the Prophets," people differed about meanings because of "the divergence of their views and minds." (¶26)
   a) Bahá'u'lláh gives the example of how a follower of one Prophet misunderstood the concept of people being "'filled with the Spirit'" to mean that the "spirit literally penetrateth or entereth into the body"; he thereby instigated an entire following that perpetrated this error. (¶26)
4. The true philosophers have not denied belief in God and have longed to "fathom His mystery." (¶27)
   a) Hippocrates, the physician, believed in God. (¶28)
   b) Socrates "dissuaded men from worshipping idols and taught them the way of God"; he is "one of the heroes in this field." He understood that the spiritual attributes of phenomenal reality precede material expression. (¶28)
   c) Plato, Socrates' student, also believed in God and in the spiritual essence underlying all created reality. (¶29)
   d) Aristotle, who discovered "the power of gaseous matter," also acknowledged belief in a Supreme Being. (¶29)
   e) I will mention the "invocation voiced by Balínús," who was also familiar with Socrates' theory of the "mysteries of creation"—the wisdom of revealed truth cannot be disputed unless one be "bereft of hearing, of vision, of understanding and of every human faculty"(¶30):
      (1) "O Lord! Thou art God and no God is there but Thee." (¶31)

VI. I have no wish "to mention anything further" but shall utter what I am told to speak. If not for My love for thee, I would "not have uttered a single word. . . ." "Appreciate the value of this station. . . ." (¶33)

A. We [the Prophets] receive Our knowledge direct from God, not from Our own devising. (¶34)

B. If We need to quote from the books "which men possess"—when We wish to "quote the sayings of the learned and of the wise"—there will appear before Us "in the form of a tablet all that which hath appeared in the world and is revealed in the Holy Books and Scriptures." (¶34)

C. This tablet, for example, is direct from God (i.e., it is not derived from the influence or teaching of others), and its wisdom is capable of being uttered by Me because "My heart as it is in itself hath been purged by God from the concepts of the learned and is sanctified from the utterances of the wise." (¶35)

VII. Beware, people of the earth, not to conclude that references to "wisdom" imply that wisdom ultimately derives from any source other than God. (¶36)

A. Every land becomes a "Seat of Wisdom" according to the divine plan of God. (¶37)

1. Greece for a "prolonged period" held such a position until "the appointed hour struck" and "its light grew dim" according to divine decree. (¶37)
2. In every land We have "set up a luminary of knowledge" that will shine "resplendent" when the "time foreordained is at hand."(¶38)

B. Indeed, in previous times things were produced that "contemporary men of knowledge have been unable to produce." (¶39)

1. Múrṭus invented an apparatus "which transmitted sound over a distance of sixty miles," and others also discovered things "which no one in this age hath beheld." (¶39)

VIII. A true philosopher "would never deny God" but would uphold His majesty. Those men of learning who "promote the best interests of humanity" we assist because "well are We able to achieve Our purpose." (¶40)

A. Don't judge the "learned" of Bahá by common standards. (¶41)
   1. Aspire to learning that benefits humankind. (¶41)
   2. "We are quit of those" who imagine that the purpose of "Wisdom" is to "give vent to one's idle imaginings and to repudiate God" as many today are doing. (¶41)

B. "The beginning of Wisdom and the origin thereof is to acknowledge whatsoever God hath clearly set forth. . . ." (¶42)
   1. This is the "foundation of statesmanship." (¶42)
   2. All the matters "related to state affairs which ye raise for discussion" are covered in these words. (¶42)

IX. Rejoice, Nabíl, that I have so honored thee: (¶43)

A. "I have mentioned thy name";
   1. I "have turned My heart and My face towards thee. . . .";
   2. I "have conversed with thee through this irrefutable and weighty exposition."
   3. Therefore, as you think on this, "Ponder in thy heart" what I (Who am the source of knowledge) have endured at the hands of those who "are truly wrapped in a grievous veil."

B. At this point the "light of utterance was quenched"; may the Glory of God "rest upon the people of wisdom." (¶44)

C. Repeat the following prayer: (¶45–47)
   1. Aid me to "extol Thy Name amongst Thy servants"
   2. and to proclaim what "will captivate the minds of men and will rejoice their souls and spirits."
   3. Strengthen me, "that I may not be hindered by the . . . oppressors . . . nor . . . the disbelievers."

4. Make me a lamp to guide those "in whose hearts the light of Thy knowledge gloweth."
5. Thou art potent "to do whatsoever Thou willest. . . ."

3. Some Conclusions about the Pattern of Ideas

Having noted the basic subjects of this tablet and having devised one possible outline of how these ideas might be subordinated, let us determine if we can now observe among these parts some pattern of ideas, some linear progression of thought.[6]

First we should note that our outline could be reshaped, refined, reorganized; it is not our presumption that we have rendered some final or official analysis of how the ideas in this work relate to one another. For example, we could reduce the number of major divisions by combining some of the sections that clearly relate to each other. By this means we might more easily demonstrate that Bahá'u'lláh is not discussing a series of distinctly different ideas, nor is He proceeding purely by association of ideas; He is, over the course of this work, discussing only a handful of closely related concepts, all of which are demonstrated by various examples and allusions.

Certainly, the first two sections to Nabíl-i-Akbar could be combined. Likewise, the third section dealing with God's reason for creating physical reality (the discussion of the "first cause") relates importantly to the fourth section regarding the sufficiency of this Revelation to provide humankind with the knowledge needed to comprehend the mysteries of God's methodology.

The fifth section relates to the fourth by establishing the evidence to prove that the knowledge set forth through the Prophets is the clearest access to understanding, not the esoteric knowledge that "strict materialists" (secular humanist scholars) produce. Bahá'u'lláh demonstrates this thesis by cataloging some of the sages of the past who are

6. Naturally, we should not presume that some form of linear progression of thought is necessarily what the Prophet intends here, nor should we presume that such a progression is a requisite for divine utterance. However, it seems likely that Bahá'u'lláh would employ a logical structure in a doctrinal treatise such as the Lawḥ-i-Ḥikmat.

generally acknowledged to have been true luminaries in the advancement of the collective ascent of human understanding. He then observes that the ultimate source of wisdom for these great thinkers—as each acknowledged—was the power of the Holy Spirit communicating with them, either directly through inspiration or indirectly through the influence of various Prophets.

Section six seems at first to be a digression about how Bahá'u'lláh is familiar with the ideas of writers and thinkers whose works He has not physically seen (i.e., their works appear before Him). However, this discussion is actually a continuation of the same point discussed in section five. He explains that the Prophets are the source of all knowledge, even for the brilliant sages who occasionally appear among us, precisely because the Prophet has direct access to all knowledge, and not because the Prophets have studied the works of others or have been influenced by others.

In other words, as we examine creatively the basic relationships the outline reveals, we can discern the unity of thought implicit in this essay. We begin to sense the progression of ideas, and we begin to perceive the focal point of Bahá'u'lláh's discussion—the idea that all knowledge ultimately derives from God, not from individual inspiration or from the singular accomplishments of certain great thinkers. Bahá'u'lláh notes that even the greatest among these individuals readily confesses his complete indebtedness and subservience to God.

This, then, is the point of section seven—that all references to true "wisdom" allude to the divine plan of God whereby one land and then another shines forth with great influence and knowledge. However, this successive rise and fall of influence among nations has not been the result of environmental determinism or of the random appearance of a group of enlightened individuals. In every case the ascent of a civilization derives from spiritual influence (divine intervention) in human affairs. Consequently, we can never presume that we know what level of intelligence, wisdom, or accomplishment was achieved in any given land.[7]

7. When Bahá'u'lláh states here that things were produced in previous times that "contemporary men of knowledge have been unable to produce," we

The eighth and ninth sections clearly go together. Bahá'u'lláh concludes in section eight that a "true philosopher" would never "deny God"; therefore, we cannot judge the "learned" of Bahá by ordinary standards.[8] Consequently, in section nine Bahá'u'lláh comforts Nabíl-i-Akbar (whom Bahá'u'lláh is implicitly designating as one of the "learned of Bahá"), urges him to have confidence, not to be awed by the apparent learning of anyone, but to utter forthrightly before others what he has discovered, to proclaim "that which will captivate the minds of men and will rejoice their souls and spirits" (¶46).

What we discover, then, as we review our schematic portrayal of the relationship of the parts of the tablet to each other is the possibility of a number of valid ways we might combine these parts. Each part grows out of, or is vitally linked to, each other part. We might also observe that analyzing the structure of ideas can provide an extremely helpful pathway by which we can gain access to the central theme or meaning of a work, something we will attempt to do more fully in Chapter 7.

---

might naturally think of physical edifices such as the pyramids or Stonehenge, whose construction still confounds modern engineers. But when Bahá'u'lláh gives the example of Múrṭus, He seems to indicate that intellectual progress is not precisely linear (i.e., that everything we can presently do or think is necessarily superior to what has gone before).

8. In the Lawḥ-i-Ḥikmat, the Kitáb-i-Aqdas, and the Kitáb-i-'Ahd, Bahá'u'lláh alludes to the "learned in Bahá" as being one of the twin branches of the Bahá'í Administrative Order (the "rulers" or elected institutions being the other branch). In this connection Shoghi Effendi interprets these passages as follows:

> In this holy cycle the *"learned"* are, on the one hand, the Hands of the Cause of God, and, on the other, the teachers and diffusers of His Teachings who do not rank as Hands, but who have attained an eminent position in the teaching work. As to the *"rulers"* they refer to the members of the Local, National and International Houses of Justice. The duties of each of these souls will be determined in the future. (qtd. in Kitáb-i-Aqdas n183)

Nabíl-i-Akbar, to whom this tablet is addressed, was designated by 'Abdu'l-Bahá as a Hand of the Cause, hence one of the "learned." However, the designation "learned" does not allude only to personages within the institution of "the learned."

For example, in light of our three-part analysis of the pattern or structure of ideas in the Lawḥ-i-Ḥikmat, we might conclude that the central theme (or unifying principle) in this work is the concept that the source of all important knowledge, wisdom, or human progress is the knowledge of God acquired through His Prophets. All human accomplishment of any sort is ultimately dependent on that fountain source. A corollary of this theme is the observation that those who deem themselves to have some knowledge independent of or unrelated to the knowledge of God are self-deluded. Related to this observation is Bahá'u'lláh's command to Nabíl-i-Akbar (and, by extension, to all humankind) that those who truly believe in and understand the ascendancy of God and His Prophets should be undaunted, undeterred, and unintimidated by those who have a "name to be wise" but who disdain the notion that an unseen reality influences human affairs.

If we proceed further to pull together the other observations we have previously made about the generic components of the Lawḥ-i-Ḥikmat, we might conclude another worthwhile point. In this work Bahá'u'lláh seems to be responding to some specific questions that Nabíl-i-Akbar has asked regarding theories of creation, just as Bahá'u'lláh in the Kitáb-i-Íqán responds to specific questions put to Him by the Báb's maternal uncle, Ḥájí Mírzá Siyyid Muḥammad. And yet, while He answers Nabíl's questions, Bahá'u'lláh incorporates these queries into a larger context—each individual question is discussed in relation to ever larger categories of thought.

B. The Pattern of Ideas in the Kitáb-i-Íqán

Because the Kitáb-i-Íqán is an expository essay (a doctrinal treatise, an apologia, an "argument"), it is highly structured around the logical exploration of the theme set forth in the first two pages of the work: if we wish to acquire certitude that a Prophet is Who He says He is (i.e., God's Viceregent), we must become detached from worldly things, must become spiritually attentive and receptive, and, most important of all, must cease regarding "the words and deeds of mortal men as a standard for the true understanding and recognition of God and His Prophets" (*Kitáb-i-Íqán* 4).

As we will see, Bahá'u'lláh constantly returns to this subject—that belief and conviction can be confirmed by logical examination and that we should not accept out-of-hand the observations and conclusions of the so-called scholars among us. Of course, Bahá'u'lláh does not place blame for the rejection of the Prophets solely on the "divines" and the "learned"; He explains that every individual has the capacity to recognize these Messengers and understand Their words. However, Bahá'u'lláh does lay the blame for the overt persecution of the Prophets and Their followers at the feet of those religious and political leaders who ignore the obvious proofs the Prophets provide of Their station and Their identity. Furthermore, Bahá'u'lláh states that the reason these leaders and "learned" ones have responded so ignominiously is that they fear the loss of prestige, power, and worldly goods which they would experience if they were to accept the claims of the Prophet.

But the Kitáb-i-Íqán is not a polemic, nor is it an ad hominem attack against certain individual clerics. It is a lucid, brilliant, straightforward, and endlessly rewarding explanation of the Divine Plan for human education as promulgated by the succession of Prophets. In the course of presenting this large subject, Bahá'u'lláh explores and analyzes with meticulous care and kindness some of the specific reasons why the Prophets are rejected in spite of the clear proofs They provide.

A careful reading of the Kitáb-i-Íqán will demonstrate that the "mysterious" nature of the Prophet's advent is not really mysterious at all. Instead, Bahá'u'lláh demonstrates that the Divine Plan of progressive revelation is a perfectly logical process which has been consistently misunderstood and misrepresented.

1. Listing the Major Groups of Ideas

At first reading, the major ideas and patterns of thought in the Kitáb-i-Íqán seem fairly obvious. The exposition contains two parts, both of which focus on questions surrounding the appearances of the Prophets. Both parts focus primarily on why the Prophets' appearances are concealed and what proofs of Their station are available to the discerning eye.

The first part seems to concentrate on the poetic or figurative nature of prophetic language to explain why the generality of humankind has failed to recognize that the clear signs provided by the Prophets have fulfilled ancient prophecies. Prophetic utterance has been misunderstood because it has been accepted as being literally true. The second part concentrates on the Prophets themselves, particularly on the nature and proofs of Their station.

As we have noted, Bahá'u'lláh is responding to the four categories of questions asked Him by Ḥájí Mírzá Siyyid Muḥammad, the unconverted maternal uncle of the Báb. According to Hasan Balyuzi, "the gist of the questions presented to Bahá'u'lláh" are as follows:

1. The Day of Resurrection. Is there to be corporeal resurrection? The world is replete with injustice. How are the just to be requited and the unjust punished?
2. The twelfth Imám was born at a certain time and lives on. There are traditions, all supporting the belief. How can this be explained?
3. Interpretation of holy texts. This Cause does not seem to conform with beliefs held throughout the years. One cannot ignore the literal meaning of holy texts and scripture. How can this be explained?
4. Certain events, according to the traditions that have come down from the Imáms, must occur at the advent of the Qá'im.[9] Some of these are mentioned. But none of these has happened. How can this be explained?

(*Bahá'u'lláh: The King of Glory* 164–65)

However, these categories of questions do not govern the structure of Bahá'u'lláh's response. Bahá'u'lláh forces Ḥájí Mírzá Siyyid Muḥammad (and all other readers) to consider the entire process of progressive

9. The Qá'im is the Twelfth Imám whose return Shí'ih Muslims await. The Báb declared Himself to be the Qá'im.

revelation. Thus, by studying the Kitáb-i-Íqán, the reader can gain certitude not only about the station of the Báb as Qá'im, but also about the process of Divine Appearances in general. The answers to the specific questions are in the tablet, but they must be uncovered in the course of studying divine methodology as a whole.

Shoghi Effendi in *God Passes By* gives a fairly complete list of the main subject groups that Bahá'u'lláh discusses during the course of this exposition on the Divine Plan:

> Within a compass of two hundred pages it [the Kitáb-i-Íqán] proclaims unequivocally the existence and oneness of a personal God, unknowable, inaccessible, the source of all Revelation, eternal, omniscient, omnipresent and almighty; asserts the relativity of religious truth and the continuity of Divine Revelation; affirms the unity of the Prophets, the universality of their Message, the identity of their fundamental teachings, the sanctity of their scriptures, and the twofold character of their stations; denounces the blindness and perversity of the divines and doctors of every age; cites and elucidates the allegorical passages of the New Testament, the abstruse verses of the Qur'án, and the cryptic Muḥammadan traditions which have bred those age-long misunderstandings, doubts and animosities that have sundered and kept apart the followers of the world's leading religious systems; enumerates the essential prerequisites for the attainment by every true seeker of the object of his quest; demonstrates the validity, the sublimity and significance of the Báb's Revelation; acclaims the heroism and detachment of His disciples; foreshadows, and prophesies the world-wide triumph of the Revelation promised to the people of the Bayán; upholds the purity and innocence of the Virgin Mary; glorifies the Imáms of the Faith of Muḥammad; celebrates the martyrdom, and lauds the spiritual sovereignty, of the Imám Ḥusayn; unfolds the meaning of such symbolic terms as *"Return," "Resurrection," "Seal of the Prophets"* and *"Day of Judgment";* adumbrates and distinguishes between the three stages of Divine Revelation; and expatiates, in glowing terms, upon the glories and wonders of the *"City of God,"* re-

> newed, at fixed intervals, by the dispensation of Providence, for the guidance, the benefit and salvation of all mankind. (139)[10]

However, as helpful and elaborate as this list is by way of indicating the vast scope of Bahá'u'lláh's exposition, this synopsis is not intended to represent the order or the manner in which these ideas appear. This we must discover for ourselves.

Within each of the two parts of the Kitáb-i-Íqán are fairly discernible divisions of thought. Bahá'u'lláh begins with a consideration of the past to demonstrate the fact that "Not one single Manifestation of Holiness hath appeared but He was afflicted by the denials, the repudiation, and the vehement opposition of the people around Him" (*Kitáb-i-Íqán* 5). What follows is a catalog of some of the Prophets and how each experienced rejection and persecution.[11]

After this recitation Bahá'u'lláh explains that "Leaders of religion, in every age" have been responsible for this rejection "inasmuch as they held the reins of authority in their mighty grasp" (15). Bahá'u'lláh observes that this rejection stemmed from the leaders' lust for power, or else from their "lack of knowledge and understanding" (17). The rest of Part One of the Kitáb-i-Íqán then focuses on the language of revelation. In particular, Bahá'u'lláh concentrates on the figurative language employed by the Prophets to foretell the advent of the next Manifestation.

The first part is not solely about language; Bahá'u'lláh discusses the physical and social circumstances of the Prophets which become "veils" to test the followers of the previous Manifestations (e.g., Moses was reputed to be a murderer, Christ was born of lowly birth and in

10. The Guardian goes on to praise this work with the following assessment of its potency: "Well may it be claimed that of all the books revealed by the Author of the Bahá'í Revelation, this Book alone, by sweeping away the age-long barriers that have so insurmountably separated the great religions of the world, has laid down a broad and unassailable foundation for the complete and permanent reconciliation of their followers" (*God Passes By* 139).

11. This parallels what Muḥammad does in the Súrih of Húd, a section of the Qur'án which, Bahá'u'lláh states, should itself be sufficient for one who is "possessed of true understanding and insight" (*Kitáb-i-Íqán* 5).

questionable circumstances, etc.). But these discussions are framed in the context of how prophetic language is fulfilled by these circumstances. In effect, the entire first part concentrates on the language of revelation, the inability of the "divines" to break the chains of their own literalism in order to interpret these utterances correctly, and the subsequent "corruption," "perversion," or "mutilation" of the Book of God that occurs when these ecclesiastical leaders impose their own faulty interpretation of scripture on their followers.

Part Two of the Kitáb-i-Íqán responds to the specific question of the proofs that the Báb is the Qá'im, but it functions as a general analysis of the station, character, power, and proof pertaining to all the Prophets. Among the subjects covered in the course of this second part are the nature of true sovereignty (spiritual ascendancy versus worldly power), the Prophets as the effective expression of Divinity in the mortal world (i.e., "attaining the Presence" of God through Them), the concept of "return" and "resurrection" as applied to each new Manifestation, the two "stations" of the Prophet (the "station of essential unity" and the "station of distinction").

The rest of Part Two would seem to focus on these two stations: each Prophet is essentially the same as all other Prophets, and yet each appears in particular historical circumstances and must, if He is to minister to the needs of humankind, fashion His appearance to respond to those conditions. However, a substantial part of the remainder of the Kitáb-i-Íqán consists of the various proofs that each Prophet brings, proofs that are available to anyone who is capable of becoming a "True Seeker." These proofs consist of (1) the verses of the Revealed Word (the City of God), (2) the pure souls who sacrificially arise in service to the new Revelation, (3) the constancy of the Prophet (who seeks neither fame nor earthly goods but only the welfare of humankind), (4) and the prophecies or traditions that are fulfilled by the advent of the Prophet (though Bahá'u'lláh frankly admits this last category of proof is not nearly so important or reliable as the first three proofs).

The Kitáb-i-Íqán thus concludes with a discussion of these prophecies or traditions (hadí<u>th</u>) to reaffirm that the Báb is indeed the Qá'im. He ends by warning the "people of the Bayán" (the Bábís themselves), that they are not immune from this same process; they, too, will soon face this same test.[12]

Of course, many other specific subjects are discussed, and the groups of ideas we have enumerated may be broken down into ever more refined subgroups—something we will attempt to demonstrate in the following extensive outline of the work. Consequently, because there is a remarkable progression to and interdependence among the various parts of the Kitáb-i-Íqán, we can derive extremely important insights about what Bahá'u'lláh is doing in this, His most important doctrinal work, by outlining how Bahá'u'lláh's "argument" proceeds.

2. Outlining the Pattern or Subordination of Ideas

Outline of the Kitáb-i-Íqán[13]

PART ONE

Thesis: To achieve certitude, you must desire it, cleanse yourself of worldliness, put your "trust in God," "follow in His way," and cease regarding the "words and deeds of mortal men as a standard for the true understanding and recognition of God and His Prophets." (3–4)

I. The history of previous Dispensations demonstrates that while many have professed to await the "advent of the Manifestations of God" (4), "they all denied Him"(4). Every Manifestation has thus experienced "the denials, the repudiation, and the vehement opposition of the people around Him" (5). The Súrah of Húd explains this clearly, and a "brief mention" of some experiences of the Prophets will illustrate the indignities They experienced: "the more closely you observe the denials of those who have opposed the Manifestations . . . , the firmer will be your faith in the Cause of God." (6)

12. And with His foreknowledge, Bahá'u'lláh knows that many will fail and that His most grievous affliction will be suffered at the hands of the Bábís as led by Mírzá Yaḥyá.

13. Parenthetic citations in the outline refer to page numbers in the U.S. Bahá'í Publishing Trust edition of the Kitáb-i-Íqán.

A. The Experience of Noah
   1. His followers were tested when what He prophesied seemed not to occur. There was divine wisdom in this.
   2. So shall all be tested, because "Do men think when they say 'We believe' they shall be let alone and not be put to proof?" (9)
B. The Experience of Húd
   1. The willful blindness of the people to whom He ministered only begat more blindness.
C. The Experience of Ṣáliḥ (Who came to the tribe of Thamúd)
   1. He tried to teach them to follow the new laws.
   2. They rejected Him because His teachings were different from their past teachings.
D. The Experience of Abraham
   1. The more He exhorted the people of the earth, "the fiercer waxed the envy and waywardness of the people." (10)
   2. Eventually He was expelled.
E. The Experience of Moses
   1. He encountered the fierce opposition of Pharaoh.
   2. Such opposition only intensifies and preserves the Revelation.

II. Major Reasons for this Consistent Opposition: "What could have prompted such behavior towards the Revealers of the beauty of the All-Glorious?"(13):
   A. Such behavior is attributed to pride, petty-mindedness, arrogance, weighing the "testimony of God by the standard of their own knowledge, gleaned from the teachings of the leaders of their faith." (15)
   B. Consequently, the leaders of religion are the main impediment.
   C. Reasons religious leaders become opposed:
      1. Some lust for leadership and don't wish to relinquish the reins of authority.

2. Others are ignorant or lack understanding.
3. Others are content with "a transitory dominion."
4. Thus the "'people of the Book'" alluded to in the scriptures (especially in the Qur'án) are "none other than the divines of that age." (16)
5. The overall reason is their "lack of knowledge and understanding." (17)

D. Only those who are spiritually inclined can discern the signs of the Manifestation.

E. When Jesus appeared, the people of Israel arose in protest:
1. They insisted the Messiah should promulgate the law of Moses, but Christ annulled the law of divorce and the sabbath day.
2. They still expect the Manifestation; therefore, God has punished them. So it is with all the "kindreds and peoples of the earth" who have likewise "deprived themselves of the clear waters streaming from the springs of purity and holiness." (19)

F. Christ forewarned His followers that He would go away and that He would send another "'Who will tell you all that I have not told you, and will fulfil all that I have said'" (20), and Muḥammad's advent fulfilled these promises. Ponder the analogy of the sun: we call days by different names, but it is the same light each day. Thus Muḥammad declared, "I am Jesus." (20–21)

III. Muḥammad fulfilled Christ's instruction about "those signs that must needs signalize the return of His manifestation" (22), because the "'bread from heaven,'" this "goodly gift" can never be "exhausted." (23)

A. "'Immediately after the oppression of those days shall the sun be darkened, and the moon shall not give her light, and the stars shall fall from heaven, and the powers of the earth shall be shaken: and then shall appear the sign of the Son of man in heaven: and then shall all the tribes of the earth mourn, and they shall see the Son of man coming in the clouds of heaven with power and great glory. And he shall send his angels with a great sound of a trumpet.'" (24–25; see also Matt. 24:29–31)[14]

1. Christian divines misunderstood, and "they therefore became deprived of . . . the Muḥammadan Revelation . . ." (26)
    a) They interpreted these words literally.
    b) They interpreted "'Heaven and earth shall pass away: but My words shall not pass away'" as meaning there would be no further revelation. (27)
    c) Therefore they refused to "submit to his law." (28)
    d) I will "share with thee a dewdrop out of the fathomless ocean of the truths treasured in these holy words." (28)

B. The phrase "'the oppression of those days'" refers to a time like today when reins of power are in the grasp of the foolish who oppress humankind. (29)
    1. These Christian divines still imagine "the door of knowledge to be closed," even though the Revelation has come and gone. (30)
    2. They seek only "their own desire," and cannot agree on anything. (30)
    3. They are like "voracious beasts" that prey upon "the carrion of the souls of men." (31)
    4. This "oppression" or "darkness of the night of error"

14. Bahá'u'lláh's "dewdrop" (*Kitáb-i-Íqán* 28) is a detailed analysis of this prophecy that continues well into Part Two. He begins discussing the last part on page 116, where He interprets the "trumpet" as the "trumpet-call of Muḥammad's Revelation: "by 'trumpet' is meant the trumpet-call of Muḥammad's Revelation, which was sounded in the heart of the universe, and by 'resurrection' is meant His own rise to proclaim the Cause of God" (116).

precedes the morning light of every new Revelation. (31)
5. Anyone interpreting this "oppression" (i.e., "pressure") as a literal condition will be lost; it implies an inability "to acquire spiritual knowledge." (32)

C. The words "'The sun shall be darkened, and the moon shall not give light, and the stars shall fall from heaven'" have many meanings, a particular one each time a Prophet employs the terms. (33)
   1. The "sun" sometimes designates the Manifestations of God. (33)
      a) They are "Luminaries" upon which depend for existence all created things. (34)
      b) The apparent limitations of the Prophets are due to our imperfect comprehension.
      c) They are exalted beyond "every descriptive attribute" and "above human understanding!" (35)
   2. In the "Prayer of Nudbih" by Imám 'Alí, the terms "sun," "moon," and "stars" refer to Prophets, saints, and their companions. (36)
      a) They shed light upon all the worlds.
   3. These terms sometimes allude to divines of the former Dispensation who live in "days of the subsequent Revelations" (36):
      a) They hold the reins of religion.
      b) If they recognize the new Revelation, they will "shine with a light everlasting." (36)
      c) Otherwise they "will be declared as darkened." (36)
   4. Another usage of "sun," "moon," and "stars" is to designate laws and teachings proclaimed in every Dispensation:
      a) In particular are the laws of prayer and fasting. (38)
      b) Example: If Islám is heaven, then """fasting is its sun, prayer, its moon."""" (40)
   5. In summary, by this prophecy is intended the idea that

the divines, the laws, the commandments, etc., of the previous Dispensation are "darkened," "exhausted," and "cease to exert their influence." (41)

a) Had the Christian divines recognized the symbolic meaning of these terms, they would not have become "oppressed by the darkness of their selfish desires." (42)

b) They still are asleep, so leave them to themselves.

c) Be steadfast, that you can understand these "mysteries with thine own eyes." (43)

IV. Other verses of prophecy regarding the continuity of Revelation and the Day of Resurrection can be similarly understood as having symbolic meaning:

A. The same symbolic manner of interpretation should be applied to understanding the prophecies about the "'cleaving of the heaven'" as a sign of the "last Hour, the Day of Resurrection." (44)

1. This means that each Revelation "is superseded and annulled" by every subsequent Revelation.
2. Symbolically this act is "mightier than the cleaving of the skies" (44) because the divine Revelation which has been securely established is "abolished at the appearance of one soul." (45)

B. The meaning of the "'changing of the earth'" in the Qur'án when Muḥammad states: "'On the day when the earth shall be changed into another earth'" (47) is explained.

1. The earth symbolizes the human heart which receives the "showers of mercy" from the "'heaven' of divine Revelation." (46)
2. When human hearts are changed (receptive), they bring forth "blossoms of true knowledge and wisdom." (46)
3. If not changed, hearts could not reflect divine attributes. (46)
4. In fact, the physical earth also becomes changed. (47)

C. Another symbolic verse regarding Resurrection Day states:

"'The whole earth shall on the Resurrection Day be but His handful, and in His right hand shall the heavens be folded together. Praise be to Him! and high be He uplifted above the partners they join with him!'" (47)

1. To interpret this in any literal sense is absurd and blasphemous, even if we assume the Prophets will do this for God. (47–48)
2. "'Earth'" means understanding and knowledge, and "'heavens'" are the heavens of "divine Revelation" (48):
   a) All previous knowledge by comparison to the new Revelation is but "a mere handful." (48)
   b) All the Dispensations of the past have been "folded together." (48)

V. The purpose of "all these symbolic terms and abstruse allusions" is to "test and prove the peoples of the world" (49)—to educate humankind. And there are other such tests associated with the advent of the Manifestations.

A. At the behest of God, Muḥammad changed the Qiblih from Jerusalem to Mecca. (50)
   1. The purpose in this "turmoil" was to "test and prove" the servants of God; it served no practical purpose. (51)
   2. No Prophet since Moses had altered the law of the Qiblih, though in the eyes of God "all the places of the earth are one and the same." (51)
   3. The purpose was to determine who would follow the Apostle (Muḥammad) when tested. These "showers of tests" (53) from God are purely for our education.

B. We also find similar tests associated with the lives of the Manifestations. To study Their deeds and words with a spiritual eye is to acquire peace and certitude.
   1. Consider Moses' reputation as a murderer.
      a) He assisted one who was being attacked, but because of this He was in danger of execution. (53–54)
      b) He received the signal to begin His ministry and

proceeded to Pharaoh to deliver the "divine Message." (55)

c) Pharaoh accused Moses of man-slaughter; Moses confessed but said He was now a Prophet. (55)

d) Surely God could have kept Moses from being placed in such position (of having to commit man-slaughter), but He was testing the people. (55–56)

2. Consider how Christ was reputed to have been born to an unchaste mother (i.e., public reputation seems to conflict with the concept of a perfected being). (56–57)

   a) How could Mary explain to those around her that the fatherless Babe she bore had been conceived of the Holy Ghost? (56)

   b) Nevertheless, God conferred Prophethood upon Jesus. (57)

C. God teaches us in this indirect manner so that we may think of Him as the "divine Charmer." (57)

1. These mysteries are "waters of mercy" to those righteous ones who understand, but "the fire of vengeance" unto the wicked. (57)

2. To those with discerning eyes and hearing ears, there is no distinction between the Revealed Word and the deeds "that have emanated from the Kingdom of divine power." (58)

3. Were the same tests to occur today, the results would be no different (58):

   a) A fatherless child would not be accepted as a Prophet.

   b) Neither would a reputed murderer.

D. In fact, the same process *has* occurred again! (59–61)

1. The Báb has been persecuted like the previous Prophets.

2. A poetic tribute to the Báb and to the present Revelation (that of Bahá'u'lláh) is given.

   a) All things are made new. (59)

   b) The mysteries are unfolded and unveiled. (59)

   - *c*) The dead are quickened. (60)
   - *d*) The universe is pregnant with "manifold bounties" (60), awaiting the hour when the effects of this outpouring will be manifest.
3. Therefore, "kindle with the oil of wisdom the lamp of the spirit within the innermost chamber of thy heart, and guard it with the globe of understanding . . ." (61)

VI. Another prophetic verse associated with the advent of a Manifestation concerns the signs that herald the event: "'And then shall appear the sign of the Son of man in heaven.'" (61)

A. By this is meant that when the power of the previous Dispensation is diminished, and the time is ripe for a new Revelation, there shall appear a star in the heaven prior to the advent of the Prophet. (61–62)

B. By this is also meant that an individual will arise immediately prior to the Revelation to announce the imminence of Revelation. (62)

C. Several examples from previous Dispensations will illustrate these twofold signs which occur with the advent of each Prophet:

1. Abraham (62–63)
   - *a*) Nimrod had a dream.
   - *b*) A star appeared.
   - *c*) A herald announced the coming of Abraham.
2. Moses (63)
   - *a*) Soothsayers told Pharaoh of a new star that signified the conception of a Child of great import.
   - *b*) A sage consoled the people of Israel with the news of a forthcoming leader.
3. Jesus (64)
   - *a*) The Magi followed the star and came to Herod asking where they might find the King of Jews.
   - *b*) John the Baptist preached of Jesus' advent.
4. Muḥammad (65)
   - *a*) Signs in the heavens appeared.

- *b*) Four men successively announced "the joyful tidings" of the advent of Muḥammad.

5. The Báb ("this wondrous and most exalted Cause") (65)
   - *a*) Many astronomers announced the appearance of a star.
   - *b*) Shaykh Aḥmad and Siyyid Káẓim prepared the way for the Báb.

VII. And now to explain the prophetic signs indicated by Christ about His return in the passage: "'And then shall all the tribes of the earth mourn, and they shall see the Son of man coming in the clouds of heaven with power and great glory.'" (66)

- A. In one sense this passage refers to the fact that the Prophets come when the influence of the previous Revelation has ebbed. (66)
- B. Of great importance in this passage is the concept of "heaven":
  1. Here "heaven" refers to the fact that the "divine Beauty," though appearing in human form, descends "from the heaven of the will of God." (67)
     - *a*) The Prophets dwell on earth but have preexisted "in the realms above." (67)
     - *b*) They walk among mortals but are constantly aware of and in communication with the kingdom of "the invisible." (67)
     - *c*) They are "raised up" by the "will of God": that is what is meant by "'coming in the clouds of heaven.'" (67)
  2. The term "heaven" can have many meanings. (68)
     - *a*) The Prophets use this term in various contexts and in "every instance" They have "given the term 'heaven' a special meaning." (68)
- C. If you "cleanse the mirror of thy heart" from malice and put aside "idle learning" that is "current amongst men," you can attain "true knowledge." (68–69) [Bahá'u'lláh's discussion of knowledge and learning]

1. There are two kinds of knowledge:
   a) Divine (69)
      (1) It derives from "divine inspiration";
      (2) Its source is "God Himself";
      (3) It produces patience, love, understanding, etc.
   b) Satanic (69)
      (1) It derives from "vain and obscure thoughts";
      (2) Its source is the "whisperings of selfish desire";
      (3) It produces arrogance, vainglory, conceit, iniquity, rebellion, hatred, and envy.
2. To acquire divine knowledge one must follow the "'snow-white Path'" (70).
   a) Pay no attention to the "idle sayings of men" (70)
   b) Become detached from "earthly affection" (70)
3. We have digressed (though in truth this confirms Our purpose). (70)
   a) There yet remain innumerable mysteries ("ḥúrís of inner meaning") which no one has yet befittingly understood. (70)
   b) When will those be found to "discover the mysteries of divine utterance?" (71)

D. Now that we have explained the meaning of "heaven," let us discuss the meaning of "clouds." (71)
1. One sense is that the Prophets bring things "contrary to the ways and desires of men" (71):
   a) Annulment of laws (71)
   b) Abrogation of former Dispensations (71)
   c) Repeal of rituals and customs (71)
   d) Exalting of the "illiterate faithful above the learned opposers" (72)
2. In another sense "clouds" concern the mortal aspect or "image" of the Prophet (72):
   a) He *seems* limited by human conditions.
      (1) Eating and drinking
      (2) Poverty and riches

(3) Glory and abasement
(4) Sleeping and waking

b) In the same way that clouds prevent us from seeing the sun, so, too, do these things prevent recognition of the Prophet. (72–73)

c) People wonder how "such a person" could be sent from God with all power and yet also be "subject to such trivial things." (73)

d) It is because of this illusion (cloud) of the Prophet's "human" limitations that the Prophets and Their followers have been so severely persecuted. (73)

3. In general, "clouds" represent changes that come with every Dispensation to challenge those who blindly imitate their fathers. (74)

a) When the Prophet (Who seems to be an ordinary human and one of them) arises to abolish "every established principle" they hold dear, they are veiled from "acknowledging His truth." (74)

b) They then confidently "pronounce the Manifestation of God an infidel." (74)

c) It is thus a test for us to pierce these "dark veils, these clouds of Heaven-sent trials" that can hinder us from recognizing the Prophet in His human form. (75)

4. This same symbolic use of "clouds" appears in the Qur'án. (75)

a) God shall come down "'over-shadowed with clouds.'" (75)

b) "[H]eaven shall give out a palpable smoke, which shall enshroud mankind: this will be an afflictive torment. . . ." (76) This smoke denotes

(1) "grave dissensions,"
(2) the abrogation of "recognized standards,"
(3) and the "utter destruction" of those who uphold these standards. (76)

5. This afflicting torment occurs even now as mankind is tested to recognize "this wondrous Cause of God." (77)
   a) The more they observe its strength, the more they become dismayed. (77)
   b) The example of the believers causes them to profess faith, but privately they "execrate His name." (77)
   c) Soon will the "standards of divine power" become evident. (78)

E. Now let us consider Christ's words, "'And He shall send His angels. . . .'" (78)
1. In general, "angels" designates those who have, through God's love, transcended human "traits and limitations" and have acquired angelic attributes. (79)
2. The sixth Imám, Ṣádiq, alluded to this same figurative image. (79)
   a) "'There stand a company of our fellow-Shí'ihs behind the Throne.'"
   b) "'A true believer is likened unto the philosopher's stone.'"
3. This symbolic language (i.e., our inability to discover the "'philosopher's stone'") signifies how difficult it is to discover a "true believer" among the Shí'ihs. (79)
4. Because the "adherents of Jesus" have failed to understand the symbolic nature of Jesus' words, they, too, have failed to recognize the Prophet. (80)
   a) Were these words to be literally fulfilled, none would fail to understand; however, without this testing, no learning takes place, and without learning, humankind would be seized by consternation. (80–81)
   b) Because Muḥammad was not literally accompanied by angels, the Christian divines rejected Muḥammad. (81)

VIII. Because the divines in every age "have literally interpreted the Word of God," they have "deprived themselves and all their people" of God's grace and mercy. (82)
   A. "'Our Word is abstruse,'" "'sorely trying,'" and "'highly perplexing.'" (82)
      1. None understand except for the "favorite of heaven," a Prophet, or "he whose faith God hath tested." (82)
      2. The divines do not fall into any of these categories. (82)
   B. The divines confidently assert that the traditions regarding the advent of the Qá'im have not yet been fulfilled. (83)
      1. Of course, they also acknowledge that none of the Christian conditions for the advent of Muḥammad have been literally fulfilled. (83–84)
      2. They then expect the literal fulfillment of their own traditions regarding the Qá'im. (83–84)
   C. Their response to Christians regarding fulfillment is that the "Books have been corrupted," but they don't understand "what is meant by corrupting the text." (84)
      1. An example of such a change by the Jewish divines is the alteration in the penalty for adultery. (85)
         a) The Pentateuch dictated death by stoning. (85)
         b) The divines changed this law to avoid the loss of manpower. (85–86)
         c) Hence, they "pervert the text" by altering the law, not by actually changing the scriptures. (86)
      2. The idea that the texts have been altered is foolish. (86)
         a) The texts have been spread throughout the world. (86)
         b) The real meaning is that texts are interpreted according to "idle imaginings" and "vain desires." (86)
         c) The same thing is happening today with the Qur'án

regarding the advent of the next Manifestation. (86)

3. In other passages Muḥammad indicates that the divines have done this quite knowingly. (86–88)
   a) Jewish divines wrote treatises refuting Muḥammad which they falsely claimed were derived from the Pentateuch. (86–87)
   b) Muslim Divines do the same today against the Bábí Faith. (88)
4. Some claim the true Gospel doesn't exist among Christians but has ascended to heaven. (89–90)
   a) God would not let this happen when His purpose is to leave behind His Word.
   b) What law would guide the people to Muḥammad (i.e., how could they be held responsible for not recognizing Muḥammad)?

D. Now when the light of a new Manifestation is shedding its radiance upon the earth, it is incumbent upon true seekers to cleanse their hearts from the things of this world in order to behold the Truth so clearly that they will need no further proof or evidence. (90–91)
   1. If you attain this station, you will recognize God's sovereignty in everything. (91)
   2. If you attain this station, you will realize that nothing is known except through recognition of God. (91)
   3. If you dwell in this land, you will understand that the greatest proof of God is the Word of God. (91–92)
   4. People of the Bayán, take heed of all I have said that you will not commit the same errors when you are tested in the "Day of God" (93) when He Who is the "Source of all light" is made manifest. (92)

PART TWO

THESIS: The purpose of these words is to "reveal and demonstrate unto the pure in heart" that the Manifestations who are sent from the spiritual world to "educate the souls of men" are invincible: "For these hidden Gems, these concealed and invisible Treasures, in themselves manifest and vindicate the reality of these holy words: 'Verily God doeth whatsoever He willeth, and ordaineth whatsoever He pleaseth.'" (97)

I. Because there can be no "tie of direct intercourse" between God and His creation, God has caused Manifestations to appear "out of the realm of the spirit" as the attributes of God perfected in the form of the "human temple." (99)
   A. They are thus empowered to convey to humankind an understanding of the realities of God. (99–100)
      1. Their knowledge, sovereignty, beauty, wisdom, etc. are but reflections of God's attributes. (99–100)
      2. In effect, there is no difference between Their reality and the reality of God except that They are created and God is preexistent. (100)
   B. In truth, all creation reflects the attributes of God. (100)
      1. This is true of physical creation: atoms and drops. (100–01)
      2. This is true to a "supreme degree" in the reality of man. (101)
         a) In humankind are "potentially revealed all the attributes of God," even as Muḥammad has said (101):
            (1) "'Man is My mystery, and I am his mystery.'" (101)
            (2) "'We will surely show them Our signs in the world and within themselves.'" (101)
            (3) "'And also in your own selves: will ye not then behold the signs of God?'" (101)
            (4) "'And be ye not like those who forget God, and whom He hath therefore caused to forget their own selves.'" (101)
            (5) "'He hath known God who hath known himself.'" (102)
   C. In summary, everything reveals the attributes of God according to its capacity:

1. Even as the tradition says: "'No thing have I perceived, except that I perceived God within it, God before it, or God after it.'" (102)
2. Because man is the "noblest and most perfect of all created things," he is a "fuller expression" of the glory of "this revelation." (102–03)
3. The most perfect man is the Manifestation. (103)

D. The station and perfection of these Beings is such that "all else . . . live by the operation of their Will, and move and have their being through the outpourings of their grace." (103)
   1. All the attributes of God are "made manifest" through them. (103)
   2. Though some Prophets excel others in outward influence or in the "intensity of their revelation" (104), all alike possess this same capacity.
   3. Because the people of the world have failed to recognize the Prophets, they have been deprived of guidance and knowledge. (105–06)

II. Having established the exalted station of the Prophets, let us return to the question of why the sovereignty of the Qá'im has not been made manifest. [Note here that the one part of the prophecy of Christ cited on pages 24–25 that Bahá'u'lláh has not explicated concerns the trumpet sounding as the angels are sent forth.]

A. In the first place, the sovereignty of the Qá'im *has* been established. (106)
   1. It is not recognized because this "sovereignty" is not the sort that people would commonly recognize. (106)
      a) Neither was this same attribute recognized in past Prophets. (106)
      b) This spiritual power takes on "earthly dominion" at the pleasure of the Qá'im; otherwise it is concealed. (107)
      c) As we have previously explained, terms like "sover-

eignty" designate the Prophet's internal "spiritual ascendancy" which is revealed to humankind according to our "receptiveness." (107–08)

2. This same process is evident when we consider the "sovereignty" of Muḥammad.
   a) Though today Muḥammad's sovereignty is "manifest among the people" (108), recall what He suffered during His lifetime.
      (1) The divines of His day "treated Him as an impostor, and pronounced Him a lunatic and a calumniator." (108)
         (*a*) The same thing hath "befallen this Servant." (109) [Here Bahá'u'lláh clearly hints at His own station.]
      (2) For this reason Muḥammad recorded these rejections in the Qur'án:
         (*a*) One verse (Qu'rán 6:35) demonstrates that there was no remedy for Him. (109–10)
      (3) Today He and His Faith are revered throughout the world, but the true sovereignty intended by the verses is the spiritual ascendancy which is an inherent part of the Prophet's reality. (111)
   b) One evidence of the sovereignty exercised by Muḥammad concerns the power of the revealed word to sever and to bind:
      (1) The faithful and the infidel "warred against each other" as if the sword of God separated the goodly from the wicked. (112)
      (2) Yet the "welding power" and "binding force" of Muḥammad's Faith united people of "divers beliefs, of conflicting creeds, and opposing temperaments." (112)
      (3) This is the significance of the verse from Isaiah regarding the wolf and the lamb feeding together. (113)

(*a*) Some await the literal fulfillment of this.
(*b*) What good would there be in such an occurrence?
(4) This is what is meant by the appearance of Muḥammad passing upon the people "the verdict of the Last Day, the verdict of resurrection, of judgment, of life, and of death." (114)

3. Because the divines and commentators of the Qur'án interpret all this literally, they pervert the grammar to infer that the Trumpet Blast foretold (in Christ's Prophecy) is yet to occur.[15]
   a) Muḥammad clearly states that it has already occurred.
      (1) By "'trumpet'" is meant the "trumpet-call of Muḥammad's Revelation." (116)
      (2) By "'resurrection'" is meant Muḥammad's rise to proclaim the Cause of God. (116)
      (3) The same symbolic significance pertains to "judgment," "paradise," and "hell," yet people still await these events. (117)
4. This same symbolic use of the terms of judgment and resurrection occurs with the advent of each Prophet.
   a) Christ spoke of being "'born again,'" by which He meant that those who recognize the Prophet are "resurrected" and those who do not are condemned to a spiritual "'death'" or "'deprivation.'"
   b) In this vein Christ spoke of letting the "'dead bury their dead.'" (119)
   c) Likewise, 'Alí employed terms like "'grave,'" "'tomb,'" "'paradise'" and "'hell'" to allude to spiritual conditions, yet people persist in thinking of these as material conditions. (120)
   d) These same terms regarding "'the dead, whom We

15. Bahá'u'lláh is still explicating the passage from Matthew which He has cited on pages 24–25 of *The Kitáb-i-Íqán.*

have quickened'" were used to describe Ḥamzih, "'Prince of Martyrs,'" but because they understood not, they caused mischief. (121–22)

e) The same misunderstanding occurs today as people look for guidance from the divines whose sole aim is "their fame and fortune." (122).

f) The only ones who will understand the symbolic nature of these terms are those who attain the knowledge of the Word of God and repudiate "manifestations of Satan." (123)

B. Clearly, then, the sovereignty of "Him Who is the King of kings" which wields power through words is superior to any earthly dominion. (123–24)

1. Were *sovereignty* to imply merely earthly dominion so that all the peoples of the world would follow the Prophet, then this would not be indicative of divine power (it would not be of God). (124)

a) The "generality of mankind is under the sway of His enemies." (125)

b) What value would there be for the Prophet to have the allegiance of such people?

2. Furthermore, if earthly sovereignty were implied, how could you explain various Qur'ánic verses alluding to this true sovereignty and dominion? (125–26)

a) If "'And verily Our host shall conquer'" were taken literally, then how do you explain the life of Ḥusayn?

(1) Ḥusayn was an incomparable warrior, yet he was martyred by "'the people of tyranny.'" (126)

b) If "'Fain would they put out God's light . . .'" (126) were taken literally, how do you explain the treatment of the Manifestations?

(1) In every age these "Lamps of God" were extinguished by the peoples of the earth—at least, "to outward seeming." (127)

(2) These "Luminaries" never found shelter or tranquillity. (127)

3. No, the terms designating sovereignty (e.g., "'ascendancy,'" "'power,'" and "'authority'") have spiritual significance, but that hidden meaning in time takes on "the outward manifestations of its potency." (128)
   a) The dust on which the drops of Ḥusayn's blood were sprinkled are now deemed powerful enough to heal and protect. (128)
   b) Likewise, Ḥusayn died alone with none to bury his body, but now pilgrims come from the "uttermost corners of the earth" to "lay their heads upon the threshold of his shrine" at this same spot. (128–29)
   c) Furthermore, even though Ḥusayn is physically dead, he benefits from this glory in the spiritual world because that "holy soul is immortal." (129)
4. Each of the "Exemplars of sacrifice," though dwelling in the dust, occupies the "seat of glory in the realms above." (130)
   a) All the fruits of Ḥusayn's martyrdom could never be recounted. (129)
   b) Let the future disclose how many hidden souls, destitute of earthly sovereignty, have aided the Cause of God. (130)
   c) These Luminaries dwell in the dust but are in glory above. (130)
      (1) They have no earthly possessions.
      (2) Though in the grip of the enemy, They are "seated on the right hand of power and celestial dominion." (130)
      (3) Though abased, They are glorified.
   d) Jesus rejoiced in His poverty, saying, "'who on earth is richer than I?'" (131)
      (1) If you understood this station, you would like-

wise "forsake the world and all that is therein. . . ." (131)

e) The sixth Imám Ṣádiq explained to a companion that possessing love for the Prophet made him rich:
   (1) Would you exchange this love for "'one thousand dinars'"? (131)
   (2) Then how can you call yourself poor if you possess something worth so much? (132)
   (3) By "riches" is thus meant being independent of all but God, and "poverty" implies the lack of "things that are of God." (132)

f) Recall the example of the examination of Jesus by the chief priests, Pilate, and Caiaphas.
   (1) He responded to their question about His claims by stating, "'Beholdest thou not the Son of Man sitting on the right hand of power and might?'" (133)
   (2) To them He was devoid of all power, so they executed Him. (133)

g) Recall how Jesus healed a man of palsy and forgave him his sins. (133–34)
   (1) The Jews thought the real power was the ability to heal.
   (2) The "real sovereignty" was the ability to forgive the man's sins. (134)

C. All these examples have but one function—to induce certitude by explaining that:
   1. True sovereignty is not dependent on earthly conditions. (134)
   2. The utterances of the "chosen Ones of God" regarding ascendancy have symbolic meanings. (134)
   3. The same accusations that caused the Jews and Christians to reject Muḥammad are now being used against the Báb. (135)

III. In addition to the question of "sovereignty," an issue that has caused the divines to reject the next Manifestation (including the Qá'im) are various questions associated with the succession of Prophets.

A. The first issue concerns the idea among some religious traditions that there will be no further revelation:
    1. The Jewish divines rejected Muḥammad saying no Prophet would appear after Moses. (135)
        a) They say the hand of God is "'chained up.'" (136)
        b) Muḥammad repudiated their inferences
            (1) By definition God's mercy never declines.
            (2) How can an omnipotent Being become powerless? (136)
    2. The Muslim divines have, for a thousand years, censured the Jews for this, but were all the while committing the same error.
        a) They contend that "all Revelation is ended." (137)
B. This demonstrates that they don't recognize the "essential Purpose" of the Cause of God—enabling humankind to "attain the Presence of God." (138) This is another issue related to the concept of succession.
    1. Numerous Qur'ánic verses allude to this concept of the purpose of Revelation as enabling humankind to attain the "'Presence of God'":
        a) "'. . . they shall ever meet Him . . .'" (138)
        b) "'. . . that they shall attain unto the Presence of their Lord . . .'" (138)
        c) "'. . . they must meet God. . . .'" (139)
        d) "'. . . who hopeth to attain the presence of his Lord . . .'" (139)
        e) "'. . . have firm faith in attaining the presence of your Lord.'" (139)
    2. There are various ways the Muslim divines misinterpret this concept of continuous revelation as expressed through the idea of "'attainment unto the Divine Presence.'"

a) Some contend that this phrase alludes to the "Day of Resurrection" when there will be a "'Universal Revelation.'" (139)
   (1) As we have explained, this condition already exists. (139)
   (2) All things express divine attributes. (140)

b) If "attainment unto the Divine Presence'" is taken to mean "attaining unto the knowledge of such revelation," then how could such a condition be restricted to the "Day of Resurrection"? (140–41)

c) If "'divine Presence'" is taken to mean a specific Revelation (the "Most Holy Outpouring" as designated by the Ṣúfís) in which the Essence itself is attained, obviously such a thing is, by definition, impossible since the finite cannot comprehend the infinite. (141)

d) If "'divine Presence'" is interpreted to mean that the "'Secondary Revelation'" will manifest the Divine Essence, clearly this is also impossible.
   (1) The Prophets manifest the attributes of God, not the Essence.
   (2) The Prophets are the most perfect Manifestation of God in creation. (142)

3. In short, to attain the "'Presence of God'" means to attain the "presence of these holy Luminaries." (142)
   a) Only through Them is all knowledge of God, His powers, and His attributes understood. (142)
   b) This attainment is available in every Dispensation. (143)

4. This attainment is possible "only in the Day of Resurrection"—i.e., "the Day of the rise of God Himself through His all-embracing Revelation." (143)
   a) This is that Day because the Báb as Qá'im has come
      (1) God has come down "'overshadowed with clouds.'" (144)

(2) Therefore, "One righteous work performed in this Day" is "immensely beyond and above the estimate of men." (144–45)

b) But the learned "have failed to apprehend the true meaning of 'Resurrection' and of the 'attainment unto the divine Presence'" (145):

(1) Because they are immersed in "material studies," they forget the "sole and fundamental purpose of all learning." (145)

(2) How can he be "justly called learned" who fails to recognize the "'Divine Presence'" in the "day of God's Revelation"? (145)

(3) Whereas he who attains this Presence "hath reached the furthermost summit of learning." (146)

c) Right now "'the Lamp of God is shining'" and is "summoning you to heed His cause." (147)

C. Also related to understanding the idea of succession is the concept of "return," the misunderstanding of which has prevented humanity from recognizing the Prophets.

1. Muḥammad identified those who failed to recognize Him as being the same people who in the past rejected previous Apostles. (148)

a) When opponents asked Muḥammad for a miracle, He responded that when this was done before, they slew the Prophets. (148)

(1) This identified them with the people in every Dispensation who persecute the Prophet. (149)

(2) Because people don't understand the enigmatic nature of these responses, they think the Prophets are ignorant. (149)

b) People denounce unbelievers and then persecute the next Prophet because He lives among them. (150)

(1) Here, too, Muḥammad identifies them as the same people. (150)

(2) He identifies Himself as the "return" of the past Prophets.

2. Clearly, the concept of "return" relates to the continuity of this process, not to the literal return of the same individual.
   a) The Prophets bring the same truth and power.
   b) The "Companions" or believers are the same few. (151)
   c) The "'infidels'" are always the so-called learned divines. (151)
3. The concept of "return" also relates to the fact that, though bringing a new message and a new Cause, each Prophet is the return of the same Divine Presence.
   a) They are regarded as "one soul and the same person." (152)
   b) They all "drink from the one Cup of the love of God, and all partake of the fruit of the same Tree of Oneness." (152)

IV. While each Prophet is the "return" of all the previous Prophets, "These Manifestations of God have each a twofold station." One of the two stations of the Prophets is the "station of pure abstraction and essential unity." (152)

A. Each Prophet has essentially the same power and mission.
   1. All alike summon humanity to the knowledge of God.
   2. All alike are "invested with the robe of Prophethood." (152)
   3. Though appearing in "divers attire," all the Prophets proclaim "the same Faith." (153–54)
   4. Such is the unity of the Prophets that each is effectively "'the return of all the Prophets'" and "every subsequent Revelation, the return of the former Revelation." (154)

B. Just as Prophets are the "return" of previous Prophets, so "chosen ones" are also the "return."
   1. The example of the followers of Noah. (154)
      a) Prior to recognizing Noah, they were concerned solely with materiality.
      b) Once transformed by belief and certitude, they renounced their kindred, their substance, their traditions, and their lives. (155)
      c) They thus exemplified "the mysteries of 'rebirth' and 'return.'" (156)
         (1) Before transformation, a thorn could "fill them with terror." (156)
         (2) After transformation, one warrior of this host would face and fight a multitude. (156)
   2. Only a "mystic transformation" (156) wrought by the "Divine Elixir" (157) could account for such change.
      a) It is like the transformation of copper into gold:
         (1) If kept in a mine in a liquid state, copper can become gold in seventy years. (157)
         (2) If the "real elixir" is applied, this transmutation occurs instantly. (157)
         (3) The touchstone will prove its essential change. (157)
      b) In the same way, the believers in the Prophet are spiritually transformed through the "Divine Elixir." (157)
         (1) It causes knowledge, guidance, and certitude. (158)
         (2) These people are essentially different. (158)
         (3) You, too, can become transformed through this unveiled understanding of the concepts of "rebirth," "return," and "resurrection." (158)
   3. So it is that in "every subsequent Dispensation" those who embrace the Faith of God "can be regarded in name, in reality, in deeds, in words, and in rank as the

'return' of those who in a former Dispensation had achieved similar distinctions." (158–59)

   a) Whether a rose blooms in the East or West, it is still a rose. Regardless of outward appearance, it has the same quality, the same fragrance. (159)

4. Reflect on the companions of Muḥammad and how they were transformed when they preceded all the peoples of the world in attaining His holy Presence. (159–60)
5. Observe now the "'return'" of these same spiritual qualities in the followers of the Báb.
   a) They exhibit the same spiritual attributes. (160)
   b) They have demonstrated the same renunciation. (160)

C. Thus it is demonstrated that the Prophet "Who is the Last" is the same as "Him Who was the First" (161):

1. They are both "Exponents of one and the same Cause." (161)
   a) As the Báb observed, the Prophets are like the Sun; though it rises at different times, it is the same sun. (161)
   b) In this sense you can understand how terms like "return," "first," and "last" are all properties of that sun. (161)
   c) Likewise, these terms apply equally to all the Prophets who have risen to "proclaim one and the same Faith." (161)
2. How, then, can people misunderstand what Muḥammad means by the term "Seal of the Prophets"?
   a) We have already noted how He declared Himself to be "'all the Prophets.'" (162)
   b) We have already noted how He declared that He was the "'first Adam.'" (162)
   c) With these phrases He demonstrates He is also the "'last Adam,'" or the "'Seal'" of the Prophets. (162)

3. The symbolic meaning of this verse has, in this Dispensation, "been a sore test unto all mankind." (162)
   a) Behold how many cling to the literal meaning of this and thus reject the Báb. (162)
   b) If they take this literally (i.e., that Muḥammad is the "last" expression of God, then why does the material world still exist? (163)
   c) When considered with a "discerning eye," it will be appreciated that these terms that are applicable to God are no less applicable to His Prophets:
      (1) The "'first'" and the "'last'" (163)
      (2) The "'manifest'" and the "'hidden'" (163)
      (3) The "'beginning'" and the "'seal'" (163)

D. There are, then, the various "veils" that deter recognition of each Manifestation as the "return" of the previous Prophet, as 'Alí himself alluded to with the phrase, "'Piercing the veils of glory, unaided'" (164):
   1. The "divines and doctors" (164) constitute one of the "veils" alluded to in this passage:
      a) They reject the Manifestation for various reasons:
         (1) They lack discernment. (164)
         (2) They desire "leadership" and thus refuse to submit or listen. (164)
      b) People follow these "pompous and hypocritical leaders" (164) for various reasons:
         (1) They refuse to think for themselves, and blindly follow. (164–65)
         (2) They refuse to believe the "divines" and the "learned" could possibly be wrong. (165)
         (3) If sheer numbers and fancy costumes were criteria for learning and truth, people of bygone ages must be accounted as superior to these "divines." (165)
      c) Every Prophet fell victim to the hatred of the "divines" and "clerics" of His day. (165–66)

(1) Woe to them for what they have done and are doing. (166)

(2) God assist those who "pierce" and "rend asunder" these "veils." (166)

2. Another sort of veil are allusive, symbolic, or "mysterious sayings" such as "Seal of the Prophets" (166), which explain the essential unity of Prophecy and the continuity of God's eternal Revelation.[16]

a) 'Alí confirms this when he states, "A thousand Fáṭimihs I have espoused, all of whom were the daughters of Muḥammad. . . ."[17] (166)

(1) How many "mysteries lie as yet unravelled within the tabernacle of the knowledge of God. . . ." (167)

(2) This same process of Revelation is eternal in the past and in the future [i.e., there have always been and always will be faithful figures like 'Alí to follow the Prophet and secure His Cause]. (167)

b) Likewise, Ḥusayn said, "I was with a thousand Adams . . ." and "I have fought one thousand battles. . . ." (167–68)

(1) This tradition also alludes to the "mysteries" of symbolic terms "'end,'" "'return,'" and "'creation without beginning or end.'" [i.e., There have always been heroic figures like Ḥusayn who appear in each Dispensation.] (168)

c) How strange that "feeble souls" (168) cling to verses that "accord with their inclinations" and "reject

16. The following section contains more detail than previous sections because Bahá'u'lláh's explication of the phrase "Seal of the Prophets" is such an important issue in the context of traditional Islámic beliefs.

17. Symbolically, these verses seem to imply that 'Alí knew a myriad mys-

those which are contrary to their selfish desires." (169)

(1) For example, when Muḥammad speaks of Himself as "Seal," He also promises the people "'attainment unto the divine Presence.'" (169)

(2) The followers cling to the first part of Muḥammad's utterance, but "turn away from the grace promised by the latter." (169)

d) In light of these allusions it is clear what these "veiled" terms mean.

(1) "Resurrection" alludes to the "rise of the Manifestation of God to proclaim His Cause." (170)

(2) "Attainment unto the divine Presence" means attainment unto the presence of God's attributes "in the person of His Manifestation." (170)

e) Because people cling to their own concept of Muḥammad as the "'seal,'" they fail to recognize the next Manifestation [the Báb]. (170)

(1) Had they recognized that God does "whatsoever He willeth, and ordaineth whatsoever He pleaseth," they would not worry about the term "seal." (170)

(2) If they really recognized their error, they could not abide their own existence. (171)

3. The main problem deterring the recognition of the Prophet is the "folly and perversity of the people" who have "turned their face toward their own thoughts and desires, and have turned their back upon the knowledge and will of God." (171)

a) Were people to recognize what these "veiled" allusions mean and recognize God's power to do

---

teries (i.e., "brides" of inner meaning or ḥúrís) that were the "daughters of Muḥammad" (i.e., could be found in the revealed statements of the Prophet).

"whatsoever He pleaseth," how could they maintain these "glaring absurdities"? (172)

(1) At the "'appointed time of a known day'" they will understand the truth.

b) For 1,280 years these "blind and ignoble people" have recited the Qur'án without true understanding. (172)

(1) The purpose of the scriptures is to understand these holy themes about the Manifestations. (172)

(2) The reading of scriptures is supposed to enable the reader to "apprehend their meaning and unravel their innermost mysteries." (172)

(3) "[R]eading, without understanding, is of no abiding profit unto man." (172)

c) Bahá'u'lláh relates an anecdote about one who asked about terms like "Day of Judgment, Resurrection, Revival, and Reckoning." (172–73)

(1) He asked about the verse regarding "'neither man nor spirit'" being asked of his sin on "'that day.'" (173)

(2) We responded that the verse means no verbal asking, because "the peoples of the world are judged by their countenance." (173)

d) Were the people to ponder the verses, they would discover the answers to all questions, great or small, and observe how all is now come to pass in this Dispensation.

(1) The departure of the Manifestations "from out their native land" would be clear [i.e., as an allusion to Bahá'u'lláh]. (174)

(2) The opposition and arrogance of "government and people" would be clear. (174)

E. "We seal Our theme" [a pun?] by alluding to the verse concerning Muḥammad regarding this place [Baghdád] and the guidance and protection people can receive from this place [from Bahá'u'lláh].

1. Accordingly, "We have . . . set forth the meaning of every theme," that all may understand. (175)
    - *a*) If one argument is not clear, then a soul may find his answer in another. (175)
2. This "Bird of Heaven" is able to "utter a myriad songs" and "unfold innumerable mysteries." (175)
    - *a*) Each word unspoken (concealed) is exalted beyond that which hath been spoken [there is yet infinitely more to tell you]. (175)
    - *b*) Let the future "disclose the hour" when these things will be revealed—the "Brides of inner meaning" will be unveiled. (175)
    - *c*) God will determine this because it is His creation, His Cause, and all knowledge discloses "mysteries of His Spirit." (176)

V. The second station of each Manifestation is the "station of distinction, and pertaineth to the world of creation and to the limitations thereof" (176).

- A. The station of distinction is defined.
    1. Each Manifestation is ordained by God to operate according to the needs and limits of the social and historical context within which He appears.
        - *a*) He possesses a "distinct individuality." (176)
        - *b*) He has a "definitely prescribed mission." (176)
        - *c*) He is endowed with a "predestined Revelation." (176)
        - *d*) He has designated limitations as to what He can reveal. (176)
    2. "Distinct individuality" is defined.
        - *a*) Each is known by a different name. (176)
        - *b*) Each is characterized by a special attribute. (176)
        - *c*) Each fulfills a definite mission. (176)
        - *d*) Each is entrusted with a particular Revelation. (176)

3. The differences in the "station" and "mission" of the Manifestations cause apparent differences in utterances.
   a) In reality They are saying the same thing. (177)
   b) "Divergences of utterance" are attributable to the fact that They must operate within the limitations of history (i.e., the "station of distinction"). (177)

B. Bahá'u'lláh compares and contrasts the "station of essential unity" with the "station of distinction":
   1. From the standpoint of essential unity, all are the same:
      a) All the Prophets "abide on the throne of divine Revelation." (177)
      b) All the Prophets are "established upon the seat of divine Concealment." (177)
      c) All the Prophets reveal the attributes of God. (177–78)
      d) Their voice is, effectively, the Voice of God. (178)
   2. From the standpoint of the "second station" ("the station of distinction"), each Prophet is differentiated from the others:
      a) Each Prophet operates within temporal limitations, characteristics, and standards. (178)
      b) Each Prophet professes unreservedly to be but the "'servant of God.'" (178)[18]

C. Some conclusions about these two stations:
   1. If any Prophet were to say "'I am God!'" He speaks the truth, for through the Prophets the attributes of God are made manifest. (178)
   2. If any Prophet were to say, "'I am the Messenger of God,'" (178) He speaks the truth, for all of the Prophets are "but Messengers of that ideal King." (179)
   3. All the Prophets alike embody "one spirit" and "one

18. That is, each Prophet describes Himself as being part of a continuous divine process, and not the unique or final expression of godliness in human history.

revelation" (179); thus, each expresses the essential attributes of God:

a) Each Prophet is the "'Beginning'" and the "'End'" ("i.e., "seal"). (179)

b) Each Prophet is also the "'First'" and the "'Last.'" (179)

c) Each Prophet is both the "'Seen'" and "'Hidden.'" (179)

D. In both stations, Prophets manifest "the uttermost state of servitude, a servitude the like of which no man can possibly attain" (179).

1. Even while claiming that Their utterance is "the Voice of divinity, the Call of God Himself," They regard Themselves "as utter nothingness" in the face of God. (180)
2. Any concept of "self" in relation to God implies "self-assertion" and "independent existence." (180)
   a) Such a "suggestion" is considered by the Prophets as "an act of blasphemy." (180)
   b) Such a "suggestion" is a "grievous transgression." (180)
3. How much more "grievous" is it for a human being to be in the presence of these Manifestations and to turn away from Their beauty? (180)

E. Clearly, then, the Prophets speak from both perspectives at the same time.

1. Whether speaking as the "Voice of Divinity" or the "Messengers of God," the Prophets have "voiced an utterance" suited to the distinct situation in which They appear (181):
   a) They speak about the celestial realm. (181)
   b) They speak about the earthly domain. (181)
2. Regardless of the perspective from which They speak, all They say is true. (181)
3. Therefore, the "divergent utterances of the Manifestations" must be "attentively considered" in this context

so that these "sayings" will no longer "agitate the soul and perplex the mind." (181)

VI. Let us consider how we can prepare ourselves to approach the utterances of the Prophets so that these veils will be lifted and true knowledge may be gained and the mysteries of these words can become unraveled [i.e., how we can become effective students of scripture] (181–82).

A. To begin with, understanding of the Prophet's words should be sought from the Prophet Himself.

1. The "divines and doctors of the age" today interpret the Prophet's words according to their own "inclination and desires." (182)

2. Were they to ask the Prophet Himself what the words meant, they would denounce Him if He disagreed with their own interpretations. (182)

a) Muḥammad was asked about the meaning of "new moons," and His answer was rejected. (182–83)

b) Muḥammad's comment about "'the Spirit'" was rejected. (183)

3. The "divines" who blindly follow Muḥammad would still reject those same answers today, even though what the Prophets say is "naught else but the truth." (183–84)

B. The rejection and persecution of the Prophets and Their utterances is due to the fact that the so-called learned ones do not truly apprehend "the meaning of Knowledge." (184)

1. The example of false knowledge is illustrated by "Guidance unto the Ignorant" by Ḥájí Mírzá Karím Khán, who, among other things, attempts to explain the "'Mi'ráj'" (Ascent) of Muḥammad.

a) He says one must have knowledge of twenty or more sciences to understand spiritual concepts. (186)

(1) One must understand metaphysical abstractions. (186)

(2) One must understand the study of alchemy. (186)
(3) One must understand natural magic. (186)

2. He upholds such "vain and discarded learning," yet he denounces the "Embodiments of God's infinite knowledge!" (186).
   a) How can he say these unworthy sciences are necessary to understand "'Mi'ráj'" when Muḥammad Himself was never concerned with them? (187)
   b) If one desires to understand the mystery of this "'Mi'ráj,'" one must put aside "the dust of these learnings." (187)
   c) These esoteric studies are "grievous veils" to true learning and understanding. (187)
3. Though Karím's clear purpose was to make himself the sole exponent of knowledge, "people hath gathered around him" and cast the knowledge of the Manifestation "behind their backs." (189)
4. Among the sciences he professes to understand is alchemy. (189)
   a) Would that a king or someone would command him to demonstrate this science. (189)
   b) If I were to undertake this same task (alchemy), the world would immediately be able to discern truth from falsehood [I could actually accomplish it]. (189–90)
   c) Yet, even then, this generation would continue to persecute Me as they have in the past—the scars on My neck bear witness to their blindness.[19] (190)

19. Here Bahá'u'lláh clearly alludes to Himself as a Prophet, something He has done somewhat indirectly earlier in the work. Towards the end of the work these allusions to His own station as a Prophet become more obvious.

5. Though Muḥammad explicitly denounces him in the Qur'án, Karím misinterprets the passage to imply praise. (190)
    a) In spite of such obvious incompetency and dissimulation, he attracts a great following. (191)

C. Only those who have divine knowledge and a pure heart can truly understand the mysteries regarding the lives and utterances of the Prophets: "A Divine Mine only can yield the gems of divine knowledge. . . ." (191) Only the "illumined in heart" can explain to you the "abstruse allusions" and "mysteries." (191) But before you can be worthy of discovering such truth, you must first become a "true seeker."[20] (192)

1. Before seeking the path to the knowledge of the Prophets, the "true seeker" must prepare with the following internal actions (192–93):[21]
    a) Cleanse and purify the heart from preconceptions derived from "acquired knowledge" or from selfish motives.
    b) Purge the breast from attraction to things of this world.
    c) Set aside prejudicial emotions (love or hate) that might distract you from the truth.
    d) Trust in God and not the "peoples of the earth."
    e) Avoid any trace of self interest in the motive for your search.
    f) Cling to patience, resignation, and silence [contemplation].

---

20. The following passage has become known by some as the Tablet of the True Seeker, though, in fact, it is an integral part of Bahá'u'lláh's ongoing exposition in the Kitáb-i-Íqán about how certitude can be acquired.

21. Though Bahá'u'lláh consistently narrates this section in the third person singular (i.e., what the "true seeker" must do), I shift to the second person, changing the "He should . . ." to a simple series of imperatives. This is inconsistent, but clearer for the purposes of our outline.

  - *g*) Avoid "idle talk," especially backbiting.
  - *h*) Be content with little, and treasure the companionship of those similarly inclined.
2. That seeker must further prepare himself with the following actions (194–95):
   - *a*) Commune with God at the dawn of every day.
   - *b*) Replace every "wayward thought" with "His loving mention."
   - *c*) Assist the "dispossessed" and the "destitute."
   - *d*) Show kindness to animals and even more to your "fellow-man."
   - *e*) Be willing to offer up your life for your "Beloved."
   - *f*) Do not allow the opinion of others to deter you from the Truth.
   - *g*) Do not wish for others what you do not wish for yourself.
   - *h*) Do not promise anything you do not fulfill.
   - *i*) Avoid the company of evildoers.
     - (1) Pray for them.
     - (2) Forgive them.
     - (3) Do not "despise" their "low estate."
   - *j*) In general, regard "all else beside God as transient," as "utter nothingness."
3. When these attributes have been attained, the following will result (195):
   - *a*) You can be called a "true seeker."
   - *b*) You will be guided in your search.
4. When the seeker is then filled with "earnest striving" and "passionate devotion," further results will occur (196):
   - *a*) Error, doubt, and misgivings will be "dissipated."
   - *b*) The "lights of knowledge and certitude will envelop" your being.
   - *c*) Spiritual insight will be conferred upon you:
     - (1) You will possess a new eye, a new ear, a new heart, a new mind.

(2) You will contemplate the "signs of the universe."

(3) You will penetrate the "hidden mysteries of the soul."

(4) With this spiritual insight, you will perceive "within every atom" confirmation of belief.

(5) You will discover spiritual meaning "in all things."

d) With ease You will be able to "discriminate between truth and falsehood" (197).

e) You will be able to understand the signs of God, the utterances of God, the works of God. (197)

5. The end result of this condition will be that the seeker enters the "City of Certitude." (197)

a) In this City the seeker will be totally content and satisfied.

b) The seeker will discover "ineffable delights" and "unnumbered mysteries" (198).

c) The seeker could not consider leaving this City. (198–99)

VII. This City of Certitude is none other than the Word of God which is periodically revealed to humankind, and we should long to attain it.[22]

A. This City is "renewed and re-adorned" approximately every thousand years. (199–200)

1. In the days of Moses it was the Pentateuch.
2. In the days of Jesus it was the Gospel.
3. In the days of Muḥammad it was the Qur'án.
4. In this day it is the Bayán.
5. In the day of "Him Whom God will make manifest," it will be His Book, which will be "transcendent and supreme" among them all. (199)

22. Here begins the first of four proofs of the Manifestation, a discussion which continues until page 247.

B. In this City there is "spiritual sustenance," the "bread of heaven," which is sufficient blessing for everyone (200):
   1. It is unity for the "detached souls."
   2. It is enrichment for the destitute.
   3. It is the cup of knowledge for those wandering in ignorance.
   4. Indeed, every spiritual bounty is within this "City."

C. One example of such a City was the Qur'án, which was "an impregnable stronghold" unto the Muslims (200).
   1. Whoever entered therein
      a) was "shielded from the devilish assaults, the menacing darts,"
      b) was given wisdom, knowledge, and "divine Unity."
   2. The Qur'án provided all the guidance that was needed after Muḥammad until 1844, when the Báb appeared. (200–01)
      a) It offered the seeker reunion with the "divine Presence" through Muḥammad.
      b) It offered infallible guidance that no "traditions" or other books could offer.
         (1) Traditions may contradict each other.
         (2) Traditions contain manifold "obscurities" (201).
      c) Muḥammad Himself stated that His "'twin weighty testimonies'" were His Family [the Imáms] and the "'Book of God.'" (201)
      d) Since the family "hath passed away" there remains only His Book as the authoritative "testimony amongst the people." (202)
   3. In the "disconnected letters" of the Qur'án, God Himself has designated Muḥammad and the Qur'án as unerring guidance unto all until the Day of Resurrection (203).[23]

---

23. The "disconnected letters" are symbols that occur throughout the Qur'án. Occurring as a prefix to various Súrihs, these mysterious letters have

a) How can people then dispute its authority or truthfulness? (203–04)
   (1) How can they allow the sayings of men to cause doubt? (203)
   (2) How can they contend that this or that did not come to pass? (204)
   (3) How could there be a "surer guide" than the Book of God? (204)

b) If we reject the truth of the Qur'án, we reject the truth of the "preceding Scriptures." (204)
   (1) This is the meaning of this verse about the station of the Qur'án. (204)

4. In another verse God states, "'if ye be in doubt'" about the Qur'án, then produce "'a Súrah like it.'" (204)

   a) The verses themselves are the surest proof to the peoples of the world. (205)
      (1) Their excellence is unrivaled.
      (2) They contain "the divine mysteries."
      (3) They are the essential link between God and His creatures.
      (4) They are the source of knowledge and wisdom.
      (5) They divide the believers from the non-believers.

   b) It is therefore incumbent upon us to submit to what God has ordained in "his divine Testimony." (205–06)

D. Various Qur'ánic passages allude to how the people are exposed to the verses of God (which are the highest proof

---

perplexed scholars down through the ages. Bahá'u'lláh states that "For lack of space We do not dwell upon them at this moment" (203), but in this same passage He explains their essential meaning.

of the station and power of the Prophet), and yet the people remain oblivious of the import of these verses.

1. It is stated, "But in what Revelation will they believe, if they reject God and His verses?" (206)
   a) By this is meant that there has never been a manifestation of divinity greater than the Prophets.
   b) And no testimony [proof] of Their station is greater than Their revealed verses.
2. In another Qur'ánic verse it is stated, "'Woe to every lying sinner, who heareth the verses of God recited to him, and then, as though he heard them not, persisteth in proud disdain! Apprise him of a painful punishment.'" (206–07)
   a) Yet even today people "disdainfully ignore" the "divinely-revealed" verses. (207)
   b) See how the people repeat the errors of their ancestors. (207)
3. In another verse of the Qur'án it is observed how the people turn "'to ridicule'" the verses of God. (207)
   a) They derisively request us to perform a miracle:
      (1) Make a part of heaven fall upon us.
      (2) Rain down "'stones upon us from heaven.'"
   b) Like the people of Israel who bartered "bread of heaven" for material prosperity, these people rejected Muḥammad. (208)
      (1) He was the same spiritual sustenance come down from heaven.
   c) They clamor for proof and guidance when the verses themselves are that proof and guidance (208–09):
      (1) They behold the sun and ask for proof of its light.
      (2) They behold the showers descending on them and ask for evidence of bounty.
   d) Proofs are unavailable to those who have no spiritual sensibilities (209):

(1) The blind cannot behold the sun.
(2) Arid soil cannot benefit from the vernal showers.
(3) The unbeliever sees in the Qur'án "naught but the trace of letters."

4. In another passage Muḥammad observes, "'And when Our clear verses are recited to them, their only argument is to say, "Bring back our fathers, if ye speak the truth!"'" (209)
   a) What foolish proof they sought [i.e., a miracle].
   b) A "single letter" of these verses can revive the spiritually dead (209).
   c) In this way the verses cause the "dead" to "'speed out of the sepulchers'" of "self and desire."
   d) These verses provide the remedy for every "ailment." (210)

E. The understanding of the verses of God is not dependent on "human learning," nor is it confined to some specific segment of learned or enlightened individuals; rather, all people have access to this testimony.
1. Some contend that understanding of the Book is not available to the "common people." (210)
   a) If the Qur'án were beyond the understanding of all people, how could it be declared as a "universal testimony"?
   b) If this were true, how could "the common people" be accountable for knowing God?
   c) Such a contention "is actuated solely by arrogance and pride."
   d) Such a contention is motivated by a desire to maintain authority over the common people.
2. True understanding of the verses of God derives from spiritual attributes, not from "the accepted standards of learning." (211)
   a) The common people who have "purity of heart," "chastity of soul," and "freedom of spirit" are

"infinitely superior and exalted above their religious leaders who have turned away from the one true God." (211)

(1) This is demonstrated by the fact that those without scholarly credentials presently are "occupying the loftiest seats of knowledge." (211)

(2) Exalted are these humble souls who are "sincere in heart." (211)

b) Whereas those who are not spiritually awake reject the verses for various reasons. (211)

(1) Some rejected Muḥammad as a """crazed poet""" and refused to abandon their gods.

(2) Some accused Muḥammad of simply compiling ancient traditions and calling them the Word of God. (212)

(3) In fact, this same accusation is being used against the Báb presently (i.e., compiling words of old). (212)

3. When the people rejected Muḥammad, claiming no independent Prophet would arise after Moses and Christ (no new law), but only one who would "'fulfill the Law,'" He reminded them of how Joseph was treated. (212)

a) The people in every age misinterpret some verse from the scriptures to contend that no further Prophet will come. (213)

b) For example, the Christian divines contend (213):

(1) that the law of the Gospel will never be annulled;

(2) that any further Prophet must confirm that law.

c) Most people are afflicted with the "same spiritual disease." (213)

(1) The followers of Muḥammad have been "veiled" by the words "'Seal of the Prophets.'"

- (2) Muḥammad warned that the "divines of the age" would be veiled by their own knowledge. (214)
- (3) They have clung to their own learning and turned away from this new Revelation. (214)

d) Muḥammad's own verses should have forewarned them of this:

- (1) You "turn aside" from a "weighty Message." (214)
- (2) They say that the Prophet is "'merely a man who would fain pervert you from your father's worship.'" (215)
- (3) They say that the verses are a "'"forged falsehood."'" (215)

e) See how the people persist in rejecting the verses of God and call the Prophet a "'calumniator'" and "'lunatic'" in spite of these warnings. (215)

F. Now the same sort of rejection Muḥammad faced is being perpetrated against God's Prophet, the Báb. (215–16)

1. In spite of these warnings in the Qur'án, the Muslims have persecuted this "Source of purity" (216) and rejected His revealed verses.

a) They reject Him even though the Báb's verses represent an "outpouring of bounty" that has never been witnessed before. (216)

b) Though the Báb has revealed innumerable verses, a score of which are "now available," many "have been plundered" or are in the "hands of the enemy." (216–17)

c) If we are wise, we will be warned by the Qur'án so we do not repeat the error of rejection committed in the past. (217)

- (1) We will then not "cavil at the Revealer of the verses."

(2) We will then accept His Cause and embrace His law.
(3) We will then benefit from His mercy.

2. When Islám was in its infancy and was "assailed by the infidels," Muḥammad noted the irony that He was persecuted for believing in God and upholding previous Revelations.
    a) At that time Islám was ostensibly "devoid of authority and power." (218)
    b) Their only claim was that "new and wondrous verses of God" had "descended upon Muḥammad" as they had in previous Dispensations.
    c) This is precisely the claim the Báb has made and for which He was persecuted. (219)
    d) Surely Muḥammad would accept as "true believers" those who now recognize the "divine verses." (219)
    e) Indeed, We have used the verses of the Qur'án as the standard for accepting the Manifestation.
        (1) Muḥammad hath "threatened with fire" anyone who would "repudiate and scoff at the verses." (220)
3. Therefore, when one arises and produces verses which could not have been "acquired through learning," is this not a proof of His station? (220–21)
    a) What response can those who reject these verses give?
    b) Do they prefer the "traditions" and "sayings" of those who wish to hold on to power?
    c) If they reject this "divine Soul" (221), to whom shall they turn for guidance?
    d) Nevertheless, though We have shown you the truth, "walk thou the way thou choosest" (221).

VIII. Besides the proof which the verses of God provide is the proof of the lives of the early followers of the Prophet [this is the second proof Bahá'u'lláh provides].

A. In every Dispensation "certain souls" (221) arise to follow:
   1. They are "obscure and detached from all worldly entanglements." (221)
   2. They seek "illumination" and "divine guidance" from the Prophet. (221)
   3. They long to "attain unto the divine Presence." (221)

B. The divines and the wealthy arise against these early believers. (221–22)
   1. They say that the Prophet is only a man like other men.
   2. They say that only the lowly ones follow the Prophet.
   3. They imply that because none of the learned, the wealthy, or the renowned believe, the Prophet must be false.

C. In this Dispensation, however, a number of learned divines have believed.
   1. I will mention the names of some so that the "timorous" and "faint-hearted" may be strengthened and encouraged. (223)
      a) Among them was Mullá Ḥusayn, without whom this Revelation would not have come to pass.
      b) Among them was Vaḥíd (Siyyid Yaḥyá), a "unique and peerless figure of his age."
      c) Among them were some four hundred others.
   2. The lives of these holy souls should be sufficient "testimony" for "the people of this day." (224)
      a) Their faith was so strong they renounced material possessions, their kindred, and their own lives.
      b) They were slaughtered for their beliefs.
      c) Their lives "witness against" those who "betrayed their faith, who bartered away immortality for that which perisheth." (224)
   3. Which testimony is more worthy? (224–25)

   a) The testimony of those whose deeds conform with their "inner life"?
   b) The testimony of "faithless souls" who are selfish, worldly, petty-minded, and oblivious of the divine Decree?

D. Consider how the proof of these martyrs compares to the early history of Islám.
   1. The martyrdom of the Imám Ḥusayn is regarded by Muslims as unprecedented and as "the greatest of all events." (225–26)
      a) No one ever demonstrated such constancy and glory.
      b) That event lasted less than a day.
   2. These "holy lights" (226), the Bábís, have endured such afflictions for eighteen years.
      a) With what devotion and rapture they sacrificed their lives. (226)
      b) If they are not "the true strivers after God," then who is? (226)
      c) Did they have any ulterior motive in this? (226)
      d) If the testimonies of these lives be false, then who can claim the truth? (226)
      e) These deeds are a "sufficient testimony" and an "irrefutable proof" to people everywhere who ponder in their hearts "the mysteries of divine Revelation." (226–27)

E. The Qur'án itself testifies to these lives as "the sign of truth." (227)
   1. Muḥammad says, "'Wish for death, if ye are men of truth'" (227), a verse which functions as a "divine touchstone." (228)
   2. These martyrs who have sacrificed all are of "unquestionable sincerity." (227)
   3. Which makes more sense?
      a) To accept the testimony of "these detached and exalted beings" (227);

b) To accept the denunciations of a faithless people who respond out of ulterior motives (227):
(1) They desire gold.
(2) They wish to retain leadership.

4. The answer is made clear by this verse through which the "true" is separated from the "false." (228)

F. But the leaders ignore the truth of this verse and instead pursue "the vanities of the world" and "earthly leadership." (228–30)

1. For example, none of those heroes whom We have mentioned as being among the divines and the learned had "rank" or "leadership." (228)
2. Religious leaders in general are unable to recognize the "Revealer of truth." (229)
   a) God endows only a select few with this capacity.
   b) In the Bábí Dispensation, not one of the "renowned divines" who have power over the people has "embraced the Faith." (229)
3. The Báb has "revealed an Epistle unto the divines of every city" (229), describing the character of their rejection of the Revelation.
   a) His purpose in discussing their opposition was to prepare the Bábís for the "day of the Latter Resurrection" [the advent of Bahá'u'lláh] when they would be similarly tested. (229)
   b) The divines to whom We have referred as having embraced the Cause of the Báb were, by the grace of God, purged of "earthly vanities" and free from "the trappings of leadership." (230)

IX. A third proof of the truth of this Revelation is constancy of the Báb in "proclaiming the Faith of God." (230)

A. Though young, and though what He revealed was contrary to the desires of the people, He was steadfast. (230)

1. He was afraid of no one.
2. He cared not of the consequences.

B. How can the people account for such constancy? (230–31)
   1. No ordinary human being could conceive of such a Revelation.
   2. Do they accuse Him of folly?
   3. Do they think He did this to acquire power or wealth?

C. If so, then why does He prophesy His own martyrdom?
   1. In the Qayyúmu'l-Asmá' He yearns for it.
   2. In His "interpretation of the letter "'Há'" He says that, but for His awareness of the necessity of His martyrdom in the "inevitable mystery" (232) of the Revelation [of Bahá'u'lláh], the people would be powerless to take aught from Him.
   3. These utterances reflect complete detachment from self and yearning for God's good pleasure.
   4. Because the persecutors in their ingratitude ignore these obvious signs of "the divine Presence" (233), they will be severely chastised in the world to come.

D. "Steadfastness in the Faith" is thus "a sure testimony" of the truth. (233–34)
   1. Muḥammad alluded to the importance of this constancy regarding His own life. (233)
   2. Behold how the life of the Báb demonstrates this quality.
      a) The more "severe the persecution," the more "His fervor increased." (234)
      b) Ultimately, He surrendered His life itself. (234)
   3. His constancy was such that "unaided and alone" He manifested spiritual power throughout the world.
      a) As soon as He declared Himself in Shíráz in 1844, the signs of the power "emanating from that Essence of Essences . . . were manifest in every land." (234)
         (1) Human knowledge and wisdom "encompassed all beings." (234)

b) Wherever holy souls arose, "divines and dignitaries rose to hinder and repress them," to torture and kill them. (234–35)

c) But the holy souls were steadfast to the last breath because of His "transmuting influence." (235)

d) Who in this world could so transform people that they would gladly endure such agony? (235)

e) This "violent commotion," this execration by the "people of the earth" of these heroes of "resignation and detachment" is the "mightiest proof" and "surest testimony" of the truth these heroes profess. (236)

X. Even though We did not intend to resort to "traditions of a bygone age" as part of the testimony or proof of Our argument, We will "cite a few" as a fourth sort of proof. (237)

A. We did not intend to do this because the things We have already said:

1. suffice [to prove the validity of Our Argument and the Bábí Cause]; (237)
2. effectively condense "all the Scriptures and the mysteries thereof"; (237)
3. enable one to discover the "mysteries of the Words of God" and "the meaning of whatever hath been manifested by that ideal King." (237)
4. However, We will do it (237–38)

a) to provide "constancy to the wavering soul,"

b) to provide "tranquillity to the troubled mind,"

c) and to make the "testimony" of God "complete and perfect" for all.

B. One tradition states: "'And when the Standard of Truth is made manifest, the people of both the East and the West curse it.'" (238)

1. Why do the people profess love and yearning for truth, and then curse it when it appears?

- *a*) They do so because the new Revelation annuls those "rules, customs, habits, and ceremonials" to which they are accustomed. (238)
- *b*) If the Prophet were to sanction "their observances," this rejection and conflict would not occur. (238)
- *c*) However, the "divine call" summons humankind to "renounce" these customs and observances. (239)

2. The people ignore these "well-founded" traditions that have been fulfilled and cling to "those of doubtful validity" that do not seem to have been fulfilled. (239)
   - *a*) The signs of truth are as obvious as the "midday sun." (239)
   - *b*) The Qur'án and recognized traditions indicate a "new Faith, a new Law, and a new Revelation" have been revealed. (239)
     - (1) The people still await one who will "uphold" the Islámic law. (239)
     - (2) The Jews likewise wait. (239–40)
     - (3) The Christians also wait. (239–40)
3. People reject the "new Law" (240) even though many traditions indicate that the new Prophet will bring this change.
   - *a*) The "'Prayer of Nudbih'" states the Mihdí[24] will "'transform the Faith.'" (240)
   - *b*) In the Zíyárat the Imám 'Alí states, "'Peace be upon the Truth made new.'" (240)
   - *c*) The sixth Imám, Abú-'Abdi'lláh, said the Mihdí will "demolish whatever hath been before Him." (240)
4. The people contend the law must not be altered even though the "object of every Revelation" is to bring about transformation, "both outwardly and inwardly." (240)

24. The Twelfth Imám, the Qá'im.

a) If change in the character of mankind does not occur, then of what value is the advent of the Manifestations? (241)

b) The collection of Shí'ih traditions called "'Aválim'" confirms that a "Youth" from the house of Muḥammad will "'reveal a new Book and promulgate a new law.'" (241)

(1) It also observes that "'Most of His enemies will be the divines.'" (241)

c) The Imám Ṣádiq confirmed this and said His Revelation would be "'Stern'" unto the Arabs.

5. The people reject this Háshimite Youth [the Báb] in spite of the explicit directions of the Imáms and the warnings of this rejection.

a) They pronounce Him an infidel, a heretic, and they persecute Him because they speak only from the promptings of selfish desires. (242)

b) When He says that which they desire not, they pronounce it contrary to the "sayings of the Imáms." (242)

c) In the "'Arba'ín'" this rejection is foretold:

(1) This tradition even makes it clear that the basis for the rejection will be the people's assertion that the Revelation is contrary to the traditions of the Imáms. (242–43)

C. It is clear in the traditions that the Revelation of the Qá'im shall itself be the standard by which these "sayings" [ḥadíth] will be measured.

1. "All else save Him are created by His command, and move and have their being through His law" (243).

2. All the major collections of Shí'ih traditions confirm the station of the Qá'im:

a) Knowledge is twenty-seven letters; all that the Prophets have thus far revealed equals two letters; the Qá'im shall "'cause the remaining twenty and five letters to be made manifest.'" (243)

   b) This utterance places the rank of the Qá'im above that of all previous Prophets and His Revelation above the "comprehension and understanding of all their chosen ones." (244)

D. Yet the people think to measure this Revelation with their own "deficient" minds, learning, and understanding, rejecting it when it fails to conform to "their standards." (244)
   1. The "divines and doctors sentence Him and His companions to death." (245)
   2. Every detail of this process was foretold in a tradition cited in three different collections (245):
      a) The Qá'im shall have an immaculate character.
      b) His chosen ones shall be abased.
      c) Their heads shall be offered as presents.
      d) They shall be slain and burnt.
      e) The earth shall be dyed with their blood.
      f) Their womenfolk shall bewail and lament.
   3. Each letter of this tradition has been fulfilled, yet no one has wondered how it could be fulfilled if the Qá'im were to bring only the laws that have already been fulfilled. (245–46)
      a) Why would strife then arise?
      b) Why would the people consider such slaughter a meritorious act "imposed upon them"? (246)
   4. An even more explicit prophecy is contained in the conversation recorded between Mu'áviyih and the Imám Abú-'Abdi'lláh:
      a) He foretold that eighty men, all worthy to be called caliphs, would be slain near Ṭihrán by Persians.
      b) As you know, this has occurred [the slaughter of the Bábís at Ṭabarsí?].
      c) The rejection of this and other obviously fulfilled traditions is due to the "faithlessness of the divines and doctors of the age" (247), even as Ṣádiq foretold.

(1) He also foretold that this same mischief would return to them. (248)

XI. These same errors of rejection We have described as applying to the followers of Muḥammad also apply to the followers of the Báb.[25]

A. Therefore, "We entreat the learned men of the Bayán" not to repeat these same errors of rejection when Mustaghá̲th̲ appears in the time of the "Latter Resurrection."

1. Be careful not to rely solely on your intellect. (248)
2. Do not rely solely on comprehension or traditional learning. (248)
3. Do not contend with the Prophet.

B. In spite of these admonitions, We foresee the suffering "the Blessed Beauty" will endure. (248)

1. "We perceive that a one-eyed man" [Siyyid Muḥammad-i-Iṣfahání] is arising "against Us." (248)
2. We foresee people in every city arising to suppress Us. (248)
3. The companions of "the Blessed Beauty" will be persecuted. (248)
    a) Some companions will flee from the oppressor and seek refuge in the wilderness.
    b) Some companions will sacrifice their lives in His path.
4. We foresee "one who is reputed for . . . devoutness and piety" who will arise to assail, resist, and oppose the Prophet. (248–49)

25. Here Bahá'u'lláh reveals that the Bábís are about to undergo the exact same test or judgment that has befallen the followers of previous Prophets. In particular, He alludes to the fact that He Himself fulfills the prophecies of the Báb regarding "Mustaghá̲th̲"—"He Who Is Invoked," the Promised Manifestation.

C. We "fain would hope" it would be otherwise, but we foreknow what will occur.[26]
   1. Would that the "people of the Bayán" would heed the warning in all that we have said [and not repeat the rejection perpetrated against themselves]. (249)
      a) Would that they could "soar in the realm of the spirit."
      b) Would that they could "discern the Truth."
      c) Would that they could recognize falsehood.
   2. However, jealousy abounds, and "such malice, envy, and hate" will occur that have never before occurred, nor will ever occur in the future. (249)
      a) A number of people have "leagued themselves against Us." (249)
      b) We recognize their intentions and their plans to attack Us.
   3. This is what will occur (and is occurring) even though We have never given anyone cause to have ill will towards us. (249–50)
      a) We have always been kindly, forbearing, and affectionate:
         (1) We have sought the fellowship of the poor.
         (2) We have been submissive and resigned "amidst the exalted and learned." (250)

D. Yet grievous as have been the assaults of "the people of the Book" against Us, these are nothing compared to what "hath befallen Us at the hand of those who profess to be Our friends." (250)[27]

---

26. Bahá'u'lláh's reference to His own foreknowledge (in this case most probably an allusion to the rebellion of Mírzá Yaḥyá) is one of several proofs here of His station, if not to His immediate audience, then to those who would read this work after the declaration of His station two years later.

27. Here again it is crucial for the reader to understand that Bahá'u'lláh's discussion of His past treatment at the hands of Mírzá Yaḥyá and His allusion to what Mírzá Yaḥyá will perpetrate in the future is not digressive. After having detailed throughout His argument the way in which each Prophet has been

1. When We first arrived in Ba<u>gh</u>dád We foresaw what was to occur. (250)
    - *a*) We retired to the wilderness before they could take place.
    - *b*) We stayed two years in complete solitude. (250)
2. Though in physical pain, Our soul was "wrapt in blissful joy." (250)
    - *a*) We often had no sustenance, no rest. (250)
    - *b*) We were oblivious to the outside world. (251)
    - *c*) In this solitude We meditated ("communed with Our spirit.") (251)
    - *d*) Our sole purpose in this was "to avoid becoming a subject of discord . . . unto Our companions . . ." (251)
    - *e*) Meanwhile, mischief abounded. (251)
3. Heeding the bidding from the "Mystic Source," We submitted Our Will to God's and returned. (251)
    - *a*) The enemies had contrived to exterminate Us. (252)
    - *b*) But "none amongst the faithful" had arisen to assist Us. (252)
    - *c*) Nevertheless, Our soul yearned to serve the Primal Point, or else We would not have remained in Ba<u>gh</u>dád. (252)

XII. We conclude Our argument with these observations:

A. "'There is no power nor strength but in God alone.'" "'We are God's, and to Him shall we return.'" (252–53)

1. Those who have "quaffed" this "Wine of love" will respond to our proofs appropriately:

---

persecuted and rejected by the followers of the previous Manifestation, He is here noting that the same Bábís (for whom this work is written as a vindication of their belief in the Báb) are at this very moment about to undergo the same judgment (i.e., of having to recognize the Musta<u>gh</u>á<u>th</u> in the person of Bahá'-u'lláh).

- *a*) They will not be governed by selfish desires.
- *b*) They will behold these "testimonies and evidences" that attest to the truth of this Faith.

B. However, the people in general ignore these proofs (253):
1. The "consummate verses";
2. The "unmistakable allusions";
3. The constancy of the Prophet Himself—"the Trust of God amongst men";
4. The "evident traditions."[28]

C. Instead, the people cling to the literal interpretation of certain traditions (253–54):
1. They find them inconsistent with their expectations.
2. They thereby deprive themselves of this "pure wine."
3. They do this even though Ṣádiq himself foretold the year when the Cause of the Qá'im would be made manifest.
4. Furthermore, the "imprisonment and afflictions" of the Qá'im were also foretold in the "'Biḥár.'"
5. None heed this "prophecy," and We shall not force those who are spiritually dead to listen.

D. Clearly the Prophets speak a twofold language whose purpose is to test and to teach.
1. The outward language is not figurative or allusive. (254)
   - *a*) This language is like a guiding lamp for the seeker.
   - *b*) These are the "unveiled traditions" and "evident verses" already mentioned [e.g., the prophecy about the imprisonment and "'the year sixty'"].
2. The other language is "veiled and concealed" to weed out the "malevolent" and to test the faithful. (254–55)
   - *a*) This language is the "Touchstone of God."
   - *b*) No one understands this, except
     - (1) Those whose hearts are assured,

28. Here, too, the reader should note that Bahá'u'lláh Himself has through the revelation of this same treatise fulfilled each of these four proofs.

   (2) Those souls who "have found favor with God,"
   (3) And those whose "minds are detached from all else but Him."

   c) In this language the literal meaning is not what is intended:
   (1) "'Every knowledge hath seventy meanings, of which one only is known amongst the people. And when the Qá'im shall arise, He shall reveal unto men all that which remaineth.'" (255)
   (2) "'We speak one word, and by it we intend one and seventy meanings; each one of these meanings we can explain.'" (255)

3. We mention this distinction between the two sorts of language, that people may not be disturbed by those traditions and utterances that do not seem to have been literally fulfilled. (256)
   a) They should attribute their "perplexity" to their "lack of understanding," and not to the "nonfulfillment of the promises." (256)
   b) The people should not let such utterances deprive them of divine bounties. (256)
   c) They should seek enlightenment from "recognized Expounders thereof." (256)
   d) In this way the "hidden mysteries may be unraveled." (256)
4. Unfortunately, none seeketh guidance concerning the "abstruse matters of his Faith" from the "divine Manifestations" (256):
   a) Most people are oblivious.
   b) Most people follow wickedness and rebellion.
   c) God will forget them even as they have "ignored His Presence in His day." (256)
   d) Those who turn away from this Beauty shall suffer the consequences. (257)
5. Peace be upon those who listen to the "Melody of the Mystic Bird calling from the Sadratu'l-Muntahá!" (257)

3. The Pattern of Ideas in the Kitáb-i-Íqán

Clearly, there are a multitude of valuable inferences we can derive from this elaborate exercise even though, for the most part, the outline speaks for itself and requires little explanation. But let us mention a few of the more useful conclusions apparent in this analysis of the pattern of thought in the Kitáb-i-Íqán.

Perhaps the most useful generalization we can make is that the work is so tight thematically that all groups overlap in such a way that we could devise a myriad different valid outlines. In this sense, it is very difficult to determine where one major division ends and another begins or what group of ideas is subordinated to what other group of ideas. In short, the Kitáb-i-Íqán is, as we have noted, one continuous statement explicating theodicy (i.e., justifying God's educational methodology). Consequently, a related valuable conclusion we immediately draw from our outline is that the wise reader will not be satisfied to study the Kitáb-i-Íqán piecemeal. To extract a phrase or two might serve to answer some particular question, but unlike The Hidden Words, the verses of which can be read out of sequence, the Kitáb-i-Íqán has a precise linear development.[29] In fact, to study the Kitáb-i-Íqán without regard for the manner in which this structure relates to Bahá'u'lláh's pattern of thought is to risk more than being deprived of the main theme of the work. Under some circumstances a random approach could well lead to erroneous conclusions.

For example, Bahá'u'lláh states in one passage, "Were any of the all-embracing Manifestations of God to declare: 'I am God!' He, verily, speaketh the truth, and no doubt attacheth thereto" (178). Out of context, this passage might be taken to imply that Bahá'ís believe that the Prophet is the incarnation of God rather the perfect incarnation of divine attributes. In context, the passage is part of Bahá'u'lláh's lengthy comparison of the two stations occupied by the Manifestations (i.e.,

29. The absence of a "linear" structure does not by any means imply a lack of some other sort of structure. For example, note William Hatcher's discussion of the structuring principles at work in the Kitáb-i-Aqdas in "*The Kitáb-i-Aqdas:* The Causality Principle in the World of Being," in *Law of Love Enshrined* 113–57.

the station of "essential unity" as compared to the "station of distinction"), a discussion in which He makes such theological and ontological distinctions absolutely clear.

Another noteworthy general observation we can make is that the outline becomes longer, more detailed, and more exacting as the argument progresses in Part Two. The reason for this is that Part One is primarily a statement of theory or doctrine. Bahá'u'lláh is discussing the concept of the poetic nature of prophetic language. He gives examples, but He has not yet begun the heart of His argument itself. Once He begins the specific proofs, Bahá'u'lláh becomes more exacting. He is not content to enunciate His thesis about the nature of the Prophets and why They have been rejected; He cites example after example so that no one can claim that these concepts are vague or ambiguous.

Another general observation we derive from our outline is that the Kitáb-i-Íqán is a truly remarkable textbook on religion. For while the work is most often alluded to as a vindication of the Báb as the Qá'im, Bahá'u'lláh during the course of this work vindicates Christ to the Jews, Muḥammad to the Christians (and to the Muslims), the Báb to the Muslims, and Himself to the "people of the Bayán." Bahá'u'lláh notes how the Muslims believe that the Christians failed to recognize Muḥammad because the true Gospel had been perverted (89). Bahá'u'lláh explains that, in fact, the reason for the failure of the Christians to recognize Muḥammad is the same reason the Muslims failed to recognize the Báb: they do not know how to understand the essentially poetic nature of scripture.

It is for this reason that Bahá'u'lláh shares the "dewdrop out of the fathomless ocean of the truths" (28) contained in the passage from Matthew—to demonstrate that the guidance leading to the recognition of Muḥammad was contained in these verses. In effect, if Muslims do not understand how to recognize in the verses of the Gospel the proof of their *own* Prophet, how can they possibly know how to discover the Qá'im by interpreting the verses of Muḥammad? So it is that Bahá'u'lláh proves the station of Christ (17–26), the station of Muḥammad—to Christians and Muslims alike (27–116); the station of the Báb (117–247); and Bahá'u'lláh's own station (248–57).

However, as Bahá'u'lláh Himself notes, the most significant point in this treatise is not the interpretation of specific proofs, but Bahá'u'lláh's establishment of the criteria by which anyone can test the claims of any Manifestation. In this sense, the final climactic passages in which Bahá'u'lláh specifically alludes both to the testing of the Bábís that will soon occur and to Himself as Mustagháth invite the wise student to apply the criteria (i.e., the "proofs" or "testimonies") articulated by Bahá'u'lláh in the Kitáb-i-Íqán to Bahá'u'lláh Himself: (1) the utterances of the Prophet, (2) the quality of the lives of those who arise to serve His Cause, (3) the constancy of the Prophet in "proclaiming the Faith of God" (230), and (4) the prophecies that the Prophet fulfills (in this case, the Prophecies of the Báb regarding Mustagháth, or "Him Whom God shall make manifest."

Another generalization we might observe about what the outline reveals concerns the theme of the standards of proof by which one judges a Prophet. A cursory reading of the Kitáb-i-Íqán might lead one to conclude that the work is an anticlerical diatribe, an indictment aimed solely at the leaders of religion. The more one studies this work, the more one becomes aware that all people in every age are charged with the responsibility of appreciating these proofs and applying these standards to the advent of a new Manifestation. The divines and the learned are particularly condemned because they are in roles of leadership and can therefore deter others from learning. But the proofs (i.e., "testimonies") are available to all alike.

Therefore, when Bahá'u'lláh warns "the learned men of the Bayán" not to "follow in such ways," not to inflict on Mustagháth "that which hath been inflicted in this day," (248) He no doubt appreciates the irony that, having just vindicated to the Bábís the validity of their own beliefs and having likewise provided them with the tools wherewith they can recognize Bahá'u'lláh as Mustagháth, He will be promptly rejected and persecuted by some of these same followers of the Báb.

In other words, even if we appreciate objectively Bahá'u'lláh's explication of the Divine plan of God and His lucid discussion of how to test the claims of a Prophet, the final proof that one understands what Bahá'u'lláh is really discussing in the Kitáb-i-Íqán is one's ability to apply these criteria to the appearance of the Prophet of the "Latter

Resurrection" (i.e., "Him Whom God shall make manifest" or Mustagháth, "He Who is invoked"). Thus, when in the last few pages Bahá'u'lláh shifts the point of view to His own perspective and describes how He is already suffering most grievously at the hands of "those who profess to be Our friends," He is clearly inviting the Bábís to apply these proofs to Himself. In particular, Bahá'u'lláh alludes—even this early (1862)—to what He will make abundantly clear in the Tablet of the Holy Mariner: the perversity of Siyyid Muḥammad of Iṣfahán, the "one-eyed man" (248) who will prove to be the anti-Christ of the Bahá'í Dispensation, and the forthcoming rebellion of Mírzá Yaḥyá.

A final generalization we observe from our outline concerns Bahá'u'lláh's allusions to Qur'ánic verses. At almost every turn Bahá'u'lláh cites passages from the Qur'án, ostensibly as authoritative support for His own statements. In fact, what becomes quickly apparent is that without the clear explanation Bahá'u'lláh renders when He cites these passages, virtually none of these abstruse verses would make any sense whatsoever. In other words, Bahá'u'lláh effectively unseals the Qur'án for the Muslims just as He has unsealed Christ's prophecies regarding the second coming to the Christians and to the Muslims.

The Kitáb-i-Íqán thus begins where the Súrah of Húd leaves off, enunciating the idea that God in His mercy continually sends to humankind selfless Teachers from the divine world, Emblems of mercy, Whom we promptly reject and persecute. After analyzing the basis for that rejection (i.e., the Manifestations tell us what we may not want to hear, and They threaten the worldly status of the religious leaders), Bahá'u'lláh discusses how to examine the basis for our belief. But where in our preliminary listing of groups we could discern the broad sense of how the work is divided, the outline particularizes the discussion into more definable segments of this overall theme.

Like the Súrah of Húd, the Kitáb-i-Íqán begins with the catalog of the Prophets. Also like the Súrah of Húd, each of these thumbnail sketches focuses on recounting how each was rejected (1–26). The catalog stops with the figure of Muḥammad. At this point Bahá'u'lláh begins explicating Christ's prophecy to prove that Muḥammad fulfills these conditions (26–116). In the second part of the Kitáb-i-Íqán, the subjects begin to overlap. Bahá'u'lláh is discussing the conditions which the Qá'im must fulfill (107–247), but within that broad discussion He discusses the concept of "sovereignty" as regards the Prophets (107–35), the concept of succession (135–52), the two stations of the Prophets (152–82), how to prepare ourselves for examining the claims of a Prophet (182–98), the four proofs of the Prophet (200–47), the judgment that will soon become the lot of the Bábís (247–51), and His conclusion (252–57).

As the outline also demonstrates, many of these longer sections can be usefully subdivided. But the essential unity of the work lies in the fact that Bahá'u'lláh both describes His methodology for inducing certitude (i.e., arguments or proofs) and demonstrates it, not once, but at length in proving that Muḥammad is the return of Christ, and even more exactingly in proving that the Báb is the Qá'im. It is, no doubt, in this context that Bahá'u'lláh Himself observes that "Our argument" (the Kitáb-i-Íqán) offers sufficient insight as to enable anyone to understand *all* the scriptures of *all* religions and all the mysteries contained therein:

> In fact, all the Scriptures and the mysteries thereof are condensed into this brief account. So much so, that were a person to ponder it a while in his heart, he would discover from all that hath been said the mysteries of the Words of God, and would apprehend the meaning of whatever hath been manifested by that ideal King. (237)

Everything in the work is subordinated to this purpose of demonstrating how the individual can vindicate his own belief (i.e., enter the City of Certitude).

If we apply these standards to Bahá'u'lláh, we quickly discover that the Kitáb-i-Íqán itself establishes Bahá'u'lláh's station. First, there is the testimony (i.e., "proof") of Divine Utterance (the Kitáb-i-Íqán itself). Second, by the time the Kitáb-i-Íqán was revealed, many "detached souls" had arisen to demonstrate their devotion to Bahá'u'lláh. Indeed, the entire Bábí community that Bahá'u'lláh had organized in Baghdád was an emblem of spirituality and detachment. Third, Bahá'-

u'lláh had repeatedly demonstrated His own constancy—during His imprisonment in the Síyáh-Chál, in His rejection of the offer to flee to Russia to escape further persecution, in His selfless return from Sulaymáníyyih to assist the Bábí community, and in His courageous stand in Baghdád against the 'ulamá arrayed against Him. Of course, though He would soon be plunged into ever more severe trials, He would persevere in revealing and promulgating the Word of God. Fourth, Bahá'u'lláh had long since fulfilled the prophecies the Báb established in the Bayán regarding the "Latter Resurrection." Certainly, this more subliminal pattern of ideas is not an accident. In 1862 when Bahá'u'lláh revealed the Kitáb-i-Íqán, He had delayed the announcement of His station for almost ten years in fulfillment of the Báb's request (mentioned in Chapter 3), that though "Him Whom God shall make manifest" would appear in the year nine (1853 A.D.), He would delay His announcement until the year nineteen (1863 A.D.).

In conclusion, though the Kitáb-i-Íqán was revealed spontaneously and without revision over the course of two days, this astounding exposition requires many readings to assess the range of ideas Bahá'u'lláh presents. But as we study our outline, we can begin to discern how the ideas of this complex exposition are coordinated around one clear thesis—that certitude can be induced by logical proofs and that the tools available for applying those proofs are available to all alike. Any particular discussion operates within this framework and must be understood in terms of its subordination to this theme; otherwise, the full import of any single idea is likely to be lost.

As we mentioned, not all of Bahá'u'lláh's works that have a complex structure may lend themselves to the sort of structural analysis that an outline provides, because, as we have noted, Bahá'u'lláh employs various types of structure, not all of which are linear. Consequently, for works like the Súratu'l-Haykal or the Kitáb-i-Aqdas, some other type of exercise (some other means of rendering a visual representation of structure in relation to subject) might prove helpful.

Chapter 7
A Close Reading of Text: Putting It All Together

O My servants! My holy, My divinely ordained Revelation may be likened unto an ocean in whose depths are concealed innumerable pearls of great price, of surpassing luster. It is the duty of every seeker to bestir himself and strive to attain the shores of this ocean, so that he may, in proportion to the eagerness of his search and the efforts he hath exerted, partake of such benefits as have been pre-ordained in God's irrevocable and hidden Tablets. If no one be willing to direct his steps towards its shores, if every one should fail to arise and find Him, can such a failure be said to have robbed this ocean of its power or to have lessened, to any degree, its treasures.

—Bahá'u'lláh

As we study the art of Bahá'u'lláh, we may find that the information we can elicit from the five questions we have posed in the preceding chapters will often guide us to a significantly increased understanding, particularly with those works in which the meaning is not readily apparent. Yet the most fruitful results will often derive from some sort of synthesis of these various queries. To a large extent, that is precisely what the sixth and final tool involves, a systematic combination of these previous studies to effect an *explication de texte.*

An *explication de texte,* "a close reading of text," helps to answer the following question: What overall meaning do we discover when we ask the first five questions and then search the text for precise meanings of enigmatic words, images, or other ambiguities? A close reading of text might thus be considered more a process of compiling, reviewing, and evaluating the information derived from applying the five previous tools rather than a separate tool of literary analysis. However, a close reading does involve a "painstaking analysis of the meanings, relationships, and ambiguities of the words, images, and other small units that make up a literary work" (*Handbook* 187).

To demonstrate this last step in action we will examine the Tablet of Aḥmad, first by applying our five questions, and then by attempting a close reading of text. Thus we will see what significant conclusions we can make about the meaning of this important tablet by applying these six tools. In short, we will attempt to discover how our concept of the meaning of the Tablet of Aḥmad is enhanced or changed by our study. It is hoped that this exercise will also enable us to arrive at a general assessment of the effectiveness of employing these and other tools of literary criticism to the art of Bahá'u'lláh.

A. Problems and Mysteries in the Tablet of Aḥmad

Obviously, any number of Bahá'u'lláh's works would serve well to illustrate the value of applying these six tools of literary analysis. An examination of the Tablet of Aḥmad offers a particularly useful model because (1) most Bahá'í readers are thoroughly familiar with this work, (2) it has a special spiritual status, and (3) it contains a significant number of mysteries and hidden treasures concealed beneath its surface.

The Tablet of Aḥmad[1]

He is the King, the All-Knowing, the Wise!

¶1 Lo, the Nightingale of Paradise singeth upon the twigs of the Tree of Eternity, with holy and sweet melodies,

1. Paragraphs are numbered for easy reference in our discussion.

proclaiming to the sincere ones the glad tidings of the nearness of God, calling the believers in the Divine Unity to the court of the Presence of the Generous One, informing the severed ones of the message which hath been revealed by God, the King, the Glorious, the Peerless, guiding the lovers to the seat of sanctity and to this resplendent Beauty.

¶2 Verily this is that Most Great Beauty, foretold in the Books of the Messengers, through Whom truth shall be distinguished from error and the wisdom of every command shall be tested. Verily He is the Tree of Life that bringeth forth the fruits of God, the Exalted, the Powerful, the Great.

¶3 O Aḥmad! Bear thou witness that verily He is God and there is no God but Him, the King, the Protector, the Incomparable, the Omnipotent. And that the One Whom He hath sent forth by the name of 'Alí was the true One from God, to Whose commands we are all conforming.

¶4 Say: O people be obedient to the ordinances of God, which have been enjoined in the Bayán by the Glorious, the Wise One. Verily He is the King of the Messengers and His Book is the Mother Book did ye but know.

¶5 Thus doth the Nightingale utter His call unto you from this prison. He hath but to deliver this clear message. Whosoever desireth, let him turn aside from this counsel and whosoever desireth let him choose the path to his Lord.

¶6 O people, if ye deny these verses, by what proof have ye believed in God? Produce it, O assemblage of false ones.

¶7 Nay, by the One in Whose hand is my soul, they are not, and never shall be able to do this, even should they combine to assist one another.

¶8 O Aḥmad! Forget not My bounties while I am absent. Remember My days during thy days, and My distress and banishment in this remote prison. And be thou so steadfast in My love that thy heart shall not waver, even if the swords of the enemies rain blows upon thee and all the heavens and the earth arise against thee.

¶9 Be thou as a flame of fire to My enemies and a river of life eternal to My loved ones, and be not of those who doubt.

¶10 And if thou art overtaken by affliction in My path, or degradation for My sake, be not thou troubled thereby.

¶11 Rely upon God, thy God and the Lord of thy fathers. For the people are wandering in the paths of delusion, bereft of discernment to see God with their own eyes, or hear His Melody with their own ears. Thus have We found them, as thou also dost witness.

¶12 Thus have their superstitions become veils between them and their own hearts and kept them from the path of God, the Exalted, the Great.

¶13 Be thou assured in thyself that verily, he who turns away from this Beauty hath also turned away from the Messengers of the past and showeth pride towards God from all eternity to all eternity.

¶14 Learn well this Tablet, O Aḥmad. Chant it during thy days and withhold not thyself therefrom. For verily, God hath ordained for the one who chants it, the reward of a hundred martyrs and a service in both worlds. These favors have We bestowed upon thee as a bounty on Our part and a mercy from Our presence, that thou mayest be of those who are grateful.

¶15 By God! Should one who is in affliction or grief read this Tablet with absolute sincerity, God will dispel his sadness, solve his difficulties and remove his afflictions.

¶16 Verily, He is the Merciful, the Compassionate. Praise be to God, the Lord of all the worlds.

(*Bahá'í Prayers* 209–13)

Shoghi Effendi has observed in a letter written on his behalf that, because Bahá'u'lláh has "invested" the Tablet of Aḥmad "with a special potency and significance," it should be recited "with unquestioning faith and confidence":

> These daily obligatory prayers, together with a few other specific ones, such as the Healing Prayer, the Tablet of Aḥmad, have been invested by Bahá'u'lláh with a special potency and significance, and should therefore be accepted as such and be recited by the believers with unquestioning faith and confidence, that through them they may enter into a much closer communion with God, and identify themselves more fully with His laws and precepts. (*Bahá'í Prayers* 209)

Of course, what Shoghi Effendi is alluding to here is Bahá'u'lláh's statement at the end of the Tablet of Aḥmad promising the one who intones this tablet several rather amazing rewards. First, Bahá'u'lláh states that the "one who chants" the tablet will receive "the reward of a hundred martyrs" and "a service in both worlds." He further assures the believer that if "one who is in affliction or grief" were to "read this Tablet with absolute sincerity, God will dispel his sadness, solve his difficulties and remove his afflictions."

The "unquestioned faith and confidence" alluded to by Shoghi Effendi should in no way be taken to imply that the believer need not attempt to understand the meaning of the Tablet of Aḥmad or to contemplate exactly *why* this work is invested with such power. After all, it is the "faith and confidence" that we need not question, not the meaning of Bahá'u'lláh's words, which Bahá'u'lláh repeatedly exhorts us to study, that we might discover the pearls of meaning concealed in His diverse utterances. This obligation to discover the "treasures" in Bahá'u'lláh's "ocean" of words is especially true with the Tablet of Aḥmad because of one crucial condition that Bahá'u'lláh incorporates into the explicit promises that this tablet makes: i.e., that "God will dispel [our] sadness, solve [our] difficulties and remove [our] afflictions" *if* we read the tablet with "absolute sincerity."

Since ordinary human beings are incapable of doing anything with "absolute sincerity," we might conclude that God will never have to make good on the promises enunciated in the Tablet of Aḥmad. However, we would hope (given the benign and loving nature of Divinity) that these assurances are not merely a celestial joke that is being made at our expense. But whether or not we can achieve "absolute" sincerity, we would still do well to understand what is implied in this condition.

Do we conclude, for example, that this "sincerity" alludes to our conviction or confidence that God will assist us? If so, then why would we be in affliction to begin with? Does this "sincerity" allude to the mental attitude with which we read (i.e., that we should not let our minds wander as we recite the Tablet of Aḥmad)? If that is the case, our challenge is one of a mundane sort of mental discipline—how not to let any other thoughts enter our mind as we read the words of the tablet.

If reading "with sincerity" means anything, surely it implies that we respond to the meaning of the words. How can we be sincere in reciting the tablet if we are not aware of what it means?

> [T]he reading of the scriptures and holy books is for no other purpose except to enable the reader to apprehend their meaning and unravel their innermost mysteries. Otherwise reading, without understanding, is of no abiding profit unto man.
> (Bahá'u'lláh, *Kitáb-i-Íqán* 172)

The first promise in the Tablet of Aḥmad is even more problematic. Bahá'u'lláh states that "God hath ordained for the one who chants it, the reward of a hundred martyrs and a service in both worlds" (¶14). With this promise there are no conditions about how the tablet should be chanted; the reward is assured.

Are we actually supposed to believe that the mere recitation of these words has the same importance as a hundred believers sacrificing their very lives to serve God? How can we accept such an equation and still believe that God is just? Furthermore, Bahá'u'lláh states that in the next world those in a higher spiritual condition will be "united in the bonds of intimacy and fellowship," while those of a lower state will not be capable of understanding the "station" of those that "rank above them":

> The people of Bahá, who are the inmates of the Ark of God, are, one and all, well aware of one another's state and con-

> dition, and are united in the bonds of intimacy and fellowship. Such a state, however, must depend upon their faith and their conduct. They that are of the same grade and station are fully aware of one another's capacity, character, accomplishments and merits. They that are of a lower grade, however, are incapable of comprehending adequately the station, or of estimating the merits, of those that rank above them. Each shall receive his share from thy Lord. (*Gleanings* 170)

This is an important point. Bahá'u'lláh here indicates an explicit causal relationship between our earthly deeds and our experience in the afterlife. Therefore, should we not presume that the eternal spiritual reward for a martyr would far exceed the eternal spiritual reward available to one whose sole virtue is to recite the Tablet of Aḥmad, especially if one is not even sure what the verse means?

But there is another pearl concealed in the shell of this promise (or should we say a "Ḥúrí" waiting to be unveiled). Why is this simple deed the equivalent of the noble acts of so *many* martyrs? It is hard enough to accept equating this act with one martyrdom, but how can we possibly maintain that our beliefs are rational and yet assert that the reciting of a tablet (even if done with faith and sincerity) could merit the same reward appropriate for a hundred detached souls who have sacrificed their lives rather than recant their beliefs?

There are other mysteries to be discovered in this brief tablet. For example, Bahá'u'lláh exhorts Aḥmad to "bear witness" that the Báb is the "true One from God, to Whose commands we are all conforming" (¶3). As we will discover in analyzing the historical background to this tablet, the Tablet of Aḥmad was revealed around 1864, after Bahá'u'lláh had announced to His followers that He was the Manifestation of God to Whom the Báb was alluding. Why would Bahá'u'lláh exhort Aḥmad to acknowledge the Báb and admonish him to obey the Báb's "commands" instead of acknowledging Bahá'u'lláh and His commands? More specifically, Bahá'u'lláh exhorts Aḥmad to be "obedient to the ordinances of God, which have been enjoined in the Bayán" (¶4). If Bahá'u'lláh in the Kitáb-i-Íqán clearly states that the Revelation of each Manifestation supersedes the ordinances of the previous Revelation, why does Bahá'u'lláh uphold the sovereignty of the Bayán even though He has already revealed many of the major works of His own Dispensation?

Even in the Tablet of Aḥmad Bahá'u'lláh identifies Himself as the Manifestation, as the "Nightingale of Paradise." Why, then, would He exhort this believer to take an action which, in light of the judgment that occurs when believers are forced to recognize the new Prophet, would seem to be regressive? Indeed, later in the tablet Bahá'u'lláh tells Aḥmad to be "steadfast in My love," a command which would again seem to confirm that Bahá'u'lláh is identifying Himself as the Prophet.

Yet another "mystery" appears when Bahá'u'lláh exhorts Aḥmad to be "as a flame of fire to My enemies" and a "river of life eternal to My loved ones" (¶9). Is Bahá'u'lláh here ordaining some specific course of action with this passage? If so, what might Bahá'u'lláh mean since His advice to believers regarding how to respond to "enemies" was, in general, to pray for them but not to contend with them? Indeed, one of the more sorrow-filled plaints of Bahá'u'lláh is His statement regarding the Bahá'ís in 'Akká who killed Siyyid Muḥammad of Iṣfahán:

> *"My captivity,"* He wrote on another occasion, *"cannot harm Me. That which can harm Me is the conduct of those who love Me, who claim to be related to Me, and yet perpetrate what causeth My heart and My pen to groan."* And again: *"My captivity can bring on Me no shame. Nay, by My life, it conferreth on Me glory. That which can make Me ashamed is the conduct of such of My followers as profess to love Me, yet in fact follow the Evil One."* (Shoghi Effendi, *God Passes By* 190)

Finally, of course, there is the mystery of the figure of Aḥmad himself. No one can long ponder the importance of this tablet without pausing to consider why a tablet of universal usage and special powers is specifically addressed to and focused on the character of this individual. Enhancing the intrigue of this mystery is a curious fact: Bahá'u'lláh revealed *two* works with the title the Tablet of Aḥmad addressed to *two* different Aḥmads in *two* different languages (one is in Arabic and the other in Persian). Are these in some way meant to be companion pieces?

Do we need to know something about the Persian Tablet of Aḥmad in order to appreciate what Bahá'u'lláh is trying to tell us with the Arabic tablet of the same name? Certainly, at the very least, we need to consider how each of the two Aḥmads responded to the tablet sent to him so that we may discover in their responses some clue about how we, too, should respond.

These, then, are some of the "Brides of inner meaning" we need to unveil in the Tablet of Aḥmad, though our quest for meaning may lead us to many others. Therefore, let us set out on this pilgrimage by using the tools of analysis we have explored thus far in our study and then proceed to apply a close reading of text.

B. The Narrative Point of View

At first glance the narrative point of view in the Tablet of Aḥmad seems simple enough. Bahá'u'lláh as Manifestation exhorts Aḥmad to be a faithful believer, not to doubt or to be "troubled" by any "affliction" or "degradation" he endures for "My sake," to "learn well this Tablet" and to chant it often. But there are some noteworthy turns in point of view during the course of this brief work.

First of all, the Tablet of Aḥmad does not begin in the first person, but in the third person—not "I" proclaim to the "sincere ones the glad tidings of the nearness of God," but "the Nightingale of Paradise" sings out this melody. Because in paragraphs three and four Bahá'u'lláh alludes to the Báb, we might conclude that this "Nightingale" also alludes to the Báb. Or, since paragraph three alludes to God as "He," the One Who hath "sent forth" the Báb, this "Nightingale" might allude to the voice of God which has from time immemorial issued forth from the "Tree of Eternity."

The opening lines of paragraph five seem to solve this mystery by making it clear that the "Nightingale" is indeed Bahá'u'lláh Himself calling out to Aḥmad "from this prison." Of course, as we become familiar with the writings of Bahá'u'lláh, we note how often the epithet "Nightingale" is used as a figurative or symbolic appellation for Bahá'u'lláh (though it has other applications as well). Our conclusion that the narrative voice is clearly that of Bahá'u'lláh is further confirmed in paragraph eight, where Bahá'u'lláh shifts from the third-person point of view to the first person, alluding to "My distress and banishment in this remote prison."

This is a very important change because it shifts the perspective from a third-person narrative voice making comments about the Manifestation to the perspective of the imprisoned Prophet Himself. From this point forward, the voice is that of Bahá'u'lláh speaking from the perspective of the "station of distinction," the Prophet as an historical figure in dire circumstances. To a certain extent, Bahá'u'lláh seems to shift back to a more detached perspective in paragraph thirteen when He again assumes a third-person point of view to assure Aḥmad that anyone who "turns away from this Beauty hath also turned away from the Messengers of the past."

There is another subtle shift in point of view in paragraph thirteen. The narrative voice tells Aḥmad that "we are all conforming" to the "commands" of the Báb. This is not the usual editorial "We" that Bahá'u'lláh uses in many tablets where, like Muḥammad throughout the Qur'án, the Prophet seems to identify Himself as a Prophet among Prophets, perhaps as an integral part of the heavenly concourse. For example, in Arabic Hidden Word number 68 Bahá'u'lláh writes: "Know ye not why We created you all from the same dust? That no one should exalt himself over the other." But here in paragraph thirteen of the Tablet of Aḥmad Bahá'u'lláh implies that the speaker is a fellow believer in the Báb. Of course, Bahá'u'lláh was a follower of the Báb prior to declaring His own station as Prophet, and this shift may allude to the fact that, in a way we shall discuss later in this chapter, Bahá'u'lláh is Himself still following the teachings of the Báb.

In summary, then, the Tablet of Aḥmad employs three distinct narrative points of view. The speaker is a third-person narrator describing the advent of the "Nightingale of Paradise," an allusion to the process by which humanity attains the "presence of God." The voice is that of a fellow believer, a Bábí, praising the station of the Báb and proclaiming obedience to the Bayán and its laws. The voice is that of the Nightingale Himself, imprisoned to be sure, but nonetheless issuing advice and commands as the Manifestation of God in whose service Aḥmad is exhorted to devote himself.

Closely allied to this variable narrative point of view is the cautionary statement that is found at the end of the Tablet of Aḥmad. This statement seems to be spoken from the perspective of the Heavenly Father, the spiritual axiom that "he who turns away from this Beauty hath also turned away from the Messengers of the past and showeth pride towards God from all eternity to all eternity" (¶13). Perhaps these three different points of view are similar to the Christian notion of the three stations of Christ symbolized by the trinitarian doctrine: Bahá'u'lláh speaks as Father, as Son, and as the Holy Spirit made manifest since the beginning of time.

C. The Historical Context

If the information we can discover by examining the narrative point of view seems relatively insignificant and somewhat tangential in conveying to us the deeper meaning of the Tablet of Aḥmad, we will find that our study of the historical context is quite the opposite. To recover Bahá'u'lláh's allusion to the figure of Aḥmad is to unearth a storehouse of hidden treasures.

As we have noted, there are two tablets entitled Lawḥ-i-Aḥmad (Tablet of Aḥmad)—one in Persian and one in Arabic. The Persian Tablet of Aḥmad is a lengthy work revealed for Ḥájí Mírzá Aḥmad of Ká<u>sh</u>án, the half-brother of the first Bábí in Ká<u>sh</u>án, Ḥájí Mírzá Jání, who was later martyred in Ṭihrán. Ḥájí Mírzá Aḥmad also became a Bábí as a result of his association with this half-brother, but unlike Ḥájí Mírzá Jání, Ḥájí Mírzá Aḥmad later "showed unfaithfulness to Bahá'u'lláh and became a follower of Mírzá Yaḥyá" (Taherzadeh, *Revelation of Bahá'u'lláh* 2:137). Nevertheless, despite Ḥájí Mírzá Aḥmad's insincerity and unseemly conduct, Bahá'u'lláh in Adrianople revealed the Persian Tablet of Aḥmad in an attempt to guide this wayward one to the right path of belief. While the effort had no effect on Ḥájí Mírzá Aḥmad, who subsequently attempted to create discord among the Bahá'ís, the tablet remains as a profound demonstration of the Prophet's "loving-kindness and forbearance" in dealing with friend and foe alike (Taherzadeh, *Revelation of Bahá'u'lláh* 2:138).

1. Aḥmad's Life

The Aḥmad who is the recipient of the Arabic Tablet of Aḥmad (the subject of our study) is quite a different sort of figure. A native of Yazd, this Aḥmad was a virtual emblem of fidelity and steadfastness. His life (ca. 1802–1902?) mirrors the progress of the Bahá'í Faith during the entire nineteenth century, spanning as it does most of the major events of Bahá'í history from the early search for the Qá'im by figures such as Shaykh Aḥmad and Siyyid Káẓim to the ministry of 'Abdu'l-Bahá after the death of Bahá'u'lláh. More importantly, Aḥmad's life serves to exemplify the qualities of a true seeker and a devoted believer inasmuch as he personally experienced every major change that the Faith itself experienced.

Bahá'u'lláh revealed the Arabic Tablet of Aḥmad around the year 1865 while in Adrianople but before being poisoned by Mírzá Yaḥyá, something Taherzadeh notes one can quickly confirm by viewing Bahá'u'lláh's exquisite calligraphy in this work.[2] The tablet was sent to Aḥmad, who at that time was en route from Baghdád to Adrianople to be with his Beloved. He had already accepted Bahá'u'lláh as "Him Whom God shall make manifest,"[3] and he found himself no longer able to accept his separation from the One Whom he regarded as the center of his existence.

Because Aḥmad was such an exemplary believer, we would naturally do well to consider with care his own reaction to the tablet so that we might discover in his response some clue to the meaning of the work and why it is endowed with such a special status. But before that response could have much meaning for us, we must first discover how he came to be on this journey at this particular time in his life.

Born into a prominent family in Yazd, Aḥmad was attracted to mysticism even while still in his teens. But his was not a mindless infatuation: his greatest longing was "to come face to face with the prom-

---

2. See *Revelation of Bahá'u'lláh* 2:107 and all of Chapter 7 in that same volume. After the poisoning, Bahá'u'lláh's hand shook for the rest of His life, and consequently everything He wrote after that point has a perceptible tremor.

3. The Manifestation of the "Latter Resurrection" Whom the Báb had promised His followers would become manifest in the year nine.

ised Qá'im" (Taherzadeh, *Revelation of Bahá'u'lláh* 2:108). During his teenage years Aḥmad associated with ascetics and dervishes, but the more he pursued this unorthodox way of life, the more his orthodox Muslim family became disturbed by his behavior and attempted to discourage him in his quest.

When their irritation increased, Aḥmad became convinced that the only solution for him was to leave home—something unthinkable in Persian society at that time. Around 1826, when he was in his early twenties, Aḥmad left his house, donned the garb of a dervish, and departed from Yazd without telling a soul. Determining to go to a more spiritually oriented country, Aḥmad headed for India and the city of Bombay. Along the way, he encountered mystics, Ṣúfís, and various self-proclaimed spiritual leaders. He also imposed upon himself a rigid spiritual discipline, "prostrating himself and repeating a certain verse of the *Qur'án* twelve thousand times" (Taherzadeh, *Revelation of Bahá'u'lláh* 2:109).

An insightful and extremely honest young man, Aḥmad found only disillusionment in his attempt to discover the Qá'im in India. He soon grew weary of the feeble claims of those who professed to have some special wisdom or thought themselves endowed with spiritual powers. In time he returned to Persia and settled in the village of Ká<u>sh</u>án.

Eventually, Aḥmad married and went to work as a weaver, though his keen longing to discover the Qá'im was never far from his thoughts. The years passed until 1844, when Aḥmad heard the news about the teachings of a young merchant in <u>Sh</u>íráz who was called the Báb. Aḥmad decided that he must investigate the claims of these teachings, but he found it difficult to discover anyone in Ká<u>sh</u>án who knew anything about this new movement.

Eventually, he discovered one who knew about the Bábí Faith, and Aḥmad was advised to proceed to Ma<u>sh</u>had, where he might discover what he wanted. The next morning Aḥmad began on foot a trek of some five hundred miles from Ká<u>sh</u>án to Ma<u>sh</u>had. Because of his arduous journey, Aḥmad fell quite ill and spent the next two months recuperating.

When he was well, Aḥmad tried to discover the whereabouts of a certain Mullá 'Abdu'l-<u>Kh</u>áliq-i-Yazdí because he had been told this individual could inform him about the Bábí movement. But at this early period in the spread of the Báb's Faith, the believers had to exercise great circumspection and care lest the community be infiltrated by agents of the government or the clergy, both of which were intent on the destruction of this new religion.

At first, Mullá 'Abdu'l-Kháliq-i-Yazdí seemed to ignore Aḥmad's request. Then, after several tests of Aḥmad's sincerity, this Bábí introduced Aḥmad to other believers, some of whom were to become the most outstanding heroes of this heroic age of the Bábí Faith. After meeting with these illumined souls, Aḥmad readily acknowledged the truth of the Báb's Cause. These Bábí teachers then urged Aḥmad to return to Káshán to his wife and family. They told him to resume his trade and to teach the Faith, but only when he was certain of the inquirer's sincerity.

After Aḥmad returned to Káshán, he discovered that there was one other believer in the city. Ironically, this believer was none other than Ḥájí Mírzá Jání, the half-brother of the "other" Aḥmad to whom the Persian Tablet of Aḥmad was written. Soon one of the most important events in the life of Aḥmad occurred. In 1847, as the Báb was being conducted to Ṭihrán (and ultimately to an imprisonment from which He would never be released),[4] Ḥájí Mírzá Jání arranged to have the Báb stay in his home for two nights. During this stay Aḥmad was able to attain the presence of the Báb and observe the young Prophet as He conversed with the divines of Káshán. This event galvanized the spiritual capacities of this stalwart believer.

Soon after the Báb's visit, the number of believers rapidly increased. The persecution of the Bábís also increased dramatically during the course of the next several years. Consequently, in time it became impossible for Aḥmad to continue living in Káshán. On one

---

4. It should be remembered here that the Báb was ostensibly en route to Ṭihrán to meet with the Sháh, but was diverted from this meeting by the infamous "Antichrist" of the Bábí Dispensation, Ḥájí Mírzá Áqásí, the Grand Vizier and spiritual guide to Muḥammad Sháh.

occasion, he was forced to hide himself in an air shaft in his house for some forty days while friends brought him food and water in secret.

Around 1858, after the Báb had been executed and Bahá'u'lláh had been exiled to Baghdád, Aḥmad set out in secret for Baghdád to attain the presence of Bahá'u'lláh. When Aḥmad at last attained His presence, he experienced firsthand the omniscience of the Prophet. Bahá'u'lláh smiled at Aḥmad and joked about how strange it was that Aḥmad had dared to become a Bábí only to hide himself in an air shaft. Aḥmad understood clearly the serious message underlying the gentle rebuke. Never again would he attempt to conceal his beliefs.

The next few years were blissful for Aḥmad. He worked as a simple hand-weaver, but he lived in the outer apartment of Bahá'u'lláh's own house, the Bayt-i-A'ẓam (the Most Great House).[5] From that perspective he was able to watch Bahá'u'lláh build a highly respected community of stalwart believers and friends from a disorganized and bewildered conglomeration of bereft followers of the Báb.

In 1863 when the Sultan issued his decree that Bahá'u'lláh leave Baghdád for Constantinople, Aḥmad was one of those souls privileged to meet with Bahá'u'lláh in the Garden of Riḍván, though, to Aḥmad's regret, he was not allowed to go with Bahá'u'lláh on the journey:

> On the twelfth day Bahá'u'lláh left for Constantinople. Some of the believers accompanied Him and some including this servant had to remain in Baghdád. At the time of His departure, all of us were together in the Garden. Those who were to remain behind were standing on one side. His blessed Person came to us and spoke words of consolation to us. He said that it was better that we remain behind. He also said that He had allowed some to accompany Him, merely to prevent them from making mischief and creating trouble. (Taherzadeh, *Revelation of Bahá'u'lláh* 2:112)

Aḥmad had long since recognized the station of Bahá'u'lláh as "Him Whom God shall make manifest," and, though he lamented the loss of

5. This house is designated in the Kitáb-i-Aqdas as a place of pilgrimage and is a holy shrine.

the "Divine Presence," he dutifully stayed behind in Baghdád as he had been told. There Aḥmad continued to teach and serve the Cause, but in time the longing to attain again the presence of the beloved of his heart was unbearable. Aḥmad set out for Adrianople, where, over the course of the forthcoming year, Bahá'u'lláh would begin to reveal tablets announcing to the world the identity of His station, just as He had done for the believers in Baghdád immediately prior to His departure from that city.

When Aḥmad arrived in Constantinople almost at his journey's end, this faithful believer received the Arabic Tablet of Aḥmad, and his life was changed forever. Immediately he changed his plans. Instead of completing the short distance to Adrianople, Aḥmad set out for Persia—something that would have been unthinkable to him prior to receiving this message from Bahá'u'lláh. The rest of Aḥmad's life was devoted to one goal—traveling the length and breadth of Persia contacting the Bábís in the various communities to tell them that "Him Whom God shall make manifest" had come in the person of Bahá'u'lláh.

This was no easy task. The Bábí community in Persia was in almost complete disarray. The Báb and most of the Bábí leaders of any note had been executed. The believers had no access to the writings and teachings of their own Faith. Furthermore, for one of their fellow believers to return after seven years of absence only to tell them that another Prophet had now appeared in fulfillment of the teachings for which their friends and family had been slaughtered and for which they themselves had endangered their very lives was, to many, blasphemy of the grossest sort.

For example, Aḥmad went to bring this news to no less a figure than Mullá Mírzá Muḥammad, one of the few survivors of the battle at Fort Shaykh Ṭabarsí. As Aḥmad spoke to this staunch Bábí and his brother, the listeners became so enraged with Aḥmad that they attacked him and broke one of his teeth. When at last the furor subsided, Aḥmad reminded them that the Báb had specifically foretold that the promised Manifestation for Whom the Báb had given His own life would bear "the name Bahá" (Taherzadeh, *Revelation of Bahá'u'lláh* 2:114–15). The brothers promised that if Aḥmad could prove this, they, too, would follow Bahá'u'lláh. They retrieved the Báb's writings from a secret hiding place in the wall of their home, whereupon Aḥmad opened a tablet and showed them conclusively a passage confirming everything he had said. The brothers immediately became Bahá'ís and, like Aḥmad, devoted their lives to defending the Cause of Bahá'u'lláh.

In this manner Aḥmad passed the remainder of his long life, teaching the Bábís about Bahá'u'lláh. Wherever he went he always he carried with him the Tablet of Aḥmad written in the exquisite calligraphy of Bahá'u'lláh. He remained a humble, simple man, but he was fearless, vigorous, and faithful; his example influenced the lives of everyone who met him. He died in 1902, having lived to be 100 according to one account (113 according to another).

2. The Implications of Aḥmad's Response

The relevance of the story of Aḥmad's life to understanding the fundamental meaning of the Tablet of Aḥmad is not difficult to discover. Because Aḥmad is clearly exemplary in the quality of his search and service, in his humility and obedience, we understandably presume that his response to the tablet might well give us a clue about what our own response should be. For however simple Aḥmad's faith may have been in some ways, his spiritual perception was acute enough for him to recognize two Prophets, to remain faithful to Their Covenants, and to discover in this tablet a call to action, a call which, for Aḥmad, superseded his fondest desire on earth—to attain the physical presence of Bahá'u'lláh. Furthermore, because this message was from a Prophet of God, Aḥmad believed it could brook no delay, but required instant, complete, and exact obedience. Aḥmad's response was immediate and unwavering, enduring to the end of his long and fruitful life: he sacrificed his own desires and subjugated his own will to what he believed to be the Will of God as conveyed through this tablet from Bahá'u'lláh. And the action he felt implicit in the commands of this tablet was for him to return to Persia to teach the Bábís about Bahá'u'lláh.

What in this brief tablet made this directive so clear to Aḥmad when it is not clear to most contemporary Bahá'ís? Is the fact that the ordinary reader cannot immediately discern this message but another index to Aḥmad's spiritual perception, or was the historical context such that Bahá'u'lláh's allusions in this work made clear what hidden meaning lies concealed beneath the surface of its language?

In short, if a principal purpose of the Tablet of Aḥmad is an exhortation to teach the Cause of God, then any attempt to intone these verses with "absolute sincerity" would seem to involve taking the action the tablet implies. Otherwise, one is merely reciting syllables and sounds, perhaps with a sincere tone, but without understanding. Certainly this issue of understanding the Tablet of Aḥmad as a command to take action is at the heart of the tablet's mystery and meaning and is directly related to the enigmatic query we raised at the outset: Why would Bahá'u'lláh state in this tablet that the Bayán is the "Mother Book" and that it is the Báb "to Whose commands we are all conforming" if the tablet was revealed after Bahá'u'lláh's Riḍván announcement?

Throughout the Bayán, the principal ordinance of the Báb to His followers, indeed the abiding theme of His entire ministry, is to recognize and follow "Him Whom God shall make manifest." In fact, He states: "At the time of the appearance of Him Whom God shall make manifest, wert thou to perform thy deeds for the sake of the Point of the Bayán, they would be regarded as performed for one other than God, inasmuch as on that Day the Point of the Bayán is none other than Him Whom God shall make manifest . . ." (*Selections from the Writings of the Báb* 95). Logically, therefore, to follow the commands of the Báb was, at the time of the revelation of the Tablet of Aḥmad in 1865, to follow Bahá'u'lláh.

Aḥmad obviously followed this precise line of reasoning implicit in the tablet: having been so favored as to have been allowed to recognize "Him Whom God shall make manifest," he should now become a "river of life eternal" to the "loved ones." That is, he should bestow upon those who had demonstrated spiritual perception in their recognition of the Báb the further opportunity to discover the Manifestation prophesied by the Báb.

In fact, Aḥmad's response thus represents a course of action, not merely a simple act of devotion or a response confined to the transition from the Bábí Faith to the Bahá'í Faith. In other words, we should not infer from Aḥmad's response that contemporary Bahá'ís are obliged to teach Bábís. No, the more universal message in Aḥmad's response is that proclaiming allegiance to a Prophet of God is only an initial step in true recognition. As Bahá'u'lláh says in His own "Mother Book," the Kitáb-i-Aqdas, the act of recognizing the Manifestation must be coupled with obedience to His commandments: "These twin duties are inseparable. Neither is acceptable without the other" (19). And one of the most important recurring commands of Bahá'u'lláh is to teach the Cause of God:

> Say: Teach ye the Cause of God, O people of Bahá, for God hath prescribed unto every one the duty of proclaiming His Message, and regardeth it as the most meritorious of all deeds. (*Gleanings* 278)

3. The Two Aḥmads

Aḥmad's response is thus crucial in resolving the mystery of why Bahá'u'lláh would exhort Aḥmad to be faithful to the commands of the Báb, but there is another even more subtle message implicit in his response that we can derive from studying the historical context of the tablet.

As we have noted, this work was written before Mírzá Yaḥyá's poisoning of Bahá'u'lláh and immediately prior to the horrendous turmoil caused by the rebellion of Mírzá Yaḥyá in Adrianople, the period foretold in the Tablet of the Holy Mariner which Shoghi Effendi designates as a "supreme crisis" (*God Passes By* 163) and which Bahá'u'lláh designated as the Ayyám-i-Shidád (Days of Stress). Of particular importance to the theme of the Tablet of Aḥmad is the fact that these events which involved Mírzá Yaḥyá's attempt to kill the Prophet and usurp His authority culminated in what Bahá'u'lláh called the "'most great separation.'" While we have already mentioned this episode in Chapter 3, let us review in more detail the events surrounding this turning point in Bahá'í history.

As the intrigues of Mírzá Yaḥyá increased, even after Bahá'u'lláh had given His younger half-brother every opportunity to reform his conduct, Bahá'u'lláh at last took decisive action. He divided in two all of His earthly possessions, gave half to Mírzá Yaḥyá, and withdrew with His family to the house of Riḍá Big. For two months Bahá'u'lláh refused to see either "friend or stranger, including His own companions" (*God Passes By* 167).

The effects of this separation were manifold, but the end result was that the believers were given free rein to choose between Bahá'u'lláh and Mírzá Yaḥyá, a choice which was indicated by an actual change in terminology to designate the two categories of believers: It was in this period that the phrase *"the people of the Bayán,"* now denoting the followers of Mírzá Yaḥyá, was discarded and was supplanted by the term *"the people of Bahá"* (Shoghi Effendi, *God Passes By* 176), henceforth designating the followers of Bahá'u'lláh. It was during this same period that the "greeting of *'Alláh-u-Abhá'* superseded the old salutation of *'Alláh-u-Akbar'*. . ." (*God Passes By* 176).[6]

In light of this context, then, the Tablet of Aḥmad was not merely implying that teaching the Bábís would be a noble gesture; in light of what Bahá'u'lláh foreknew was about to occur, this was a critical task. For while the "temporary breach" (Shoghi Effendi, *God Passes By* 170) of "the most great separation" would stain the name of the Bábí Faith, the Báb had clearly prophesied that this testing would beset His followers. Consequently, a vital mission now fell to stalwart followers like Aḥmad—to convey to those followers of the Báb in Persia who had long been deprived of Bahá'u'lláh's leadership the message of His subsequent Revelation and the truth surrounding these events.

Such a mandate was no doubt apparent after the "most great separation," but we must keep in mind that the Tablet of Aḥmad was revealed prior to any hint of such rebellion, as was the Persian Tablet of Aḥmad. Indeed, in his biography of Bahá'u'lláh, Hasan Balyuzi cites comments by Áqá Riḍá that life in the house of Amru'lláh (God's command) was quite felicitous in the early part of the Adrianople period:

> In this house of Amru'lláh, Áqá Riḍá comments, they were all together at night, and in the daytime, some went about their trades, while others served in the house. Áqá Muḥammad-Báqir-

6. Both phrases mean essentially the same thing (God is the Greatest), but the Bahá'í version employs *Abhá* (Greatest Glory), a form of the Greatest Name *Bahá* (Glory).

> i-Qahvih-chí and Ustád Muḥammad-'Alíy-i-Salmání saw to the preparation and serving of tea, coffee and other refreshments. . . .
>
> . . . "We were all very happy together in that house of Amru'lláh," he comments, "and no thought of separation ever crossed anyone's mind." This state of affairs lasted for about a year. (Balyuzi, *Bahá'u'lláh: The King of Glory* 222)

Yet, while all might have seemed well enough at the time Aḥmad received the tablet (no doubt one reason he was determined to join that happy entourage), Aḥmad knew that he could hardly become "a river of life eternal" to the "loved ones" by secluding himself in the shelter of Bahá'u'lláh's presence.

While all this detail might seem unnecessary to our objective of assessing the theme of the Tablet of Aḥmad, it is at the very heart of the tablet's central theme. During the second year in this house the "treachery and insubordination" (Balyuzi, *Bahá'u'lláh* 222) foretold so dramatically in the Tablet of the Holy Mariner began to appear. At the center of this intrigue were Mírzá Yaḥyá and the so-called Antichrist of the Bahá'í Revelation, Siyyid Muḥammad-i-Iṣfahání. However, another prominent source of this rebellion was the "other" Aḥmad, Ḥájí Mírzá Aḥmad, the very one to whom the Persian Tablet of Aḥmad is addressed.

Bahá'u'lláh had brought the rebellious Aḥmad (Ḥájí Mírzá Aḥmad) with Him to Adrianople so that this wavering follower could not cause trouble among the Bahá'í community in Baghdád:

> It will be recalled that Bahá'u'lláh had brought Ḥájí Mírzá Aḥmad with Himself from Baghdád, lest he might again fall foul of the Persian consul-general because of his uncontrollable tongue, as a result of which he had been detained and jailed. The Persian Tablet of Aḥmad, resonant with power and authority, is addressed to this Ḥájí Mírzá Aḥmad. . . . (Balyuzi, *Bahá'u'lláh* 222)

This information is obviously of strategic importance to our study of the Arabic Tablet of Aḥmad, for during this same period of time Bahá'-

u'lláh penned *two* tablets to *two* believers named Aḥmad, and both tablets have the exact same title. One Aḥmad remained faithful and obedient, and the other became increasingly perfidious and ignored the loving attempts of Bahá'u'lláh to assuage his prideful rebellion:

> In Adrianople Bahá'u'lláh revealed a Tablet addressed to him, to call him back to a high destiny. In this Tablet the ringing tone of divine authority is stern, yet the word of counsel is loving and tender. But Ḥájí Mírzá Aḥmad failed to rise to the station to which he was summoned. (Balyuzi, *Edward Granville Browne and the Bahá'í Faith* 64)

Knowing the supreme wisdom and foresight with which Bahá'u'lláh performed every act, we have to believe that this was hardly a coincidence—the historical juxtaposition of two believers with the same name, both having lived in the same village (Káshán) at the same time, both simultaneously receiving exalted messages from the Prophet of God Himself, both, presumably, having the same opportunity to become spiritual heroes. One becomes a hero, and the other becomes an inveterate enemy of the Cause of God. So precisely mathematic is the equation of these two individuals, that an examination of the historical context of the Tablet of Aḥmad begs us to compare these two diametrically opposed responses to the same set of circumstances and leads us to one inevitable conclusion: it is not circumstances that determine our spiritual destiny but our volitional response to the Revelation.

Returning to the central task at hand, then, we can hardly pose the question of how to approach the Arabic Tablet of Aḥmad with "absolute sincerity" (or with any sincerity whatsoever) without bearing in mind that each of us has the opportunity to succeed or fail. And the most obvious sign of success or failure is the extent to which our espoused belief is borne out in action, or, as Shoghi Effendi so eloquently and succinctly describes belief in action, "the extent to which our own inner life and private character mirror forth in their manifold aspects the splendor of those eternal principles proclaimed by Bahá'u'lláh" (*Bahá'í Administration* 66).

D. A Generic Analysis of the Tablet of Aḥmad

It would not seem that we could gain much of value by examining the Tablet of Aḥmad from the standpoint of genre. In our discussion of genre we grouped the Tablet of Aḥmad with "Prayers and Tablets of Special Potency." The work is most often thought of as a prayer, though it is actually a type of epistle or mandate for Aḥmad, spiritual guidance for him to recite, almost as his credo.

The Tablet of Aḥmad thus has no precise characteristics that would designate it as typical of any established category of literary form. It might be grouped with other brief tablets containing spiritual guidance, but, like the Fire Tablet, the Long Healing Prayer, and other works of special potency or status, the Tablet of Aḥmad is, more or less, *sui generis* (its own category).

However, just as we can hardly appreciate the work apart from the historical context which informs its meaning (especially as the context relates to the two Aḥmads), so, too, we can hardly study this work without considering how the Arabic Tablet of Aḥmad compares generically to the Persian tablet of the same name. The more familiar we become with both tablets, the more we begin to discern an important contrast between the genres of these two works. For example, we might well expect that both tablets would take more or less the same form because both tablets are revealed to two Aḥmads from the same general background and because both tablets are revealed in the same set of historical circumstances. Such is not the case.

We have generally assessed the fundamental form and nature of the Arabic Tablet of Aḥmad as being a tightly structured exhortation in which the recipient is guided to pursue a handful of goals. The explicit nature of these objectives might be summarized as follows: (1) to follow the commands of the Báb, (2) to call to mind Bahá'u'lláh's "bounties" and suffering, (3) to be steadfast, (4) to be "as a flame of fire to My enemies," and (5) "a river of life eternal to My loved ones," (6) not to entertain doubts, and (7) to learn this tablet and chant it often. Of course, after examining the historical context, we now realize that the most important exhortation, though "concealed" from the ordinary reader, was clear enough to the faithful Aḥmad: (8) to explain to the "loved ones" of God that the Promised Manifestation has appeared in the person of Bahá'u'lláh.

The Persian Tablet of Aḥmad is totally different in form, though very similar in theme. In the second volume of *The Revelation of Bahá'u'lláh* Adib Taherzadeh devotes an entire chapter to the Persian Tablet of Aḥmad. He describes this as a "lengthy" work in which "Bahá'u'lláh has poured out His loving counsels and exhortations upon the Bábís in general and Aḥmad in particular" (137, 138). Also revealed "prior to Mírzá Yaḥyá's attempt to assassinate" Bahá'u'lláh, this work is, according to Taherzadeh, Bahá'u'lláh's attempt to retrieve the few wayward souls who were gathering around Mírzá Yaḥyá, individuals who sought means for "creating dissension, poisoning the minds of the believers, and devising evil plans to uproot the Cause of God and bring division within its ranks" (Taherzadeh, *Revelation of Bahá'u'lláh* 2:138–39).

The result is that the Persian Tablet of Aḥmad is a lengthy doctrinal discourse, two-thirds of which is translated into English by Shoghi Effendi (see *Gleanings* CLII and CLIII, 322–29). This treatise takes the form of a series of very explicit but lovingly phrased exhortations, most of which begin with the epithet, "O My servants!" Some of these caution the believer against the very conduct that the recipient was embracing: "vain desires," "the thirst of heedlessness," "vain hopes and idle fancies," and "evil and corrupt affections." Likewise, many passages clearly imply that the recipient has already endangered his soul: "Why have ye struggled to hinder the Manifestation of the Almighty and All-Glorious Being from shedding the radiance of His Revelation upon the earth?" (324); "How vain, how contemptible, are the imaginations which your hearts have devised, and are still devising!" (326); "Who else but yourselves is to be blamed if ye choose to remain unendowed with so great an outpouring of God's transcendent and all-encompassing grace . . . ?" (328); "Follow not, therefore, your earthly desires, and violate not the Covenant of God, nor break your pledge to Him" (328).

These caveats are neither indirect nor veiled. There is little "mystery" here. Bahá'u'lláh obviously knows every iniquitous thought these malefactors have and every pernicious act they have committed or intend to perpetrate. Therefore, Bahá'u'lláh's concern in this is not for His own safety or station nor even for the protection of the Cause of God, which, He repeatedly states, is beyond their power to deter: "Can ye imagine that the wondrous works that have proclaimed My divine and resistless power are withdrawn, or that the potency of My will and purpose hath been deterred from directing the destinies of mankind?" (324). No, the dominant theme of this tablet is the enunciation in the most obvious terms of what course of action these endangered souls must take if they choose to save themselves from their own rejection of the Holy Spirit: "Break not the bond that uniteth you with your Creator, and be not of those that have erred and strayed from His ways" (328).

Therefore, throughout the Persian Tablet of Aḥmad Bahá'u'lláh alludes to affirmative actions these individuals can take to cease their waywardness and salvage their imperiled souls: "Be as resigned and submissive as the earth, that from the soil of your being there may blossom the fragrant, the holy and multicolored hyacinths of My knowledge" (322); "Let the flame of search burn with such fierceness within your hearts as to enable you to attain your supreme and most exalted goal" (323); "Let the flame of the love of God burn brightly within your radiant hearts" (325); ". . . I have brought forth and revealed unto you the pearls that lay concealed in the depths of His everlasting ocean" (327).

The best-known passage from this tablet is Bahá'u'lláh's assurance in a concluding verse that these individuals should not gauge the success of their lives in terms of earthly comfort or the opinion of others because the important rewards of their constancy will be experienced in the continuation of their lives in the world beyond:

> O My servants! Sorrow not if, in these days and on this earthly plane, things contrary to your wishes have been ordained and manifested by God, for days of blissful joy, of heavenly delight, are assuredly in store for you. Worlds, holy and spiritually glorious, will be unveiled to your eyes. You are destined by Him, in this world and hereafter, to partake of their benefits, to share

> in their joys, and to obtain a portion of their sustaining grace. To each and every one of them you will, no doubt, attain. (329)

Obviously, we could benefit from studying further this important tablet, but our sole purpose here is to demonstrate one very particular point regarding genre: While both tablets have the same general purpose and are focused on the same general theme of steadfastness in following the commandments of God, the Persian Tablet of Aḥmad contains a detailed explanation of the rationale for such fidelity. The Arabic Tablet of Aḥmad contains very little explanation or elaboration; it is succinct, allusive, and, in terms of its primary theme, somewhat abstruse and concealed.

In this sense the two tablets establish a symbiotic relationship to each other, a complementarity somewhat similar in nature to the relationship between the two most important works of the Bahá'í Revelation, the Kitáb-i-Íqán and the Kitáb-i-Aqdas. The Kitáb-i-Íqán is a lengthy doctrinal treatise in Persian which vindicates a belief in divine authority by unmasking prophecy and by elucidating the errors derived from applying standards of human knowledge to the language and process of progressive revelation. The Kitáb-i-Aqdas is a succinct but sometimes abstruse and allusive work in Arabic that commands action and fidelity. The Kitáb-i-Íqán thus establishes the basis for belief or certitude, and the Kitáb-i-Aqdas enunciates the course of action, the right path—how belief can assume a course of human behavior. The parallel is obvious: the Persian Tablet of Aḥmad discusses the reason that fidelity to the Revelation of Bahá'u'lláh is valid, despite the appeal of earthly treasures and worldly powers. The Arabic Tablet of Aḥmad states the course of action that translates certitude as an abstraction (a sense of conviction) into an existential response. The statement of Bahá'u'lláh in the preamble to the Kitáb-i-Aqdas that recognition without obedience is insufficient ("neither is acceptable without the other") is thus borne out in the response of the two Aḥmads. The true Aḥmad abandons the physical presence of the Beloved to devote the rest of his life to serving the "loved ones" of God, thereby effectively combining recognition of Bahá'u'lláh's station with obedience to His commands. The "false" Aḥmad, while having professed recognition of the Manifestation, refuses to be obedient and becomes immersed in his own desire for self-aggrandizement.

We can thus hardly avoid the conclusion that it is Bahá'u'lláh's intent that we compare these two works and the responses of the two Aḥmads. The end result of our comparison confirms this assumption. No matter how generous, loving, convincing, and clear Bahá'u'lláh is in His words to the false Aḥmad, it is ultimately the believer's own decision as to how he will respond, and he chooses to follow Mírzá Yaḥyá. Conversely, however brief, indirect, and allusive Bahá'u'lláh may be in His words to the faithful Aḥmad, this true believer needs only the hint of guidance from his Beloved, and he eagerly accepts the desire of Bahá'u'lláh as being synonymous with his own will and his own best interest. Stated axiomatically, no power can save us against our will, and, conversely, no power can deter us if we are willing to direct our lives according to the Prophet's guidance.

E. Figurative Language in the Tablet of Aḥmad

Relatively speaking, the Arabic Tablet of Aḥmad contains little metaphorical language. However, some of the figurative images in the work are worth noting as part of our close reading of text.

The first and most obvious figurative expression stems from Bahá'u'lláh's appellation for Himself as "the Nightingale of Paradise." As we have previously noted, this frequently used epithet implicitly describes the melodious voice of the Prophet as singing out in the darkness of night when most of humanity is spiritually asleep. Because most are asleep, only the "sincere ones" hear the song. Likewise, only those like Aḥmad will perceive in these "sweet melodies" the "glad tidings of the nearness of God."

As we discovered in Chapter 6, Bahá'u'lláh carefully delineates in the Kitáb-i-Íqán the symbolic or metaphorical meaning of "nearness" and "the court of the Presence of the Generous One."[7] In that discus-

---

7. See *Kitáb-i-Íqán* 138–42.

sion, Bahá'u'lláh states that "attaining the Presence of God" or the "divine Presence" means recognizing the Manifestation:

> The knowledge of Him, Who is the Origin of all things, and attainment unto Him, are impossible save through knowledge of, and attainment unto, these luminous Beings who proceed from the Sun of Truth. By attaining, therefore, to the presence of these holy Luminaries, the "Presence of God" Himself is attained. From their knowledge, the knowledge of God is revealed, and from the light of their countenance, the splendour of the Face of God is made manifest. (*Kitáb-i-Íqán* 142)

As we have already observed, Bahá'u'lláh, though speaking here in the third person, clearly identifies His voice as the voice of the new Prophet.

Because Bahá'u'lláh also goes on to acknowledge that the Báb is one of these "Nightingales," we discover here a twofold perspective. On the one hand, the Bábís have already been tested to recognize the voice of the Nightingale in the personage of the Báb, and they have passed that test. Hence, however much Bahá'u'lláh forewarns the "false" Aḥmad about the need to recognize Bahá'u'lláh as the Báb's successor, Bahá'u'lláh still addresses him in the Persian Tablet of Aḥmad as a "banished and faithful friend" (*Gleanings* 323), one who has suffered banishment by virtue of his belief in the Báb.

On the other hand, Bahá'u'lláh cautions the Bábís that, however attentive they were in recognizing the Báb, they are now being tested again, as is humankind as a whole. In short, this process of hearing the melody and attaining the Presence is endless. Therefore, early in the Tablet of Aḥmad Bahá'u'lláh alludes to the "Tree of Eternity" upon which the Nightingale perches. As we noted in the chapter on patterns of imagery (Chapter 5), this second image is a frequently recurring symbol in Bahá'í scripture, representing the succession of Prophets from time immemorial. Therefore, when Bahá'u'lláh alludes to Himself as the new Prophet ("that Most Great Beauty"), He also employs the figurative image of the "Tree of Life that bringeth forth the fruits of God," a tree, like the Sadratu'l-Muntahá, "through Whom truth shall be distinguished from error." As we have also discussed, the metaphor "fruits of God" can designate the bounties of spiritual knowledge and guidance bestowed on humankind, as well as the "ever-advancing civilization" which humankind carries forth as a result of this divine assistance.

Going back to Bahá'u'lláh's first use of the "tree" image in this work, we note that instead of portraying the Prophet as the Tree, the Prophet is a Nightingale singing "upon" this Tree. This image alludes to the continuity among the Prophets, and, more importantly, to the fact that each Prophet is able to perform His task because of the work done by the preceding Prophets. This is the "Divine Unity" to which Bahá'u'lláh alludes in that same sentence—i.e., ". . . calling the believers in the Divine Unity to the court of the Presence of the Generous One. . . ."

The reason this image is so important will become more apparent when we trace the pattern of ideas. For now it is sufficient to recall that Aḥmad's task is to inform the Bábís that "Him Whom God shall make manifest" has come. Consequently, Bahá'u'lláh focuses on that transition: Bahá'u'lláh is "that Most Great Beauty, foretold in the Books of the Messengers," and yet Bahá'u'lláh is also a believer in the Báb, "to Whose commands we are all conforming."

This motif is made abundantly clear toward the end of the tablet when Bahá'u'lláh cautions that whoever turns away from "this Beauty" (Himself) has also "turned away from the Messengers of the past" (including the Báb). In short, it is well and good that a Bábí has discovered that the Báb is the promised Qá'im, but if such a believer subsequently rejects Bahá'u'lláh, then he has not really recognized the Báb, for to recognize the Báb is to be "obedient to the ordinances of God, which have been enjoined in the Bayán" by the Báb. And, as we have noted, foremost among the ordinances of the Báb was that His followers turn to the new Manifestation when He appeared because "on that Day the Point of the Bayán is none other than Him Whom God shall make manifest . . . " (*Selections from the Writings of the Báb* 95).

There are other images worth noting: the image of the Prophet as "this resplendent Beauty" and as "that Most Great Beauty." But for the purposes of demonstrating the effectiveness of our procedures, let us content ourselves by discussing briefly an obvious but unexpectedly effective image—Aḥmad as a "flame of fire" and as a "river of life eternal."

These metaphorical terms are, to a certain extent, commonplace and obvious. Aḥmad is to assist the "loved ones" and deter the "enemies." We have noted how Aḥmad helps provide eternal life to the "loved ones" by leading them to Bahá'u'lláh, but in what sense does he become a "flame of fire" to the enemies of God? Certainly, he is not to attack them or persecute them, as the term "a flame of fire" might be taken to imply. What, then, would enable Aḥmad to become a "flame of fire" to the enemies?

Naturally, we might think of fire in regard to those who sin against the Prophet in terms of hellfire or spiritual retribution—that which tortures the soul of a malefactor. Because any understanding of what the malefactor has lost through willful rejection of the Holy Spirit is clear only in the afterlife (unless he or she repents), we must ask what it is in this life that most rankles the spirit of one attempting to overthrow the Prophet of God.

The answer we discover in most portrayals of such figures in fictional works (such as Milton's Satan in *Paradise Lost*) and by observing such figures in history (such as Omar or Siyyid Muḥammad of Iṣfahán) is that the serenity and certitude of the faithful most disturbs them. This is precisely the reason that such impious ones attempt to win others to their cause or cynically try to stir up doubts among the faithful. The conviction and peace of mind of the true believers is like a fire to the heart of those who, by perceiving such ones, understand exactly what they have lost or have cast aside. Even more terrifying to these "enemies" are those who, like Aḥmad, overtly demonstrate fidelity and certitude by winning over the hearts of others, thereby further securing the Faith of God in spite of the mischievousness of the Covenant-breakers.

When Aḥmad is attacked for telling the Bábís in Persia that Bahá'u'lláh is the promised Manifestation foretold by the Báb (when Aḥmad is "overtaken by affliction in My path" and "degradation for My sake"), he is not "troubled thereby." Aḥmad's serenity and acquiescence are thus like a fiery torment to the "enemies" who have lost their faith and conviction.

Of course, anyone who provides access for others to the "Presence of God" by teaching the Faith becomes a source of eternal well-being, "a river of life eternal." Here, as throughout literature, water symbolizes life and life-giving sustenance. And in this passage Aḥmad is exhorted to be a veritable "river" of such nourishment, unceasing and abundant, the very qualities this believer in fact demonstrated. But we would be derelict even in such a brief analysis of these poetic terms if we neglected to note the obvious but no less profound relationship between these twin images. Aḥmad is being exhorted to become *one* thing, not two. By becoming a "river of life eternal" to the "loved ones," he automatically becomes a "flame of fire" to the "enemies" of God. In short, that which is life-sustaining water to the thirsty soul is a searing fire to the faithless ones.

F. A Structural Analysis of the Tablet of Aḥmad

At this point we may feel we have largely explicated the major themes and ideas of this brief tablet. But as we apply our two remaining tools (structural analysis and a close reading of text), we will begin to appreciate that there is always much more going on in works of genius than we are conscious of, even after many readings.

As we have observed in our discussion of point of view, the work begins in the third person with the imagistic description of the Prophet as a nightingale singing upon the limbs of the divine Lote-Tree. We also observed that this is an obvious allusion to the continuity of prophecy in human history and an explicit reference to Bahá'u'lláh, a theme that is expanded in the second paragraph where Bahá'u'lláh ("that Most Great Beauty") is described in terms of fulfilling ancient expectations. Of course, now that we know the context in which this tablet was revealed, we can appreciate how in this same paragraph Bahá'u'lláh is alluded to as the divine touchstone "through Whom truth shall be distinguished from error and the wisdom of every command shall be tested."

After this identification of the speaker as the long-awaited Prophet, the voice of Bahá'u'lláh speaks to Aḥmad in a precise historical context, giving Aḥmad specific instructions. But what follows can be viewed in terms of several organizational patterns. For example, in paragraph three Bahá'u'lláh tells Aḥmad to "Bear . . . witness" (testify or make evident through his actions) that "we are all conforming" to the teachings of the Báb. Paragraphs four, five, and six might then represent the specific things Aḥmad is to tell the Bábís. They are to "be obedient to the ordinances of God" that the Báb has revealed by making a "clear" choice as to whether or not Bahá'u'lláh ("the Nightingale") is the "path" to God (i.e., is the promised Manifestation the Báb has prophesied). Aḥmad is then to tell them that if they "deny" these verses (i.e., reject the "Nightingale"), then, logically, they are also violating their professed beliefs in the Báb.

Paragraph seven then shifts back to Bahá'u'lláh's conversation with Aḥmad. Consequently, paragraphs seven through thirteen convey to Aḥmad specific helpful information that will assist him as he goes about conveying the message to the Bábís that the promises in the Bayán about "Him Whom God shall make manifest" have been fulfilled in the person of Bahá'u'lláh. One sort of assistance Bahá'u'lláh gives is to forewarn Aḥmad that he will be tested because the Bábís will not necessarily believe him and may denounce what they perceive to be blasphemy in his statements. Of course, when He forewarns Aḥmad that the "swords of the enemies" may "rain blows" upon Aḥmad, He may be alluding to the figurative swords of denial and denouncement rather than to literal physical attacks.[8] When Bahá'u'lláh further warns Aḥmad that he may be "overtaken by affliction" and "degradation," and thus find himself in "grief" (i.e., in anxiety or consternation from finding himself rejected for telling the truth), Bahá'u'lláh provides information calculated to assuage the difficulties Aḥmad will encounter. For example, Bahá'u'lláh arms Aḥmad by giving him insight into why the Bábís may reject his good news. Instead of thinking for themselves, the Bábís may heed the false advice of people like Mírzá Yaḥyá, or else they

8. In other passages it seems clear that Bahá'u'lláh often employs the vehicle *sword* for the tenor *tongue*. For example, in Persian Hidden Word no. 72 (discussed in Chapter 5), the sheathed sword might represent the tongue of a believer that remains quiet when it should be proclaiming the advent of the Manifestation.

may be veiled in their perception by adhering to a traditional understanding of their scriptures (i.e., "superstitions"):

> For the people are wandering in the paths of delusion, bereft of discernment to see God with their own eyes, or hear His Melody with their own ears. Thus have We found them, as thou also dost witness.
>
> Thus have their superstitions become veils between them and their own hearts and kept them from the path of God, the Exalted, the Great.

Another sort of assistance Bahá'u'lláh provides is to reassure Aḥmad that no matter how bleak things may seem, he can remain steadfast by following certain steps. First, he should never forget that Bahá'u'lláh is always assisting him, even while He is physically absent: "O Aḥmad! Forget not My bounties while I am absent." Second, when Aḥmad feels distressed and alone, he should remember that the Prophet of God Himself is having to endure even worse distress: "Remember My days during thy days, and My distress and banishment in this remote prison." Third, Aḥmad can overcome whatever affliction he will face if he will be "steadfast in My love" and rely "upon God." Of course, related to this third piece of advice is the means by which he can accomplish this steadfastness and reliance—the chanting of the tablet which, Bahá'u'lláh assures him, will "dispel his sadness, solve his difficulties and remove his afflictions," providing, of course, that he intones the tablet "with absolute sincerity."

The tablet proper seems to end in paragraph thirteen, where Bahá'u'lláh commands Aḥmad, "Learn well this Tablet" and "Chant it during thy days." What follows this, as we have already noted, are the several assurances to Aḥmad (and to everyone else) that the recitation of this tablet can have astounding benefits: "the reward of a hundred martyrs," "a service in both worlds," the dispelling of "sadness," the solving of "difficulties," and the removal of "afflictions."

To sum up, then, the structure of the Tablet of Aḥmad would seem to have four general parts. Part one (paragraph one and paragraph two) is a somewhat formal preface proclaiming the station and purpose of the speaker (Bahá'u'lláh) as a Manifestation of God. Part two (paragraphs three through seven) contains the message (and the choice) that Bahá'u'lláh indicates Aḥmad should convey to the Bábís. Part three (paragraphs eight through thirteen) gives advice to Aḥmad about what he will encounter on this mission and how he can protect himself, and part four (paragraphs fourteen and fifteen) describes the exalted status of this tablet and the benefits that can be derived from it.

The theme that seems to hold these parts together is the announcement that Bahá'u'lláh is the fulfillment of the Báb's promise in the Bayán that God would send the Prophet of the Latter Resurrection—"Him Whom God shall make manifest"—the One to Whom all Bábís should turn. This idea is most forcefully and plainly indicated in the second paragraph, where Bahá'u'lláh announces, to both the "sincere ones" (those who are awaiting this fulfillment) and the "severed ones" (those who seek to undermine Bahá'u'lláh's authority) that "this [Bahá'u'lláh's Revelation] is that Most Great Beauty, foretold in the Books of the Messengers. . . ."

G. A Close Reading of the Tablet of Aḥmad

Everything we have done so far by way of explicating the Tablet of Aḥmad is part of a close reading of text. But in addition to assembling the information we have already gleaned into a unified statement of theme, a close reading also implies a creative study of individual words and phrases that might seem to have an important bearing on that theme. Even more important to our present task, a close study of text should attempt to render some final resolution to those remaining enigmatic questions with which we began. Therefore, let us examine those words or phrases that seem to need some additional attention.

As we observed in our survey of the fundamental structure of this work, in the second structural division (¶3–7) Bahá'u'lláh seems to instruct Aḥmad in what he should convey to the people of the Bayán. Bahá'u'lláh first tells Aḥmad to testify that "we" are in total compliance with the law of the Bayán and recognize the Báb as "the King of the Messengers." This information is important because it focuses on the repeated theme that to recognize one Prophet is to recognize all those

Who have gone before and, more to the point, to recognize all those Who will come in the future.

Consequently, it might well be that the "Say:" which begins paragraph four is not God's command to Bahá'u'lláh, but Bahá'u'lláh's instruction to Aḥmad about what to tell the people: "O people be obedient to the ordinances of God. . . ." We find this same vocative ("O people") in the sixth paragraph: "O people, if ye deny these verses, by what proof. . . ." These phrases seem to confirm that the specific instructions to Aḥmad regarding what he is to do and say are contained in paragraphs three through six and possibly seven; paragraph seven may be the continuation of Bahá'u'lláh's challenge to those who would reject "these verses" to prove the basis for their rejection. However, because Bahá'u'lláh shifts from talking directly to the "people" and refers to them as "they" ("they are not, and never shall be able to do this . . ."), we might assume that paragraph seven is part of Bahá'u'lláh's aside to Aḥmad. In effect, Bahá'u'lláh seems to be telling Aḥmad not to worry when he challenges the people, because there is no way that they can contrive a valid refutation of the truth.

Another point of interest in these instructions occurs in paragraph five, where Bahá'u'lláh identifies Himself as the Nightingale. Since this is part of the direct quote Aḥmad is to deliver (as opposed to the general admonition in paragraph three about bearing witness to the station and the authority of the Báb), Bahá'u'lláh has, in effect, freed Aḥmad from being perceived as the source of these observations. Aḥmad is to tell the people that this command (that they "be obedient to the ordinances of God . . .") is from Bahá'u'lláh, as is the more explicit command that they choose which path they will take. And what are the paths they can choose? (1) They can choose to "turn aside from this counsel" (presumably, to follow Mírzá Yaḥyá and those who reject Bahá'u'lláh as the "Nightingale" and successor to the Báb), or (2) they can "choose the path to [their] Lord" by following Bahá'u'lláh.

Extremely relevant to this issue is the ambiguous phrase "these verses" in paragraph six. Are "these verses" the information Aḥmad is conveying to the people of the Bayán? Are "these verses" the Tablet of Aḥmad as a whole? Are "these verses" the passage in the Bayán in which the Báb forewarns His followers that at the "time of the appearance of

Him Whom God shall make manifest," the "the Point of the Bayán" will be "none other than Him Whom God shall make manifest" (*Selections from the Writings of the Báb* 95)? Of course, in one sense "these verses" may well allude to all the revealed verses of God. In effect, to deny any of the verses of God is to deny all the verses of God. However, inasmuch as Bahá'u'lláh is exhorting Aḥmad to confront the as yet unconverted Bábís and tell them that the Promised One of the Báb has come in fulfillment of the Báb's own prophecy, it would seem most likely that "these verses" alludes to the promise of the Báb in the Bayán.

The logic of this interpretation is important. Bahá'u'lláh is first giving the Bábís an explicit choice to make: believe that I am "Him Whom God shall make manifest," or reject such a belief. However, if you choose to reject that belief, then what is the basis of your professed beliefs in the Báb, since He has explicitly forewarned you that this judgment would occur and since I come with manifest proof of my identity?

This is not to say that the first two paragraphs are unimportant in Bahá'u'lláh's message to the Bábís. In eloquent and poetic phrases, Bahá'u'lláh announces essentially the same thing, that He, the Nightingale, is "that Most Great Beauty" prophesied by all the previous Manifestations. In this sense, Bahá'u'lláh is repeating the announcement He made in private to the believers assembled in the Garden of Riḍván before His departure from Ba<u>gh</u>dád—the same announcement He was about to issue from Adrianople to all the world's rulers: "Almost immediately after the 'Most Great Separation' had been effected, the weightiest Tablets associated with His sojourn in Adrianople were revealed" (Shoghi Effendi, *God Passes By* 171).

The Bábís in Persia had not been privy to the Riḍván announcement. Therefore, as Aḥmad went about teaching the followers of the Báb, he would show them the Tablet of Aḥmad itself, not just the passages that seem explicitly aimed at the people of the Bayán. In effect, while some parts seem specifically geared to the choice or judgment laid upon the Bábís, the overall meaning of the tablet, as well as its promised rewards, are applicable to all people from all backgrounds. Bahá'u'lláh makes this clear when He states that its bounties descend upon anyone "who is in affliction or grief." Its effectiveness is not confined to Aḥmad or to any one group.

This same general applicability is likewise appropriate to Bahá'u'lláh's exhortation to Aḥmad that he become "as a flame of fire" and "a river of life eternal." As we already noted, nothing is so vexing to the enemies of religion as those who are confirmed and secure in their beliefs. Likewise, nothing is more vivifying to those who aspire to belief than to witness one like Aḥmad, who has been tested time and time again but who remains confirmed, steadfast, and detached from aught else but fidelity to the task with which the Prophet of God has honored him.

This brings us to another key word that has an important relation to the mystery we have as yet left unsolved, the ostensibly hyperbolic reward of "a hundred martyrs and a service in both worlds." It is clear from all accounts of Aḥmad's life that he not only understood immediately what assignment was implied for him in this tablet; he also accepted this daunting task as the highest honor and greatest gift that could have been bestowed upon him. Therefore the word "service" is a critical clue to the "bounty" that Bahá'u'lláh assures will become bestowed upon Aḥmad and those who chant the prayer.

The point is that service and servitude are, in the context of Bahá'í belief, the highest station which a human being can attain. This belief is most obviously demonstrated by the fact that the exemplary Bahá'í 'Abdu'l-Bahá took a name designating Himself as the "Servant of Bahá'u'lláh." Indeed, 'Abdu'l-Bahá specifically describes the station of servitude as His highest aspiration:

> My name is 'Abdu'l-Bahá, my identity is 'Abdu'l-Bahá, my qualification is 'Abdu'l-Bahá, my reality is 'Abdu'l-Bahá, my praise is 'Abdu'l-Bahá. Thraldom to the Blessed Perfection is my glorious refulgent diadem; and servitude to all the human race is my perpetual religion. (*Tablets of Abdul-Baha* 2:430)

Likewise, in Bahá'u'lláh's delineation of spiritual ascent in The Seven Valleys, the highest station to which one can aspire is the state of servitude and selflessness, which Bahá'u'lláh calls "True Poverty and Absolute Nothingness." Even in the Kitáb-i-Aqdas Bahá'u'lláh exalts this station with the following words:

> Say: The liberty that profiteth you is to be found nowhere except in complete servitude unto God, the Eternal Truth. Whoso hath tasted of its sweetness will refuse to barter it for all the dominion of earth and heaven. (¶125)

Consequently, when Bahá'u'lláh alludes in the Tablet of Aḥmad to the "favors" that "We bestowed upon thee," He is in part referring to the reward of a "hundred martyrs," but he is also alluding to the "service in both worlds." In short, the greatest gift the Prophet can bestow upon Aḥmad, or upon anyone else, is the privilege of being allowed to serve God. In this context, service to Bahá'u'lláh begets neither rest nor retirement, but ever more sublime levels of service.

This brings us at long last to the question of the "hundred martyrs." Again, the simple solution to this phrase might seem to be to accept it as a hyperbolic assurance that the true believer will be *extremely* blessed. A slightly more complex solution might be to read in it that all who believe shall achieve salvation, though as we noted earlier, this interpretation produces certain theological dilemmas. A more satisfying solution relates to the concept of service as a gift of God. In particular, the best solution may well play off of the concept that there is "service" in the spiritual world as well as service in the physical plane of existence. Bahá'u'lláh hints at this kind of otherworldly service in the Kitáb-i-Aqdas when He assures the believers that He and the heavenly concourse will behold them from the spiritual realm and, more to the point, that He will send heavenly hosts to assist whoever arises to serve His Cause:

> In My presence amongst you there is a wisdom, and in My absence there is yet another, inscrutable to all but God, the Incomparable, the All-Knowing. Verily, We behold you from Our realm of glory, and shall aid whosoever will arise for the triumph of Our Cause with the hosts of the Concourse on high and a company of Our favored angels. (Kitáb-i-Aqdas ¶53)

And who, we might ask, could be more "favored" among these angelic hosts who will serve the servants of God than those martyrs who joyfully sacrificed every earthly delight in order to serve the Cause of God?

Thus "the reward of a hundred martyrs" may have nothing to do with implying that the suppliant will receive the *same* reward as a hundred martyrs receive, but rather that the suppliant (especially if he be sincere) will receive the reward of being *assisted by* a hundred martyrs if he arises to teach. Indeed, we can imagine that those who sacrificed their all in this life (and thereby lost opportunities to teach others during their earthly existence) would take special pleasure in assisting those in the physical realm who teach the Cause of God.

H. Some Major Conclusions about the Tablet of Aḥmad

The end result of our effort to find some simple statement of meaning for the Tablet of Aḥmad thus seems to lead us to the conclusion that this brief work is not only a call to action, but, more specifically, an exhortation to teach. If so, then the rewards and promises the tablet contains would be directly related to that command. Any "sincerity" with which one might intone the verses of this work must surely involve some attempt to respond to the injunctions it imposes, because "reading, without understanding, is of no abiding profit unto man" (Bahá'u'lláh, *Kitáb-i-Íqán* 172). Likewise, the tablet would seem to indicate that one's "sadness," "difficulties," and "afflictions" will be dispelled when the believer devotes himself or herself to teaching others. In this sense, the Tablet of Aḥmad does not depict a process of waiting passively for unseen forces to bring about transformation; it is a call to action, a teaching tablet, an exhortation to appreciate and accept the "bounty" of "a service in both worlds."

Naturally, this interpretation does not nullify Shoghi Effendi's exhortation that the believer recite this verse "with unquestioning faith and confidence." If we learn nothing else from studying the bounty of God as elucidated in the Bahá'í scriptures, we should learn that God in His graciousness and mercy rewards all of us who sincerely seek to progress, however perfectly or imperfectly we understand what is going on. The sincere motive behind an action has more import than some quantifiable index to the worth of an act (which we can never understand anyway because we can never appreciate the ultimate consequence of any action).

Yet equally clear is the fact that spiritual development, like any other organic growth, is never static. We are either progressing or regressing. Consequently, while at one stage it may be adequate for us to recite the Tablet of Aḥmad with sincerity but with little understanding, clearly our goal should be to achieve some degree of enlightenment about what Bahá'u'lláh is trying to tell us so that, in addition to having confidence that assistance will be delivered, we may also gain valuable information about how to govern our lives according the Prophet's advice as indicated in the Tablet of Aḥmad.

I. Conclusion

There is, then, a wisdom to be found in approaching the art of Bahá'u'lláh with systematic rigor. Yet no approach to the Revelation of Bahá'u'lláh, however studied and thorough, can ever substitute for the individual's personal determination, inventiveness, and inspiration—the motive forces that must needs complement any successful venture into the bountiful waters of this vast ocean. In short, there is no need to make rigid distinctions between a "spiritual" study of Bahá'í scripture and a "scholarly" study. Good scholarship must necessarily consider the unseen spiritual forces that empower and unify the Prophet's art, and the enthralled believer must (if he or she is to make progress in understanding and applying the words of Bahá'u'lláh) never disdain the systematic work of the scholar whose earnest labors often provide essential tools for even our most personal reflection and meditation. The objective of either approach is the same—to search beneath the surface of the Prophet's eloquence to discover the treasured themes, the jeweled verities, the priceless pearls of wisdom that lie waiting there for each of us.

Postscript

On a visit to the National Bahá'í Archives located in the House of Worship in Wilmette, Illinois, after the publication of the first edition of *The Ocean of His Words: A Reader's Guide to the Art of Bahá'u'lláh,* I was surprised and delighted to see on display the original Tablet of Aḥmad, which is penned in Arabic in Bahá'u'lláh's own exquisite calligraphy. Even more exciting to me was the appended note, which I had never before seen or heard of:

> The well-known Tablet of Ahmad in Arabic, which Shoghi Effendi, in a letter written on his behalf, states is "invested by Bahá'u'lláh with a special potency and significance." In an account of the life of Ahmad by the Hand of the Cause A. Q. Faizi in *Bahá'í News,* March–April 1967, Mr. Faizi quotes Ahmad as saying, "I received the Tablet of 'The Nightingale of Paradise' and reading it again and again, I found out that my Beloved desired me to go and teach His Cause. Therefore I preferred obedience to visiting Him." The original Tablet was given to the National Bahá'í Archives in 1953 by Hand of the Cause Jináb-i-Varqá, who had received the Tablet from Jamal, the grandson of Ahmad.

Upon reading this caption, I was doubly thankful that I had no knowledge of Aḥmad's comment prior to using the Tablet of Aḥmad as the sample exercise for the final chapter of the book. For while I had proffered my study as a tool to assist others in their own personal investigation of the Bahá'í writings, I suddenly realized that the process had worked for me too, inasmuch as Aḥmad's comment confirmed an interpretation of the work that the tools of literary analysis had led me to infer.

John Hatcher, 2001

Appendix

*Events in the Life of Bahá'u'lláh and Some of His Revealed Works**

Before the Birth of Bahá'u'lláh's Revelation (1817–1852)

Birth of Bahá'u'lláh	12 November 1817
Birth of the Báb	20 October 1819
Declaration of the Mission of the Báb in Shíráz	23 May 1844
Birth of 'Abdu'l-Bahá	23 May 1844
Conference of Badasht	June 1848
Death of Muḥammad Sháh; Accession of Náṣiri'd-Dín Sháh	4 September 1848
Beginning of the Mázindarán upheaval at Shaykh Ṭabarsí	10 October 1848
Imprisonment of Bahá'u'lláh in Ámul	December 1848
End of the upheaval at Shaykh Ṭabarsí	10 May 1849
Martyrdom of the Báb	9 July 1850

* Based on "Events in the Life of Bahá'u'lláh," in *Call to Remembrance: Connecting the Heart to Bahá'u'lláh,* comp. Geoffrey W. Marks (Wilmette, Ill.: Bahá'í Publishing Trust, 1992), 278–85.

Ṭihrán (1852)

Attempt on the life of Náṣiri'd-Dín Sháh by three misguided Bábís	15 August 1852
False accusation and imprisonment of Bahá'u'lláh in the Síyáh-Chál of Ṭihrán	August 1852

Some Works Revealed during this Period

Rashḥ-i-'Amá (Revealed in the Síyáh-Chál)

Baghdád (1853–1863)

Banishment of Bahá'u'lláh to Baghdád	12 January 1853
Withdrawal of Bahá'u'lláh to Kurdistán	10 April 1854
Return of Bahá'u'lláh from Kurdistán	19 March 1856
Public declaration of the mission of Bahá'u'lláh in the Garden of Riḍván in Baghdád	22 April 1863
Departure from the Garden of Riḍván for Constantinople	3 May 1863

Some Works Revealed during this Period

Az-Bágh-i-Iláhí
Báz-Áv-u-Bidih-Jámí
Chihár-Vádí (The Four Valleys)
Ghulámu'l-Khuld (The Youth of Paradise)
Haft-Vádí (The Seven Valleys)
Halih-Halih-Yá Bishárat
Ḥúr-i-'Ujáb (The Wondrous Maiden)
Ḥurúfát-i-Állín (The Exalted Letters)
Javáhiru'l-Asrár (The Essence of Mysteries)
Kalimát-i-Maknúnih (The Hidden Words) (circa 1858)
The Kitáb-i-Íqán (The Book of Certitude) (1862)
Lawḥ-i-Kullu'ṭ-Ṭa'ám (Tablet of All Food)
Lawḥ-i-Bulbulu'l-Firáq (Tablet of the Nightingale of Bereavement)
Lawḥ-i-Fitnih (Tablet of the Test)
Lawḥ-i-Hawdaj (Tablet of the Howdah) (Revealed on the journey to Constantinople)
Lawḥ-i-Ḥúríyyih (Tablet of the Maiden)
Lawḥ-i-Malláḥu'l-Quds (Tablet of the Holy Mariner) (Naw-Rúz 1863)

Lawḥ-i-Maryam
Madínat'ur-Riḍá (The City of Radiant Acquiescence)
Madínatu't-Tawḥíd (The City of Unity)
Munáját-i-Ḥúríyyih (Prayer of the Maiden of Heaven)
Prayers (Revealed in Kurdistán)
Qaṣídiy-i-Varqá'íyyih (Revealed in Kurdistán)
Ṣaḥífiy-i-Shaṭṭíyyih (Book of the River)
Sáqí-Az-Ghayb-i-Baqá (Revealed in Kurdistán)
Shikkar-Shikan-Shavand
Subḥána-Rabbíya'l-A'lá
Súratu'lláh (Súrih of God)
Súriy-Nuṣḥ
Súriy-i-Qadír (Súrih of the Omnipotent)
Súriy-i-Ṣabr (Súrih of Patience, also known as Lawḥ-i-Ayyúb, Tablet of Job) (First day of Riḍván, 1863)
Tafsír-i-Hú
Tafsír-i-Ḥurúfát-i-Muqaṭṭa'ih (Interpretation of the Isolated Letters, also known as Lawḥ-i-Áyiy-i-Núr, Tablet of the Verse of Light)

Constantinople (1863)

Arrival of Bahá'u'lláh in Constantinople	16 August 1863

Some Works Revealed during this Period

Lawḥ-i-'Abdu'l-'Azíz Va-Vukalá (Tablet to Sulṭán 'Abdu'l-'Azíz)
Mathnavíy-i-Mubárák
Subḥánáka-Yá-Hú (also known as Lawḥ-i-Náqús, Tablet of the Bell) (19 October 1863)

Adrianople (1863–1868)

Arrival of Bahá'u'lláh in Adrianople	12 December 1863
Departure of Bahá'u'lláh from Adrianople	12 August 1868

Some Works Revealed during this Period

Alváḥ-i-Laylatu'l-Quds
Kitáb-i-Badí'
Lawḥ-i-Aḥmad-i-'Arabí (Tablet of Aḥmad, Arabic) (circa 1865)
Lawḥ-i-Aḥmad-i-Fársí (Tablet of Aḥmad, Persian)
Lawḥ-i-Ashraf (Tablet of Ashraf)
Lawḥ-i-Bahá (Tablet of Bahá)
Lawḥ-i-Khalíl

Lawḥ-i-Nápulyún I (First Tablet to Napoleon III)
Lawḥ-i-Naṣír
Lawḥ-i-Nuqṭih (Tablet of the Point)
Lawḥ-i-Qamíṣ (Tablet of the Shirt or Robe)
Lawḥ-i-Riḍván
Lawḥ-i-Rúḥ (Tablet of the Spirit)
Lawḥ-i-Salmán I (Tablet of Salmán)
Lawḥ-i-Sayyáḥ (Tablet of Sayyáḥ)
Lawḥ-i-Siráj
Lawḥ-i-Sulṭán (Tablet to the S͟háh of Persia, Náṣiri'd-Dín S͟háh)
Lawḥ-i-Tuqá (Tablet of Piety or the Fear of God)
Munáját͟háy-i-Ṣiyám (Prayers for Fasting)
Riḍvánu'l-Iqrár
Súriy-i-Aḥzán
Súriy-i-Amr (Súrih of the Command)
Súriy-i-Aṣḥáb (Súrih of the Companions)
Súriy-i-Bayán
Súriy-i-Damm (Tablet of Blood)
Súriy-i-G͟huṣn (Tablet of the Branch)
Súriy-i-Ḥajj I (Tablet of Pilgrimage for the House of the Báb)
Súriy-i-Ḥajj II (Tablet of Pilgrimage for the Hosue of Bahá'u'lláh)
Súriy-i-Hijr
Súriy-i-'Ibád (Súrih of the Servants)
Súriy-i-Mulúk (Tablet of the Kings)
Súriy-i-Qalam
Súriy-i-Qamís
Súriy-i-Ra'ís (Revealed on the journey to 'Akká)
Súriy-i-Vidád

'Akká (1868–1877)

Arrival of Bahá'u'lláh in 'Akká	31 August 1868
Death of Mírzá Mihdí, the Purest Branch	23 June 1870
Release from prison barracks to house within 'Akká	4 November 1870
Murder of Siyyid Muḥammad and two of his companion Covenant-breakers in 'Akká	23 January 1872
Marriage of 'Abdu'l-Bahá and Munírih K͟hánum	August–September 1872

Some Works Revealed during this Period

Kitáb-i-Aqdas (The Most Holy Book) (1873)
Lawḥ-i-'Abdu'l-Vahháb
Lawḥ-i-Aḥbáb (Tablet of the Friends)
Lawḥ-i-Fu'ád
Lawḥ-i-Haft Pursish (Tablet of Seven Questions)
Lawḥ-i-Ḥikmat (Tablet of Wisdom)
Lawḥ-i-Hirtík
Lawḥ-i-Ittiḥád (Tablet of Unity)
Lawḥ-i-Malik-i-Rús (Tablet of the Czar)
Lawḥ-i-Malikih (Tablet to Queen Victoria)
Lawḥ-i-Mánikchí Ṣáḥib
Lawḥ-i-Nápulyún II (Second Tablet to Napoleon III)
Lawḥ-i-Páp (Tablet to the Pope)
Lawḥ-i-Pisar-'Amm (Tablet to the Cousin)
Lawḥ-i-Qad Iḥtaraqa'l-Mukhliṣún (The Fire Tablet) (circa 1871)
Lawḥ-i-Ra'ís
Lawḥ-i-Ru'yá (Tablet of Vision) (1 March 1873)
Lawḥ-i-Salmán II (Tablet of Salmán)
Lawḥ-i-Tibb (Tablet of Medicine)
Súriy-i-Haykal (Súrih of the Temple)

Mazra'ih and Bahjí (1877–1892)

Bahá'u'lláh's departure from 'Akká for the Mansion at Mazra'ih and His first visits to the Riḍván Garden	early June 1877
Bahá'u'lláh's occupation of the Mansion of Bahjí	September 1879
Visit by Bahá'u'lláh to Haifa	1883
Death of Navváb in 'Akká	1886
Two visits by Bahá'u'lláh to Haifa; revelation of the Tablet of Carmel; and Bahá'u'lláh's identification of the site of the future Shrine of the Báb	Spring 1890 and Summer 1891
Bahá'u'lláh's revelation of Epistle to the Son of the Wolf	1891
Revelation of the Kitáb-i-'Ahd, Bahá'u'lláh's Book of the Covenant, the last Tablet revealed before His death	1892

Ascension of Bahá'u'lláh	29 May 1892
Unsealing and reading of Bahá'u'lláh's Kitáb-i-'Ahd, the Book of the Covenant, at Bahjí	7 June 1892

Some Works Revealed during this Period

Bis͟hárát (Glad-Tidings)
Epistle to the Son of the Wolf (1891)
Is͟hráqát (Splendors)
Kalimát-i-Firdawsíyyih (Words of Paradise)
Kitáb-i-'Ahd (The Book of the Covenant) (1892)
Lawḥ-i-Aqdas (The Most Holy Tablet)
Lawḥ-i-Arḍ-i-Bá (Tablet of the Land of Bá) (1879)
Lawḥ-i-Burhán (Tablet of the Proof)
Lawḥ-i-Dunyá (Tablet of the World)
Lawḥ-i-Karmil (Tablet of Carmel) (1891)
Lawḥ-i-Maqṣúd (Tablet of Maqṣúd)
Lawḥ-i-Siyyid Mihdíy-i-Dahají
Súriy-i-Vafá (Tablet to Vafá)
Tablet of Trustworthiness (circa 1879)
Tablet revealed in the house in the Garden of Riḍván
Tablet to *The Times* of London (1891)
Tajallíyát (Effulgences) (1885–86)
Ṭarázát (Ornaments)

Works Cited

Writings of Bahá'u'lláh

*Á**th**ár-i-Qalam-i-A'lá* (The Traces of the Supreme Pen). A compilation of the Writings of Bahá'u'lláh, Vol. 7. Ṭihrán: Bahá'í Publishing Trust, 134 B.E. (1978).

Epistle to the Son of the Wolf. 1st ps ed. Translated by Shoghi Effendi. Wilmette, Ill.: Bahá'í Publishing Trust, 1988.

Gleanings from the Writings of Bahá'u'lláh. 1st ps ed. Translated by Shoghi Effendi. Wilmette, Ill.: Bahá'í Publishing Trust, 1983.

The Hidden Words. Translated by Shoghi Effendi. Wilmette, Ill.: Bahá'í Publishing Trust, 1939.

The Kitáb-i-Aqdas: The Most Holy Book. 1st ps ed. Wilmette, Ill.: Bahá'í Publishing Trust, 1993.

The Kitáb-i-Íqán: The Book of Certitude. 1st ps ed. Translated by Shoghi Effendi. Wilmette, Ill.: Bahá'í Publishing Trust, 1983.

Prayers and Meditations. Translated by Shoghi Effendi. 1st ps ed. Wilmette, Ill.: Bahá'í Publishing Trust, 1987.

The Proclamation of Bahá'u'lláh to the Kings and Leaders of the World. Haifa: Bahá'í World Centre, 1967.

The Seven Valleys and The Four Valleys. New ed. Translated by Marzieh Gail and Ali-Kuli Khan. Wilmette, Ill.: Bahá'í Publishing Trust, 1991.

Surat 'ul Hykl: Sura of the Temple. [Translated by Anton F. Haddad.] Chicago: Behais Supply and Publishing Board, 1900.

Tablets of Bahá'u'lláh revealed after the Kitáb-i-Aqdas. Compiled by the Research Department of the Universal House of Justice. Translated by Habib Taherzadeh et al. 1st ps ed. Wilmette, Ill.: Bahá'í Publishing Trust, 1988.

Writings of the Báb

Selections from the Writings of the Báb. Compiled by the Research Department of the Universal House of Justice. Translated by Habib Taherzadeh et al. Haifa: Bahá'í World Centre, 1976.

Writings of 'Abdu'l-Bahá

Paris Talks: Addresses Given by 'Abdu'l-Bahá in Paris in 1911. 12th ed. London: Bahá'í Publishing Trust, 1995.

The Promulgation of Universal Peace: Talks Delivered by 'Abdu'l-Bahá during His Visit to the United States and Canada in 1912. Compiled by Howard MacNutt. 2d. ed. Wilmette, Ill.: Bahá'í Publishing Trust, 1982.

Selections from the Writings of 'Abdu'l-Bahá. Compiled by the Research Department of the Universal House of Justice. Translated by a Committee at the Bahá'í World Centre and Marzieh Gail. Haifa: Bahá'í World Centre, 1978

Some Answered Questions. Compiled and translated by Laura Clifford Barney. 1st ps ed. Wilmette, Ill.: Bahá'í Publishing Trust, 1984.

Tablets of Abdul-Baha Abbas. 3 vols. New York: Bahai Publishing Society, 1909–16.

Will and Testament of 'Abdu'l-Bahá. Wilmette, Ill.: Bahá'í Publishing Trust, 1944.

Writings of Shoghi Effendi

The Advent of Divine Justice. 1st ps ed. Wilmette, Ill.: Bahá'í Publishing Trust, 1990.

Bahá'í Administration: Selected Messages 1922–1932. 7th ed. Wilmette, Ill.: Bahá'í Publishing Trust, 1974.

Directives from the Guardian. New Delhi: Bahá'í Publishing Trust, n.d.

God Passes By. New ed. Wilmette, Ill.: Bahá'í Publishing Trust, 1974.

The Promised Day Is Come. 1st ps ed. Wilmette, Ill.: Bahá'í Publishing Trust, 1996.

The Unfolding Destiny of the British Bahá'í Community: The Messages from the Guardian of the Bahá'í Faith to the Bahá'ís of the British Isles. London: Bahá'í Publishing Trust, 1981.

The World Order of Bahá'u'lláh: Selected Letters. 1st ps ed. Wilmette, Ill.: Bahá'í Publishing Trust, 1991.

Writings of the Universal House of Justice

Issues Related to the Study of the Bahá'í Faith. Wilmette, Ill.: Bahá'í Publishing Trust, 1999.

The Seven Year Plan, 1979–86: Statistical Report, Riḍván 1983. Haifa: Bahá'í World Centre, 1983.

Compilations of Bahá'í Writings

Bahá'í Prayers: A Selection of Prayers Revealed by Bahá'u'lláh, the Báb, and 'Abdu'l-Bahá. New ed. Wilmette, Ill.: Bahá'í Publishing Trust, 1982.

Bahá'í World Faith: Selected Writings of Bahá'u'lláh and 'Abdu'l-Bahá. 2d ed. Wilmette, Ill.: Bahá'í Publishing Trust, 1976.

The Compilation of Compilations: Prepared by the Universal House of Justice 1963–1990. 2 vols. Maryborough, Australia: Bahá'í Publications Australia, 1991.

Lights of Guidance: A Bahá'í Reference File. Compiled by Helen Hornby. 2d ed. New Delhi: Bahá'í Publishing Trust, 1988.

Scholarship: Extracts from the Writings of Bahá'u'lláh and 'Abdu'l-Bahá and from the Letters of Shoghi Effendi and the Universal House of Justice. Prepared by the Research Department of the Universal House of Justice. Mona Vale, Australia: Bahá'í Publications Australia, 1995.

Other Sacred Texts

The Holy Bible. King James Version.

The Koran. Translated by J. M. Rodwell. London: J. M. Dent, 1909. Reprint, New York: E. P. Dutton, Everyman's Library, 1978.

Other Works

Balyuzi, H. M. *Bahá'u'lláh: The King of Glory.* Oxford, England: George Ronald, 1980.

———. *Edward Granville Browne and the Bahá'í Faith.* Oxford: George Ronald, 1970.

———. *Muḥammad and the Course of Islám.* Oxford: George Ronald, 1976.

Ciardi, John. "Dialogue with the Audience." *Saturday Review* 22 (November 1958): 42.

Gail, Marzieh. *Bahá'í Glossary.* Wilmette, Ill.: Bahá'í Publishing Trust, 1955.

Hatcher, John S. *The Arc of Ascent: The Purpose of Physical Reality II.* Oxford: George Ronald, 1994.

———. *The Purpose of Physical Reality: The Kingdom of Names.* Wilmette, Ill.: Bahá'í Publishing Trust, 1987.

———. *From the Auroral Darkness.* Oxford, England: George Ronald, 1984.

———. *A Sense of History: A Collection of Poems by John S. Hatcher.* Oxford, England: George Ronald, 1990.

Hatcher, John S., and William S. Hatcher. *The Law of Love Enshrined: Selected Essays by John Hatcher and William Hatcher.* Oxford: George Ronald Publishers, 1996.

Hayden, Robert E. *Collected Poems of Robert Hayden.* Ed. Frederick Glaysher. New York: Liveright Publishing Corporation, 1985.

Holley, Horace. "The Writings of Baha'Ullah." *Star of the West* 13, no. 5 (August 1922): 104–07.

Holman, C. Hugh, and Harmon, William. *A Handbook to Literature.* 6th ed. New York: MacMillan, 1992.

Mírzá Abu'l-Faḍl. *The Bahá'í Proofs (Ḥujaja'l-Bahíyyih) and A Short Sketch of the History and Lives of the Leaders of This Religion.* Translated by Ali-Kuli Khan. Facsimile of 1929 edition. Wilmette, Ill.: Bahá'í Publishing Trust, 1983.

Momen, Wendi, ed. *A Basic Bahá'í Dictionary.* Oxford, England: George Ronald, 1989.

Nabíl-i-A'ẓam [Muḥammad-i-Zarandí]. *The Dawn Breakers: Nabíl's Narrative of the Early Days of the Bahá'í Revelation.* Translated and edited by Shoghi Effendi. Wilmette, Ill.: Bahá'í Publishing Trust, 1932.

Norton Anthology of Poetry. 3d. ed. Eds. Allison, Barrows, Blake, Carr, Eastman, and English. New York: W. W. Norton & Company, 1983.

Taherzadeh, Adib. *The Covenant of Bahá'u'lláh.* Oxford: George Ronald, 1992.

———. *The Revelation of Bahá'u'lláh.* 4 vols. Oxford: George Ronald, 1974–87.

Index

A

'Abdu'l-'Azíz, Sulṭán, 128, 131
'Abdu'l-Bahá
  as Center of the Covenant, 79, 154–56, 161–63, 217
  as Most Mighty Branch, 162n
  prayer in life of, 58–59
  as servant of Bahá'u'lláh, 355
'Abdu'l-Kháliq-i-Yazdí, Mullá, 332
Abraham
  rejection of, 253
  twofold signs of, 260
action
  belief in, 340
  mysticism and, 106, 107
Adamic myth, 217, 219
"Adam's Curse" (Yeats), 14
Afnán, 216
Aghṣán, 163, 216
Aḥmad, of Káshán, Ḥájí Mírzá
  rebellion of, 339–40, 345
  Tablet of Aḥmad (Persian) addressed to, 329, 339–40, 345, 346
Aḥmad, of Yazd
  instructions from Bahá'u'lláh, 349–51, 353
  meets Bahá'u'lláh, 333
  meets the Báb, 332
  responds to tablet with action, 335–37, 344–45, 355
  searches for Qá'im, 330–32
  Tablet of Aḥmad (Arabic) addressed to, 334
  travel teaches in Persia, 334, 335, 359
Aḥmad, Shaykh, 261
alchemy, 207–8, 288
Alexander II, Czar, 129
Alláh-u-Abhá. *See* Greatest Name
allegories
  defined, 49, 133–34, 187
  in Hidden Words, 109
  in parables of Christ, 134
  in Seven Valleys, 134–35
  in Súratu'l-Haykal, 49, 100, 138
  in Tablet of the Holy Mariner, 49–50, 135–37
allusions, 175
Amru'lláh, house of
  epistles revealed in, 126
  happiness in, 338–39
andarz literature. *See* gnomic verse
angels, symbols of, 264

L

M

Muḥammad, Ḥájí Mírzá Siyyid
  Kitáb-i-Íqán addressed to, 85, 112, 248
Muḥammad, Mullá Mírzá
  accepts Bahá'u'lláh, 334–35
Muḥammad-'Alí, Áqá
  Kitáb-i-Badí' dictated to, 85–86
Muḥammad-'Alí, Mírzá
  in Kitáb-i-'Ahd, 163
Muḥammad Báqir, Shaykh (the Wolf), 132–33
Muḥammad Ḥusayn
  addressee of Súriy-i-Vafá, 114
Muḥammad Ḥusayn Báqir Isfahání (Imam-Jum'ih of Iṣfahán), 133
Muḥammad-i-Ḥasan, Mírzá (King of Martyrs), 132–33
Muḥammad-i-Ḥusayn, Mírzá (Beloved of Martyrs), 132–33
Muḥammad-i-Qá'iní, Áqá. *See* Nabíl-i-Akbar
Muḥammad of Iṣfahán, Siyyid
  as Antichrist of Bahá'í Faith, 93n, 315, 339
  killing of, 81, 326
  in Kitáb-i-Badí', 86
  rebellion of, foretold, 315
Muḥammad Taqíy-i-Najafí, Shaykh
  addressee of Epistle to the Son of the Wolf, 42, 45, 67, 86–87, 147–48
Muḥammad (the Prophet)
  familiarity of, with Jewish scripture, 24
  had no formal training, 23
  rejection of, 255, 257, 273, 287
  as return of Prophets, 254–57, 277, 279, 298
  reveals Word of God, 9
  as Seal of the Prophets, 279–80, 281–82, 296
  sovereignty of, 269–70
  steadfastness of, 302
  suffering of, 269
  transformation of companions of, 279
  twofold signs of, 260–61
Muḥyi'd-Dín, Shaykh
  addressee of Seven Valleys, 87, 105
Muir, Sir William, 24
Múrtus, 241, 244n–245n
Muslims, await new Revelation, 304
Mustagháth, 73
  See also Bahá'u'lláh
mysticism, 103–7

N

Nabíl-i-Akbar (Áqá Muḥammad-i-Qá'iní)
  in house of Majíd, 239
  Lawḥ-i-Ḥikmat
    charge to, 236, 238, 245
    prayer for, 242–43
    revealed for, 117–19, 148, 235–36, 237, 242, 246
  as "learned" of Bahá, 245n
Napoleon III, Emperor
  epistle to, 67, 130
  rejects Bahá'u'lláh, 80, 128–29
narrative perspective
  Bahá'u'lláh used various, 35–36
  effects of, on reader, 34, 36
  in Epistle to the Son of the Wolf, 41–45
  first person defined, 34
  in Hidden Words, 36–41
  in Kitáb-i-Íqán, 46–48, 73–74
  omniscient defined, 35
  in prayers, 53–59, 61
  in *Prayers and Meditations,* 54–55
  in Súratu'l-Haykal, 49–51
  in Tablet of Aḥmad, Arabic, 327–29
  in Tablet of Carmel, 51–52

narrative perspective *(continued)*
in Tablet of the Holy Mariner, 39, 49–50, 157
third person defined, 34
as tool of literary criticism, 32
See also first-person perspective; third-person perspective
Náṣiri'd-Dín Sh͟áh, 17–18, 128, 238
nature, metaphors of, 214–15
nearness, symbolic meaning of, 345–46
New Critics, 101
New Jerusalem, 224, 225
next world, 60
analogy describing, 177
rewards of, 343–44
stations in, 324–25
Nightingale, 327, 328, 345, 346, 353, 354
Nimrod, 260
nine, 99–100
Noah
rejection of, 253
story of, as allegorical, 136–37
transformation of followers of, 278
Nudbih, prayer of, 256, 304

O

objectivist criticism, 101–2
obligatory prayers
power of, 323
three, 140
ocean, 319
olfactory imagery, 212–14

P

parables
of Christ, 72
as allegories, 134
compared with Persian Hidden Word no. 78, 187, 189
matrices for, 187, 189–94, 195–96 table 5.8, 220, 221
reasons for, 172, 180
workers in the vineyard, 193, 220–21, 223–24
in Seven Valleys, 135, 194, 196–201
Pentateuch, 265, 266
persona
of Bahá'u'lláh as father, 157
Bahá'u'lláh veils capacity in, 59
defined, 52
philosophers
belief in God, 240, 242, 245
knowledge of, from God, 239–40, 244, 246
philosopher's stone, 207–9, 264
philosophical essay. *See* doctrinal essays
physical reality, 21–22, 166–67
Pius IX, Pope, 129–30
Plato, 240
point of view. *See* narrative perspective
poverty, 273
prayers
in 'Abdu'l-Bahá's life, 58–59
in Bahá'u'lláh's life, 148–49
becoming creative readers of, 140–41
for Nabíl-i-Akbar, 242–43
narrative perspective of, 53–59, 61
of Nudbih, 256, 304
obligatory, 140
occasional, 141–44
of potency, 144–46
provides nourishment, 58–59, 139–40, 149

for Queen Victoria, 147
for Shaykh Muḥammad Taqíy-i-Najafí, 147–48
use of persona in, 52–53
Prayers and Meditations, 54–55
preexistence, 39–40, 216
Proclamation of Bahá'u'lláh, The, 78
progressive revelation, 281–82, 285–86, 291
analogy for, 214–15
in Kitáb-i-Íqán, 72, 247, 315
misunderstandings about, 274–77
prophecies
advent of new Prophet, 260–61
Christ's return, 254–57, 261–64, 270n, 313
Day of Resurrection, 74, 248, 257–58, 275–76, 283
Latter Resurrection, 74–75, 307, 317, 330n
Prophets
afflictions of, intended for humanity, 60
and artists, 5–6, 14–16, 19
aware of Prophethood, 18
as being God, 8–9, 285, 312
continuity among, 347, 349
as distinct creation, 10, 28
distinctness of each, 63, 72, 284–85
equal status of, 71–72
figurative language of (*see* figurative language, of Prophets)
had no formal training, 15–16, 24, 119
knowledge of, direct from God, 241, 244, 246
language as medium of, 6
proofs of, 314
Divine Utterance, 28, 251, 293–94, 298, 314
followers as, 299–300, 303, 314
list of, 251
prophecies fulfilled, 314
steadfastness of Prophets, 314
recognition of, 6
need for spiritual sensitivity, 212, 266
by religious leaders, 250–51, 253–54, 255–57
through their art, 5
veils to, 280–83
reflect God's attributes, 267–68, 275, 280, 285–86, 312
rejection of, 5, 252, 268, 293–97
reasons for, 113
by religious leaders (*see* religious leaders)
relationship of, with God, 19, 24
religious context, 76
return of, misunderstood, 276–77, 279–80
reveal Word of God, 9
servitude of, 286
submit to will of God, 60–61
test followers of previous Prophets, 72–73, 191–92, 250–51, 258–60, 263–64
transformation of believers, 278–79
two stations of, 251, 277, 284, 287, 312–13
unity of, 277, 285
veiled language of, 310–11
See also art of Prophets
Proverbs, 120
Pythagoras, 240

Q

Qá'im. *See* Báb, the
Qaṣídiy-i-Varqá'íyyih, 110
Qayyúmu'l-Asmá', 204–5, 302

U

V

W